DISTRIBUTION-FREE
TESTS

DISTRIBUTION-FREE TESTS

H. R. NEAVE
and
P. L. WORTHINGTON

London
UNWIN HYMAN
Boston   Sydney   Wellington

Published by the Academic Division of
Unwin Hyman Ltd
15/17 Broadwick Street, London W1V 3FP, UK

Unwin Hyman Inc.,
8 Winchester Place, Winchester, Mass. 01890, USA

Allen & Unwin (Australia) Ltd,
8 Napier Street, North Sydney, NSW 2060, Australia

Allen & Unwin (New Zealand) Ltd in association with the
Port Nicholson Press Ltd
60 Cambridge Terrace, Wellington, New Zealand

First published in 1988

British Library Cataloguing in Publication Data

Neave, Henry R. (Henry Robert) *1942–*
    Distribution-free tests.
    1. Distribution free statistical methods
    I. Title. II. Worthington, P.L.
    519.5
ISBN 0-04-519019-4

Library of Congress Cataloging in Publication Data

Neave, Henry R.
    Distribution-free tests.

    Bibliography: p.
    Includes index.
    1. Nonparametric statistics. 2. Statistical
hypothesis testing. I. Worthington, P.L. II. Title.
QA278.8.N43   1988   519.5   88-17204
ISBN 0-04-519019-4 (alk. paper)
ISBN 0-04-519020-8 (pbk.). alk. paper)

Typeset in 10 on 12 point Times by Columns of Reading
and printed in Great Britain by Biddles of Guildford

It's Distribution Free

by G. E. P. Box

To be sung to the music of Gilbert and Sullivan's 'When The Foeman Bares His Steel'
(TR = Ta-ran-ta-ra)

It's distribution free! TR TR
Due to Mann and Whit-en-nee TR
And to them we give our thanks TR TR
As we fiddle with the Ranks TR
In complex calculations you need never be involved
A child of three could do it easily
But the thing we like the best
About this ad-mir-a-ble test
Is it's distribution free!

When your data's rather skew TR TR
And you don't know what to do TR
When decision is a must TR TR
And the calculator's bust TR
And although you're pretty sure they dropped the beaker on the floor
And the data isn't all it ought to be
Your alternative hypothesis will feel a rosy glow
Chosen by a test that's distribution free!

Oh it's distribution free! TR TR
(Well . . . I think it *ought* to be) TR
No problems need delay TR TR
We've assumed them all away TR
We declared our independence in this country long ago . . .
And isn't independence here the key?
So as they sound the bugle at the ending of the day
Be proud your test was distribution free!

When your alpha must be right TR TR
And your limits must be tight TR
If, with care, you rank the ties TR TR
So that none can criticize TR
Then whatever kind of errors you have made along the way
The first kind we will gladly guaranty
It is clearly evident
It's exactly five percent
If it's distribution free!

When you want a Ph.D. TR TR
Full of Mathematistry TR
In this you should invest TR TR
A NON-PARAMETRIC TEST TR
A thesis full of lemmas and theorems by the score
Your committee all will welcome that with glee
For you, their heads they'll bare
And create a special chair
If it's DISTRIBUTION FREE!

It's distribution free TR TR
It's not like Students' t TR
No Normality implied TR TR
Takes the Cauchy in its stride TR
You could have a distribution like a stalagmitic mass
(Inverted stalactitic, don't you see?)
And I very greatly doubt
That you'd be a fraction out
For it's Distribution Free!

When outliers abound TR TR
And John Tukey can't be found TR
Missing data everywhere TR TR
Here's a test beyond compare TR
This procedure's not most powerful, but we know how power corrupts
We therefore, rightly, shun this property
But we're going to mark the spot
Where this concept was begot
To be distribution free!

(With thanks to Professor G.E.P. Box)

Preface

We intend this book to be read (and used!) by people from a wide range of disciplines: the social sciences, business studies, sport and recreational studies, medicine, management science, engineering, science and mathematics. The examples and exercises have been carefully selected to show the versatility of distribution-free statistics in these various disciplines.

All the necessary statistical background material (including a very important chapter on the philosophy of statistical tests) is given, so that no previous knowledge is required. Furthermore, the presentation of the material in the chapters has been designed so that those readers who have studied mathematics to an elementary level can derive the same benefit as those having a deeper mathematical background.

We have taken care to develop the various ideas by intuitive reasoning so that the reader readily grasps 'what is going on'. In fact, the very nature of distribution free statistics encourages such a common-sense approach to analysing statistical problems.

For the main procedures and tests in the book, we have provided BASIC computer programs. These will be of particular use to owners of 'home computers' and others who have access to a computer. However, many distribution-free tests are so easy to apply that usually all one needs is a pencil and paper!

We are grateful to Kathryn, Fiona and Richard Worthington for their assistance in the preparation of this book. Our thanks go to Jack Gillett for his helpful suggestions and to the staff of Unwin Hyman for their patience and forebearance during the development of this book.

Peter Worthington & Henry Neave

Contents

How to use this book

Naturally the authors would like to think that you will avidly read this book with all-consuming interest from cover to cover. However, we are realistic enough to appreciate that some readers will have neither the time nor the inclination to manage that. So here are a few comments about the structure of the book which may help you to gain the most benefit if you only have time for an abbreviated reading.

If you are essentially a beginner at statistics, having had either no formal training or just a brief introductory course in the subject, you should take the time to read carefully through Part I. This is an introduction to the most essential ideas of probability and statistics which will be needed for a proper understanding of the techniques described in the rest of the book. On the other hand, if you already have a sound basic knowledge of the subject, you could just skim through the pages of Chapter 1, making sure that everything covered there looks reasonably familiar. However, we do strongly recommend that you carefully read Chapter 2 on statistical testing, even if you already know something about this important area of statistics. The reason is that the main ideas of hypotheses testing are often badly taught and, as a result, misunderstood – sometimes by people who have been using them for years. To ensure you do not fall into that trap, please read Chapter 2, no matter what is the level of your previous experience, as it is the foundation on which virtually all the rest of the book is built.

Parts II, III, IV and V deal, respectively, with tests suitable for when one sample, two samples, association between two samples and more than two samples (or data of a more complex form) are available for analysis. Most chapters present two tests (or procedures) for the same or similar situations; often one test is of a 'quick and simple' nature and the other is rather more sophisticated. You should not try to read about the second test in a chapter before reading about the first, as the practical situation and illustrative numerical example are usually the same for both tests and so are only described once. On the other hand, you do not have to read chapters in their entirety. The coverage of most of the tests and other techniques is divided into normal-type and small-type sections. The normal-type part provides a fairly self-contained introduction to the technique, including the full treatment of a numerical example, and may well be quite sufficient for a first reading. The small-type sections contain 'optional extras', which you may dip into as and when you wish. These include such topics as the treatment of tied observations, adaptation of the tests for one-sided or two-sided alternatives, some basic theory, and what to do if the samples are so large that the tables in the back of the book or elsewhere are insufficient. All of these aspects are important for full understanding of a particular technique; however, it will probably be sensible for you to skip, at least initially, most or all of the small type, thus giving you more time to read about a wider variety of the methods contained in the book and so getting a better 'feel' for the ideas of distribution-free statistics.

Finally, Part VI contains three chapters. The first two contain a brief summary of some other tests for situations met in earlier chapters, and also some applications to new situations of tests covered in the main part of the book. The other chapter describes some distribution-free methods of forming confidence intervals; these methods are quite interesting but often rather cumbersome in practice, and so have not been included earlier in the book.

One problem about a book of this kind, which covers a wide variety of statistical methods, is that a very substantial part of it can be taken up with tables. However, one of the authors has separately produced a set of tables (H. R. Neave's *Elementary statistics tables*, Allen & Unwin, 1981), which gives very comprehensive coverage of many of the topics contained in this book. As these tables are now in wide circulation, particularly as the standard book of tables for new statistics courses in the Open University, it seemed unnecessarily extravagant to reproduce them here. Accordingly, any required table that is included in *Elementary statistics tables* (indicated henceforth by *EST*) appears only in an abbreviated form in this book. Page references to *EST* are given throughout this book wherever appropriate.

PART I
Essential background

1
Some statistical ideas

Introduction

In this chapter we provide the background for the main business of the book. We do not intend to give a comprehensive treatment of all aspects of elementary statistics and probability; we shall just concentrate on what is required for understanding the procedures in the rest of the book. No doubt some readers will be quite familiar with many of the ideas presented here – nonetheless we do recommend such readers to glance through this chapter to see which main concepts of basic statistics are most relevant to distribution-free methods.

To set the scene, let us first look at some situations that are typical of those often encountered by statisticians.

SITUATION 1

A dietician ponders about the effectiveness of a new weight-reducing diet. The weights (kg) of 10 patients were recorded before and after use of the diet:

Patient	A	B	C	D	E	F	G	H	I	J
before	98.0	105.0	107.3	99.0	84.0	102.2	115.1	103.4	119.3	116.7
after	96.0	101.5	106.9	97.1	84.5	98.0	113.7	103.4	112.0	117.0

We ask: is there sufficient evidence here to support the claim that the new diet is effective in reducing weight?

SITUATION 2

The contents of a family-size packet of Corn Flakes are quoted as weighing 750 g. However, because of a suspected malfunction in the machinery, the management are concerned that the average weight might be less than 750 g. Sixteen packets are weighed giving the following results:

749.3	754.4	748.3	756.4	746.4	752.7	752.2	749.1
757.4	758.8	747.1	748.6	753.8	749.1	750.5	754.3

We ask: is there evidence to support the management's concern?

SITUATION 3

As part of a survey on shopping habits, information is sought on the number of items purchased by customers in supermarkets and local shops. On a particular day, the following data were collected:

supermarket	10	23	13	27	36	5	20	15	42	21	39
local shop	11	2	9	15	4	12	13				

We ask: what can we conclude about customers' purchasing habits?

SITUATION 4

A market-research organization seeks information on consumer preferences regarding the colour of bread wrappers. Six people are asked for their opinions on four different coloured wrappers. (In practice, of course, the number of people questioned would be far greater.) The information gathered is shown below, where 1 corresponds to the preferred choice, 2 to the second choice, and so on.

Consumer	Red	Blue	Yellow	Green
A	3	1	2	4
B	1	2	3	4
C	3	1	4	2
D	1	2	3	4
E	2	1	3	4
F	2	3	1	4

We ask: is there evidence of any colours being preferred or disliked compared with others?

Let us now spend a few moments discussing the different types of data featured in the above situations.

In situations 1 and 2, the data were *measurements* of something (weights in both of these cases). In other situations, measurement data might be, for instance, volumes, or lengths, or heights, or densities, or times, or tempertatures. Such data can (if measured precisely) generally take any values within certain limits; thus, for example, the weights of the dieters could be anywhere between, say, 28 kg and 140 kg. Such measurement quantities are said to be *continuous* variables because their values can be anywhere within a *continuous* range.

In contrast to this, consider situation 3, where the variable being recorded was the number of purchases. Here the values were obtained by *counting* and so they could only be *whole numbers*, (i.e. *integers*). Other such integer variables are (a) the number of teeth in a cat, (b) a team's baseball scores, (c) the number of cups of coffee sold at Heathrow Airport on a particular day, (d) the number of times the word 'Bond' occurs in the James Bond novels and (e) the number of fleas on your pet dog. These are typical of what are known as *discrete* variables, where the value of the variable is usually obtained by counting something*.

In situation 4, the data just consisted of preferences, and so were not obtained by either accurate measuring or counting. Such data, although possessing much important information about what has been sampled, are obviously less detailed and less precise than the previous types of data. A big advantage of distribution-free techniques is that they can easily cope with such less-detailed data, unlike more traditional statistical methods. Other instances where preference data can arise are in (a) the grading of wine from different regions, (b) the weekly top-ten pop records and (c) judging the Miss World contest. The essential feature is that we are able to list the data in some kind of order – a process commonly known as *ranking*. Thus, for example, a judge testing four wines (A, B, C and D) might grade them as: 'A is the best, C is next best, D is third best, and B is worst'. To these grades we could assign the numerical ranks 1, 2, 3 and 4; so we would say that A has rank 1, B has rank 4, C has rank 2 and D has rank 3. Note that we do not attempt to attribute any actual 'marks' or 'scores' to the items being compared. As long as we can rank them, we have enough information to use distribution-free techniques. (Again, this is something of a simplification; a few distribution-free techniques do need numerical information. However, the large majority do not and, in these cases, numerical information has to be reduced to ranked data in order to use the techniques.)

Before beginning to analyse problems such as these, we will first discuss some basic statistical ideas which will help your understanding of what follows later.

STATISTICAL POPULATIONS

The 'population' is the collection of things about which our investigation and analysis are designed to provide some insight and information. More specifically, we may be concerned with the way in which a particular

---

* This is only a very restricted idea of 'discreteness', but it covers the majority of applications. The general meaning of discreteness is that there are definite gaps between the possible values, unlike *continuous* variables whose values may be arbitrarily close together (apart from any limitations imposed by the imprecision of the measuring device). So, for example, the variable that represents the proportion of heads when 10 coins are tossed (the possible values being 0, 0.1, 0.2, . . . , 0.9 and 1) is *discrete*, although it takes some non-integer values.

quantity or characteristic *varies*, i.e. is *distributed*, in the things comprising the population (for example, in the above situations, weights or numbers of items bought or opinions concerning colours of wrappers). We attempt to obtain information about such *distributions* by analysing *samples* drawn from these populations.

For our purposes, there are two meanings to the term 'population'. First, we have populations that arise directly from practical situations, such as the one dissussed below. Such populations may be called 'real-life' populations. We also need 'ideal' or 'model' populations, whose distributions may not really exist in real life but which nonetheless are used by statisticians to model real-life population distributions. Later in this chapter we shall examine the most important features of some of these ideal population distributions.

'REAL-LIFE' POPULATIONS

To a lay person, the word 'population' usually means the inhabitants of a region or country. However, statisticians impart a much broader meaning to the word, so that it does not have to relate just to groups of humans (or animals). In its most general form, a population is the collection of *all* items under investigation. More specifically, it is the collection of the values of the characteristic of those items that we wish to study.

Examples of such populations could be:

(a)   The average petrol consumptions of Ford automobiles manufactured in Great Britain last year.
(b)   The yield (kg) of tomatoes from each plant of a certain variety.
(c)   The current ages of everybody living in Great Britain.
(d)   The weight of contents of nominally 750 g packets of Corn Flakes filled by a particular machine.

At this point, several words of caution are appropriate. As we indicated above, a population is ideally a specific collection of 'things' on which unambiguous and relevant measurements or counts can be made on the characteristics of interest. It is also explicitly or implicitly assumed that so-called 'random samples' (see later in this chapter) can be taken of these things or their values. Although many teachers of statistics and books on the subject seem to assume (apparently, with scarcely a second thought) that the world is like that, a few moments of mature consideration will reveal that this is often not the case. For instance, consider the above four examples.

(a)   *The average petrol consumptions of Ford automobiles manufactured in Great Britain last year*
How is 'average petrol consumption' measured? What is meant by that expression? Perhaps we are referring to one of the standard Government or

consumer-organization tests; but which one? Is the consumption at a steady 56 mph or at a steady 70 mph or under 'simulated city driving' (whatever that is)? How about some real consumption figures from actual driving? But that depends very much on who is driving, how they are driving and where they are driving. Maybe we *want* to take such features into account and maybe we do not. Maybe Ford are a particularly popular choice as company cars, which might imply a rather large proportion of high-speed driving. How is that to be taken into account in comparing consumption figures for other makes of car (assuming we want it to)?

Let us turn to the other part of the definition of this population: 'manufactured in Great Britain last year'. This sounds simple enough – but wait! These days, different parts of cars are made in different companies and countries. Also, assembly may take place in still further locations. Thus it is difficult to define exactly what is meant by 'Made in Great Britain'. Perhaps it does not really matter, in which case why include it in the description of the population?

Even 'manufactured . . . last year' is hard to define. Different components are made at different times and different sections are assembled at different times. Perhaps we mean 'completed last year'. But when is a car 'complete'? Is it when it is painted or when its accessories are incorporated or when it is delivered to a distributor or when it is sold or when it is registered.

It may even be difficult to define what is meant by 'Ford'. There are various companies (e.g. Iveco-Ford and Ford New Holland) which are only partly owned by Ford, and that status may change during the year. Do we involve them in our study?

All these may be irritating questions, but until they are answered, how can we know which vehicles we should regard as candidates for our sample?

(b) *The yield (kg) of tomatoes from each plant of a certain variety*
In some respects, this is even more difficult to pin down than the Ford cars in (a). At least in that case there was an attempt (albeit rather unsuccessful) to define the population in terms of time and location. Here there is no such attempt. For one thing, this 'population' is forever increasing, at least until this variety of tomato plant becomes extinct. Also the yield may change over time because of changes in growing techniques. Even at any fixed time, yield (however one attempts to define it at a 'fixed time') will depend on a number of factors, such as location, climate, soil preparation, frequency and amount of watering, frequency of picking, etc. To put it mildly, it will be rather difficult to define what we mean by the selection of a random sample from this 'population', let alone actually to take it!

(c) *The current ages of everybody living in Great Britain*
You should by now be getting the drift of our argument, so we will make our discussions on both (c) and (d) quite brief. In (c) the difficulty is that the population of individuals is perpetually changing since rather a lot of babies are born and lots of people die each day. In any case, can we define exactly who lives in Britain and who does not? What about dual-nationals, or those who are in the process of emigrating, or those 'of no fixed abode', or those whose life is mostly spent at sea? As regards the actual ages to be recorded, there is also the little problem that everybody is continually growing older!

(d)   *The weights of contents of nominally 750 g packets of Corn Flakes filled by a particular machine*

The particular problems here are that (as in (b)) the number of things (packets) to be included in the population keeps on growing, and that the contents may depend very much on factors such as who is operating the machine, the machine settings used, and so on. Even for a given collection of flakes, the total weight will vary according to, say, humidity of the environment, which affects moisture content.

So, in summary, there can be (and usually are) many problems associated with the basic conditions assumed for statistical sampling and inference procedures. The population of 'things' may be continually changing, with extra items being created and, possibly, others dropping out; consequently, in practice, a 'random sample' is difficult to define, let alone take. Further, the characteristic(s) being measured may be continually changing for any given member of the population. Also, they may be very dependent on extraneous factors, as opposed to being a property of the population member itself.

These problems are usually impossible to solve completely. Therefore, the best that the able statistician can do, if he is going to use standard statistical inference techniques, is to be continually aware of such problems, to evaluate their seriousness, and to alleviate their effects as far as possible. He takes particular care to reduce looseness in the definitions as far as possible, and to define measurements on population items which are meaningful and informative. Also, if populations are to be compared with each other, he tries to ensure that these comparisons are as 'fair' as is feasible. He will also 'grasp the nettle' of saying that standard statistical techniques are inappropriate and should not be carried out when conditions are too far from what the theory assumes. In particular when either the population, or the measurements of the characteristics of interest, are varying in an unstable and unpredictable way, a sampling experiment carried out at the present time may have little bearing on the future, and may mislead. Indeed, the concept of stability is paramount for the use of the techniques covered in this book, and for most other statistical procedures as well; after all, if the subjects of our study are unstable over time, how can the 'now' tell us anything about what is to come?

All the examples and illustrations in this book are to be read with the understanding that these matters have been fully considered, and the researchers are satisfied that the situations are sufficiently stable for inference techniques to be meaningful.

One type of situation that is relatively 'safe' as regards the problems we have been discussing is anything based on census data. The population is usually fairly clear-cut and stability problems are not normally relevant since census studies, by definition, relate to a fixed time or time period, and do not pretend to forecast the future.

Accordingly, in order to illustrate a few ideas about populations, we have chosen data collected by the Office of Population Censuses and Surveys. The data relate to numbers of live births in England and Wales during 1980. The table below gives information on the distribution of births according to the age of the mother:

Age of mother (years)	Number of births
15 to 19	60 754
20 to 24	201 541
25 to 29	223 438
30 to 34	129 908
35 to 39	33 893
40 to 44	6 075
45 to 49	625
Total	656 234

Such a table is often called a *frequency distribution* table since, as in this case, it shows how the frequencies of births are *distributed* according to the age of the mother. From it, we can glean a lot of information about the population. For instance, only about 1% (i.e. 6075/656 234 + 625/656 234 = 0.0102) of all births were to mothers aged 40 or above. About 9% (60 754/656 234 = 0.0926) of the mothers were under 20 years old. Also, not surprisingly, the majority of the births were to women aged between 20 and 35. This type of information can be nicely illustrated in a picture called a histogram, in which the frequencies are represented diagrammatically by rectangular blocks. A histogram for the births data is shown in Figure 1.1.

Our statement about the majority of births being to women between 20 and 35 years can now be seen 'at a glance'. A particularly important feature of the distribution is also immediately revealed by the histogram, namely its lack of symmetry. Indeed, the actual shape of the distribution agrees with common sense – most births are to mothers in their 20s, and the numbers decline steadily but not abruptly as age increases. The shape

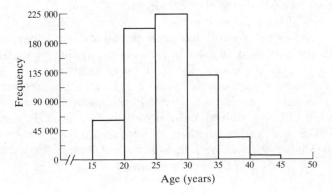

Figure 1.1

of the distribution would only be symmetric if birth rates rose in the first half of the maternal age range in a similar pattern to which they decline in the second half. There is really no reason why this should be so, and yet many traditional statistical techniques depend on distributions being symmetric. Of course, in other countries and cultures, the shape of the distribution of ages might be quite different, though it is unlikely to be symmetric!

In addition to extracting information regarding proportions and shape of the distribution, it is also useful to obtain some *numerical measures* that summarize the main features of the population. The two typical numerical measures of greatest importance are: (a) *averages*, which, in some sense, locate the 'centre' of the distribution – such averages are therefore called *measures of location*; and (b) measures of *dispersion*, which indicate, for example, whether the majority of the population are closely clustered around the average or are more widely dispersed.

Measures of location

There are many ways of measuring the 'centre' or 'average' of a population. The two most popular measures are the *mean* and the *median*.

The *mean* of a population (usually denoted by the Greek letter (mu) μ, pronounced 'myew' as in 'music') is equal *to the sum of all the values divided by the size of the population*. For the births data we obtain

$$\mu = \frac{17\ 521\ 448}{656\ 234} = 26.7 \text{ years}$$

Although the mean is a much-used measure of location, it does suffer some disadvantages. We will go into details later; suffice to say here that some of these disadvantages make it quite unsuitable for most distribution-free work, and so therefore we will generally use the median as our location measure in this book.

The *median* (which we will denote by the Greek letter (phi) ϕ)* is very simple in concept: it is just the middle value of the population in the sense that half the population lies below it and half above it. This is, of course, an eminently reasonable measure of location; in fact, many would say that it is a more natural measure than the mean – it certainly satisfies the criterion of being 'central' more obviously than does the mean. If the population is not too large, then the median is easily obtained after simply arranging the numbers into ascending order; for example, the numbers 4, 8, 7, 5, 8, 5 and 6 are arranged as

* We have chosen to represent the median of a population by ϕ as this represents a population split into two equal parts – which is just what the median does!

4   5   5   6   7   8   8

from which we clearly see that the median ϕ is equal to 6.

Should there be an even number of observations, for example, 5, 5, 7, 7, 8, 8, 8, and 11, then the median is taken to be halfway between the middle pair, i.e. $\phi = \frac{1}{2}(7+8) = 7.5$. However, most populations are too large for this simple technique to be suitable and a more appropriate method of obtaining the median is from the so-called *cumulative distribution function* (cdf). First, the *cumulative* frequencies are calculated by simply summing successive frequencies in the frequency table. A table of cumulative frequencies for the above data on maternal ages is given below:

Age of mother (years)	Frequency	Cumulative frequency	Percentage cumulative frequency
15 to 19	60 754	60 754	9.26
20 to 24	201 541	60 754+201 541 = 262 295	39.97
25 to 29	223 438	262 295+223 438 = 485 733	74.02
30 to 34	129 908	485 733+129 908 = 615 641	93.81
35 to 39	33 893	615 641+33 893 = 649 534	98.98
40 to 44	6 075	649 534+6 075 = 655 609	99.90
45 to 49	625	655 609+625 = 656 234	100
Total	656 234		

You will see that we have added a final column of percentage frequencies; these will make the identification of the middle value (the 50% value) easier. Before we calculate the median using this table, it is worth observing that facts concerning proportions of births in the different age groups, such as those illustrated above, are very readily computable from this cumulative distribution function. Thus, we immediately see that 9.26% of the mothers were in their teens, that (100−98.98)%, or about 1%, were in their 40s and that (93.81−9.26)% = 84.55% (i.e. the large majority) were between 20 and 34 years old inclusive. We mention this importance of the cdf in readiness for its use in later chapters. Once the cumulative distribution table has been obtained, a close approximation to the median can be easily obtained by drawing a graph of the cdf. Figure 1.2a shows the correct representation of the cdf of this population while Figure 1.2b shows the sort of graph that is usually drawn when one wants to obtain an estimate of ϕ by locating the 50% point.

In Figure 1.2b, the broken line 'shows the way' and gives a median value for the population of about 26.5 years. Of course, this estimate of the median is not absolutely accurate, but will generally be good enough

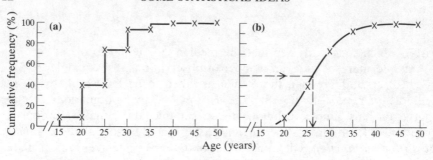

Figure 1.2

'for most practical purposes' – and is certainly to be preferred to putting 656 234 items into ascending order!

Measures of dispersion

The second vitally important characteristic of a population is the *dispersion* (or *spread*, or *variability*) of its members. It might be that the members of a population are tightly bunched, in which case there is little dispersion in the population (e.g. see Fig. 1.3a). Low dispersion is most desirable in many populations; for instance, those relating to the manufacture of scientific instruments, the weights of foodstuffs, filling operations – indeed, virtually every kind of measurement on virtually every production process. On the other hand, large variability, or dispersion, between items in any such situations (see Fig. 1.3b) may indicate faulty machinery, slap-dash methods, erratic quality of raw material, etc. – which certainly would cause displeasure to the customer. In other contexts, high dispersion of a population might be an entirely expected and natural phenomenon, such as, for example, with the weights or heights of a human population.

For the purposes of this book, it will be sufficient for the reader to understand the general ideas of dispersion in populations, rather than becoming deeply involved in calculating values of particular measures of dispersion. However, we should briefly say something about the *standard deviation* of a population, which is the quantity most commonly used in classical statistics to measure dispersion.

As we shall see shortly, the standard deviation does not arise in a particularly obvious manner. One 'natural' measure of dispersion is the average of the differences between the values of the population and the 'centre' of the population. Now, in classical statistics, 'averages' and 'centres' are usually described in terms of means and so, if a population has N members (denoted by $X_1, X_2, X_3, \ldots, X_N$), a 'natural' measure of dispersion is

(a)

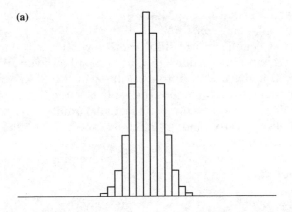

(b)

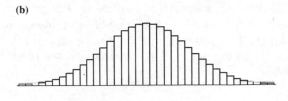

Figure 1.3

$$\frac{|X_1 - \mu| + |X_2 - \mu| + |X_3 - \mu| + \ldots + |X_N - \mu|}{N}$$

where the quantities $|X_1 - \mu|$, $|X_2 - \mu|$, etc. are the distances of each member from the mean μ of the population. (The vertical bars denote what are called 'absolute values' or 'sizes'. So, for example, if $\mu=10$ and $X_1=13$ then $|X_1-\mu| = |13-10| = 3$; and if $X_2 = 7$ then $|X_2-\mu| = |7-10| = |-3| = 3$. Both of these sizes are 3, since 13 and 7 are each 3 units from $\mu=10$.) The above measure of dispersion is sometimes referred to as the 'mean absolute deviation' and is often abbreviated by MAD. By using some standard mathematical notation, the above expression for the MAD can be abbreviated to

$$\text{MAD} = \frac{\sum_{i=1}^{N} |X_i - \mu|}{N}$$

where $\sum_{i=1}^{N}$ is a summation notation which stands for 'in the expression that follows, set i equal to 1, then 2, then 3, and so on up to N, and then add up (sum) all those expressions obtained'. You may like to check that this 'short-hand' version of the MAD expression is indeed equivalent to the previous 'long-hand' version.

Unfortunately, mathematical statisticians have never been too fond of the MAD; the absolute values $|X_i-\mu|$ are a bit awkward to handle algebraically. But the use of absolute values in the MAD expression is necessary in order to prevent positive and negative differences (deviations) cancelling each other out. (In fact, it is quite easy to show that $\Sigma(X_i-\mu)$ is always zero, and so it could never form the basis for a measure of anything!)

However, there is an alternative way of preventing this – and that is to square the deviations. The resulting measure is

$$\frac{(X_1 - \mu)^2 + (X_2 - \mu)^2 + \ldots + (X_N - \mu)^2}{N} = \frac{\sum_{i=1}^{N} (X_i - \mu)^2}{N}$$

This measure is known as the *variance* of the population. However, this is really not at all a proper measure of dispersion. For example, if you are comparing two populations where the deviations in one are three times as big as in the other, then you will find that the variance of that population is nine times as big as the other. This we can easily see from the following two populations:

Population 1	X_i	7	8	10	15	($\mu=10$)
	$X_i-\mu$	−3	−2	0	5	

variance = (9 + 4 + 0 + 25)/4 = 38/4

Population 2	X_i	1	4	10	25	($\mu=10$)
	$X_i-\mu$	−9	−6	0	15	

variance = (81 + 36 + 0 + 225)/4 = 342/4 = 9 × 38/4

Similarly, if the deviations were four times as big, the variance would be 16 times that of the other. The remedy is simple – we take the *square root* of the variance to give a valid measure of dispersion; this overcomes the problem just mentioned (check this out with the above example). It is this measure that is known as the *standard deviation* of the population. The standard deviation is usually denoted by the Greek letter (sigma) σ. Thus we have

$$\sigma = \sqrt{\frac{\sum_{i=1}^{N} (X_i - \mu)^2}{N}}$$

The standard deviation of the ages of mothers is equal to 5.4 years. A much smaller value would have indicated that most of the ages were closer to the mean value (so there would not be much dispersion); while a much greater value (for example, $\sigma=10$) would have indicated that the ages were spread more evenly and broadly over the possible range of 15 to 50 years, for example.

SAMPLES

More often than not, it is impracticable for us to obtain the various population features we have mentioned: the histogram, the median, the mean and the standard deviation. This is likely to be because of the high cost or sheer impossibility of measuring or observing every member of a large population. So we are obliged to take a *sample* from the population in the hope that the sample characteristics (sample median, sample mean, etc.) will be close to the corresponding population characteristics. Indeed, this is really what much of the subject of statistics is all about: we are finding out things about populations by investigating samples taken from them.

To illustrate a few of these sample characteristics, we have taken a random sample of 40 from the population of mothers. (The word 'random' implies that all possible selections from the population are equally likely.) The ages of the 40 mothers (measured to the nearest tenth of a year) were:

32.1	29.8	29.3	24.9	29.5	30.8	23.5	26.0
23.1	22.3	27.0	25.8	28.6	17.6	15.0	26.8
28.9	34.9	31.2	25.8	30.5	34.2	27.2	27.1
34.3	22.4	35.1	15.2	31.7	21.5	18.2	30.1
25.6	27.3	23.7	31.9	20.9	26.4	23.4	18.8

It is particularly interesting to calculate the various sample characteristics in this case, since we will be able to compare them with the known corresponding population values. First let us construct the sample histogram. To help with this, we have formed the frequency table using the same intervals as for the population:

Age of mother (years)	Frequency	Cumulative frequency	Percentage cumulative frequency
15–19	5	5	12.5
20–24	9	14	35.0
25–29	15	29	72.5
30–34	10	39	97.5
35–39	1	40	100
40–44	0	40	100
45–49	0	40	100

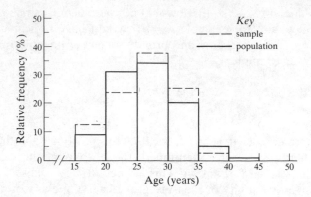

Figure 1.4

Figure 1.4 shows the sample histogram superimposed on the population histogram. Similarly, Figure 1.5 shows a graph of the sample cdf superimposed on a graph of the population cdf (note that in both cases we have drawn the *true* graphs of the cdfs rather than the smoothed versions such as we drew in Figure 1.2b in order to obtain a value for ϕ).

The notable feature of these figures, particularly when we remember how tiny is the sample compared to the size of the population (40 compared to 656 234), is how well the pictures for the sample reflect the corresponding population pictures. Let us see whether the numerical measures for the samples similarly bear any resemblance to those for the population.

The sample *mean*, which we will denote by $\bar{x}$, is calculated using the analogous formula to that for the population, namely

$$\text{sample mean} = \frac{\text{sum of all the values}}{\text{number of values}}$$

$$\bar{x} = \frac{\sum_{i=1}^{n} x_i}{n}$$

where we have denoted the n values in the sample by $x_1, x_2, x_3, \ldots, x_n$. Using this formula on our sample gives

$$\bar{x} = \frac{1058.3}{40} = 26.5 \qquad \text{(to one decimal place)}$$

The sample *median*, which we will denote by $\tilde{x}$, is the halfway point in the sample, which here, with a sample of 40, is halfway between the 20th and 21st members when the data have been ordered. A clever way to

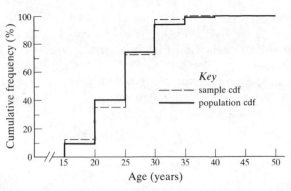

Figure 1.5

reduce the labour involved is to note from the cumulative frequency table that these two values must be in the age group '25 to 29', and so in fact we need only sort through the 15 values in this group. Doing this, we find that the 20th and 21st values are 26.8 and 27.0 respectively, giving

$$\tilde{x} = \tfrac{1}{2}(26.8 + 27.0) = 26.9$$

The standard deviation (sd) of the sample is also calculated in a similar fashion to its population counterpart. The formula for sd is

$$sd = \sqrt{\frac{\sum_{i=1}^{n} (x_i - \bar{x})^2}{n}}$$

and for our sample this produces sd = 5.15. These sample statistics are remarkably close to their population counterparts as the following table shows:

	Mean	Median	Standard deviation
population	$\mu = 26.7$	$\phi = 26.5$	$\sigma = 5.4$
sample	$\bar{x} = 26.5$	$\tilde{x} = 26.9$	sd = 5.15

Of course, one cannot depend on the sample statistics always being as close as this to their population counterparts. However, with a sample as large as 40, it is quite usual for them to be fairly close. Indeed, classical statistical methods very largely depend on this being the case.

We have calculated the sample statistics in this instance for interest only, since we already know the population equivalents. In real-life situations, these population 'parameters' are unknown, and the sample statistics are used to provide information about them – this example shows that they can be quite effective in so doing.

Although in classical statistics the sample mean $\bar{x}$ is used to estimate μ, the sample standard deviation sd is not generally used to estimate σ. The reason for this is that sd tends to under-estimate σ, particularly with small samples. The remedy for this problem is to use a modified version of the sample deviation, which is defined by

$$s = \sqrt{\frac{\sum_{i=1}^{n} (x_i - \bar{x})^2}{n-1}}$$

i.e. s is the same as sd with the n in the denominator replaced by $n-1$. So whenever we need to estimate σ, we shall invariably use s.

THEORETICAL DISTRIBUTIONS

Census data provide us with the relatively unusual situation of having comprehensive information about 'real-life' populations. In particular, this permits accurate evaluation of their important numerical characteristics. In most other cases, it is either too difficult or too expensive to obtain such complete data, and so then we need to sample the populations in order to find out something about these characteristics. To do this, we need knowledge of some common theoretical distributions which have proven good at modelling 'real-life' distributions. Fortunately, some of these distributions are also very useful in dealing with the theory of many of the test procedures we shall examine throughout the book.

Before looking at these theoretical distributions, we shall use the distribution of maternal ages to help introduce us to some of the concepts of theoretical distributions and also to some notions of probability which will be important later.

What information do probabilities give us? The probabilities of events are numerical assessments of the chance or likelihood of these events occurring. To begin with extreme cases, an impossible event is said to have the probability of 0 of occurring, while an event that is certain to occur is said to have a probability of 1. Usually, the probability of an event occurring lies somewhere between these extremes; a probability close to 0 (say, less than 0.05) indicates that there is only a small chance of the event happening and a probability close to 1 (say, greater than 0.95) indicates that there is a very strong chance of the event occurring. A probability of $\frac{1}{2}$ indicates an even (or '50–50') chance of the event happening; a probability below $\frac{1}{2}$ indicates that the odds are against the event happening, while a probability above $\frac{1}{2}$ indicates that the event is 'odds on'. A probability of $\frac{2}{3}$ indicates that, in the long run, the event happens '2 times out of 3', and a probability of 0.9 indicates that in the long run the event happens '9 times out of 10'.

With these thoughts in mind, let us now look again at the distribution of maternal ages. Suppose that these maternal ages are just part of the details held on a computer filing system in a regional health authority. Then, when we speak of selecting a mother 'at random' in a particular age band, we are referring to selecting the appropriate computer reference rather than the actual mother!

For the moment, our ideas will be based on the histogram (Fig. 1.1) for this population, and we reproduce this in Figure 1.6 with the frequency scale replaced by a relative frequency scale (which effectively goes from 0 to 1 instead of from 0 to $N = 656\ 234$), since this is the most helpful scale for our purposes. For convenience, we have also indicated the actual relative frequency on each block. From this figure we see that the proportion of ages over 40 is $0.009+0.001 = 0.010$, i.e. 1%. We can interpret this result as being the chance that when a mother is selected at random from the population, she was of age at least 40 when her child was born (obviously, quite a small chance). As a further example, consider the probability of selecting a mother whose age at the birth was between 20 and 29 years inclusive. From the histogram in Figure 1.6 we see that the proportions for the two blocks covering this age range are about 0.31 and 0.34, and so the probability of selecting a mother in the age band 20–29 years is about $0.31+0.34 = 0.65$, which indicates nearly a 2 in 3 chance of selecting someone from the population in this age range.

Now, of course, the sum of the proportions for all the individual classes is 1, and so the histogram in Figure 1.6 is showing us how the total probability of 1 is distributed over the various age groups, and this immediately gives us what is known as the *probability distribution* of the ages. Sometimes it is more convenient to display the probability distribution as a table:

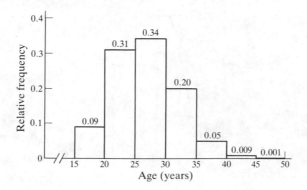

Figure 1.6

Age	Probability
15–19	0.09
20–24	0.31
25–29	0.34
30–34	0.20
35–39	0.05
40–44	0.009
45–49	0.001
Total	1

Actually we are combining ideas of both discrete and continuous distributions in this presentation. The age of a person is a continuous variable (it is a measurement of length of life), and so the above distribution is really a *discrete* approximation to what is essentially an underlying continuous distribution. In the case of a continuous variable, it is usual to have some kind of an algebraic description of the probability distribution, i.e. a formula, which can be used to draw a picture of the distribution. Clearly in this instance this is not possible. However, we can supply a graphical indication of the behaviour of the ages when they are viewed as a continuous variable. By a judicious use of free-hand on Figure 1.6, we obtain the sketch shown in Figure 1.7.

If we use such a curve to represent the probability distribution, then the probability of an age being 20 and 30 years will now correspond to the area indicated on the sketch in Figure 1.8. This is just a generalization of what happens in the histogram; if you think about it, you will realize that areas represent probabilities there as well.

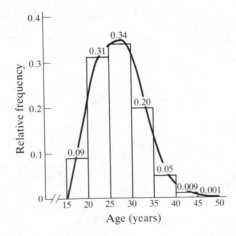

Figure 1.7

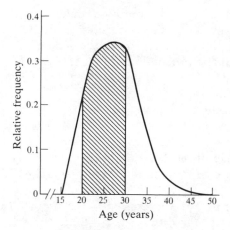

Figure 1.8

Now consider two age groups of equal lengths, say 20–24 years and 40–44 years. The probabilities associated with these groups are represented in Figure 1.9. Just by visually comparing the two areas, we see that the probability of selecting a mother between 20 and 24 years is, of course, far greater than for the other group. This feature is often expressed by saying that there is a greater 'density' of probability in the first group than in the second.

Because a curve such as that in Figure 1.9 indicates this relative density of probability, it is called a *probability density function* (or pdf for short). If the distribution is derived from theoretical arguments (instead of empirically, as here), then we are usually fortunate enough to find an algebraic representation of the pdf; this often allows us to obtain

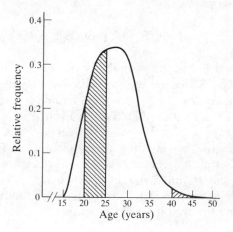

Figure 1.9

probabilities quite easily and more accurately.

Once we have available the probabilities of some events (either by empirical or theoretical means), there are a number of probability laws that can be used to find probabilities of other events in which we might be interested. We shall only mention here the few which we need for the purpose of this book.

First, consider again the two events, and their probabilities, highlighted in Figure 1.9. They are

Prob(age of mother is between 20 and 24) = 0.30
Prob(age of mother is between 40 and 44) = 0.01

Suppose now that we were interested in the probability of the mother's age being in either of these two groups. Since the area representing this probability is obviously obtained by adding the two individual shaded areas in Figure 1.9, we have

Prob((age is between 20 and 24) or (age is between 40 and 44))
= Prob(age is between 20 and 24) + Prob(age is between 40 and 44)
= 0.30+0.01 = 0.31

This is a direct application of the simple form of the so-called *addition law* of probability, which states that if two events, E_1 and E_2 say, are *mutually exclusive* (that is, they cannot occur simultaneously, which is indeed the case in our example), then

$$\text{Prob}(E_1 \text{ or } E_2) = \text{Prob}(E_1) + \text{Prob}(E_2)$$

If E_1 and E_2 are *not* mutually exclusive, then a more general addition law is needed; this is

$$\text{Prob}(E_1 \text{ or } E_2) = \text{Prob}(E_1) + \text{Prob}(E_2) - \text{Prob}(E_1 \text{ and } E_2)$$

where $\text{Prob}(E_1 \text{ and } E_2)$ is the probability of both E_1 and E_2 occurring.

The addition law is one of the two most-used probability laws. The other is the *multiplication law*. As the name implies, the *independence* of two events E_1 and E_2 states that the occurrence or non-occurrence of either event does not, in any way, affect the occurrence or non-occurrence of the other event; thus, the probability of E_1 (say) occurring does not depend at all on whether E_2 does or does not occur. When we have two events that are independent in this sense, the multiplication law provides us with a way of calculating the probability of both events occurring. The multiplication law is given by

$$\text{Prob}(E_1 \text{ and } E_2) = \text{Prob}(E_1) \times \text{Prob}(E_2)$$

If we have more than two events, say, E_1, E_2, . . . , E_n, which are all mutually independent, then similarly

Prob(E_1 *and* E_2 *and* . . . *and* E_n) = Prob(E_1)×Prob(E_2)×. . .×Prob(E_n)

To illustrate this law, suppose that, in the population of mothers, we have information on the colour of the mothers' eyes. In particular, suppose that 40% of the mothers have blue eyes, so that the probability of selecting a mother with blue eyes is 0.40. Then, making the reasonable assumption that eye colour is *independent* of age, we can calculate the probability of, for example, selecting a mother who is both aged between 20 and 24 years *and* has blue eyes in the following manner:

Prob(aged between 20 and 24 *and* blue-eyed)
  = Prob(aged between 20 and 24)×Prob(blue-eyed)
  = 0.30 × 0.40
  = 0.12

– quite a small chance! Having sown the seeds of a few of the main concepts of theoretical distributions, we now progress to a slightly more formal approach.

RANDOM VARIABLES

Undoubtedly, all of us at some time or other have thrown a die (or dice) in playing some game – Ludo, Monopoly, etc. Now before we throw a die, we have no idea as to which of the scores 1, 2, 3, 4, 5 or 6 will occur; all we know is that, *if* the die is fair, then each score has an equal probability (1 chance in 6, or $\frac{1}{6}$) of occurring. So we have a variable quantity (the score) whose values 1, 2, 3, 4, 5 or 6 occur according to a rule of chance: associated with each score is the probability of $\frac{1}{6}$. Other examples of variables whose outcomes depend on some rule of chance are: the number of defectives in a sample of, say, 20 electronic components; the number of shoppers arriving at a supermarket checkout over a prescribed period of time; the actual (as opposed to intended) time of arrival of buses at a particular stop; and the total score on two dice in a game of Monopoly. However, we note that the rules of chance for these variables are not so easily predetermined as with the score on a die!

In each case, we are dealing with variable quantities whose values (sometimes called *realizations*) occur according to a law of chance, i.e. its *probability distribution*. Such variables are called *random variables* to distinguish them from the sort of variables we get in algebra, which are determined by definite formula (e.g. $y = 2x + 6$) rather than by chance behaviour.

Random variables can be classified as being either *discrete* or *continuous*. A discrete random variable can take on only certain values, usually (but not always) just integers, as with the scores 1, 2, 3, 4, 5 and 6 of a die. On the other hand, a continuous random variable can take any value over its possible range, as with the times of arrivals of buses at a stop. More often, the values of a discrete random variable are obtained by a counting process, while those of a continuous random variable are derived by a measurement process.

It is usual to denote random variables by upper-case (capital) letters and their realizations by lower-case letters. So, for example, if we are interested in the scores from throwing a die we would perhaps denote 'score on die' by D and then write its probability distribution as:

d	1	2	3	4	5	6
Prob($D = d$)	1/6	1/6	1/6	1/6	1/6	1/6

To illustrate these ideas further, let us consider the situation that arises in the game of Monopoly: a player throws two dice and then moves his marker the number of squares indicated by the total score of the dice. Let us use T to denote this random variable, i.e.

$$T = \text{total score on the two dice}$$

The possible values of T are 2, 3, 4, 5, 6, 7, 8, 9, 10, 11 and 12, and the probabilities associated with these scores are easily obtained. Observe first that when two dice are thrown, 36 *equally likely* realizations are possible:

(1,1)	(1,2)	(1,3)	(1,4)	(1,5)	(1,6)
(2,1)	(2,2)	(2,3)	(2,4)	(2,5)	(2,6)
(3,1)	(3,2)	(3,3)	(3,4)	(3,5)	(3,6)
(4,1)	(4,2)	(4,3)	(4,4)	(4,5)	(4,6)
(5,1)	(5,2)	(5,3)	(5,4)	(5,5)	(5,6)
(6,1)	(6,2)	(6,3)	(6,4)	(6,5)	(6,6)

where, say, the dice are of different colours (blue and red), and the first number in each pair represents the outcome on the blue die and the second number the outcome on the red die. We can then immediately see, for example, that a total score of 2 can be achieved in only one way, by (1,1), and so Prob($T=2$) = 1/36. Similarly there are two ways out of 36 of scoring a total of 3, and so Prob($T=3$) = 2/36. Continuing in this way, we obtain the distribution of T as:

t	2	3	4	5	6	7
Prob($T = t$)	1/36	2/36	3/36	4/36	5/36	6/36

t	8	9	10	11	12
Prob($T = t$)	5/36	4/36	3/36	2/36	1/36

These probabilities should be consistent with the experience of avid players of Monopoly; for example, the most likely score is 7 (but it still only occurs 1 time in 6 on average) while the scores of 2 and 12 each only occur 1 time in 36 in the long run.

Once the probability distribution of a random variable, which for generality we call X, has been obtained, we can derive its *cumulative distribution function* (cdf). This function, which is usually denoted by $F(x)$, gives probabilities of events of the type: $X \leq x$ (i.e. the event that X takes a value that is no larger than x) – and such events are often of considerable importance. The cdf can be obtained in a manner similar to that for the distribution of ages, i.e. we simply add successive probabilities. Doing this for the random variable T (the total score from two dice), we obtain

$$F(t) = \text{Prob}(T \leq t) = \begin{cases} 0 & t < 2 \\ 1/36 & 2 \leq t < 3 \\ 3/36 & 3 \leq t < 4 \\ 6/36 & 4 \leq t < 5 \\ 10/36 & 5 \leq t < 6 \\ 15/36 & 6 \leq t < 7 \\ 21/36 & 7 \leq t < 8 \\ 26/36 & 8 \leq t < 9 \\ 30/36 & 9 \leq t < 10 \\ 33/36 & 10 \leq t < 11 \\ 35/36 & 11 \leq t < 12 \\ 1 & t \geq 12 \end{cases} \quad \text{for}$$

Figure 1.10 shows a graph of this cdf. Notice that the cdf is specified for all real numbers and not just the individual scores 2, 3, . . . , 12. Thus (if one wished!) we could say that Prob($T \leq 4.5$) = 6/36 and Prob($T \leq 20$) = 1; these results are undoubtedly true, though they are hardly likely to be very useful. However, the cdf does help us to find probabilities of more sensible events such as:

Prob($T \leq 7$) = $F(7)$ = 21/36

Prob($T > 10$) = 1 − Prob($T \leq 10$) = 1 − $F(10)$ = 1 − 33/36 = 3/36

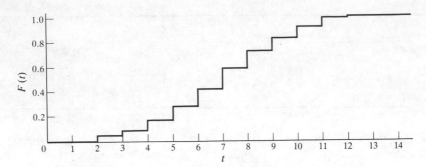

Figure 1.10

$$\text{Prob}(T\geqslant 8) = 1 - \text{Prob}(T\leqslant 7) = 1 - F(7) = 1 - 21/36 = 15/36$$

and, slightly more involved,

$$\text{Prob}(6\leqslant T\leqslant 9) = \text{Prob}(T\leqslant 9) - \text{Prob}(T<6)$$
$$\text{Prob}(T\leqslant 9) - \text{Prob}(T\leqslant 5)$$

$$= F(9) - F(5) = 30/36 - 10/36 = 20/36$$

Although our discussion on probabilities has so far been concerned with discrete random variables, a similar analysis can be performed with continuous random variables (though not always as easily). As an example, consider a random variable, U, whose realizations (expressed to any prescribed number of decimal places) are equally likely to take *any* value over the range 0 to 1. This random variable may not be as new to some of you as you may imagine, for it is this random variable that creates the unpredictability in most computer games*.

The graph (see Fig. 1.11) of its probability density function, which we denote by $f(u)$, reflects this property of equal chances very well. Also note that the area is equal to 1. The mathematical formula for its pdf is simply

$$f(u) = \begin{cases} 1 & 0\leqslant u\leqslant 1 \\ 0 & \text{otherwise} \end{cases}$$

In fact, since this is such a useful distribution, it has been given a name: it is 'the *uniform* distribution over $(0,1)$', a name that clearly reflects its characteristics.

---

* The BBC Micro function RND(1) gives a realization of this random variable, as do buttons marked RND or RAND, etc., on many pocket calculators.

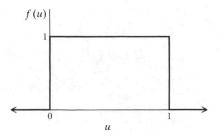

Figure 1.11 Graph of the pdf of the uniform distribution over (0,1).

Probabilities relating to this distribution are easily obtained. For instance

$$\text{Prob}(0.5 \leqslant u \leqslant 0.75) = (\text{area under the pdf curve between } u=0.5 \text{ and } u=0.75)$$
$$= 0.25 \times 1 = 0.25$$

and

$$\text{Prob}(u \geqslant 0.8) = (\text{area between } u=0.8 \text{ and } u=1) = 0.2 \times 1 = 0.2$$

These areas are illustrated in Figures 1.12a and b respectively.

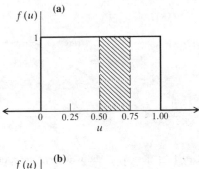

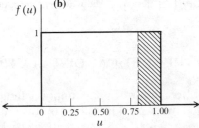

Figure 1.12 (a) Area between $u = 0.5$ and $u = 0.75$. (b) Area between $u = 0.8$ and $u = 1$.

The cdf of U is just as easy to derive. We know that $F(U) =$

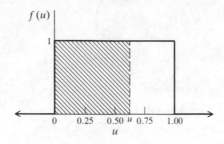

Figure 1.13 Area between $U = 0$ and $U = u$.

$\text{Prob}(U \leqslant u) = $ (area between $U=0$ and $U=u$) $= u \times 1$ (see Fig. 1.13). Thus a complete description of its cdf is

$$F(U) = \text{Prob}(U \leqslant u) = \begin{cases} 0 & u < 0 \\ u & 0 \leqslant u \leqslant 1 \\ 1 & u > 1 \end{cases}$$

The graph of the cdf also has a simple form and is shown in Figure 1.14.

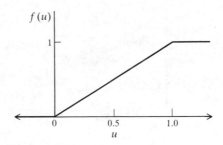

Figure 1.14 Graph of the cdf of the uniform distribution over (0,1).

SOME STANDARD THEORETICAL DISTRIBUTIONS

It is fortunate that the behaviour of many unpredictable events in real life can often be modelled by well known theoretical distributions whose properties are well documented. In this section we briefly look at just three of these standard distributions – the binomial, the normal and the chi-squared distributions – each of which, in one way or another, is needed in various parts of the book.

The binomial distribution

One of the remarkable things about the binomial distribution is the large number of situations to which it can be applied. To quote just two situations we have:

EXAMPLE 1

A multiple-choice examination paper contains 18 questions, each having just two possible answers. Now, if a candidate were to choose each answer solely by guesswork, then the probability of choosing the correct answer is $\frac{1}{2}$ in each case. If the candidate needs 12 or more correct answers to pass, then by using the binomial distribution we can calculate the probability of a pass being obtained purely by such guesswork!

Here we have a situation where each guess (outcome) is one of two possibilities (right or wrong) and, unless the candidate is operating a 'scheme', the outcome of a particular guess is independent of all the others.

EXAMPLE 2

Suppose it is known that 25% of all males suffer to some extent from colour-blindness. If a random sample of, say, 20 males were selected then, for instance, we could calculate the probability of at least two males in the sample being colour-blind.

As in example 1, the outcome of each trial or inspection is one of two possibilities, namely colour-blind or not colour-blind. Also, whether or not one person is colour-blind is quite independent of the condition of other people in the sample. (This is still effectively true even if colour-blindness tends to run in families, since the members of our sample are randomly selected from the population.)

Both of these situations have the common features characteristic of binomial distributions. In each case we have:

(a) A number, n, of independent similar trials ($n=18$ in the first example and $n=20$ in the second).
(b) The outcome of each trial is one of just two possibilities. In general, let us refer to these two possibilities as success (S) and failure (F). The probability of a success in any one trial is commonly denoted by p and remains the same in every trial; similarly the probability of a failure at any trial is denoted by q. Of course, since success and failure are the only two possible outcomes, it is clear that $p+q=1$.

To fix our ideas, consider an experiment in which $n=5$ independent trials are conducted. Each outcome will be either a success (with probability p) or a failure (with probability q). Suppose we want to find the probability of getting just two successes out of the five tries.

It might happen that the first two tries were successes followed by three failures. We can represent this realization by

$$S \quad S \quad F \quad F \quad F$$

Now, since it is assumed that the outcomes of all trials are independent of each other, the probability of this particular arrangement or configuration is obtained by using the multiplication law:

$$p \times p \times q \times q \times q = p^2 q^3$$

But, since we want the probability of two successes out of five, *irrespective* of whether they are the first two, or the first and third, or the second and the fifth, etc., we need to take into account *every* configuration that can give rise to two successes and three failures. There are in fact 10 such arrangements. We display them below, and their probabilities are computed alongside:

Configuration	Probability
S S F F F	$p \times p \times q \times q \times q = p^2 q^3$
F S S F F	$q \times p \times p \times q \times q = p^2 q^3$
F F S S F	$q \times q \times p \times p \times q = p^2 q^3$
F F F S S	$q \times q \times q \times p \times p = p^2 q^3$
S F S F F	$p \times q \times p \times q \times q = p^2 q^3$
F S F S F	$q \times p \times q \times p \times q = p^2 q^3$
F F S F S	$q \times q \times p \times q \times p = p^2 q^3$
S F F S F	$p \times q \times q \times p \times q = p^2 q^3$
F S F F S	$q \times p \times q \times q \times p = p^2 q^3$
S F F F S	$p \times q \times q \times q \times p = p^2 q^3$

So, each such configuration has the same probability, $p^2 q^3$, of occurrence. As there are 10 of them, the total probability of having precisely two successes out of five is $10 p^2 q^3$.

This and all similar binomial probability computations are composed of two parts. The '$p^2 q^3$' part is easy – it comes straight from the multiplication rule. The '10' part, which counts the number of possible configurations, is not so easy. In practice, it would certainly be extremely tedious to have to resort to listing every arrangement to determine this number! Luckily, there is a well known formula which gives us the number without all that tedious work. To understand the formula, you will need to know what is meant by 'factorials'. For any positive integer n, 'factorial n', which is denoted by $n!$, is computed as

$$n! = n \times (n-1) \times (n-2) \times \ldots \times 3 \times 2 \times 1$$

so that, for example, $5!=5\times4\times3\times2\times1=120$. Other examples that you might like to check are: $2!=2$, $3!=6$, $4!=24$ and $6!=720$. An exception to this rule is $0!$, which is simply taken to have the value of 1.

Now we can state our important result: the number of configurations of exactly x successes and $n-x$ failures in n trials is given by

$$\frac{n!}{x!(n - x)!}$$

This quantity is called a *binomial coefficient*, and is usually denoted by either $\binom{n}{x}$ or ^nC_x.

In our problem above, the number of configurations of two $(=x)$ successes and three $(= n-x)$ failures in five $(=n)$ trials is computed by the formula as

$$\binom{5}{2} = \frac{5!}{2!3!} = \frac{5\times4\times3\times2\times1}{2\times1\times3\times2\times1} = 10$$

which is in agreement with our previous method.

Note that we can write the probability of getting two successes out of five as

$$\binom{5}{2} p^2 q^3$$

It is therefore easy to see how to generalize the result to any case where we have, say, n trials and want the probability of getting precisely x successes. Writing X for the number of successes in n trials, we have

$$\text{Prob}(X=x) = \text{Prob}(x \text{ successes out of } n \text{ trials})$$
$$= \binom{n}{x} p^x q^{n-x} \qquad (x = 0,1,2, \ldots ,n)$$

Notice what each part of this expression represents:

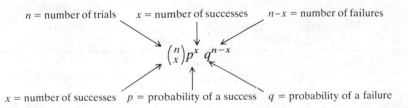

This general result gives the probabilities of *every* possible number x of successes($x = 0,1,2, \ldots ,n$) in a binomial situation, and so is called the *binomial distribution*.

To illustrate this important distribution further, let us consider the student in Example 1. In this case, $n=18$ and the probability of correctly answering a question is $\frac{1}{2}$, i.e. $p=\frac{1}{2}$ (and so also $q=\frac{1}{2}$). If we let X denote his total number of correct answers out of the 18, we find, by substituting $p=q=\frac{1}{2}$ and $n=18$ in the above formula, that

$$\text{Prob}(X=x) = \binom{18}{x}\left(\frac{1}{2}\right)^{x}\left(\frac{1}{2}\right)^{18-x} \qquad (x = 0,1,2, \ldots ,18)$$

So, for instance, if we wanted the probability of the student only guessing four answers correctly, we simply put $x=4$ in the above formula. This gives

$$\text{Prob}(X = 4) = \binom{18}{4}\left(\frac{1}{2}\right)^{4}\left(\frac{1}{2}\right)^{14}$$

Now

$$\binom{18}{4} = \frac{18!}{4!14!} = \frac{18\times17\times16\times15}{4\times3\times2\times1} = 3060$$

and so

$$\text{Prob}(X = 4) = 3060 \times \left(\frac{1}{2}\right)^{4} \times \left(\frac{1}{2}\right)^{14}$$

$$= 0.0117 \quad \text{(to four decimal places)}$$

In the same way we could calculate the probability of his guessing correctly any number from 0 to 18. The results for this are shown in the following table:

x	0	1	2	4	4	5	6
Prob($X = x$)	0.0000	0.0001	0.0006	0.0031	0.0117	0.0327	0.0708

x	7	8	9	10	11	12
Prob($X = x$)	0.1214	0.1669	0.1855	0.1669	0.1214	0.0708

x	13	14	15	16	17	18
Prob($X = x$)	0.0327	0.0117	0.0031	0.0006	0.0001	0.0000

It is interesting to look at the histogram (shown in Fig. 1.15) of this

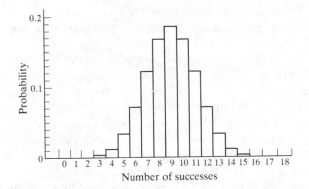

Figure 1.15

distribution which, because $p=q=\frac{1}{2}$, is symmetrical about $x = 9$ (the average number of successes).

Of course, once we have the full set of probabilities like this, it is easy to determine the chances of the student passing the examination on guesswork alone. We need to find the probability of his getting 12 or more correct answers, and so we have

$$
\begin{aligned}
\text{Prob}(X \geqslant 12) &= \text{Prob}(X=12) + \text{Prob}(X=13) + \ldots + \text{Prob}(X=18) \\
&= 0.0708 + 0.0327 + 0.0117 + 0.0031 + 0.0006 + 0.0001 \\
&\quad + 0.0000 \\
&= 0.1190
\end{aligned}
$$

So the student has about a 1 in 8 chance of passing by guesswork alone. Although obviously the odds are against this happening, the probability is by no means negligible. To counteract this, in practice most multiple-choice papers have more than two suggested answers to each question. Suppose there were four options per question. Then with $p=\frac{1}{4}$ and $q=\frac{3}{4}$, the probability of passing on guesswork alone, i.e. $\text{Prob}(X \geqslant 12)$, is now only 0.0002.

Even for quite small values of n, calculating binomial probabilities can be very tedious, particularly probabilities of *ranges* of values like the $X \geqslant 12$ in the last example. However, for $n \leqslant 20$ and a wide selection of values of p, binomial probabilities can be read directly from pages 4 to 11 of *EST* – individual probabilities like $\text{Prob}(X=12)$ from the left-hand pages, and cumulative probabilities like $\text{Prob}(X \leqslant 12)$ or $\text{Prob}(X \geqslant 12)$ from the right-hand pages.

For some purposes we need to know the mean and standard deviation of the number of successes. We state the results without proof (although the result for the mean is fairly obvious):

The mean (or 'expected') number of successes is $\mu = np$.
The standard deviation of the number of successes is $\sigma \sqrt{npq}$.

In the case of the 18-question examination paper with two options per question ($n=18$, $p=\frac{1}{2}$), the average number of correct answers obtained by guesswork is $\mu=np=18\times\frac{1}{2}=9$ (as you would surely 'expect'). The standard deviation of the number of correct answers is $\sigma=\sqrt{npq} = \sqrt{18\times\frac{1}{2}\times\frac{1}{2}} = \sqrt{4.5} = 2.12$. It is interesting to compare these figures with what we get when there are four options per question ($n=18$, $p=\frac{1}{4}$). Then, $\mu=np= 18\times\frac{1}{4} = 4.5$ – much lower, again as you would 'expect'; the standard deviation $\sigma=\sqrt{npq} = \sqrt{18\times\frac{1}{4}\times\frac{3}{4}} = 1.84$. Note that this is also lower than before, indicating a smaller variability around the mean value; whereas with $p=\frac{1}{2}$ there is a relatively large chance of the number of correct answers being substantially different from the average (either high or low), with $p=\frac{1}{4}$ it is more likely that we will definitely get a score close to the mean value.

The normal distribution

The normal distribution is the most important of all continuous probability distributions. One reason for this is that it very adequately describes the behaviour of results of many measuring processes. Typical examples are:

(a)   the heights of females (or males) in a community;
(b)   the net weights of cans of petfood, packets of breakfast cereals, etc.;
(c)   the lengths of mass-produced components;
(d)   the *actual* time of arrival of, say, the '8 o'clock bus'.

All have histograms that first gradually rise in height to a maximum and then similarly decrease to give an approximately symmetrical shape. The normal curve (or *density* function) is a continuous curve which behaves in a similar way and has a perfectly symmetrical shape. A typical normal curve is shown in Figure 1.16.

Such a curve is often described as being 'bell-shaped'. The problems

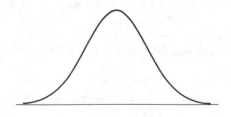

Figure 1.16

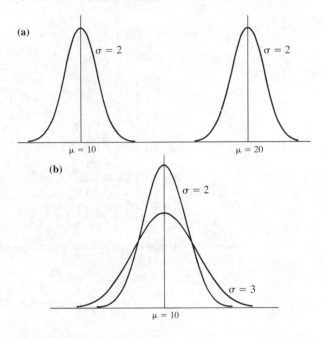

Figure 1.17

about where the curve is centred, and how wide or narrow it is, depend
on its values of μ and σ. What would be the effect on the shape of the
normal curve if the mean and/or standard deviation were different?
Figure 1.17 illustrates normal distributions for varying means μ and
standard deviations σ.

It is common to refer to a normal distribution whose mean is μ and
standard deviation is σ (i.e. variance is σ^2) by the notation $N(\mu, \sigma^2)$.
Thus the two distributions in Figure 1.17a could be denoted by N(10,4)
and N(20,4) and those in Figure 1.17b by N(10,4) and N(10,9). In each
case, we see that the basic shape is retained. Changing the mean does not
alter the shape of the curve at all – it simply shifts its position. Increasing
the standard deviation flattens the shape (which is to be expected since
the total area of 1 has to be spread out over a greater range of values).
On the other hand, a small standard deviation results in the curve being
narrow and more pointed. To illustrate how well the normal curve
describes real data, we recorded the heights of 200 female students who
attended our college. Figure 1.18 shows the histogram produced from this
sample.

This histogram is reproduced in Figure 1.19, and superimposed on it is
the normal curve whose mean and standard deviation are the same as
those of the sample.

A vitally important feature of normal distributions is that, regardless of

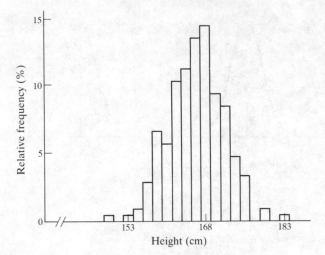

Figure 1.18

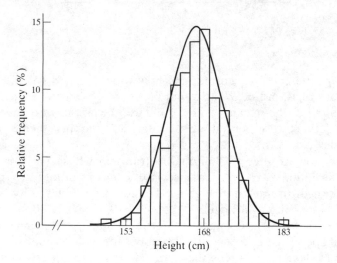

Figure 1.19

their means and standard deviations, results such as the following are always true:

(a)   68% of its area lies within 1 standard deviation of μ;
(b)   95% of its area lies within 1.96 (i.e. roughly 2) standard deviations of μ;
(c)   99% of its area lies within 2.58 standard deviations of μ.

See Figure 1.20 for illustration of this point.

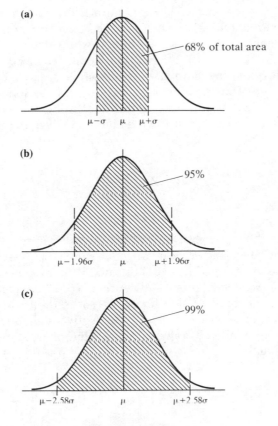

Figure 1.20

A useful interpretation of this feature is that the probability of obtaining an observation more than 2 standard deviations away from the mean is about 5%, and more than 2.5 standard deviations away is about 1%. Thus if we observed a value that is more than, say, 2 standard deviations away from the mean, then we might classify it as a somewhat unusual event which might cast doubt as to whether the observation even comes from this distribution – more of this idea later!

We recall that, for a continuous distribution, the probability of an observation lying between two specified values is given by the corresponding area under the graph of the pdf. Now, as we have said, normal distributions are encountered (at least approximately) in a wide variety of situations. Since different situations are likely to give rise to different values of the mean μ and/or standard deviation σ, we need some easy way of calculating areas under different normal curves. Clearly, it is impossible to provide a table for every possible normal distribution!

Fortunately, it is easy to relate *any* normal distribution to *one* particular normal distribution: this is the so-called *standard* normal distribution, which is simply the normal distribution whose mean is 0 and standard deviation is 1, i.e. $N(0,1^2)=N(0,1)$. So all we need in order to get probabilities for any normal distribution is a table of areas for the standard normal distribution. The basic idea is as follows. Suppose we have a variable X which is normally distributed with mean μ and standard deviation σ. Then if we define a new variable Z as

$$Z = \frac{X - \mu}{\sigma}$$

it turns out that the distribution of Z is always the *standard* normal distribution. Since any event involving X can be easily expressed in terms of an event involving Z (as we illustrate in the examples below), then a table of the *standard* normal distribution $N(0,1)$ is indeed all we need. Table A at the back of this book (or pages 18–19 of *EST*) gives the probabilities $\text{Prob}(Z \leqslant z)$, i.e. the cumulative distribution function of $N(0,1)$, which is often denoted by $\Phi(z)$. Here are some examples of the use of this table.

(a) $\Phi(2) = \text{Prob}(Z \leqslant 2)$
     $= 0.9772$

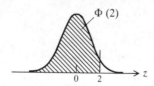

(b) $\text{Prob}(Z>1.5) =$ (area to the right of $z=1.5$)
                     $= 1 - \text{Prob}(Z \leqslant 1.5)$
                     $= 1 -$ (area to the left of 1.5)
                     $= 1 - \Phi(1.5)$
                     $= 1 - 0.9332$
                     $= 0.0668$

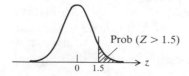

(c)   Prob(Z<−1.42) = Φ(−1.42)
                    = 0.0778

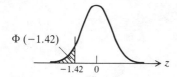

Φ (−1.42)

(d)   Prob(−1.6⩽Z⩽0.3) = (area to the left of 0.3) −
                                        (area to the left of −1.6)
                             = Φ(0.3) − Φ(−1.6)
                             = 0.6179 − 0.0548
                             = 0.5631

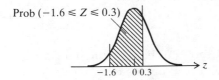

Prob (−1.6 ⩽ Z ⩽ 0.3)

The uses of the relation $Z = (X-\mu)/\sigma$ on 'non-standard' normal
distributions is shown in the following examples.

EXAMPLE 1

Suppose that turn-round time for servicing an aircraft between flights is
normally distributed with mean 25 min and standard deviation 3 min.
What is the probability that the turn-round will exceed 30 min?
   Let X denote the servicing time – its normal curve is:

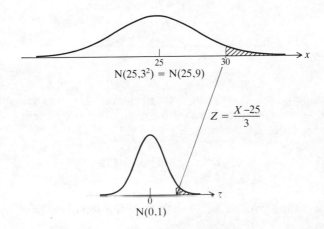

The shaded area corresponds to Prob($X>30$) and this is equal to the shaded area under the standard normal curve, if Z is defined according to the above rule, i.e.

$$Z = \frac{X-\mu}{\sigma} = \frac{X-25}{3}$$

Using $Z = (X-\mu)/\sigma$, we find that $X=30$ corresponds to $Z = (30-25)/3$ = 1.67. So, we can now use Table A to obtain the required probability:

$$\begin{aligned}
\text{Prob }(X>30) &= \text{Prob}(Z>1.67) \\
&= 1 - \text{Prob}(Z\leqslant1.67) \\
&= 1 - \Phi(1.67) \\
&= 0.0475
\end{aligned}$$

EXAMPLE 2

In the same situation, suppose we want to find the servicing time x, say, which is exceeded on 1% of occasions, i.e. Prob($X>x$) = 0.01.

In the diagrams below, both shaded areas correspond to what is sometimes called an *upper-tail* probability of 0.01:

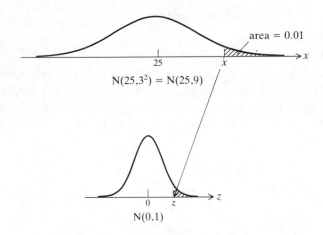

The shaded area corresponds to Prob($X>30$) and this is equal to the shaded area under the standard normal curve if Z is defined according to the above rule, i.e.

$$Z = (X-\mu)/\sigma = (x-25)/3$$

First we use Table A to find z. As there has to be an area of 0.01 to the right of z (and thus an area of 0.99 to the left), we have

$$\text{Prob}(Z<z) = 0.99 \qquad \text{i.e.} \qquad \Phi(z) = 0.99$$

and so, reading from Table A, we obtain $z = 2.326$. But

$$z = \frac{x - \mu}{\sigma}$$

where $\mu=25$ and $\sigma=3$, and so

$$2.326 = \frac{x - 25}{3}$$

From this

$$x = 3\times2.326 + 25 = 31.98$$

What does this result imply? Simply that there is a chance of only about 1% that the servicing time will exceed 32 min.

As these two examples show, by using the relation $Z=(X-\mu)/\sigma$ in conjunction with the standard normal table (Table A), we are able to obtain probabilities in any normal distribution regardless of the value of its mean and standard deviation.

The normal approximation to the binomial distribution

Calculating binomial probabilities can get quite painful for large values of n (and remember that the tables in *EST* only go up to $n=20$). Fortunately, unless the probability p of success is close to 0 or 1, normal distributions can provide quite a good approximation to the binomial distributions.

To illustrate how this approximation is used (and how good it is), let us again consider the binomial distribution with $n=18$ and $p=0.5$. This particular distribution arose in the previous section as the distribution of the number of correct answers obtained by guessing between the two choices in each question. We found that $\mu=9$ and $\sigma=2.12$. Figure 1.21 shows the histogram of this distribution together with the normal distribution $N(9,2.12^2)$. Immediately we see just how well the normal distribution describes the behaviour of this binomial distribution. In fact, it can be shown that the closeness of these two distributions continually improves as n increases – in technical terms, we say that the binomial distribution is *asymptotically* normally distributed.

The calculation of approximate binomial probabilities from the normal distribution is really quite straightforward. For example, let us calculate

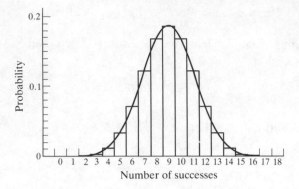

Probability

0.2

0.1

0

0 1 2 3 4 5 6 7 8 9 10 11 12 13 14 15 16 17 18
Number of successes

Figure 1.21

the probability of having 12 or more correct answers on the multiple-choice paper. Figure 1.22 indicates the area under the normal curve needed to approximate the required probability. Note that the shaded region on the normal scale starts at 11.5 rather than 12. This is to compensate for the fact that the binomial variable is discrete (integer-valued) while the normal variable is continuous – the 'correction' of 0.5 is called the *continuity correction*. The reason for its use is clear from the diagram: the area to the right of 12 would clearly be too small.

The value of Z corresponding to the 'corrected' binomial value 11.5 is

$$z = \frac{11.5 - 9}{2.12} = 1.18$$

(where, you will recall, $\mu = np = 18 \times \frac{1}{2} = 9$ and $\sigma = \sqrt{npq} = \sqrt{18 \times \frac{1}{2} \times \frac{1}{2}}$ =2.12). From the normal table (Table A)

$$\text{Prob}(Z \geq 1.18) = 1 - \Phi(1.18)$$
$$= 1 - 0.8810$$
$$= 0.1190$$

which agrees (to four decimal places) with the true probability of 0.1190 obtained earlier using exact binomial calculations.

As a general rule, if $n \geq 20$ and p is between $5/n$ and $1 - 5/n$, quite good results will be obtained using this normal approximation to the binomial distribution (and the larger n is, the better!). The continuity correction gives

$$\text{Prob}(X \leq x) = \Phi\left(\frac{x + 0.5 - \mu}{\sigma}\right)$$

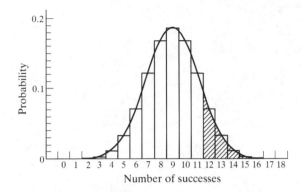

Figure 1.22

$$\mathrm{Prob}(X{=}x) \;=\; \Phi\!\left(\frac{x + 0.5 - \mu}{\sigma}\right) \;-\; \Phi\!\left(\frac{x - 0.5 - \mu}{\sigma}\right)$$

and

$$\mathrm{Prob}(X{\geqslant}x) \;=\; 1 \;-\; \Phi\!\left(\frac{x - 0.5 - \mu}{\sigma}\right)$$

where $\mu{=}np$ and $\sigma{=}\sqrt{npq}$ are the mean and standard deviation of the binomial distribution.

In later chapters you will find that the normal distribution is the asymptotic distribution of very many of the test statistics that we use.

The chi-squared distribtion

The final distribution we need to mention is the so-called *chi-squared* (χ^2) distribution (denoted by the Greek letter (chi) χ, pronounced 'ki'). It was discovered in 1876 by Friedrich Robert Helmert and rediscovered in 1900 by Karl Pearson. Since then it has been used in a wide variety of contexts but, although we too shall use it in later chapters, its complexity prevents us from examining its features in much detail. The shape of its probability density curve varies according to a quantity known as its number of degrees of freedom (denoted by the Greek letter (nu) v in the tables). To give you some idea of how the shape depends on v, we reproduce in Figure 1.23 the density curves for chi-squared distributions for $v{=}1$, 2, 4 and 10. As you see, it is difficult to speak of a typical shape for a chi-squared distribution! However, the sort of information about chi-squared distributions which we shall need later is summarized in Table B. This table gives the end-points for areas of certain sizes. For example, the entry for $v{=}2$ and $q{=}0.95$ is 5.991, and this tells us that the

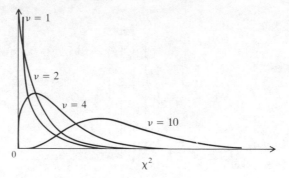

Figure 1.23

area to the left of 5.991 under the chi-squared pdf with $\nu=2$ degrees of freedom is 0.95, as shown in Figure 1.24. It follows that, in this case, with two degrees of freedom, the probability of a chi-squared value being *greater* than 5.991 is $1 - 0.95 = 0.05$, i.e. 5%.

The values tabulated in Table B are referred to as percentage points since they are the values for areas of 95% and 99% of the total (a more extensive range of percentage points of the chi-squared distribution is given on page 21 of *EST*).

A note on the use of the median instead of the mean

In this chapter we have referred to the median and the mean as measures of 'location' or 'average'. Classical statistical tests for location almost always use the mean; however, the mean is not used in distribution-free methods. There are a number of reasons for this. First, there are a few probability distributions that do not even have a mean! Thus, if our distribution-free techniques are to be valid for *all* (continuous) distributions, the mean must clearly be inappropriate. Further, even if a population's mean does exist, the distribution of the sample mean depends very much on that population's probability distribution (unless the sample size is large) – thus the sample mean is not useful for distribution-free purposes.

So, when a measure of location or average is needed in a distribution-free context, we shall invariably use the median. All continuous probability distributions have a median – it is defined as the point, ϕ, that divides the area under the probability density function into two equal parts. For symmetric distributions, ϕ is equal to the mean μ (if μ exists). For non-symmetric (or asymmetric) distributions, ϕ is different

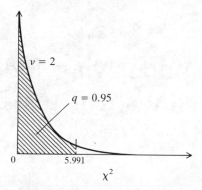

Figure 1.24

from μ; however, in some senses ϕ is then a *better* measure of 'average' or 'typical value' than μ since it is often the case in asymmetric distributions that the minority of extreme values have an undue influence on μ, making it 'untypical' of the distribution as a whole.

2
The underlying ideas of statistical tests

Introduction

Tests (usually called *hypothesis tests* or *significance tests*) often play a major part in statistical investigations. This book is almost entirely concerned with statistical tests, and it is important for us to be quite clear from the start on both the usefulness and the limitations of such procedures. To be honest, many people tend to look upon statisticians, and their techniques and conclusions, with suspicion or even downright distrust. 'You can prove *anything* with statistics' is a common gibe, and this is often supported by Benjamin Disraeli's famous definition of the three kinds of lies.* In this chapter, which in a sense is the most important (and perhaps the most difficult) one in the book, not only will we hope to dispel some of the myths about statistics (and statisticians!), but we shall lay the essential foundations for almost all subsequent chapters.

The basic idea of most statistical techniques is to increase our knowledge about populations using information in samples taken from them. In statistical testing, we are concerned with examining the truth, or otherwise, of hypotheses (suppositions, proposals, claims, guesses, etc.) about some feature(s) of one or more populations. For instance, we might find ourselves considering claims such as:

(a) There are no differences between the average yields from four different types of wheat.
(b) A new medical treatment is more effective than the existing treatment.
(c) Urban children are less healthy than rural children.
(d) There is no connection between sales of luxury goods and unemployment.

* That is, his 'lies, damned lies, and statistics'. Actually, although this famous saying is indeed usually ascribed to Disraeli, John Bibby writes in his amusing little book *Quotes, damned quotes, and . . .* (Demast Books, 1983) that: 'as far as I'can tell, Winston Churchill knew that Mark Twain wrote that Benjamin Disraeli had said the oft-quoted phrase. However, it sounds most un-Disraelite to me. Lord Blake, biographer of Dizzy, has confirmed as much in a personal letter.

. . . and so on.

Whether or not particular hypotheses are eventually assessed to be reasonable will depend on the weight of evidence contained in data from the relevant population(s). Actually, as opposed to the gibe mentioned at the start of the chapter, we never claim to *prove* anything completely by means of a statistical test: we simply pronounce a judgement based on the available evidence, and give an assessment of the strength of that evidence. Of course, sometimes the evidence may be so overwhelming that a hypothesis may be regarded as proved (or disproved) 'for all practical purposes'.

The wary reader will note, both from the preamble and from the examples of hypotheses just given, that the use of statistical tests presupposes the meaningful existence of 'populations'. Traditionally, statisticians and users of statistical techniques seem to have paid scant attention to the validity of this presumption in their areas of application. However, as we have seen in Chapter 1, such validity is by no means a foregone conclusion. Partly because of this, other statisticians have more recently tended to suggest that the complete topic of statistical testing is inappropriate to the real world. The countless thousands of users of statistical tests over the last half-century might find it difficult to agree with such an extreme a view! We agree that more care and attention need to be paid to the questions of existence and identification of the populations under study than has normally been the case in traditional practice, but that, subject to the context being considered suitable as the result of such considerations, tests do have an important and useful role to play in helping to interpret data. As implied in Chapter 1, both the descriptions and the illustrations of the use of the techniques in this book should be read with the understanding that the circumstances of applications are deemed to be appropriate.

Anyone involved with statistical testing should always pay considerable attention to each of the following matters:

(a) understanding the logical structure of the statistical testing procedure;
(b) choosing the most appropriate hypotheses;
(c) stating the conclusions as accurately and as informatively as possible;
(d) interpreting these conclusions 'in English' rather than merely using mathematical or statistical terminology.

To these ends, in the next section we present five main steps which may be used to govern the formulation and execution of *any* statistical test. The use of these five steps virtually guarantees that the important points listed above are all properly covered. We shall present that section as if we were designing a test 'from scratch'; however, in practice, our task will usually be easier than this, for the whole of step 2 and parts of steps 4 and 5 will follow automatically as soon as any specific test from the remaining chapters of this book has been chosen. However, this comprehensive discussion will show you more clearly what really happens in a complete sense in a statistical test, and all the examples given in later chapters effectively consist of these five steps plus some 'technical aids'.

CONCEPTS OF STATISTICAL TESTING

Rather than presenting the underlying ideas of statistical testing 'in the abstract', it seems more sensible to discuss them with reference to a specific problem. So, consider the following situation.

A car-accessory manufacturer has developed what it claims to be an 'improved' car wax polish. A motoring magazine decides to carry out an experiment to compare the new polish with the old so as to test the manufacturer's claim. Eighteen car owners were selected and asked to treat half the roof of their car with the new polish and half with the old. The owners were told to judge which polish gave the better finish and to send their findings to the magazine.

Let us now describe our five steps in terms of this experiment.

STEP 1   FORMULATION OF THE PRACTICAL PROBLEM IN TERMS OF HYPOTHESES

We shall begin by attempting to clarify exactly what is meant by the word 'hypothesis'. According to the authors' edition of the Concise Oxford Dictionary, a hypothesis is defined as 'a supposition made as basis for reasoning, without reference to its truth, or as a starting-point for investigation' and then, maybe rather pessimistically, as a 'groundless assumption'. The dictionary's definition is certainly quite appropriate for one of the hypotheses we use when setting up a test – the so-called *null* hypothesis, which is usually denoted by H_0. This null hypothesis usually represents the proposition that there is no difference between two or more populations (at least in respect of the feature(s) in which we are interested); or, when we are studying just one population, it might represent maintenance of the *status quo*, i.e. *no* difference now from what has been the case before, or no difference from the manufacturer's specifications, and so on. However, as we shall see, any test always involves (at least) *two* hypotheses, namely

(a)   the *null* hypothesis, H_0, and
(b)   an *alternative* hypothesis (denoted by H_1 or H_A).

It is perhaps unfortunate that the word 'alternative' can give the impression that H_1 is somehow inferior to H_0; for it is, in fact, the *more important* hypothesis from the practical point of view. The 'A' might better stand for 'action' rather than 'alternative' since H_1 or H_A *indicates the range of situations that we want the test to be able to recognize or 'diagnose'* should they be true. A positive diagnosis will indicate that we should perhaps take action of some kind (for example, to adopt a new medical treatment if the test indicates it to be better than the existing one, or to recommend a new paint if it is judged better than the rest), or at least to take steps to investigate the situation further.

Although of less practical interest, the null hypothesis plays a fundamental role in the formal details of the test procedure. Remember that, in situations where we have two or more samples, the null hypothesis usually states that there is no difference between the populations being compared; while in a situation involving only one population, it expresses something like the maintenance of the *status quo*. Thus H_0 is *basically a standard or control against which the strength of evidence in favour of the type of difference described by H_1 can be measured.*

The hypotheses appropriate for the problem of the car wax polish can now be immediately identified as:

H_1: The new polish is an improvement on the old one.
H_0: The two polishes are equally good.

Once the hypotheses have been selected, we can proceed to the crux of the formal argument in statistical testing. This may be stated in the following terms:

At the outset, we tentatively *assume* the truth of H_0 (whether or not we actually believe it!). Then, with *this assumption*, if the data lead to a result that is relatively unlikely and would be much better explained if H_1 were true, then we have reason to reject H_0 in favour of H_1 by what is essentially an 'argument by contradiction'.

It is this argument that we pursue in steps 3 to 5.

STEP 2   CHOICE OF THE TEST STATISTIC

How can the data be used in some reasonable and convenient way to test the hypotheses? The first point to make is that, in general, it would be too complicated and cumbersome to use each piece of available data *explicitly* in the test procedure. Instead, what we almost invariably do is to carry out some calculation on the data so as to summarize them in terms of a single representative figure. Any such quantity calculated from the data is called a *statistic* and, for the time being, we shall denote our chosen statistic by T. Obviously we want T to relate to those aspects of the data that are relevant to the particular problem we are trying to solve. There are two important properties that T must satisfy in order to be of use in testing the hypotheses:

(a) Since T is to be used to indicate the weight of evidence pointing to the truth of H_1 as opposed to H_0, then T must tend to behave differently when H_1 is true from when H_0 is true; and, in general, the greater the difference in the real situation from that expressed by H_0, the greater should be the difference in the behaviour of T.

(b) The probability distribution of T must be calculable (at least approximately) under the assumption that H_0 is true. This distribution is called the null distribution and provides the guide as to what are or are not reasonable values of T under H_0.

So how can we devise an appropriate test statistic T for the car wax problem? Let us consider the following simple procedure:

A car owner has to judge between the two polishes. Suppose we denote his judgment by '+' or '−' according to whether he judges the new or the old polish to be the better. Let us define T as the total number of '+'s, i.e. T is the number of car owners who judged the new polish as the better of the two.

Is this test statistic T appropriate for the job? The answer is clearly 'yes'. It certainly satisfies the former of the above two criteria; for if the new polish is a real improvement (i.e. H_1 is true), then we can expect T to have a high value, whereas if the polishes were just as good as each other (i.e. H_0 is true) we would expect the numbers of '+'s and '−'s to be fairly similar, leading to a more moderate value of T. Thus the behaviour of T depends on whether H_0 or H_1 is true, as required. The second criterion is also satisfied since, if H_0 is true, the car owners' decisions as to which is the better polish will be rather like tossing a coin, i.e. they will each produce a '+' or a '−' with probability of $\frac{1}{2}$ each; consequently the null distributioin of T is binomial with $n=18$ and $p=\frac{1}{2}$ (cf. the example regarding the mutliple-choice exam paper in Chapter 1).

Once we have discovered the null distribution of T (i.e. its probability distribution when H_0 is true), we can discriminate between what are and are not reasonable values of T under H_0.

STEP 3   THE CRITICAL REGION AND HOW IT IS USED

Once the test statistic T has been selected, we ask: 'What kind of values of T will most strongly point to H_1 being true rather than H_0 being true?' Such a collection of values of T is called a *critical region*. Then, if we find that the value of T calculated from our data lies in such a critical region, our conclusion is that we may 'reject H_0 in favour of H_1'; when this happens, the value of T is said to be *significant*. But if T does not lie in the critical region then we do not have sufficient evidence to reject H_0 in favour of H_1 and the value of T is then said to be *not significant*.

Unlike many books and teachers, we avoid talking about 'accepting H_0' in this latter case. The reason is that there is invariably a wide range of possible situations under which any particular value of T can be regarded as reasonable and, since we cannot discriminate between such situations, then there is no reason why we should believe (i.e. 'accept') H_0 rather than any of the other (possibly countless) possibilities under which our value of T may be regarded as reasonable. For example, suppose an investigation involves the hypotheses

H_0: Average length = 60 cm.
H_1: Average length > 60 cm.

To speak of accepting H_0 in this case seems to imply that we believe the average length is *definitely* 60 cm and not 59.7 cm or 60.1 cm or any other possible value for which the same value of T is still unsurprising. Furthermore, tests are always constructed so that lack of information, especially through having too little data, tends to produce *non-significant* values; in this case, it is obviously even more misleading to talk positively about 'accepting H_0'. So we prefer the less ambitious description of 'not rejecting H_0', which gives a more accurate impression of what the test has found (or rather, not found!).

In the car wax problem, remember that if H_1 is true then we expect more '+'s than '−'s (i.e. a high value of T); otherwise if H_0 is true we expect similar numbers of '+'s and '−'s (a moderate value of T) or, of course, fewer '+'s than '−'s (a low value of T) if the new polish is inferior to the old one. So we should reject H_0 in favour of H_1 (i.e. have positive evidence that the new polish is better) only if T is *large*, i.e. in symbols, if $T \geqslant c$, where c is some appropriately chosen 'critical value'. This critical value c is determined using our knowledge of the null distribution of T, which in this example is binomial with $n=18$ and $p=\frac{1}{2}$. Since the average value of T under this distribution is 9 (from $\mu=np=18\times\frac{1}{2}$), values of c that are possibly worth considering are, say, 10 or 11 or 12, . . . or 17, or even 18. The selection of a suitable critical value from these possibilities is the subject of step 4.

STEP 4 DECIDING ON A SIGNIFICANCE LEVEL, AND HENCE DETERMINING THE CRITICAL VALUE

We have now decided on the *type* of critical region appropriate for our test, namely $T \geqslant c$. But how do we decide on the details of precisely how large the critical region should be, i.e. how do we choose c? To help us with this, we need to consider what are the acceptable levels of risk of the test giving incorrect conclusions from the data; for it is a sad fact of life that, *however* we decide on the criteria for rejecting or not rejecting H_0, incorrect conclusions will always be possible.

If, for example, the critical region is relatively large, then H_0 may often be rejected when it should not be (an injustice!). On the other hand if, in order to avoid this type of error, we make the critical region very small, then we will find ourselves frequently *failing* to reject H_0 when we should be doing so (another injustice!). In practice, the decision on whether or not to reject H_0 depends on what is known as the *significance level* (or the size) of the test. This is defined as the *risk we are prepared to take of committing the error of rejecting H_0 when it is in fact true*. (This kind of risk is sometimes referred to as a type I error. A type II error refers to the other risk, i.e. of not rejecting H_0 when it is in fact false.) In other words, it is the probability of obtaining a significant value of T when H_0 is true. The larger or smaller the significance level, the larger or smaller will be the critical region.

We use significance levels of between about 0.1% and 10%, depending on the practical seriousness of making this kind of error. Our standard practice throughout the book, for all tests and choices of hypotheses, is to provide details for significance levels of 5% and 1%, which are the ones most commonly used, and sometimes a couple of others.

Suppose that for the car wax problem we decide, at least in the first instance, on a significance level of about 5%. We would say 'about 5%' since it is usually impossible with a discrete null distribution to obtain critical regions that correspond *exactly* to a given nominal probability such as 5%. So, for this approximate significance level, what is the appropriate critical region? Now, as we have already seen, the null distribution of the test statistic T is binomial with $n=18$ and $p=\frac{1}{2}$, and we seek a value c such that $P(T \geqslant c) = 0.05$ when H_0 is true. Using the table of probabilities for the binomial distribution given in Chapter 1 (page 32) we see that $P(T \geqslant 13) = 0.0481$, which is the closest we can get to 0.05. Thus, we may state the test's decision rule as follows:

If $T \geqslant 13$ we shall reject H_0 in favour of H_1 at a significance level of about 5%, otherwise we shall not reject H_0 (at this level).

In other words, we are saying that such values of T are so much more likely under H_1 than under H_0 that we claim positive support for the truth of H_1. Otherwise, if $T \leqslant 12$, we cannot reject H_0 in favour of H_1, for then either the value of T is 'middling' and so entirely reasonable under H_0, or T is small – in which case, although it is unlikely to occur under H_0, it would be even more unlikely under H_1.

Now suppose that the results from the 18 car owners were

$+$ $+$ $+$ $-$ $+$ $+$ $+$ $+$ $+$ $+$ $+$ $-$ $+$ $+$ $+$ $+$ $+$ $+$

Counting the number of '+' signs gives $T=16$.

STEP 5   CONCLUSION

Referring to the above decision rule, we see that there is sufficient evidence (at the 5% level of significance) to reject the null hypothesis that the car waxes are equally good in favour of the alternative hypothesis that the new wax polish is indeed an improvement.

We could leave the issue there. However, a conclusion like this, which is based merely on whether we are or are not able to reject H_0 in favour of H_1 at some prescribed significance level (5% in this case) can be very wasteful of the information in the data. Suppose the investigation had produced the even more extreme result that all 18 signs were '+'s, i.e. *every* car owner preferred the new wax. Then, of course, again we would have rejected H_0 in favour of H_1 at the 5% significance level. But this conclusion would also have been reached had there been 17, 16 (as above), 15, 14 or even 13 '+'s! In practice, a much more informative conclusion may be reached by considering *various* significance levels and determining how big the critical region needs to be in order for the observed value of T to fall just into it. How accurately one can do this depends of course on how much detail is available on the null distribution – we do not always have the complete information available as we do in our current example.

In practice, though, no great accuracy is necessary; all that is really needed is a rough assessment of the weight of evidence supporting H_1. Even a fairly approximate idea of the 'borderline' significance level leads to much more useful and meaningful interpretations. Typical conclusions could be that there is:

(a)   very little, if any, evidence (if the 'borderline' significance level exceeds 10%);
(b)   some suspicion, but nowhere near conclusive evidence (between 5% and 10%);
(c)   considerable evidence (between 1% and 5%);
(d)   very strong evidence (between 0.1% and 1%);
(e)   practically conclusive evidence (less than 0.1%).

How does this discussion affect our conclusion in the car wax problem? Previously we described the result $T=16$ as being significant at the 5% level. But the table on page 32 in Chapter 1 gives $P(T \geqslant 16)=0.0007$. Therefore the result is far stronger than merely 'significant at the 5% level'; it is in fact significant at the 0.07% level (or at any weaker level, i.e. at any level exceeding 0.07%). So, in the words of the preceding paragraph, we have 'practically conclusive evidence' to support the manufacturer's claim that the new polish is better than the old.

SUMMARY

The above ideas on statistical testing are conveniently summarized in the flowchart shown in Figure 2.1. In this flowchart, notice that there is a choice to be made on whether or not to follow the *simple* route. The non-mature, relatively 'simple-minded', route (the left-hand side) follows our initial description of fixing a significance level and then essentially just answering yes or no to the question of whether the result is significant at this specific level. This rather unimaginative approach is still used in some textbooks but, as we have seen, it can be very wasteful of the information actually presented in the data. Nevertheless, if the ideas of statistical testing are new to you, you may find it easier to stay with this approach for the time being. The more sophisticated route (the right-hand side) summarizes the approach covered in all but the first paragraph in step 5 above.

Finally, we should remind the reader that, in practice, substantial parts of the above procedure will be simplified once we have decided which test to use. The test we have devised for the car wax problem is a standard procedure known as the 'sign test', to be covered in more detail in Chapter 3. The main practical simplifications are that, as soon as we have decided to use such a standard test,

(a)   the statistic to be calculated is automatically decided upon, and
(b)   details of critical values for particular significance levels are made directly available to us in tables, without us having to investigate the null distribution ourselves.

One-sided and two-sided tests

We have already seen the fundamental role played by the alternative hypothesis H_1 in determining the critical region; for, if you recall, the critical region represents the types of samples which, if they occur, would most strongly influence us to believe in H_1 rather than H_0. In the above problem, this led to critical regions of the form $T \geqslant c$. We shall now see that H_1 is responsible for classifying a test as being either *one-sided* or *two-sided*.

In the car wax problem it seemed that the most appropriate alternative hypothesis for the situation was

H_1: The new polish is an improvement on the old one.

But suppose, more generally, that we were interested in finding out

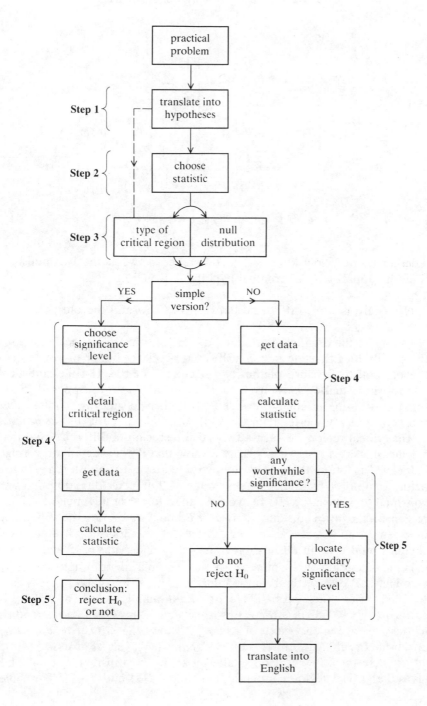

Figure 2.1 Flowchart for statistical testing.

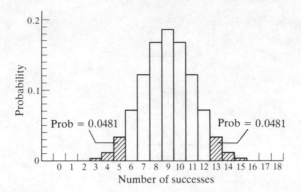

Figure 2.2   Critical region $T \leqslant 5$ and $T \geqslant 13$.

whether there is *any* kind of real difference between the two polishes, then the appropriate alternative hypothesis would be

H_1: There is *some* difference between the new and the old polishes.

Now, unlike the original alternative, this H_1 of some difference allows for the possibilities that the new polish could be either better or worse than the old polish. Because of the 'two-sidedness' of this H_1, the statistical test for this situation is referred to as a *two-sided test*, as opposed to the test based on the original 'one-sided' H_1 (which specifically required that the new polish be better than the old), which is called a *one-sided test*.

The critical region for such a two-sided test is quite different from that for the one-sided test. Under H_0, we know that the 'expected' or average value of T is 9 (i.e. $18 \times \frac{1}{2}$). For the two-sided test, it is a difference in the actual value of T from its expected value of 9 in *either* direction that will constitute evidence for H_1. In symbols, therefore, we now need a critical region of the form 'distance between T and 9' $\geqslant c^*$ i.e. the difference between T and 9 is at least c. For example, if we choose $c=4$, the critical region would contain all possible values of T satisfying $T \leqslant 5$ and $T \geqslant 13$.

However, using the symmetry of the binomial distribution with $p = \frac{1}{2}$ (see Fig. 2.2) or directly from the table on page 32 in Chapter 1, it is easy to find that the probability of T attaining such a value is $2 \times 0.00481 = 0.0962$ or 9.62%; this is the significance level corresponding to this critical region – and, of course, it shows the critical region to be unsatisfactory if we are interested in significance levels of around 5%. So let us make the critical region smaller by taking $c=5$ instead of $c=4$. This gives the critical region containing the values $T \leqslant 4$ and $T \geqslant 14$. The table

* This statement is sometimes written as $|T-9| \geqslant c$, where as we mentioned in Chapter 1 the vertical bars mean 'take the absolute value of $T-9$'.

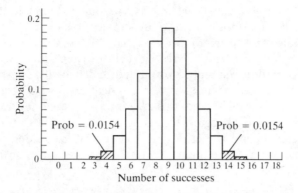

Figure 2.3   Critical region $T \leqslant 4$ and $T \geqslant 14$.

on page 32 shows us that the corresponding significance level is $2 \times 0.0154 = 0.0308$(See Fig. 2.3) – rather less than 0.05 but certainly more appropriate than the 0.0962 significance level for $c=4$.

So our decision rule for the two-sided test is to reject H_0 in favour of H_1 if $T \leqslant 4$ or $T \geqslant 14$, and otherwise not to reject H_0. This rule is the best we can find for the nominal significance level of 5% although, as we have just seen, the actual significance level is more like 3%.

The question of which form of alternative hypothesis is relevant, and so whether a one-sided or two-sided test should be used, should always be decided *before* the data are inspected (or preferably even collected). The deciding factor is whether one is concerned in practice with diagnosing a difference in *either* direction or in *just one* direction, should H_0 be untrue; and this is ruled out by the practical circumstances of the problem being investigated. For instance, a company might be interested in discovering whether one of its products differs in quality from its rivals (giving a two-sided test); or on the other hand it might only be interested in testing whether its product is *inferior* (giving a one-sided test) since evidence of this might necessitate action involving redesign, price cutting, etc. A one-sided test is more *sensitive* (more likely to reject H_0) if there is actually a difference in the prescribed direction – but this is at the expense of having *no* sensitivity at all for recognizing differences in the opposite direction. This is well illustrated by the car wax problem. The value $T=13$, which is quite a likely result if the new polish is rather better than the old, is significant at the 5% level in the one-sided test, but not in the two-sided test. On the other hand, very small values are significant in the two-sided test (with its nominal 5% critical region $T \leqslant 4$ and $T \leqslant 14$) but not in the above-one-sided test.

The choice between one- and two-sided tests is usually easier to make when dealing with actual practical problems (when the details of the problem are well understood) than with some textbook problems (when such details may be lacking). However, we shall attempt in this book to give sufficient description of the illustrative problems to allow well informed choices to be made.

Of course, in our tables, etc., it will be necessary to distinguish between information relating to one-sided and two-sided tests. We shall use α_1 and α_2 to denote the significance levels corresponding respectively to one-sided and two-sided tests. Thus, for example, we would write the critical region for the above one-sided test as $T \geqslant 13$ for $\alpha_1 = 5\%$ (nominal) and the critical region for the two-sided test as $T \leqslant 4$ and $T \geqslant 14$ for $\alpha_2 = 5\%$ (nominal).

Best conservative critical values

We mentioned earlier that it is often impossible to obtain a critical region that exactly corresponds to a desired significance level (this was very marked in the above two-sided test!). So we follow what is in fact standard practice of indicating the largest critical region whose significance level is *no greater* than the nominal figure, i.e. we use the so-called '*best conservative*' critical regions. For example, suppose that, in the one-sided version of the car wax problem, we wanted to use a nominal significance level of $\alpha_1 = 1\%$ (so as to lessen the risk of rejecting H_0 when it is in fact true). From the table on page 32 we find that, if H_0 is true,

$$\text{Prob}(T \geqslant 14) = 0.0154$$
$$\text{Prob}(T \geqslant 15) = 0.0038$$

The 1% best conservative critical region is $T \geqslant 15$, even though $\text{Prob}(T \geqslant 14) = 0.0154$ is actually slightly closer to $0.01 = 1\%$ than 0.0038, the $\text{Prob}(T \geqslant 15)$; so we are erring 'on the safe side'! The practice of using best conservative critical values is adopted in *EST* and virtually all other books of statistics tables as well as in the tables in this book.

Power of tests

We shall often present more than one test for a given problem. How then do you, the reader, decide which to use in practice? We shall discuss the pros and cons of the tests as we go along. For example, one test may be particularly quick and simple to execute whereas a second, more complicated, test may be better able to diagnose when H_1 is true, i.e. it may be more *sensitive* or *powerful*. Whether one goes for the simple test or instead decides that the extra sensitivity or power justifies the harder work needed for the second test will be a matter of personal taste and circumstances.

Exact power comparisons are usually difficult or impossible, so we will usually make only qualitative comments. However, in some cases approximate power calculations have been done (usually from computer simulations) and then we will be able to be more specific.

Finally, we shall go into a little more detail on some problems of interpretation and application of statistical tests. We have already mentioned, near the beginning of the chapter, that difficulties involved with clearly defining relevant populations rightly cause concern to some statisticians. Presuming that these difficulties can be overcome, an even nastier logical obstacle awaits us; namely, that the *null hypotheses are virtually never true*!

For illustration, let us consider again the example of the car polishes. We established earlier that the appropriate null hypothesis was

H_0: The two polishes are equally good.

'Equally good'? *Exactly* equally good? Even if the two polishes are made by the same manufacturer, there are bound to be some differences in chemical formulations and the conditions under which they were made, and consequently in their properties. The differences may be substantial, or they may be slight, but nonetheless differences there will be.

Further, again consider the four examples at the beginning of the chapter. The appropriate null hypotheses are as follows:

(a) There are no differences between the average yields from four different types of wheat. *No* differences? That implies they are all *precisely* the same. How likely is that?
(b) A new medical treatment is exactly as effective as the existing treatment. Perhaps the only way this can be envisaged as being possible is if both treatments were entirely useless, which is not a very interesting situation!
(c) Urban children are just as healthy (or unhealthy) as rural children. Apart from the supreme difficulties of uniquely defining what we mean by urban and rural and of measuring 'health', could anybody really even consider the possibility of exact equality of 'healthiness' in the two groups?
(d) There is no connection between sales of luxury goods and unemployment. No connection? Do we really mean none at all?

Put in more formal terms, null hypotheses are almost always expressed in terms of an exact identity of two or more distributions, or at least identity of various aspects of them; or, when just one population is the subject of study, H_0 usually proposes a specific value for some characteristic such as the mean or median, or an exact specification of that population's distribution. Consider the standard textbook example of testing a coin for unbiasedness or fairness, usually expressed in terms of H_0: $p=\frac{1}{2}$, where p is the probability of the coin turning up heads when tossed. There are, incidentally, plenty of problems here of the type discussed in Chapter 1 regarding definitions, stability, etc. As the coin is repeatedly tossed, its properties will change – it will become worn, quite possibly more on one side than the other, and it may pick up some dirt; thus p could keep changing. In any case, is it really true that the outcome is wholly independent of *how* the coin is tossed, and *who* tosses it? But, setting all that aside, and supposing that the event of throwing a head really does have a meaningful probability p, is it really feasible that p could be equal to 0.5? That means *precisely* 0.5 and not 0.499 999 9999 or 0.500 000 0001 or anything else. Also, we have only used 10 decimal places here, whereas p (being a *continuous* quantity) should strictly be expressed to infinitely many decimal places for complete precision; and 0.500 000 00 . . . is only one possibility out of 'infinitely many'. Realizing this, would you bet on H_0 being true for any particular coin.

Having become aware of such uncomfortable facts of life, some statisticians have come to the rather extreme conclusion that statistical tests have no value. The authors of this book, along with the majority of researchers, do not concur with this extreme attitude. However, we do believe that users of tests should be a lot more aware of such conceptual problems, and their consequences, than is usually the case. What are the implications?

First, you must *never* make the common mistake of inferring from a non-significant result in a test that H_0 is somehow 'proved' or even supported in any positive way. For, as we have indicated, the chances are that you will never come across a true null hypothesis in your lifetime! This is why we were careful earlier in the chapter to talk of 'not rejecting' H_0 when we obtain a non-significant result, as opposed to 'accepting it'. It also follows that, when we are carrying out a two-sided test, the alternative hypothesis is essentially *always* true (we do not need any data at all to establish that!). Of course, in the one-sided case it is quite feasible for *both* H_0 and H_1 to be untrue – the true state can be the other side of H_0 from H_1; however, let us just consider two-sided cases for now.

The vital point to realize is that a two-sided H_1 contains absolutely every possibility other than the single case comprising H_0; in particular, it includes cases very close to H_0, and it includes everything in between. With this more refined way of looking at the situation, what is it that a statistical test does, and what do we want it to do? Bearing in mind what we have just been saying, what we want is for the test to tell us when H_0 is *substantially* in error. Very small differences between yields from various types of wheat, or between medical treatments, or between car polishes, are (usually) unimportant for us to know about. We certainly do want to know about larger differences; and the larger the differences, the more important it is that we know about them. This idea reflects very nicely what a test does. It is a good thing that generally we do not want to know about very small differences, because normally a test will not be able to tell us about them, for the distribution of the test statistic T will then be only minutely different from its null distribution. But if the differences are substantial, the distribution of T (and hence its behaviour) will be *considerably* different from the null distribution, and this will generally considerably increase the chance of T falling into the critical region, i.e. giving a significant result. The practical effect of all this is that, in some quite unquantifiable way, significant results from tests will tend to correspond to relatively substantial (and perhaps important) differences from H_0; i.e. tests will usually do just the kind of thing that we want them to do.

But beware! There is a way to upset this happy state of affairs; and that, believe it or not, is to collect a *lot* of data. Now usually, of course, it is imagined that the more information we collect, the better able we are to get the 'right' answer; and, strictly speaking, that is also true with statistical tests. The unusual aspect of tests is that, as we have already established, we know what the 'right' answer is even before we look at any data. The 'right' answer is that H_0 is false and H_1 (at least, if it is two-sided) is true! So (paradoxically) a very large amount of data can make a test more sensitive (at least from a practical point of view) than does a moderate amount of data. A large amount of data makes it very likely that a test will give a significant result, irrespective of whether the difference from H_0 is large or small, whereas using the test with moderate amounts of data will tend to give significant results when the difference from H_0 is important and non-significant results when the difference is unimportant.

This is why, in spite of the basic logical difficulties, tests have been found so useful over the years by countless users of statistical techniques. For reasons of economy of time and effort, amounts of data used in tests have tended to be 'moderate' rather than 'very large'. So, maybe more by luck than by judgement, users of tests have found themselves getting what they perceive to be useful and 'correct' results from tests, i.e. correct from the point of view of practical importance, as opposed to correct from the point of view of the formal definitions of the hypotheses.

Nobody can define exactly what is meant by terms as 'moderate' or 'very large', so we will not try. The sort of sample sizes that we use in the illustrations in this book are typical of standard practice, which has stood up well to the test of time. A moral that results from this discussion is that you should not decry the use of small samples nor, following a related argument, the use of relatively unsophisticated tests. Remember that a significant result using a small sample and/or an unsophisticated test will, far more often than not, indicate a more important difference from H_0 than a result of the same significance using a larger sample and/or a more sophisticated test!

Conclusion

You may have found some of the discussion in this chapter quite difficult to take in. That would not be surprising, for several of the points we have made here are poorly understood by many users of statistical methods, with the result that such users tend to over- or under-estimate the extent of the evidence in their data. We would recommend that you now read the next one or two chapters, and then come back and reread this chapter a little later. You will then find these important ideas taking shape and meaning much more than they may have done at the first reading.

PART II

Tests involving one sample

The two chapters in this part of the book are both concerned with investigating a single population, as opposed to comparing two or more populations. In Chapter 3 we test hypotheses about the median of the population, and two tests are presented for this situation. First, we return to the sign test which, as we saw in Chapter 2, is extremely simple to apply and needs only minimal assumptions about the underlying population. The other test, Wilcoxon's signed-rank test, uses more detailed information from the sample and so naturally is more powerful than the sign test; however, the conditions for its validity are more restrictive than with the sign test.

Chapter 4 deals with a quite different one-sample problem, usually called 'goodness-of-fit'. In this case the hypotheses being tested concern the nature of the whole population distribution rather than just the median. Again, two tests are presented. One of these tests, the Kolmogorov–Smirnov test, is particularly appropriate for continuous populations, while the other one, the chi-squared test, is more convenient with discrete populations. However, as we shall see, both tests can be used for either type of population. More important differences between these two tests relate to the kind of null hypothesis being tested. If H_0 proposes a completely specified distribution (for example, that the population is normally distributed with mean 10 and standard deviation 2), then the Kolmogorov–Smirnov test is the more powerful of the two – though it is more time-consuming to apply. However, if H_0 just specifies that the population has one of a family of distributions (for example, that it is some unspecified binomial distribution) then, in general, only the chi-squared test can be used.

3
One-sample location tests

THE SIGN TEST

Introduction

The sign test is almost certainly the oldest of all formal statistical tests as there is published evidence of its use long ago by J. Arbuthnott (1710)! It exists in several forms, but the version presented here is the one already introduced in Chapter 2, i.e. a test for the median value of a population. However, in this section we examine the procedure in more detail then previously.

PRACTICAL EXAMPLE

The managing director of a mail-order company is concerned about the possible slow progress of orders through his administration department. He tells the administration manager to ensure that at least half of the orders received are processed within one day (eight working hours). Some weeks later he times 18 orders selected at random to check whether his demand has been met.

HYPOTHESES

Being somewhat distrustful of his administration manager's ability, the managing director's main aim in performing the test is to check for evidence that his instructions have *not* been met. This happens when *less* than half of the order are being processed within eight working hours, or in other words, that the median processing time ϕ exceeds 8 h. The hypotheses may be summarized as follows:

$$H_0: \phi = 8 \text{ h.}$$
$$H_1: \phi > 8 \text{ h.}$$

Clearly, H_1 indicates that the test is *one-sided*. Therefore, we shall initially present the details appropriate for such a one-sided test; the amendments needed for the two-sided version of the test will be given later.

DATA

The times spent by the 18 orders in the administration process were recorded as:

16 h 30 min	14 h 00 min	5 h 40 min	9 h 10 min	11 h 45 min
4 h 20 min	7 h 55 min	10 h 15 min	7 h 45 min	16 h 05 min
10 h 05 min	7 h 30 min	9 h 15 min	11 h 55 min	9 h 25 min
10 h 35 min	8 h 20 min	10 h 10 min		

STATISTIC

The test is called the *sign* test because the statistic used is computed from data that are in (or have been reduced to) the form of '+' and '−' signs. So here let us write a '+' for all those times greater than 8 h and a '−' for those times less than 8 h. The above data can thus be represented as:

+	+	−	+	+	−
−	+	−	+	+	−
+	+	+	+	+	+

It is worth mentioning here that, once he had definitely decided to use the sign test, the managing director could have saved himself some trouble in collecting these data. Rather than bothering to produce the detailed information above, all he really had to do was to check the progress of each order at precisely eight working hours (i.e. at the same time next day) after receipt at administration; those which had then been processed through administration would be recorded as '−'s, and the rest as '+'s.

The test statistic, which we will denote by S, may be either the number of '+' signs or the number of '−' signs, according to context. Clearly, if H_0 is true we would expect the number of '+'s and '−'s to be roughly equal, whereas if H_1: $\phi > 8$ h is true, we would expect a relatively large number of '+'s and correspondingly few '−'s. The table of critical values (Table C at the back of the book) is given in terms of *small* values of the statistic, and therefore here we need to define S as the number of '−' signs.

CRITICAL REGIONS

With S defined in this way, the smaller the value of S then the more evidence there is to support H_1. Thus critical regions are of the form:

$$S \leq \text{critical value}$$

Following the convention we introduced in Chapter 2, we denote significance levels relevant to one-sided tests by α_1 (and those relevant to two-sided tests by α_2). Thus from Table C (or the more detailed table on page 29 of *EST*) we see that, with a sample size $n=18$, the critical regions are $S \leqslant 5$ and $S \leqslant 3$ for significance levels $\alpha_1 = 5\%$ and 1% respectively.

SOLUTION

The 18 signs include only five minuses and so $S=5$. This result is significant at the $\alpha_1 = 5\%$ level, and consequently the managing director has obtained some evidence in favour of H_1, i.e. it seems quite likely that his requirement is not being met by the administration department.

DISCUSSION

The sign test is clearly an extremely quick and simple one-sample test for the median value. The fact that the numerical data are dispensed with and only the limited information, as summarized by the '+' and '−' signs, is retained, does mean, however, that relatively large differences between the numbers of '+' and '−' signs are necessary for the test to produce significant results, particularly if the sample is small. In other words, the test tends to support H_1 only when it is intuitively obvious from the data that H_1 is probably true! However, this criticism becomes less true for larger sample sizes, as can be seen by inspection of the more extensive table of critical values in *EST*; for example, with $n=100$, a 41/59 split of signs is sufficient to reject H_0 at the $\alpha_1 = 5\%$ significance level.

It is worth mentioning at this point that, in order to produce tests which are truly distribution-free (i.e. make no detailed assumptions about the form of population distribution), it turns out to be *necessary* to use statistics that do not depend on the actual numerical values in the data, but instead rely on a cruder summary of them (such as '+' and '−' signs in the sign test). In two-sample and other situations to be covered in later chapters, the reduction in information needed is not so drastic as in the one-sample case, so that the resulting test procedures tend to have rather greater power and sensitivity than the sign test. However, it will still always be the case that actual numerical values from the data will *never* be used in the formation of the test statistics in order that the 'distribution-freeness' property be retained. A by-product of this policy is that the resulting test statistics will generally be rather quicker and easier to calculate than their equivalents in classical statistical methods.

One-sided and two-sided tests
As we have said, a choice has to be made between defining S as the number of '+' signs or as the number of '−' signs. For a one-sided test, the appropriate choice is the one *which would be expected to have the smaller value when H_1 is true.* For a two-sided test, we define S simply as whichever of the two choices actually gives the smaller number. Thus in the above example, had we been testing H_0: $\phi=8$ against the two-sided alternative H_1: $\phi \neq 8$, S would take the value 5 *either* if there were 13 '+'s and 5 '−'s (as in our problem) or if there were 5 '+'s and 13 '−'s. But in the one-sided case above, had there been 13 '−'s and 5 '+'s, the test

value would have been $S=13$ (since in that problem S is equal to the number of '$-$' signs) and, of course, this would have provided no evidence in favour of the stated alternative H_1: $\phi>8$.

So in the two-sided case, the critical regions are of the form

$$S \leqslant \text{critical value}$$

where S is *either* the number of '$+$' signs *or* the number of '$-$' signs, whichever is the smaller. Thus, for example, either 3 '$-$'s or 3 '$+$'s would lead to the rejection of H_0: $\phi=8$ in favour of H_1: $\phi\neq8$ at the $\alpha_2=2\%$ level of significance.

What happens if any observations are equal to the hypothesized value of ϕ?
If we are sampling from a continuous distribution and recording observations to sufficient accuracy, it is extremely unlikely that any observations will be *exactly* equal to the hypothesized value (8 h 00 min in the above example). However, usually data cannot be measured to such extreme accuracy and, in any case, it is often convenient to round values to relatively large units even if greater accuracy is possible. (For example, the above data have clearly been rounded to the nearest 5 min, although it would surely have been possible to measure the times more accurately than that.) It is then quite likely that one or two observations might be recorded as equal to the hypothesized value. The usual procedure with the sign test is to discard such values from the sample and to reduce the sample size accordingly. So, for example, if the first observation in the above sample had been 8 h 00 min instead of 16 h 30 min, we would then have considered the sample to be of size 17, consisting of 5 '$-$'s and 12 '$+$'s (which would still have produced evidence significant at the $\alpha_1=5\%$ level in favour of H_1: $\phi>8$). This procedure is quite satisfactory unless there are *several* observations at the crucial value; then there is a case for retaining the original sample size and sharing out these awkward observations equally, i.e. regarding half of them as '$-$'s and half as '$+$'s.

Null distributions
The null distribution of S, which we recall is its distribution when H_0 is true, has already been discussed in Chapter 2. However, for completeness, here are the details again.

If H_0 is true, then every one of the n observations in the sample gives rise to a '$+$' or a '$-$' sign with probability $\frac{1}{2}$ each. Now as all observations are *independent* of each other (which follows from the concept of a random sample), we know that the total number of '$-$' signs (or of '$+$' signs) has the binomial distribution with parameters n (the sample size) and $p=\frac{1}{2}$ (see page 31).

Thus if S represents the statistic used in the above practical problem (i.e. the number of '$-$' signs in a sample of $n=18$ signs), then all probabilities to do with S may be read directly from the table given on page 32 (or from pages 10–11 in *EST*). In particular, recalling that our critical regions are of the form $S \leqslant$ critical value, we quote the following:

$$\text{Prob}(S\leqslant3) = 0.0038$$

$$\text{Prob}(S\leqslant4) = 0.0154$$

$$\text{Prob}(S \leqslant 5) = 0.0481$$

$$\text{Prob}(S \leqslant 6) = 0.1189$$

As we mentioned in Chapter 2, with a discrete-valued statistic it is not generally possible to find critical regions corresponding exactly to the nominal 5% or 1% figures traditionally used for significance levels. The convention that is commonly adopted, and which is used in our tables (and in *EST*), is to indicate the largest critical region whose significance level is no greater than the nominal figure (the so-called best conservative critical region). Thus, using the above probabilities, we see that the best conservative critical region corresponding to $\alpha_1 = 1\%$ is $S \leqslant 3$; in fact, it corresponds to a significance level of 0.38% whereas the next larger critical region, $S \leqslant 4$, corresponds to a significance level of 1.54%, which is *larger* than the nominal 1%. Similarly, the best conservative critical region for a nominal significance level of 5% is $S \leqslant 5$.

In the two-sided case, S is defined as the number of either '−' or '+' signs, whichever is the smaller: for example, that $S \leqslant 3$ corresponds to the number of '−' (or '+') signs being 0, 1, 2, 3, 15, 16, 17 or 18. Since binomial distributions with $p = \frac{1}{2}$ are symmetric, it is clear that $\text{Prob}(S \leqslant 3)$ is now $2 \times 0.0038 = 0.0076$; similarly all other probabilities in the above list need doubling. You will then see the justification for using the same list of critical values in Table C for both cases, but with the α_2 significance levels being *double* those of α_1.

Large sample sizes

If n exceeds 50, critical values are not obtainable from Table C. However, it is easy to see how approximate critical values may be calculated. For large n, we have seen in Chapter 1 that binomial distributions are well approximated by normal distributions, particularly when $p = \frac{1}{2}$. In the one-sided case, we know that the null distribution of S is the binomial distribution with parameters n and $p = \frac{1}{2}$. This distribution has mean $\mu = np = \frac{1}{2}n$ and standard deviation $\sigma = \sqrt{np(1-p)} = \sqrt{n/4} = \frac{1}{2}\sqrt{n}$.

We can therefore obtain good approximate critical values using the integer part of $\mu - z\sigma - \frac{1}{2} = \frac{1}{2}n - \frac{1}{2}z\sqrt{n} - \frac{1}{2}$, where z is the required percentage point of the standard normal distribution (from Table A) and where we have used the continuity correction (see Ch. 1). For $\alpha_1 = 5\%$ and 1% the respective values of z are 1.6449 and 2.3263. So, for example, with $n = 50$ and $\alpha_1 = 5\%$, the approximate critical value of S is the integer part of $\frac{1}{2} \times 50 - \frac{1}{2} \times 1.6449\sqrt{50} - \frac{1}{2} = 18.68$, i.e. 18, which is the same as the entry in Table C.

Critical values for the two-sided test are obtained similarly using the appropriate values of z; for example, with $\alpha_2 = 5\%$ and 1%, z is 1.96 and 2.5758 respectively.

THE WILCOXON SIGNED-RANK TEST

Introduction

We have already remarked on the fact that the representation of the data in the sign test by just '+'s and '−'s is a rather drastic reduction of the original numerical information. For example, no use is made of the fact that two out of the 18 processing times in the above practical problem are actually greater than 16 working hours, i.e. *two* days! Unfortunately, as we have discussed (see page 67) there is no way of using such more detailed information without upsetting the distribution-free property of the procedure. Nevertheless the signed-rank test, published by Wilcoxon (1945), does make some use of the sizes of the differences between the observed values and the hypothesized median. The price to be paid is a restriction on the form of the population distribution for which the procedure is valid. Not only should the distribution be continuous (as usual), but also its probability density function must be *symmetric*. This is, of course, by no means as severe a restriction as that of normality, which is required by the classical statistical methods, but it does mean that the test is not truly distribution-free.

PRACTICAL PROBLEM

We shall illustrate Wilcoxon's signed-rank test with the same practical problem as for the sign test, i.e. using the times that 18 orders took to be processed by an administration system.

HYPOTHESES

As before, we have

$$H_0: \phi = 8 \text{ h.}$$
$$H_1: \phi > 8 \text{ h.}$$

STATISTIC

For each observation we compute the difference between the time taken and the hypothesized median value of 8 h. These differences are shown below:

+8 h 30 min	+6 h 00 min	−2 h 20 min	+1 h 10 min	+3 h 45 min
−3 h 40 min	−0 h 05 min	+2 h 15 min	−0 h 15 min	+8 h 05 min
+2 h 05 min	−0 h 30 min	+1 h 15 min	+3 h 55 min	+1 h 25 min
+2 h 35 min	+0 h 20 min	+2 h 10 min		

To check whether the symmetry condition on the distribution of differences seems reasonable, we could construct the 'dot diagram' shown

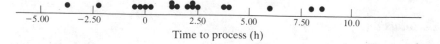

Figure 3.1 Dotplot of the data.

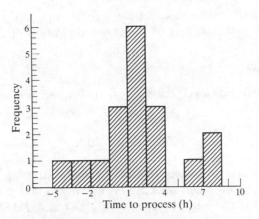

Figure 3.2 Histogram of the data.

in Figure 3.1 or the histogram shown in Figure 3.2. Neither diagram gives cause for concern about the symmetry assumption.

Next, these differences are ranked, *ignoring whether they are positive or negative*, from 1 for the smallest to 18 for the largest. The table below shows these ranks together with the differences:

Difference	Rank	Difference	Rank
+8 h 30 min	18	+8 h 05 min	17
+6 h 00 min	16	+2 h 05 min	8
−2 h 20 min	11	−0 h 30 min	4
+1 h 10 min	5	+1 h 15 min	6
+3 h 45 min	14	+3 h 55 min	15
−3 h 40 min	13	+1 h 25 min	7
−0 h 05 min	1	+2 h 35 min	12
+2 h 15 min	10	+0 h 20 min	3
−0 h 15 min	2	+2 h 10 min	9

The Wilcoxon signed-rank statistic T is then calculated as the sum of the ranks of *either* the positive differences or the negative differences, *whichever the one-sided alternative hypothesis suggests should be the smaller* (see later for the procedure with a two-sided alternative hypothesis). In our problem, H_1 suggests that there should be a smaller number of *negative* differences than positive ones, and so we take T to be the sum of the ranks of the *negative* differences.

Clearly, if H_0 is true, we would expect the sums of the ranks of the negative and positive differences to be roughly equal. On the other hand, if H_1 is true, we would expect one of these sums to be large and the other small. As with Table C for the sign test, the critical values in Table D are given in terms of *small* values of the signed-rank statistic, which is the reason for the italicized part of the above definition of *T*.

CRITICAL REGIONS

As we have just indicated, critical regions for the Wilcoxon signed-rank test are of the form

$$T \leq \text{critical value}$$

Table D gives critical values of *T* for sample sizes up to 50 (a more extensive table is on page 29 of *EST*). For $n=18$ and significance levels $\alpha_1 = 5\%$ and 1%, the critical regions are $T \leq 47$ and $T \leq 32$ respectively.

SOLUTION

The sum of the ranks for the negative differences (-2 h 20 min, -3 h 40 min, -0 h 05 min, -0 h 30 min and -0 h 15 min) is given by

$$T = 11+13+1+2+4 = 31$$

CONCLUSION

The result is within in the 1% critical region, and so we have strong evidence to support the alternative hypothesis that the median processing time is greater than 8 h.

Discussion

As we have previously stated, the null distribution of *T* is only valid if the underlying probability density function is symmetric; if this density function is non-symmetric then the given critical values will not be valid. Thus, if we have reason to believe that the underlying distribution is symmetric, then the Wilcoxon signed-rank test may be used instead of the sign test and will usually have superior power. Indeed, in our practical problem, Wilcoxon's test gave a result that was significant at $\alpha_1 = 1\%$ whereas the result from the sign test was significant at only $\alpha_1 = 5\%$. Wilcoxon's test should not be used if there is any substantial doubt about the symmetry assumption.

One-sided and two-sided tests

We know that a one-sided alternative hypothesis is supported by small values of a particular one of the two rank sums (i.e. the sums of the ranks of either the negative or positive differences). But if the alternative hypothesis is two-sided then *T* is defined as the smaller of these two rank sums. In this case, critical regions are again of the form $T \leq$ critical value, but now the significance levels are those indicated by α_2 in the tables.

What happens if any of the differences are zero, or if any of the differences are equal to each other?

The answer to the first of these questions is usually the same as for the sign test, i.e. we ignore those data and reduce the sample size accordingly. As regards the second question, the problem is of course that the ranks are not then uniquely defined. The way out of this problem is to average the ranks that would have been taken by these tied observations had we been able to discriminate between them, and then allocate this *average* to *each* of the tied values. This important device for dealing with tied values will also be used in many of the other tests in this book. To illustrate the idea, let us suppose the previous times had been recorded to the *nearest 15 min*; this is a nice way of showing how ties can occur by imprecise measuring (as opposed to being 'really' present in the data). These times are:

16 h 30 min	14 h 00 min	5h 45 min	9 h 15 min	11 h 45 min
4 h 15 min	8 h 00 min	10 h 15 min	7 h 45 min	16 h 00 min
10 h 00 min	7 h 30 min	9 h 15 min	12 h 00 min	9 h 30 min
10 h 30 min	8 h 15 min	10 h 15 min		

which now give the following differences:

+8 h 30 min	+6 h 00 min	−2 h 15 min	+1 h 15 min	+3 h 45 min
−3 h 45 min	0 h 00 min	+2 h 15 min	−0 h 15 min	+8 h 00 min
+2 h 00 min	−0 h 30 min	+1 h 15 min	+4 h 00 min	+1 h 30 min
+2 h 30 min	+0 h 15 min	+2 h 15 min		

In the ranking process, the difference of 0 h 00 min is discarded, leaving just 17 differences to rank. The ranks of these remaining differences are:

Difference	Rank	Difference	Rank
+8 h 30 min	17	+8 h 00 min	16
+6 h 00 min	15	+2 h 00 min	7
−2 h 15 min	9	−0 h 30 min	3
+1 h 15 min	4.5	+1 h 15 min	4.5
+3 h 45 min	12.5	+4 h 00 min	14
−3 h 45 min	12.5	+1 h 30 min	6
0 h 00 min	–	+2 h 30 min	11
+2 h 15 min	9	+0 h 15 min	1.5
−0 h 15 min	1.5	+2 h 15 min	9

The two differences +0 h 15 min and −0 h 15 min are (remembering that signs are ignored) in positions that would normally have been assigned ranks of 1 and 2, and so the average of these ranks, 1.5, is assigned to each of these differences. The two differences of +1 h 15 min are treated similarly, as are the differences +3 h 45 min and −3 h 45 min. The three differences −2 h 15 min, +2 h 15 min and +2 h 15 min are in positions 8, 9 and 10 and so each is assigned the average rank of 9.

The test statistic T, the sum of the ranks of the negative differences, is now equal to $9+12.5+1.5+3 = 26$. Since the effective sample size is now 17, we see that this result falls in the $\alpha_1=1\%$ critical region of $T \leqslant 27$.

Null distributions

Under the null hypothesis, the true median of the differences is zero. Thus, assuming that the distribution of the differences is *symmetric* about zero, the chances are *even* ('50–50') that the smallest difference (with rank 1) is positive or negative; the same is true for the next smallest difference (with rank 2); and similarly for every one of the ranked differences. (The theory assumes there are no ties.) It follows that all possible allocations (2^n in all) of signs to ranks are equally likely. So if one generates these 2^n allocations (either manually or by computer) and calculates the value of T for each, a frequency distribution for T can be constructed and then the null probability distribution of T is obtained by simply dividing the frequencies by 2^n.

We now outline this procedure for $n=6$, and thus confirm the critical values given for this value of n in Table D. We will consider the one-sided case where T is the rank sum of negative differences. With $n=6$ there are $2^6=64$ possible alocations of signs; we show below just a small part of the layout:

		Ranks				
1	2	3	4	5	6	Value of T
+	+	+	+	+	+	0
−	+	+	+	+	+	1
+	−	+	+	+	+	2
−	−	+	+	+	+	3
+	+	−	+	+	+	3
⋮	⋮	⋮	⋮	⋮	⋮	⋮
+	−	−	−	−	−	20
−	−	−	−	−	−	21

If you complete the details, you will find that the distribution of T is symmetric (why?). Figure 3.3 shows the histogram of the distribution. In particular notice that

$$\mathrm{Prob}(T=0) = 1/64 = 0.015\ 625$$

$$\mathrm{Prob}(T\leqslant 1) = 2/64 = 0.031\ 250$$

$$\mathrm{Prob}(T\leqslant 2) = 3/64 = 0.046\ 875$$

$$\mathrm{Prob}(T\leqslant 3) = 5/64 = 0.078\ 125$$

Thus the best conservative critical regions for $\alpha_1=2\frac{1}{2}\%$ and 5% are $T=0$ and $T\leqslant 2$ respectively, while there are no critical regions corresponding to significance levels of 1% or $\frac{1}{2}\%$; these results confirm the entries for $n=6$ in Table D.

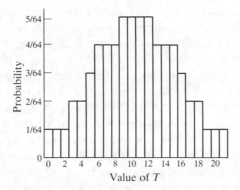

Figure 3.3

Large sample sizes

Figure 3.1 (earlier) showed that for $n=6$ the distribution of T is symmetric. Indeed, as the sample size increases, the shape becomes ever closer to that of the normal distribution. This enables us to obtain approximate critical values for T when n is large. It can be shown that T has mean $\mu=n(n+1)/4$ and standard deviation $\sigma= \sqrt{n(n + 1)(2n + 1)/24}$.

So approximate critical values of T may be obtained by taking the integer part of $\mu-z\sigma-\frac{1}{2}$, where z is the appropriate percentage point of the standard normal distribution and the '$-\frac{1}{2}$' is the continuity correction.

To illustrate the reliability of this approximation, consider the case when $n=50$ (the largest sample size in Table D). Then $\mu=50\times51/4=637.5$ and $\sigma=\sqrt{50\times51\times101/24} = 103.59$, and so the formula for approximate critical values is the integer part of $637.5-103.59z-0.5$. For example, for $\alpha_1=5\%$ we have $z=1.6449$. This gives an approximate critical value of 466.6, and the integer part of this, 466, actually agrees with the entry in Table D.

Critical values for the two-sided test are obtained in a similar manner using the appropriate values of z; for example, for $\alpha_2=5\%$ and 1%, z is 1.96 and 2.5758 respectively.

A note on the computer programs

At the end of this and subsequent chapters we are providing computer programs for most of the statistical procedures discussed in that chapter. The programs are written in BASIC since this language is so widely known and available. However, we are well aware that there are many versions of BASIC in use. Consequently, to make our programs directly usable on as many different types of computer as possible, we have written them in a fairly rudimentary version of BASIC. If your computer supports a more sophisticated BASIC, you may well be able to improve and shorten the programs.

Our programs can be described as 'utilitarian' – they do their job of implementing the test procedures but do not cater for sound, mistakes, flashing messages, colour, etc.! (No doubt computer buffs will add such effects.) However, in the program that follows, we have included a routine to allow correction of mistakes made in entering the data (this is particularly useful when dealing with large samples) – these few lines of the program can be easily incorporated into other programs if desired.

For small sample sizes, most of the tests in the book are quicker to do 'by hand' than to use the computer – which, of course, is one of the appeals of distribution-free tests. Further, some of the simpler tests (for example, the sign test and Tukey's location test in Chapter 5) can usually be carried out manually in less time than it would take to type in the data, even with large data sizes! Therefore, we have not provided programs for tests of this particularly 'quick-and-easy' type.

Assignments

The first assignment is more suited to the sign test than to Wilcoxon's signed-rank test since it is well known that the distribution of times between arrivals at queues is asymmetric (the sample bears this out!). The second assignment is equally suited for either test and so you may like to try both of them and compare conclusions.

1   Arrivals at check-out
A supermarket chain employed a consultancy firm to investigate service times at their newest store. One aspect that was examined was the time between successive customers arriving at a check-out. Times between arrivals (minutes) were obtained for various periods of a week and those for part of Monday morning are given below:

6.0	7.5	2.7	2.0	2.8	2.6	5.0	11.7	1.3	1.7
3.9	1.2	0.6	0.7	1.7	6.7	2.1	9.6	3.7	4.5
0.5	5.9	1.2	3.1	3.3	0.2	1.9	0.2	2.4	2.0
4.4	0.2	1.2	8.6	0.3	1.9	5.1	0.4	10.4	10.3

Task: Use a histogram or a dot diagram to see whether or not it is reasonable to suggest that these data could have come from a symmetric distribution.

The average time for established stores for a corresponding period is 1.2 min. Is there evidence to suggest that the median time for the new store is greater than this average?

2   Serum sodium levels
The data give the results of analyses of 20 samples of serum measured for their sodium content. The average value for the method of analysis used is 140 ppm.

| 140 | 143 | 141 | 137 | 132 | 157 | 143 | 149 | 118 | 145 |
| 138 | 144 | 144 | 139 | 133 | 159 | 141 | 124 | 145 | 139 |

(*Source*: National Quality Control Scheme, Queen Elizabeth Hospital, Birmingham, referenced in *Data* by D.F. Andrews and A.M. Herzberg, Springer, 1985.)

Task: Is there evidence that the median level of sodium in this serum is different from 140 ppm?

Program 3.1   The Wilcoxon signed-rank test

```
100 REM *** WILCOXON SIGNED-RANK ONE SAMPLE TEST ***

110 REM ** INPUT THE DATA **
120 INPUT "SAMPLE SIZE ? ";N
130 DIM A(N),D(N),RK(N)
140 PRINT "INPUT THE OBSERVATIONS :"
150 FOR I=1 TO N
160 INPUT A(I)
170 NEXT I

180 REM ** CHECK ENTRIES **
190 INPUT "ARE THE ENTRIES CORRECT ? (Y/N) ";Z$
200 IF Z$="Y" THEN GO TO 300
210 INPUT "WHICH OBSERVATION ? ";L
220 INPUT "NEW OBSERVATION ? ";A(L)
230 PRINT "THE SAMPLE VALUES ARE NOW :"
240 PRINT
250 FOR I=1 TO N
260 PRINT A(I);"   ";
270 NEXT I
280 PRINT
290 GO TO 190

295 REM ** CALCULATION OF THE TEST STATISTIC **
300 INPUT "HYPOTHESISED VALUE OF THE MEDIAN = ";M
310 FOR I=1 TO N
320 LET A(I)=A(I)-M
330 NEXT I

340 REM ** REMOVE ZERO DIFFERENCES **
350 LET NC=0
360 FOR I=1 TO N
370 IF A(I)=0 THEN GO TO 400
380 LET NC=NC+1
390 LET A(NC)=A(I)
400 NEXT I

405 REM ** RANK SAMPLE **
410 LET N=NC
420 FOR I=1 TO N
430 LET D(I)=ABS(A(I))
440 NEXT I
450 GO SUB 1000
```

Continued overleaf

Program 3.1   Continued

```
460 REM ** CALCULATION OF RANK SUMS **
470 LET SN=0
480 LET SP=0
490 FOR I=1 TO N
500 IF A(I)<0 THEN LET SN=SN+RK(I)
510 IF A(I)>0 THEN LET SP=SP+RK(I)
520 NEXT I
530 PRINT
540 PRINT "SUM OF THE POSITIVE RANKS = ";SP
550 PRINT "SUM OF THE NEGATIVE RANKS = ";SN
560 PRINT
570 IF N<=50 THEN STOP
580 REM ** CALCULATION OF APPROXIMATE CRITICAL VALUES (N > 50) **
590 INPUT "PERCENTAGE POINT OF STANDARD NORMAL DISTRIBUTION ";Z
600 LET SD = SQRT(N*(N+1)*(2*N+1)/24)
610 LET MN = N*(N+1)/4
620 PRINT "CRITICAL VALUE = ";INT(MN-Z*SD-.5)

1000 REM ** SORT SAMPLE **
1010 FOR I=1 TO N
1020 LET T=0
1030 LET S=0
1040 LET C=D(I)
1050 FOR J=1 TO N
1060 IF D(J)>C THEN GO TO 1110
1070 IF D(J)<C THEN GO TO 1100
1080 LET S=S+1
1090 GO TO 1110
1100 LET T=T+1
1110 NEXT J
1120 LET RK(I)=T + (S + 1)/2
1130 NEXT I
1140 RETURN
```

4
Goodness-of-fit tests

Introduction

Quite a number of important practical problems require the use of so-called *goodness-of-fit* tests. The following example illustrates the meaning of goodness-of-fit.

A market-research company was given the task of finding out consumer preferences for three new flavours of toothpaste. In the investigation, the new flavours, whisky, brandy and champagne, were tested along with a traditional mint flavour. The four toothpastes were identically packaged; only a letter A, B, C or D identified them. In all, 400 people took part in the experiment and each was asked to state which flavour (as identified by the letter) they preferred. At the end of the experiment, the market researcher would know how many of the 400 people preferred each flavour. Now if there is no general preference for any particular flavour the mean or *expected* number of votes for each flavour would be 400/4=100; the expected* frequencies of votes would be as follows:

Flavour	whisky	brandy	champagne	mint
Number expected in each category	100	100	100	100

What we shall examine is how well the observed data *fit* this expected pattern; hence the term *goodness-of-fit*. Because of natural sample variations, we cannot expect the fit to be exact; but if the fit of the 'observed frequencies' to the 'expected frequencies' is worse than might be reasonably caused by sampling variations, then we have evidence against the equal-preference hypothesis, and so the researcher would then have some specific likes and dislikes to report.

The above example illustrates just one of many different situations

---

* Although seemingly in universal use, the term *expected* frequency is misleading. Even if there were no general preferences, it would be remarkable indeed if *precisely* 100 votes for each flavour were obtained, and so this could hardly be an 'expected' occurrence in the normal sense of the word. However, in statistics, 'expected' has to come to be used as analogous to 'mean value of'. In the same way, when 1000 000 fair coins are tossed, the mean ('expected') number of heads is 500 000; however, the probability of getting exactly this number is minute.

where a goodness-of-fit test is appropriate. As with other hypothesis tests, it often serves as a preliminary to a larger experiment. For instance, most people experience queues – in the supermarket, at the traffic lights, in the doctors' surgery – and in order to obtain reliable information concerning, say, the average waiting time, or the average queue length, it is very helpful to have some idea of the distributions of arrival times and service times. Data need to be collected and a goodness-of-fit test performed to see whether or not it is reasonable to use a particular probability model.

Another application of goodness-of-fit tests arises when applying classical tests. We have already mentioned (a number of times) that one of the fundamental assumptions of classical statistical tests is that the observations should come from normal distributions. Clearly, it is sensible and important to check whether this assumption seems valid before using such procedures, i.e. we need goodness-of-fit tests to check for normality.

So, in performing a goodness-of-fit test, we are interested in seeing just how well observed data fit a theoretical model or hypothesized distribution. In this chapter we shall examine three popular goodness-of-fit tests: the chi-squared test, the Kolmogorov–Smirnov test and Lilliefors' test (which is a special type of Kolmogorov–Smirnov procedure designed specifically for testing normality).

THE CHI-SQUARED GOODNESS-OF-FIT TEST

Introduction

This versatile and widely used test was introduced by Karl Pearson (1900), which makes it the oldest procedure in this book except for the sign test. It owes its popularity to the fact that it is easy to use and is valid over a very wide range of situations. Indeed, all that the test demands is that the n independent observations are capable of being classified into a number, say k, non-overlapping categories (for example, the preferred flavours of toothpaste, where $k=4$) and that the probabilities of observations falling into these categories can be calculated when the appropriate null hypothesis is assumed true. The procedure has the name 'chi-squared' because (except for small samples) the null distribution of the test statistic is approximately a chi-squared distribution.

PRACTICAL PROBLEM

The sales director of a major pottery company predicted the 1986 sales (as proportions of the total sales) of their five leading designs of bone china dinner sets. The predicted proportions were:

Design	Clementine	Ice rose	Cottage garden	Birds of paradise	Arden
Predicted percentage total sales	35	20	20	10	15

Following usual company practice, at the end of the first quarter, the accounts department samples 400 invoices for dinner sets. The production manager would like to use this sample to indicate whether or not the sales predictions are being fulfilled.

HYPOTHESES

The production manager is interested in seeing whether the sales of the five designs is following the pattern predicted by the sales director. If not, then he will need an indication of the changes so as to take action to adjust production accordingly. The appropriate null hypothesis states that the sales of the five designs is following the predicted pattern and the alternative hypothesis states that this pattern is not being followed. So we have:

H_0: The percentage of sales for Clementine, Ice rose, Cottage garden, Birds of paradise and Arden designs are 35%, 20%, 20%, 10%, and 15% respectively.

H_1: The percentages of sales for the five designs are not 35%, 20%, 20%, 10% and 15%.

DATA

The breakdown of the 400 sampled invoices between the five designs was:

Design	Clementine	Ice rose	Cottage garden	Birds of paradise	Arden
Number	108	102	92	42	56

We shall refer to these data as the *observed* frequencies (Ob. for short) to distinguish them from the frequencies expected (Ex.) under H_0.

STATISTIC

What we need is some method of comparing the observed frequencies (Ob.) with the mean or *expected* frequencies (Ex.) when H_0 is true, i.e. we seek a statistic that measures the discrepancies between the observed and expected frequencies. Now if H_0 is true, then the mean or expected number of Clementine orders is 35% of 400, i.e. 140. Likewise, the expected frequencies for the remaining designs are $20\% \times 400 = 80$, $20\% \times 400 = 80$, $10\% \times 400 = 40$ and $15\% \times 400 = 60$, respectively. These observed and expected frequencies are shown in the following table:

Frequency	Clementine	Ice rose	Cottage garden	Birds of paradise	Arden
Ob.	108	102	92	42	56
Ex.	140	80	80	40	60

If H_0 *is* true, then the observed frequencies should roughly fit the expected frequencies so that the differences Ob.−Ex. will be relatively small. It is in fact these differences that form the basis of the χ^2 (chi-squared) statistic. Although it might at first sight seem reasonable to form a test statistic by simply summing these differences, this turns out to be useless since the negative differences always cancel out the positive ones to give a sum of zero. Pearson overcame this problem by squaring the differences before performing a summation; in fact his actual test statistic was

$$\chi^2 = \sum \frac{(\text{Ob.} - \text{Ex.})^2}{\text{Ex.}}$$

where the sum is over the k categories. In this formula, each squared difference $(\text{Ob.}-\text{Ex.})^2$ is divided by the appropriate Ex. before summing; this compensates for the effect that the differences (Ob.−Ex.) naturally tend to be larger for large values of Ex. even when H_0 is true.

Therefore, if H_0 is true, the observed frequencies will tend to be relatively close to the expected frequencies, resulting in a corresponding small value of χ^2; on the other hand, if there are large discrepancies between the observed and expected frequencies, indicating that H_1 is true, then χ^2 will tend to be large.

CRITICAL REGIONS

We have seen that, if H_1 is true, then χ^2 will tend to take large values. This immediately leads us to critical regions of the form

$$\chi^2 \geqslant \text{critical value}$$

Critical values are usually obtained from the chi-squared distribution (Table B) since for large samples (see the section entitled 'A note on small expected frequencies' below for more particulars) the null distribution of χ^2 is approximately chi-squared. This approximation is very reliable for large sample sizes, which is fortunate since, in general, the exact null distribution of χ^2 cannot be calculated. The appropriate number of degrees of freedom of the null distribution is $k-1$, where k is the number of categories.

In our problem, we have $k=5$, and so the approximate critical values for χ^2 are found by consulting the chi-squared distribution (Table B) with four degrees of freedom. Doing this gives the 5% and 1% critical regions as $\chi^2 \geqslant 9.488$ and $\chi^2 \geqslant 13.277$ respectively.

SOLUTION

The calculation of χ^2 is most conveniently performed by carrying out the following sequence:

(1) For each category, calculate the differences Ob.−Ex.
(2) Square the differences to get $(Ob.-Ex.)^2$.
(3) Divide each $(Ob.-Ex.)^2$ by the appropriate Ex.
(4) Sum the quantities $(Ob.-Ex.)^2/Ex$ to obtain the value of χ^2.

These stages are shown in the following table for the data of our practical problem. (Notice that the sum of the differencs Ob.−Ex. does indeed equal zero as we mentioned above.)

	Clementine	Ice rose	Cottage garden	Birds of paradise	Arden
Ob.	108	102	92	42	56
Ex.	140	80	80	40	60
Ob.−Ex.	−32	22	12	2	−4
$(Ob.-Ex.)^2$	1024	484	144	4	16
$(Ob.-Ex.)^2/Ex.$	1024/140	484/80	144/80	4/40	16/60
	= 7.31	= 6.05	= 1.80	= 0.10	= 0.27

The value of χ^2 is now easily obtained by summing the quantities $(Ob.-Ex.)^2/Ex.$, thus

$$\chi^2 = 7.31 + 6.05 + 1.80 + 0.10 + 0.27$$
$$= 15.53$$

This value of χ^2 falls in the $\frac{1}{2}$% critical region, which well and truly indicates that we have very strong evidence to support the alternative hypothesis that the percentage of sales does not agree with the sales director's predictions.

Rather than leaving the problem at this stage, it is usually fruitful (whenever H_1 is supported) to see what else can be deduced from the data. Looking at the discrepancies between the observed and expected frequencies – and, in particular, at the individual values of

$(Ob. - Ex.)^2/Ex.$ – we see that the sales for the last three categories are more or less on target, while those for Clementine and Ice rose are not. It would seem that the sales for these two designs are roughly equal rather than reflecting the predicted sales pattern.

A note on small expected frequencies

The chi-squared approximation for the null distribution of χ^2 runs into trouble when the expected frequencies are small; this can happen when some proportions predicted under H_0 are small and/or the sample size is small. The approximation may then be poor and so in this case it is necessary to modify the procedure. As a rough guide:

(a)　no expected frequency should be less than 1, and
(b)　no more than a fifth of the expected frequencies should be less than 5.

But what should we do if this criterion is not satisfied? The usual approach to this problem is to combine some of the categories in order to avoid the small expected frequencies. To illustrate this idea, suppose that in our practical problem the predicted sales had been 40%, 25%, 20%, 8% and 7%, and that only 50 sales invoices had been sampled, yielding observed frequencies 14, 13, 11, 5 and 7 for the five designs. The table of observed and expected frequencies would now be:

Frequency	Clementine	Ice rose	Cottage garden	Birds of paradise	Arden
Ob.	14	13	11	5	7
Ex.	20	12.5	10	4	3.5

The expected frequencies in the last two categories fail to satisfy condition (b) above – both are less than 5. In this case, the solution is simple; we combine these two offending categories to give the modified table of frequencies:

Frequency	Clementine	Ice rose	Cottage garden	Birds of paradise + Arden
Ob.	14	13	11	12
Ex.	20	12.5	10	7.5

We can now proceed with the usual calculation for χ^2, happy in the knowledge that the critical values from the chi-squared distribution (now based on $k-1 = 4-1 = 3$ degrees of freedom) are reliable. In fact, the reader may verify that the value of χ^2 for these data is 4.62, which does not fall in the 5% critical region of $\chi^2 \geqslant 7.815$, and so these results would not give cause to reject the production manager's predictions.

Discussion

Whenever there is a natural choice of categories into which the data can be classified, the chi-squared test is the obvious 'goodness-of-fit' procedure. However, even when natural categories do not exist (as when the distribution specified under H_0 is continuous), the test may still be used by creating 'artificial' categories. On the other hand, in these circumstances, one may prefer the Kolmogorov–Smirnov test (see later in this chapter), which is designed specifically for use with continuous distributions. Nevertheless, since it is still quite common practice to use the chi-squared test on continuous distributions, we now give two examples of this kind of application. We have chosen the same scenario for both examples; in each case we are interested in whether it is likely that a sample could have been taken from a normal distribution – the difference between the two cases is that in the first one the mean and the standard deviation are specified in the null hypothesis, whilst in the second case they are not.

Example on the normal distribution with mean and standard deviation specified

PRACTICAL PROBLEM

A major elevator manufacturer bases its safety standards on the principle that the weights of adults are normally distributed with a mean 62 kg and a standard deviation 11 kg, i.e. $N(62,121)$. However, it was recently brought to their notice that this information dates from over 45 years ago! Naturally, their R&D department wish to find out whether this distribution of weights is still appropriate; for, if the distribution has changed, it might necessitate a revision in the recommendation for the maximum number of people permitted in their elevators.

HYPOTHESES

The R&D department's concern is whether there has been a change in the distribution of weights of the adult population. So the alternative hypothesis relevant to them is that the distribution of weights is not normal with $\mu=62$ kg and $\sigma \leqslant 11$ kg.

H_0: The sample is from the normal distribution with mean 62 and standard deviation 11.

H_1: The sample is not from the normal distribution with mean 62 and standard deviation 11.

DATA

In the actual survey, the R&D team sampled 500 adults. However, for our purpose in illustrating the chi-squared technique (and later the Kolmogorov–Smirnov test), we will use just 50 of these weights. The weights (kg) were:

72.2	64.0	53.4	76.8	86.3	58.1	63.2	73.1	78.0	44.3
85.1	66.6	80.4	76.0	68.8	76.8	58.9	58.1	74.9	72.2
73.1	39.3	52.8	54.2	65.3	74.0	63.2	64.7	68.8	85.1
62.2	76.0	70.5	48.9	78.0	66.6	58.1	32.5	63.2	64.0
68.8	65.3	71.9	72.2	63.2	72.2	70.5	80.4	45.4	59.6

SOLUTION

Our first job is to group these data into intervals (which we have arbitrarily chosen to be roughly 5 kg in width) to form the 'grouped' frequency table:

Interval	Frequency
less than 40 kg	2
40–49.9 kg	3
50–54.9 kg	3
55–59.9 kg	5
60–64.9 kg	8
65–69.9 kg	7
70–74.9 kg	11
75–79.9 kg	6
80–89.9 kg	5
90 kg or more	0

Next, based on the supposition that the null hypothesis is correct, i.e. the data are from the $N(62,121)$ distribution, we calculate the expected proportion of the distribution in each interval; the expected frequencies are then obtained by multiplying these proportions by the sample size, 50. Using the relation $Z=(X-\mu)/\sigma$ ($= (X-62)/11$, in our case), which we first used in Chapter 1, we compute the value of the standard normal variable corresponding to each interval boundary in the above frequency table. The following table shows the details:

Interval	Left-hand boundary, x	$z=(x-62)/11$	$\Phi(z)$	Expected proportion in interval	Expected frequency in interval
					$50 \times 0.0228 =$
< 40				0.0228	1.140
40–49.9	40	−2.00	0.0228	0.1151	5.755
50–54.9	50	−1.09	0.1379	0.1232	6.160
55–59.9	55	−0.64	0.2611	0.1675	8.375
60–64.9	60	−0.18	0.4286	0.1778	8.890
65–69.9	65	0.27	0.6064	0.1609	8.045
70–74.9	70	0.73	0.7673	0.1137	5.685
75–79.9	75	1.18	0.8810	0.0685	3.425
80–89.9	80	1.64	0.9495	0.0451	2.255
≥ 90	90	2.55	0.9946	0.0054	0.270

To satisfy the requirements of the chi-squared approximation, we combine the last three categories; then only one expected frequency – the first one – out of the remaining eight is less than 5, and so the conditions mentioned previously are satisfied. The value of χ^2 is obtained in the usual manner from the resulting eight categories:

Interval	< 40	40–49.9	50–54.9	55–59.9	60–64.9	65–69.9	70–74.9	≥ 75
Ob.	2	3	3	5	8	7	11	11
Ex.	1.140	5.755	6.160	8.375	8.890	8.045	5.685	5.950
$(Ob.-Ex.)^2/Ex.$	0.649	1.319	1.621	1.360	0.089	0.136	4.969	4.286

Hence

$$\chi^2 = 0.649 + 1.319 + 1.621 + 1.360 + 0.089 + 0.136 + 4.969 + 4.286$$
$$= 14.429$$

We have not been able to specify the decision rule before now since we need to know the number k of categories available for calculating χ^2, and this was unknown until the expected frequencies were computed.

In this problem, we have $k=8$ categories and hence $k-1=7$ degrees of freedom. Hence, from Table B, we see that we reject H_0 in favour of H_1 at the 5% and 1% levels of significance if $\chi^2 \geqslant 14.067$ and $\chi^2 \geqslant 18.475$ respectively. We see that the calculated value of $\chi^2=14.429$ lies in the 5%, but not in the 1%, critical region, and so we have some (but not strong) evidence to support H_1. In other words, it seems unlikely that the sample is from $N(62,121)$ – indeed, it may not be from a normal distribution at all or it could be from a normal distribution but having mean and standard deviation different from 62 and 11 respectively.

In the next example of the use of the chi-squared test, we again look at the problem where the sample is hypothesized to come from a normal distribution but now where the mean and standard deviation are not specified in H_0, i.e. we are now concerned with the general 'parentage' of our sample but not in the particular member of the family!

Example involving the normal distribution – mean and standard deviation not specified

PRACTICAL PROBLEM AND DATA

We will use the same problem and data as in the previous example.

HYPOTHESES

This time the R&D department's concern is simply whether or not it is reasonable to claim that the sample came from some normal distribution, without assuming anything about the mean and standard deviation of the distribution. So we have:

H_0: The sample of adult weights is from some normal distribution.
H_1: The sample is not from a normal distribution.

SOLUTION

The solution follows the same pattern as before, except now the mean and standard deviation have to be estimated from the sample using the formulae from Chapter 1. The sample mean $\overline{X}=66.35$ estimates μ while σ is estimated by the modified sample standard deviation, $s=\sqrt{\sum(X-\overline{X})^2/(n-1)}$ = 11.61. So, by using the relation $Z=(X-66.35)/11.61$ (from $Z=(X-\mu)/\sigma$ with μ and σ replaced by their estimates X and s respectively) we can now calculate the value of the standard normal variable corresponding to each interval boundary. The details of this calculation and that for the expected frequencies is given in the following table.

Interval	x	$z=$ $(x-66.35)$ 11.61	$\Phi(z)$	Expected proportion	Expected frequency
< 40				0.0116	$50 \times 0.0116 =$ 0.580
40–49.9	40	−2.27	0.0116	0.0677	3.385
50–54.9	50	−1.41	0.0793	0.0842	4.210
55–59.9	55	−0.98	0.1635	0.1277	6.385
60–64.9	60	−0.55	0.2912	0.1610	8.050
65–69.9	65	−0.12	0.4522	0.1695	8.475
70–74.9	70	0.31	0.6217	0.1487	7.435
75–79.9	75	0.75	0.7734	0.1076	5.380
80–89.9	80	1.18	0.8810	0.0983	4.915
⩾ 90	90	2.04	0.9793	0.0207	1.035

This time, to satisfy the validity conditions for the chi-squared approximation, we combine the first three and the last two categories. The value of χ^2 is calculated in the usual manner from the resulting seven categories:

Interval	< 55	55–59.9	60–64.9	65–69.9	70–74.9	75–79.9	⩾ 80
Ob.	8	5	8	7	11	6	5
Ex.	8.175	6.385	8.050	8.475	7.435	5.380	5.950
$(Ob.-Ex.)^2/Ex.$	0.004	0.300	0.000	0.257	1.709	0.071	0.152

from which $\chi^2 = 2.493$.

Recall that in our previous examples, the number of degrees of freedom has been $k-1$. However, in this problem, both the mean and the standard deviation of the population have had to be estimated from the data in order to compute the expected frequencies. This tends to make the expected frequencies closer to the observed frequencies than would otherwise be the case. Fortunately, this effect is easily compensated by *reducing* the number of degrees of freedom by the number (two, in this example) of such estimated quantities. So our decision rule is now based on $k-1-2=7-1-2=4$ degrees of freedom, and rejects H_0 in favour of H_1 at the 5% and 1% levels of significance if $\chi^2 \geqslant 9.488$ and $\chi^2 \geqslant 13.277$ respectively.

The calculated value of $\chi^2 = 2.493$ is nowhere near any of these critical regions. Consequently, there is no evidence at all of the population being non-normal.

KOLMOGOROV–SMIRNOV TEST

Introduction

This test was devised by A. N. Kolmogorov (1933), and a similar technique was developed by N. V. Smirnov (1939); consequently it is commonly known as the Kolmogorov–Smirnov test. It is specifically designed for analysing goodness-of-fit situations where the underlying distribution is continuous. One immediate consequence is that we are saved the awkwardness of creating arbitrary categories as needed in the chi-squared test. Another useful feature of their test is that it can be carried out using either an arithmetical method or an equivalent graphical approach; the latter may not be any quicker, but it does aid the understanding of the principles behind the technique.

In Chapter 1 we saw that the sample cdf can be expected to reflect the main features of the population cdf (unless the sample is very small). Basically, the Kolmogorov–Smirnov procedure compares the sample cdf (denoted here by $F_n(x)$ with n referring to the sample size) with the hypothesized population cdf (denoted here by $F_0(x)$ with the '0' indicating that this is the cdf predicted under H_0). If H_0 were true, we would expect $F_0(x)$ and $F_n(x)$ to stay reasonably close together; on the other hand, large differences between $F_0(x)$ and $F_n(x)$ constitute evidence against H_0. There are several tests available based on comparing $F_0(x)$ and $F_n(x)$, essentially differing only in their methods of comparison. The Kolmogorov–Smirnov test is the best-known of these tests, and its measure of difference between the cdfs is simply the maximum (vertical) distance between $F_0(x)$ and $F_n(x)$.

It is worth noting that, although this test was primarily designed for continuous distributions, nevertheless it can be applied to discrete distributions, though in this case the critical values may be over-conservative (i.e. the true α may be less than the nominal α).

PRACTICAL PROBLEM

We have chosen to use the same example as before, i.e. the elevator problem. This will give us the advantage of seeing how the Kolmogorov–Smirnov test performs relative to the chi-squared test, which if you recall is *not* ideally suited for dealing with continuous distributions.

HYPOTHESES

The R&D department's concern is whether there has been a change in the distribution of the weights of the adult population. So the alternative hypothesis to them is that the distribution of weights is not normal with $\mu=62$ kg, $\sigma=11$ kg; clearly this is a *two-sided* alternative hypothesis since the alternative cdf could lie above or below that of the hypothesized distribution. Thus, the hypotheses may be written as follows:

  H_0: The sample is from the normal distribution with mean 62 and standard deviation 11.
  H_1: The sample is not from the normal distribution with mean 62 and standard deviation 11.

Should the evidence favour H_1, then, of course, further analysis will be needed to examine what kind of model distribution of weights might now be appropriate.

Note that we have specifically stated that H_1 is a two-sided hypothesis rather than saying 'nothing' as we did when we used the chi-squared test to analyse this problem. As we discuss later, the Kolmogorov–Smirnov test has the advantage of being easily adaptable for use with either one-sided and two-sided alternative hypotheses as appropriate.

DATA

For convenience we reproduce below the data for this problem:

72.2	64.0	53.4	76.8	86.3	58.1	63.2	73.1	78.0	44.3
85.1	66.6	80.4	76.0	68.8	76.8	58.9	58.1	74.9	72.2
73.1	39.3	52.8	54.2	65.3	74.0	63.2	64.7	68.8	85.1
62.2	76.0	70.5	48.9	78.0	66.6	58.1	32.5	63.2	64.0
68.8	65.3	71.9	72.2	63.2	72.2	70.5	80.4	45.4	59.6

STATISTIC

If H_0 is true, then we would expect the sample cdf to bear some resemblance to the cdf of the normal distribution $N(62,121)$. On the other hand, if H_1 is true, then the two cdfs may differ markedly in some respect. For example, they may have similar shapes but with one of them displaced from the other, indicating that only the means differ; or, one may be steeper than the other, indicating a difference in spread; or, the shapes may be very different, indicating that it is unlikely that the sample comes from any normal distribution.

The closeness, or otherwise, of the two cdfs is measured by calculating the greatest vertical difference, D_n, between them; if D_n is large, then we can claim it is unlikely that the sample comes from the hypothesized distribution, i.e. $N(62,121)$. We recall that the sample cdf, $F_n(x)$, is given by

$F_n(x)$ = proportion of sample observations less than or equal to x

i.e.

$$F_{50}(x) = \frac{\text{number of observations} \leq x}{50}$$

The sample cdf, $F_{50}(x)$, for our problem is calculated in Table 4.1, where you should note that we have rearranged the observations into ascending order. Also, whether one opts for the graphical or the arithmetical method, it is advantageous to convert the observed values to standardized values, z, using the transformation $Z = (X-\mu)/\sigma$, where μ and σ are the values given in H_0, i.e. we use $z=(x-62)/11$. We then obtain the results in Table 4.1.

Since the hypothesized distribution is normal, we may make use of graph paper on which the standard normal distribution has already been drawn (such as the one on page 27 of *EST*). Then the 'standardized' sample cdf (i.e. using the z values just calculated) may be drawn and the largest vertical difference, D_{50}, found. Figure 4.1 shows the result. We have indicated the greatest vertical difference, D_{50}, on Figure 4.1, it

Table 4.1

Observation, x	Standardized value, z	Frequency	Cumulative frequency	$F_{50}(x)$
32.5	−2.68	1	1	0.02
39.1	−2.06	1	2	0.04
44.3	−1.61	1	3	0.06
45.4	−1.51	1	4	0.08
48.9	−1.19	1	5	0.10
52.8	−0.84	1	6	0.12
53.4	−0.78	1	7	0.14
54.2	−0.71	1	8	0.16
58.1	−0.35	3	11	0.22
58.9	−0.28	1	12	0.24
59.6	−0.22	1	13	0.26
62.2	0.02	1	14	0.28
63.2	0.11	4	18	0.36
64.0	0.18	2	20	0.40
64.7	0.25	1	21	0.42
65.3	0.30	2	23	0.46
66.6	0.42	2	25	0.50
68.8	0.62	3	28	0.56
70.5	0.77	2	30	0.60
72.2	0.93	5	35	0.70
73.1	1.01	2	37	0.74
74.0	1.09	1	38	0.76
74.9	1.17	1	39	0.78
76.0	1.27	2	41	0.82
76.8	1.35	2	43	0.86
78.0	1.45	2	45	0.90
80.4	1.67	2	47	0.94
85.1	2.10	2	49	0.98
86.3	2.21	1	50	1.00

occurs at just before $z=0.11$ (corresponding to $x=63.2$) and is approximately equal to 0.26.

As we mentioned in the introduction, an alternative to the graphical method is an equivalent arithmetical procedure, the details of which are given below. First note that the maximum vertical distance must occur at or just before one of the steps of $F_{50}(x)$. So we only need to find $F_0(x)$ ($\Phi(z)$ in this case) at each of the data values of $F_{50}(x)$ – using either the bottom or the top of the step in each case, whichever gives the greater distance. The details of these computations are given in Table 4.2. From this table we see immediately that the value of D_{50} is 0.2638.

CRITICAL REGIONS

Since large values of the Kolmogorov–Smirnov statistic D_n indicate that the sample cdf $F_n(x)$ is not similar to the hypothesized cdf $F_0(x)$, the

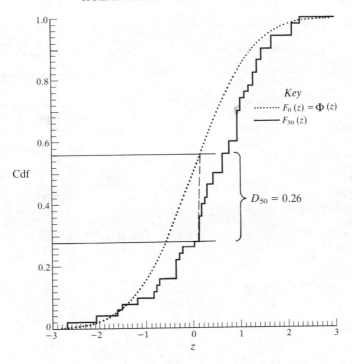

Figure 4.1

critical regions must have the form

$$D_n \geq \text{critical value}$$

Consulting Table E (or page 26 of *EST*) we find that for $n=50$, the $\alpha_2=5\%$, 2% and 1% critical regions are $D_{50} \geq 0.1884$, $D_{50} \geq 0.2107$ and $D_{50} \geq 0.2260$ respectively.

SOLUTION

We found that $D_{50}=0.2638$, which falls well inside the $\alpha_2=1\%$ critical region. In other words, we have strong evidence to support the alternative hypothesis that the data are not from the normal distribution $N(62,121)$. A glance at the graph in Figure 4.1 shows that the sample cdf roughly follows what would be expected of a normal distribution, but it seems to be shifted to the right. So one possibility is that the observations are from a normal distribution whose mean is greater than 62.

Discussion

It is worth bearing in mind that the Kolmogorov–Smirnov test does not look *specifically* for changes in location, or dispersion (or in anything so specific). It

GOODNESS-OF-FIT TESTS

Table 4.2

Observation, x	Standardized value, z	$F_{50}(x)$	$\Phi(z)=$ $F_0(x)$	Differences At step	Differences Before step
< 32.5		0			
32.5	−2.68	0.02	0.0037	0.0163	0.0037
39.1	−2.06	0.04	0.0197	0.0203	0.0003
44.3	−1.61	0.06	0.0537	0.0063	0.0137
45.4	−1.51	0.08	0.0655	0.0145	0.0055
48.9	−1.19	0.10	0.1170	0.0170	0.0370
52.8	−0.84	0.12	0.2005	0.0805	0.1005
53.4	−0.78	0.14	0.2117	0.0717	0.0917
54.2	−0.71	0.16	0.2389	0.0789	0.0989
58.1	−0.35	0.22	0.3632	0.1432	0.2032
58.9	−0.28	0.24	0.3897	0.1497	0.1697
59.6	−0.22	0.26	0.4129	0.1529	0.1729
62.2	0.02	0.28	0.5080	0.2280	0.2480
63.2	0.11	0.36	0.5438	0.1838	0.2638*
64.0	0.18	0.40	0.5714	0.1714	0.2114
64.7	0.25	0.42	0.5987	0.1787	0.1987
65.3	0.30	0.46	0.6179	0.1579	0.1979
66.6	0.42	0.50	0.6628	0.1628	0.2028
68.8	0.62	0.56	0.7324	0.1724	0.2324
70.5	0.77	0.60	0.7793	0.1793	0.1193
72.2	0.93	0.70	0.8238	0.1238	0.2238
73.1	1.01	0.74	0.8438	0.1038	0.1438
74.0	1.09	0.76	0.8621	0.1021	0.1221
74.9	1.17	0.78	0.8790	0.0990	0.1190
76.0	1.27	0.82	0.8980	0.0780	0.1180
76.8	1.35	0.86	0.9115	0.0515	0.0915
78.0	1.45	0.90	0.9265	0.0265	0.0665
80.4	1.67	0.94	0.9525	0.0125	0.0525
85.1	2.10	0.98	0.9821	0.0021	0.0421
86.3	2.21	1.00	0.9864	0.0136	0.0064

was designed to signal *any* kind of substantial difference in distribution from that proposed in H_0. Sometimes though, as appears to be the case in our current problem, the general shape of the sample cdf is roughly the same as that of the theoretical distribution, in which case it may be possible to be more specific about the kind of difference present.

It should be noted that had we worked in terms of the original x values instead of the standardized z values, we would have finished up with precisely the same picture after an appropriate adjustment in scale, and so would still have obtained precisely the same value of D_{50}.

Also, the Kolmogorov–Smirnov test has given us a much stronger conclusion than did the χ^2 test for the same problem. This follows from examining the levels at which significance has been attained. In the chi-squared test, χ^2 only just fell into the 5% critical region, thus indicating only moderate evidence against H_0. But here, D_{50} has finished up in the 1% critical region, indicating very strong evidence against H_0. This is not really surprising, for as we have already remarked, the Kolmogorov–Smirnov procedure is specifically designed for dealing with situations where the underlying distribution is continuous.

One-sided alternatives
Although our problem involved a two-sided alternative hypothesis (i.e. comprising all kinds of differences from $F_0(x)$), the Kolmogorov–Smirnov procedure can be easily applied to one-sided alternatives. All we do, instead of considering *all* the differences (positive *and* negative ones), is to consider *only* the positive or the negative differences, *whichever are expected under the one-sided alternative hypothesis*. So, for example, suppose the alternative hypothesis was:

H_1: The population from which the sample is taken has a cdf which is *greater* than the hypothesized cdf, $F_0(x)$, for at least part of the range of possible x values.

For evidence that this particular H_1 is true, we need $F_n(x)$ to be substantially higher than $F_0(x)$ for some value(s) of x. Such an alternative hypothesis might be chosen because it is suspected that the population under investigation has a lower average than the distribution in H_0 or, more generally, that the overall characteristics of the population are such as to give mainly lower values than would be expected under H_0. In such cases, $F_n(x)$ will tend to rise earlier (i.e. for those lower values of x) than $F_0(x)$; consequently the differneces $F_n(x) - F_0(x)$ will tend to be *positive*. The appropriate test statistic which reflects this behaviour is:

$$D_n^+ = max[F_n(x) - F_0(x)]$$

(where the '+' sign in D_n^+ *denotes that* $F_n(x)$ is expected to be greater than $F_0(x)$).
Conversely, suppose the chosen alternative hypothesis were:

H_1: The population being sampled has a cdf which is *less* than $F_0(x)$ for all or at least some values of x.

Then the differences $F_n(x) - F_0(x)$ will tend to be negative. This suggests that the appropriate test statistic is:

$$D_n^- = max[F_0(x) - F_n(x)]$$

(where the '−' sign in D_n^- denotes that $F_n(x)$ is expected to be less than $F_0(x)$).
In either case, the larger the value of the statistic, the stronger is the evidence for that particular H_1. In other words, critical regions are of the form $D_n^+ \geq$ critical value or $D_n^- \geq$ critical value, respectively, where the critical values are obtained from Table E (or page 26 in *EST*). As usual, since we now have a one-sided test, it is the α_1 significance levels that are appropriate, so that, for example, the $\alpha_1 = 5\%$ critical value for a sample of size 50 is 0.1696.
We will illustrate the one-sided version of the Kolmogorov–Smirnov test with the same problem and data as previously for the two-sided case. The null hypothesis is the same as before:

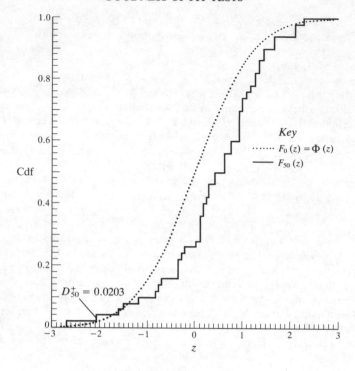

Figure 4.2

H_0: The sample is from a normal distribution with mean 62 and standard deviation 11.

However, whereas previously H_1 comprised essentially *all* other distributions, we can now have a more selective H_1. There are two possibilities. (Imagine, for the moment, that you have not yet seen the data, so that we are still in the early stages of formulating the type of hypothesis test appropriate for particular versions of the practical problem.) First, suppose that in order to make his product more marketable, the manufacturer is considering the possibility of *raising* the permitted number of people in the elevator. He may only do this if there is evidence that adult weights are generally *less* than expected under H_0. This gives rise to the one-sided alternative hypothesis:

H_1: The population being sampled has a cdf which, for some or all values of x, is *higher* than $F_0(x)$, the cdf of $N(62,121)$.

The statistic that would then be expected to give large values when this one-sided H_1 is true is $D_n^+ = \max [F_n(x) - F_0(x)]$. But, of course, when we consider the graphs of $F_n(x)$ and $F_0(x)$ in Figure 4.2, we see that the step function $F_n(x)$ is mostly below $F_0(x)$, i.e. $F_n(x) - F_0(x)$ is mostly *negative*. It does creep above $F_0(x)$ very occasionally but the furthest it gets above $F_0(x)$ is by an amount 0.0203 (as indicated in Fig. 4.2), and so the value of the statistic D_{50}^+ is 0.0203. Obviously this

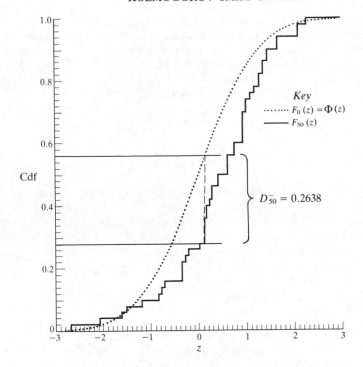

Figure 4.3

is nowhere near the $\alpha_1 = 5\%$ critical region of $D_{50}^+ \geq 0.1696$ and so we have no evidence at all to support this one-sided H_1.

However, now consider the different practical situation where the manufacturer is worried that the weights may now be generally *higher* than indicated in H_0, so that he may have to *reduce* the number of people permitted in the elevator. In this case his alternative hypothesis would be:

H_1: The population being sampled has a cdf $F_0(x)$ which, for some or all values of x, is *lower* than that of the normal distribution in H_0.

Now the appropriate test statistic is $D_n^- = \max[F_0(x) - F_n(x)]$, since this is the one which would be expected to be large if this H_1 were true. We are now inspecting those parts of the graphs where the step function $F_{50}(x)$ is *below* $F_0(x)$, i.e. virtually the whole picture! So the value of D_{50}^- is 0.2638, the same as D_{50} in the two-sided case. Figure 4.3 shows the two cdfs and D_{50}^-. However, as usual when comparing one-sided and two-sided versions of tests, the significance level has been halved, with the result that $D_{50}^- = 0.2638$ is well into the $\alpha_1 = \frac{1}{2}\%$ critical region, giving practically conclusive evidence of a general increase in adult weights.

Large sample sizes
It was shown by L.A. Goodman (1954) that the null distribution of $4nD_n^{+2}$ (or $4nD_n^{-2}$) is approximately chi-squared with two degrees of freedom. To see how

this can be used to obtain approximate critical values of D_n^+, D_n^- or D_n, consider $\alpha_1=5\%$. From Table B, the $\alpha_1=5\%$ critical value of the chi-squared distribution with two degrees of freedom is 5.991. Identifying this with $4nD_n^{+2}$, for example, the approximate $\alpha_1=5\%$ critical value of D_n^+ (or D_n^-) is $\frac{1}{2}\sqrt{5.991/n} = 1.2238/\sqrt{n}$.

The table below gives the multipliers of $1/\sqrt{n}$ required to obtain approximate critical values for the usual levels of significance:

α_1	5%	$2\frac{1}{2}\%$	1%	$\frac{1}{2}\%$
α_2	10%	5%	2%	1%
	1.2238	1.3581	1.5174	1.6276

To see how good these approximations are, we consider $n=50$, which is the largest sample size in Table E. The above formula approximates the $\alpha_1=5\%$ critical value as $\frac{1}{2}\sqrt{5.991/50} = 0.1731$, compared with the value of 0.1619 given in Table E. So this approximation method, though useful, is not wonderfully accurate for moderate sample sizes, and the reader is recommended to use the table in *EST* on page 26 for all n up to 100.

Discrete distributions

Although specifically designed for continuous distributions, the Kolmogorov–Smirnov test can be used successfully with discrete distributions. However, in this case the tabulated critical values are conservative; for example, a tabulated 5% critical value might in actual fact represent, say, an actual 4% level of significance.

We will briefly illustrate the procedure for discrete distributions with a set of data from 'Is goal scoring a Poisson process?' By D.J. Colwell and J.R. Gillett (1981, *Mathematical Gazette*). In this article, the scores for the 1978–79 season of 22 football teams are analysed to see whether the Poisson distribution could be a reasonable model for the results. The hypotheses for this problem are:

H_0: The number of goals scored by QPR were from a Poisson distribution with mean 1.

H_1: The number of goals scored by QPR were not from a Poisson distribution with mean 1.

The goals per match scored by QPR in the 1978–79 season were as follows:

Goals scored	0	1	2	3	4	5	6+
Frequency	11	23	4	3	0	1	0

The decision rule for this two-sided test is, at a (nominal) 5% significance level, to reject H_0 in favour of H_1 if $D_{42} \geqslant 0.2052$.

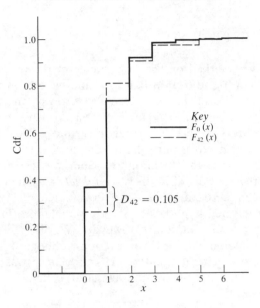

Figure 4.4

The hypothesized cdf, $F_0(x)$, is calculated from

$$F_0(x) = \sum_{r=0}^{x} e^{-1}/r!$$

where $x = 0,1,2, \ldots$ (alternatively the table on page 14 in *EST* may be used to obtain $F_0(x)$). The following table gives the sample cdf $F_{42}(x)$ and $F_0(x)$:

Score	0	1	2	3	4	5	6+
Frequency	11	23	4	3	0	1	0
Cumulative frequency	11	34	38	41	41	42	42
$F_{42}(x)$	0.262	0.810	0.905	0.976	0.976	1	1
$F_0(x)$	0.343	0.710	0.906	0.976	0.995	0.999	1

Figure 4.4 shows the graphs of $F_{42}(x)$ and $F_0(x)$ and also the maximum difference D_{42} equal to 0.105 (approximately). A more accurate value of D_{42} can be obtained from the above table and is $F_0(0) - F_{42}(0) = 0.3679 - 0.2619 = 0.1060$. This value of D_{42} does not lie in the $\alpha_2 = 5\%$ critical region and so we have no evidence at all to support H_1. (As a matter of interest, the reader might like to check that the chi-squared test also reaches the same conclusion.)

LILLIEFORS' TEST FOR NORMALITY

We have already remarked on the importance of the problem of testing for normality when μ and σ are unknown, and have shown how the chi-squared test may be used in this context. However, there are two big disadvantages of using the chi-squared test for this problem: (a) it involves an arbitrary choice of categories into which the data are classified, and (b) it needs a fairly large sample size.

In its standard form, the Kolmogorov–Smirnov test cannot be used unless the hypothesized distribution is *completely* specified (for example, normal with mean $\mu=62$ and standard deviation $\sigma=11$); it cannot be used for testing the null hypothesis that the population simply has some unspecified normal distribution. However, W. H. Lilliefors (1967) produced a special table of critical values for a Kolmogorov–Smirnov type of test for this more general situation. His procedure was to estimate μ by the sample mean $\overline{X}$, and σ by the 'classical' estimator

$$s = \sqrt{\frac{\sum\limits_{i=1}^{n}(X-\overline{X})^2}{n-1}}$$

(where the sample is denoted by $X_1, X_2, \ldots, X_n$), and then to calculate a D_n statistic with reference to that normal distribution with mean $\overline{X}$ and standard deviation s. (This is, of course, similar in principle to how we adapted the chi-squared test in this general case.) Critical regions for the resulting D_n are obtained from a special table of critical values rather than from the ones we have been using so far. (Unfortunately, Lilliefors' table of critical values was rather inaccurate. A far more accurate table is given in Table F (or on page 27 of *EST*).)

PRACTICAL PROBLEM AND DATA

We will illustrate Lilliefors' test for normality with the same problem and data as before, i.e. the elevator manufacturer.

HYPOTHESES

The manufacturer is now solely concerned with whether or not the data are from some normal distribution. This leads to the more general kind of hypotheses:

   H_0: The sample is from some normal distribution.
   H_1: The sample is not from a normal distribution.

Here H_1 is a two-sided hypothesis since no interest is being shown as to whether the cdf $F(x)$ of the population is higher or lower than the hypothesised cdf $F_0(x)$.

CRITICAL REGIONS

As with the Kolmogorov–Smirnov test, critical regions are of the form

$$D_n \geqslant \text{critical value}$$

Table F gives the $\alpha_2=5\%$ and 1% critical regions as $D_{50} \geqslant 0.1246$ and $D_{50} \geqslant 0.1454$ respectively.

SOLUTION

As before, the easiest way to calculate the statistic is to use standardized values, which in this case are calculated using the relation $Z=(X-\overline{X})/s$. For the data of our problem $\overline{X}=66.35$ and $s=11.61$. These standardized values, arranged in ascending order, together with the sample cdf, $F_{50}(x)$, are given in Table 4.3. (Note that F_{50} is the same as before.)

Figure 4.5 shows the graphs of $F_{50}(x)$ and $F_0(x)$. The value of D_{50} is approximately 0.12 and occurs just before $z= -0.27$ (corresponding to

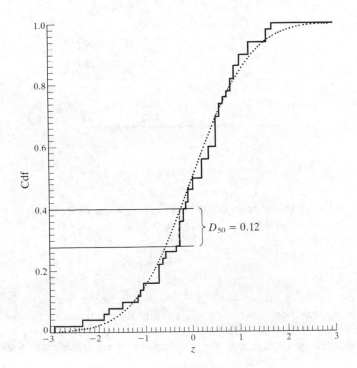

Figure 4.5

Table 4.3

Observation, x	Standardized value, z	$F_{50}(x)$
32.5	-2.92	0.02
39.1	-2.33	0.04
44.3	-1.90	0.06
45.4	-1.80	0.08
48.9	-1.50	0.10
52.8	-1.17	0.12
53.4	-1.12	0.14
54.2	-1.05	0.16
58.1	-0.71	0.22
58.9	-0.64	0.24
59.6	-0.58	0.26
62.2	-0.36	0.28
63.2	-0.27	0.36
64.0	-0.20	0.40
64.7	-0.14	0.42
65.3	-0.09	0.46
66.6	0.02	0.50
68.8	0.21	0.56
70.5	0.36	0.60
72.2	0.50	0.70
73.1	0.58	0.74
74.0	0.66	0.76
74.9	0.74	0.78
76.0	0.83	0.82
76.8	0.90	0.86
78.0	1.00	0.90
80.4	1.21	0.94
85.1	1.61	0.98
86.3	1.72	1.00

$x=63.2$). Using the normal cdf tables (Table A), a more accurate value of D_{50} is found to be $\Phi(-0.27)-0.28 = 0.3936-0.28 = 0.1136$.

CONCLUSION

The calculated value $D_{50}=0.1136$ does not lie in the $\alpha_2=5\%$ critical region, and so these data certainly contain no evidence of non-normality. It would seem that the company can be fairly confident that, at least on the evidence of the sample, the population of adult weights is something like normally distributed.

Large sample sizes
Approximate critical values may be found by dividing the constants in the following table by $\sqrt{n}$:

α_1	5%	$2\frac{1}{2}$%	1%	1%
α_2	10%	5%	2%	$\frac{1}{2}$%
	0.8255	0.8993	0.9885	1.0500

So, for example, with $n=50$ (which is the largest sample size in Table F) the $\alpha_2=5\%$ approximate critical value is given by $0.8993/\sqrt{50} = 0.1272$, which is only 0.0026 different from the value given in Table F. Again, if possible, the table on page 27 of *EST* is recommended if n is less than 100.

Assignments

1 Genetics

In 1982, a group of our college students performed an experiment to examine some genetic characteristics of flies. The characteristics were:

(a) length of wing – (i) vestigial and (ii) long;
(b) eye colour – (i) sepia and (ii) red;
(c) body colour – (i) pale and (ii) ebony;

giving eight possible mutations:

(1) long, red and pale;
(2) long, sepia and pale;
(3) long, red and ebony;
(4) vestigial, red and pale;
(5) long, sepia and ebony;
(6) vestigial, sepia and pale;
(7) vestigial, red and ebony;
(8) vestigial, sepia and ebony.

If all these mutations are independent of each other, then the respective proportion of each, according to genetic theory, should be $27 : 9 : 9 : 9 : 3 : 3 : 3 : 1$. In fact, the number of flies in each of the eight mutations categories was respectively:

$$83 \quad 21 \quad 47 \quad 18 \quad 14 \quad 3 \quad 2 \quad 1$$

Task: Apply a goodness-of-fit test to these data to see whether the genetic theory is a reasonable explanation of the results.

2 Bus arrival times

As part of a public transport survey, the times at which buses actually arrived at a particular stop were recorded. The following data give the number of minutes 40 buses were late or early ('early' being denoted by a negative value).

−0.5	0.7	0.1	1.4	0.6	1.6	−0.5	1.6
1.5	2.7	1.2	1.1	0.6	−1.7	1.7	0.2
0.4	0.1	0.9	−2.3	−1.6	5.5	0.9	−1.3
−1.0	0.1	−3.6	1.9	−0.4	−1.6	2.0	0.6
−1.4	−2.9	1.5	−1.3	−0.2	0.9	−1.5	−3.9

Task: Use Lilliefors' test to see whether it is reasonable to suppose that these times could be normally distributed.

Program 4.1   Chi-squared goodness-of-fit test

```
100 REM *** CALCULATION OF CHI-SQUARED GOODNESS-OF-FIT STATISTIC ***

110 REM ** INPUT NUMBER OF CATEGORIES **
120 INPUT "NUMBER OF CATEGORIES ? ";N
130 DIM OB(N),EX(N)

140 REM ** INPUT OBSERVED AND EXPECTED FREQUENCIES **
150 LET L=0
160 LET Z=0
170 PRINT "INPUT THE OBSERVED FREQ. AND THE CORRESPONDING EXPECTED FREQ."
180 FOR I=1 TO N
190 INPUT OB(I),EX(I)
200 IF EX(I)<5 THEN LET L=L+1
210 IF EX(I)=0 THEN LET Z=Z+1
220 NEXT I
230 PRINT

240 REM ** CHECK FOR ZERO AND LOW EXPECTED FREQUENCIES **
250 IF Z=0 THEN GO TO 280
260 PRINT "THERE ARE ";Z;" EXPECTED FREQUENCIES EQUAL TO ZERO!"
270 STOP
280 IF L=0 THEN GO TO 310
290 PRINT "WARNING ... THERE ARE ";L;" EXPECTED FREQUENCIES LESS THAN 5"

300 REM ** CALCULATION OF TEST STATISTIC **
310 Q=0
320 FOR I=1 TO N
330 Q=Q+(OB(I)-EX(I))^2/EX(I)
340 NEXT I
350 PRINT
360 PRINT "VALUE OF THE TEST STATISTIC = ";INT(1000*Q+.5)/1000
```

Program 4.2   Lilliefors' test for normality

```
          PROGRAM 4.2: LILLIEFORS' TEST FOR NORMALITY


100 REM *** LILLIEFORS' STATISTICS FOR NORMALITY ***

110 REM ** INPUT THE SAMPLE SIZE **
120 INPUT "NUMBER OF X-VALUES ? ";N
130 DIM F1(N),F(N),S(N),D(N)
140 LET SUM=0
150 LET SS=0
160 LET TF=0

170 REM ** INPUT VALUES  & FREQUENCIES **
180 PRINT "INPUT THE ";N;" VALUES & THEIR FREQUENCIES"
190 FOR I=1 TO N
200 INPUT D(I),F(I)
210 NEXT I
220 GO SUB 1000

230 REM ** CALCULATION OF SAMPLE CDF, MEAN & SD **
240 FOR I=1 TO N
250 LET TF=TF+F(I)
260 LET S(I)=TF
270 LET SUM=SUM+D(I)*F(I)
280 LET SS=SS+D(I)^2*F(I)
290 NEXT I
300 FOR I=1 TO N
310 S(I)=S(I)/TF
320 NEXT I
330 LET M=SUM/TF
340 LET SD=SQRT((SS/TF-M^2)*TF/(TF-1))
350 FOR I=1 TO N
360 LET D(I)=(D(I)-M)/SD
370 NEXT I

375 REM ** CALCULATION OF THE NORMAL CDF **
380 FOR I=1 TO N
390 LET X=ABS(D(I))
400 LET X1=1/(X*.231642+1)
410 LET X2=(((((X1*.530701-.726578)*X1+.710708)*X1-.142248)*X1+.12742)
    *X1)*EXP(-X*X/2)
420 IF D(I)>0 THEN LET F1(I)=1-X2
430 IF D(I)<=0 THEN LET F1(I)=X2
440 NEXT I
450 LET DF=0
460 FOR I=1 TO N
470 LET AD=ABS(S(I)-F1(I))
480 IF AD>DF THEN LET DF=AD
490 LET AD=ABS(S(I-1)-F1(I))
500 IF AD>DF THEN LET DF=AD
510 NEXT I
520 PRINT "VALUE OF LILLIEFORS' STATISTIC = ";DF
530 STOP

1000 REM ** SORT INTO ASCENDING ORDER **
1010 LET N1=N
1020 LET N1=INT(N1/2)
1030 IF N1=0 THEN GO TO 1190
1040 FOR I=1 TO N-N1
1050 FOR J=I TO 1 STEP -N1
```

Continued overleaf

Program 4.2   Continued

```
1060 LET J1=J+N1
1070 IF D(J)>D(J1) THEN GO TO 1100
1080 LET J=0
1090 GO TO 1160
1100 LET T=D(J)
1110 LET T1=F(J)
1120 LET D(J)=D(J1)
1130 LET F(J)=F(J1)
1140 LET D(J1)=T
1150 LET F(J1)=T1
1160 NEXT J
1170 NEXT I
1180 GO TO 1020
1190 RETURN
```

PART III

Tests involving two samples

This part of the book is involved with comparisons of various kinds between two populations, the comparisons being made on the basis of samples drawn from the populations. In each of these four chapters in this part, we present two tests: one that has fairly high power, and one where the emphasis is more on speed and simplicity.

The tests in Chapter 5 are designed for detecting differences in 'location' between the populations, i.e. differences between their averages (in particular, their medians). On the other hand, the tests in Chapter 6 are designed to detect differences in the *spread* (or dispersion) of the populations. Remember that by 'spread' we mean a measure of the variability of observations about the average value; thus if the observations tend to be close to the median then the population has small spread, whereas if many of them tend to be a long way from the median then the population has large spread.

The tests in Chapters 5 and 6 work best if the difference (in location or spread respectively) is the only substantial difference between the populations; in particular, the ability of the tests in Chapter 6 to recognize a difference in spread can be severely impaired if there is a difference in location as well. However, with many processes it is often the case that location and spread are related; if one is high, the other tends to be high as well. A quick test presented in Chapter 7 is particularly effective in this situation, and the other test in that chapter has power to detect just about any kind of substantial difference between the populations.

Chapter 8 deals with data in the form of so-called 'matched pairs'. This is where each observation in one sample has some kind of natural link with an observation in the other sample. An obvious example is where the two samples consist of observations on the same set of patients before and after some treatment. It turns out that the analysis of such data is quite unlike the analysis of other two-sample situations and, in fact, uses techniques that you have already seen in Part II.

5

Two independent samples – tests for differences in location

THE MANN–WHITNEY TEST

Introduction

This extremely good and widely used test was published by H. B. Mann and D. R. Whitney (1947). As long as the samples are not too large, the computations required are neither excessive nor difficult. Also, the test has high power; indeed, in the special case of sampling from normal distributions having equal variances – the only circumstances when the two-sample t-test (which is the standard test from classical statistics for this particular two-sample problem) is valid – the Mann–Whitney test is virtually as powerful as the t-test. In addition, as with all the distribution-free procedures, it retains its validity over a vastly broader range of sampling situations.

A version of the Mann–Whitney test was introduced two years earlier by Wilcoxon (1945) in the same article as that in which his signed-rank test (see Ch. 3) first appeared. However, Wilcoxon only dealt with equal sample sizes and used a rank-sum calculation which involves slightly heavier arithmetic than the Mann–Whitney method. Nevertheless, we shall cover the Wilcoxon version also, not only for historic reasons but also because it is closely related to a test for dispersion differences that we shall present in Chapter 6.

PRACTICAL PROBLEM

In 1980 a consumer magazine published a table showing the percentage of new cars, of a wide selection of makes and models, that broke down at least once in the first year's motoring. One aim of the survey was to investigate the truth (or otherwise) of the widely held opinion that Japanese cars are more reliable than British cars. The data for the Japanese models and those models wholly or mainly manufactured in Britain were extracted from the table to enable appropriate comparisons to be made.

HYPOTHESES

Presumably, the null hypothesis H_0 of equal reliabilities of Japanese and British cars implies approximately equal overall percentages of Japanese and British cars suffering breakdowns during their first year. However, this would not be the case if there were some tendency for the usage of the two nations' cars to differ appreciably and, in practice, this question may need considering first. If this is a problem, one might have to collect different data (e.g. the numbers of cars suffering breakdowns during their first 10 000 miles, say). In any case, the data obviously concern only this one particular aspect of reliability, and any conclusions to be drawn from the analysis should of course be limited to this alone.

The survey is investigating the truth of the idea that Japanese cars are more reliable than British ones, and so this, or rather its implication in the current context, is the alternative hypothesis H_1 that we shall use. Therefore, our hypotheses are:

H_0: On average, equal proportions of Japanese and British cars suffer breakdowns during their first year.

H_1: On average, a higher proportion of British cars than Japanese cars suffer breakdowns during their first year.

DATA

The survey included eight Japanese models and 12 British models. The percentages of cars of each type breaking down during their first year were as follows:

Japanese	3	7	15	10	4	6	4	7				
British	19	11	36	8	25	23	38	14	17	41	25	21

Regrettably for the British manufacturers, these data tell their own story without much need for a formal statistical test! Nevertheless, we shall pursue the detailed analysis in order to illustrate the two tests of this chapter; besides, it will be interesting to see whether the weight of evidence formally assessed by the tests agrees with our intuitive interpretation of the data.

STATISTIC

Just suppose for the moment that H_0 were true so that, on average, Japanese and British cars are equally reliable, at least during their first year. Then, if we were to select a Japanese model and a British model at random from the lists available, there should be an even chance as to which will suffer the greater percentage of breakdowns. On the other hand, if Japanese cars really are the more reliable on average then, although it is of course not certain that the Japanese model selected would fare better than the British model in this particular survey, the odds will be in favour of this happening. So it seems reasonable that, if several such comparisons were made, it must be highly likely that a *majority* of these comparisons would favour the Japanese models. The Mann–Whitney test is based directly on this idea.

For consistency with later work, let us denote the data on the eight Japanese models as sample A and the data on the 12 British models as sample B. The sizes of the samples will be denoted n_A and n_B, so that $n_A=8$ and $n_B=12$ in our problem. The Mann–Whitney test compares every item in sample A in turn with every item in sample B, a record being kept of the number of times, say, that the item from sample A is the greater. In all, there are of course $n_A n_B$ comparisons to be made.

Even with the fairly small samples concerned in our example, this procedure would seem at first to involve a rather hefty amount of work – for, with $n_A=8$ and $n_B=12$, we have 96 comparisons to make. Fortunately there is a simple method, which we now describe, that carries out this computation extremely efficiently.

The first task is to arrange all the data into ascending order, though with the samples still retaining their separate identities. An effective way of doing this is to place the values roughly on a linear scale as shown in Figure 5.1.

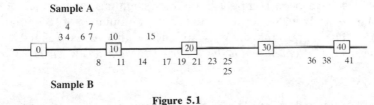

Figure 5.1

It is now easy to write down a list of 'A's and 'B's corresponding to the origins of the numbers in the ordered sequence, thus obtaining the *letter sequence*:

A A A A A A B A B B A B B B B B B B B B

This indicates that the six lowest readings came from sample A, the next lowest from sample B, the next from sample A, the next two from sample B, and so on. Next let us write under each A the number of 'B's that precede it in the sequence:

A A A A A A B A B B A B B B B B B B B B
0 0 0 0 0 0   1   3

Each of these numbers is actually the result of 12 (i.e. n_B) comparisons, obtained by comparing the corresponding A with every one of the 'B's. The numbers recorded show how many of the B values are exceeded by the A value, i.e. in relation to our particular example, the number of cases in which the Japanese model suffered more breakdowns than a British model. Note especially that these numbers are expected to be *small* if our one-sided alternative hypothesis H_1 is true. Since there are eight (i.e. $n_A=8$) such numbers, we have effectively carried out all the required 96 (i.e. $n_A n_B=8\times12$) comparisons. To determine how many of these 96 comparisons have the A value *exceeding* the B value we simply add together these eight figures, giving a value which we denote by U:

$$U = 0 + 0 + 0 + 0 + 0 + 0 + 1 + 3 = 4$$

Note that the same total would of course have been obtained had we instead written under each B the number of 'A's that *follow* it in the sequence; we would then have computed U as

$$U = 2 + 1 + 1 + 0 + 0 + 0 + 0 + 0 + 0 + 0 + 0 + 0 = 4$$

Of course, had the alternative hypothesis been that British cars are more reliable on average than Japanese, then U would have been defined as the number of comparisons in which the B value *exceeds* the A value. This would have been computed either by counting the number of 'A's preceding each B in the letter sequence or the number of 'B's following each A. The important thing is to ensure that U is defined to be *whichever type of count would be expected to be small when H_1 is true*.

CRITICAL REGIONS

Since it is *small* values of U that are significant, critical regions are of the form

$$U \leq \text{critical value}$$

The critical values for U are tabulated on page 30 of *EST* for all sample sizes n_1, $n_2 \leq 25$ and also for $n_1=n_2 \leq 50$; here n_1 represents the smaller of n_A and n_B, and n_2 the larger. Table G is an abbreviated version of this table. As we are carrying out a one-sided test in this example, the significance levels are indicated by α_1 in the tables.

Hence, for sample sizes 8 and 12, we see that the critical regions for significance levels $\alpha_1=5\%$, $2\frac{1}{2}\%$, 1% and $\frac{1}{2}\%$ are $U \leq 26$, $U \leq 22$, $U \leq 17$ and $U \leq 15$ respectively.

SOLUTION

Not unexpectedly, the value of the statistic U obtained from the breakdowns data, i.e. $U=4$, is well inside even the $\frac{1}{2}\%$ critical region. It is indeed obvious that, if the tables had given details for still smaller values of α_1, this value of U would have remained significant even at much more stringent levels. The Mann–Whitney test has therefore confirmed our initial impressions about the data, and has judged there to be essentially conclusive evidence that the Japanese models have better average reliability (certainly during the first year) than the British models.

WILCOXON'S VERSION OF THE TEST

As with his one-sample test, the statistic for Wilcoxon's version of this two-sample test is computed by adding together certain ranks (which explains why his version is often referred to as the *rank-sum* test). The *ranks* of the observations in the two samples are obtained by simply numbering the letters in the letter sequence from 1 to N, where N is the total number of observations. For our problem, $N = n_A + n_B = 20$, and we obtain:

A	A	A	A	A	A	B	A	B	B	A	B	B	B	B	B	B	B	B	B
1	2	3	4	5	6	7	8	9	10	11	12	13	14	15	16	17	18	19	20

The rank-sum statistic is then simply either

the sum R_A of the ranks of the 'A's

or

the sum R_B of the ranks of the 'B's

The choice between R_A and R_B must be the one that you would expect to be smaller when H_1 is true than when H_0 is true. Our H_1 is that the Japanese cars are the more reliable, which would imply that the 'A's monopolize the start of the letter sequence and the 'B's monopolize the end (which of course does happen in this case) – this will result in R_A being smaller than expected under H_0 and R_B being larger. Thus R_A is the required rank sum in this case; you should check that $R_A = 40$.

Special tables of critical values for the rank-sum statistic have been produced elsewhere. However, it is very easy to convert R_A and R_B to the value of U found by the Mann–Whitney method. We shall prove later that

$$U = R_A - \tfrac{1}{2} n_A (n_A + 1)$$

or, had R_B been the appropriate rank sum, by

$$U=R_B-\tfrac{1}{2}n_B(n_B+1)$$

In this case, we have $U=R_A-\tfrac{1}{2}n_A(n_A+1) = 40-\tfrac{1}{2}\times8\times9 = 40-36 = 4$, as before.

Discussion

As we have said previously, the Mann–Whitney procedure really is an excellent test for the two-sample location problem, being reasonably easy to execute, having power almost reaching that of the classical t-test under normality, and of course being much more widely applicable than the t-test. In fact, it can be shown that, when sampling from other distributions, the Mann–Whitney test is often more powerful than the t-test would be even if valid critical values for t were then available. Perhaps the only real drawback of the Mann–Whitney test is that it does require knowledge of the complete letter sequence; and, if the samples are large, ordering the whole set of observations can be quite a time-consuming operation; use of Program 5.1 is then recommended. However, as we shall shortly see, the other test to be described in this chapter contrasts sharply with the Mann–Whitney test in that it only requires knowledge of what is happening in the very extremes of the letter sequence, so that complete ordering is unnecessary. As a result, this other test is very quick to execute however large the samples may be.

One-sided and two-sided tests

The relation between one-sided and two-sided Mann–Whitney tests is analogous to that with the sign test and Wilcoxon's signed-rank test of Chapter 3. Previously we have seen that, in the one-sided case, U has been defined as either

the number (U_A, say) of comparisons having the A value less than
the B value

or

the number (U_B, say) with the A value exceeding the B value

according to which is expected to be the *smaller when the one-sided H_1 is true*. With the Wilcoxon rank-sum version, there was a similar choice to be made between R_A and R_B.

However, if the alternative hypothesis is *two-sided*, both eventualities must be catered for, since unusually low values of either U_A or U_B (or equivalently, of either R_A or R_B) would indicate the truth of H_1. In this case, we proceed as follows:

Perform any one of the pairs counts described in the 'Statistic' section above but, for the moment, denote the answer by U^* instead of U. In other words, U^* is obtained by adding together either

(a)   the number of 'B's preceding each A (or equivalently, the number of 'A's following each B), or
(b)   the number of 'A's preceding each B (or equivalently, the number of 'B's following each A).

Similarly, if using Wilcoxon's version, compute either $R_A - \frac{1}{2}n_A(n_A+1)$ or $R_B - \frac{1}{2}n_B(n_B+1)$, and again call the answer U^*.

In general, there are two possible values that can be obtained for U^*: either

the number of pairs with the A greater than the B (case (a) above)

or

the number of pairs with the B greater than the A (case (b) above)

As you know, the tables of critical values are appropriate only for small values of the statistic. Thus we must ensure that we finish with the smaller of the two possible values of U^*.

Now let us be clever. Note that, having computed one value of U^*, the other possible value must be $n_A n_B - U^*$, since the two values have to add up to the total number of comparisons made, which is $n_A n_B$. Consequently, for whichever value of U^* has been computed, U is defined simply as the smaller of U^* and $n_A n_B - U^*$. Critical regions are then of the form $U \leqslant$ critical value, with the significance levels now being denoted by α_2.

Incidentally, if you are smart, you would probably have chosen to calculate what turns out to be the smaller value of U^* in any case – for the arithmetic is then easier! You can soon see this if you try out computation (b) on the breakdowns data, i.e. one of the counts which gives $U^*=92$. If you need to check whether you have indeed obtained the smaller value of U^*, the easiest way is to compare it with $\frac{1}{2}n_A n_B$ (=48 in our problem); as long as your U^* does not exceed $\frac{1}{2}n_A n_B$, then it is the required value, i.e. U is equal to that U^* value.

How do we deal with ties?

Tied (that is, equal) observations in the same sample cause no difficulty; indeed there are three such pairs of tied values in the breakdowns data, but that has been of no consequence in the above work. However, if ties occur between observations from both samples, the letter sequence is no longer uniquely defined, and so we then need to generalize the definition of the test statistic.

We have noted that, if we are sampling from continuously distributed populations and record the data with sufficient accuracy, we are extremely unlikely to find any ties. However, ties do occur in practice, either because the populations have discrete distributions or, in the case of continuous distributions, because the data may only have been recorded (for instance) to one or two decimal places, or even just to the nearest whole number. We have already seen an example of this situation in Chapter 3 when using the Wilcoxon signed-rank test in the problem of times to process orders. There we found that, although there happened to be no problems with tied observations in the original version of the data, ties did occur when the directions were later rounded to the nearest 15 min. This very phenomenon motivates a very reasonable method of dealing with ties, not only in the Mann–Whitney test but quite generally. Imagine that the data are remeasured with sufficient accuracy to break all the ties. It is surely possible to claim that all possible ways of breaking the ties are about equally likely. Thus, if we consider the set of letter sequences obtained by breaking the ties in all possible ways, and calculate the statistic for each, the mean of the values thus obtained must be a sensible 'compromise' value for the statistic.

If there are several tied values in the data, this procedure could become tedious, but at least it provides a principle on which to work. Fortunately, in the Mann–Whitney test, this mean value of the statistic may be found by an alternative, and much quicker, method. If using the rank-sum calculation, tied observations should be given the average rank of the positions they cover in the letter sequence, just as we did for Wilcoxon's signed-rank test in Chapter 3. Or, if using the Mann–Whitney pairs-count method, the same result is obtained by regarding every tied (A,B) pair as simply contributing $\frac{1}{2}$ to whichever count is being carried out. To illustrate this, let us slightly alter the numbers in our example. Suppose that the best-performing British model suffered a 7% breakdown rate instead of the original 8%, and also that the model originally recorded as 14% is now 15%. The ordered combined samples and the corresponding letter sequence are now as follows, where tied values (involving items from both samples) are boxed:

Percentage	3	4	4	6	7	7	7	10	11	15	15	17	19	21
	A	A	A	A	A	A	B	A	B	A	B	B	B	B
Position	1	2	3	4	5	6	7	8	9	10	11	12	13	14

Percentage	23	25	25	36	38	41
	B	B	B	B	B	B
Position	15	16	17	18	19	20

Consider first the Wilcoxon rank-sum calculation. The three tied values at 7 occupy positions 5, 6 and 7 in the letter sequence, so we assign the average rank $(5+6+7)/3=6$ to all three. The two tied values at 15 occupy positions 10 and 11, and so we give each a rank of $10\frac{1}{2}$. So now

$$R_A = 1+2+3+4+6+6+8+10\frac{1}{2} = 40\frac{1}{2}$$

giving $U=40\frac{1}{2}-\frac{1}{2}\times8\times9 = 4\frac{1}{2}$, which is of course still extremely significant.

Alternatively, consider the direct calculation of U as the number of (A,B) pairs with the B less than the A. If we compute this as above by summing the number of 'B's less than each A, we now say there is $\frac{1}{2}$ of a B preceding each of the two 'A's at value 7, and $2\frac{1}{2}$ 'B's preceding the A at 15. This gives:

$$U = 0+0+0+0+0+\tfrac{1}{2}+\tfrac{1}{2}+1+2\tfrac{1}{2} = 4\tfrac{1}{2}$$

as before.

In practice we treat ties in this way, whether they arise from inaccurate measurements of data from continuous distributions or because the population distributions are in fact discrete.

Null distributions
To compute the null distribution we need a stronger form of the null hypothesis than that stated earlier, namely one that states that the populations from which the two samples are drawn have identical continuous probability distributions.

Equivalently, the 'A's and the 'B's can effectively be regarded as being drawn from the same source. In other words, given the $N=n_A+n_B$ numbers constituting the data, all allocations of n_A of these numbers to sample A and the rest to sample B have the same probability. This implies that, *when H_0 is true, all possible letter sequences* (having n_A 'A's and n_B 'B's) *are equally likely*. (As usual in theoretical considerations, we assume there to be no ties.)

This important idea provides the principle upon which the null distribution of *any* two-sample distribution-free statistic may be calculated. There are

$$\binom{N}{n_A} = \binom{N}{n_B} = \frac{N!}{n_A!n_B!}$$

possible letter sequences. (This follows since, for example, each letter sequence depends on the choice of the n_A out of N positions into which the 'A's are placed; the number of ways of choosing n_A positions out of N available is $\binom{N}{n_A}$.) If the test statistic is computed for each of them, then the probability of the statistic taking any specified value is given by the proportion of times it takes that value in these $\binom{N}{n_A}$ sequences. Of course this is an impracticable proposition if the sample sizes are large. But it is viable for smallish sample sizes, especially with a computer; more efficient methods, usually involving recurrence relations, can often be devised for finding these probabilities for larger samples.

Consider, for example, the one-sided Mann–Whitney test with sample sizes $n_A=3$ and $n_B=6$, where U is defined as the number of (A,B) pairs having the A greater than the B. The number of possible letter sequences is $\binom{9}{3} = 84$. As a partial illustration, let us calculate the probabilities of $U=0$, 1, 2 and 3. There is clearly only one letter sequence giving $U=0$, namely AAABBBBBB. There is also only one giving $U=1$, namely AABABBBBB. Two can be found giving $U=2$: they are AABBABBBB and ABAABBBBB. There are three with $U=3$: AABBBABBB, ABABABBBB and BAAABBBBB. Thus Prob($U=0$) = Prob($U=1$) = 1/84, Prob($U=2$) = 2/84 and Prob($U=3$) = 3/84. As critical regions are of the form $U \leqslant$ critical value, let us check the validity of the entries for these sample sizes in Table G. Our calculations give

$$\text{Prob}(U=0) = 1/84 = 0.0119$$
$$\text{Prob}(U \leqslant 1) = \text{Prob}(U=0)+\text{Prob}(U=1) = 2/84 = 0.0238$$
$$\text{Prob}(U \leqslant 2) = 4/84 = 0.0476$$
$$\text{Prob}(U \leqslant 3) = 7/84 = 0.0833$$

Thus there are no critical regions available for $\alpha_1=1\%$ or $\frac{1}{2}\%$, but the best conservative critical regions for $\alpha_1=2\frac{1}{2}\%$ and 5% do exist and are $U \leqslant 1$ and $U \leqslant 2$ respectively. These results concur with the tabulated critical values in Table G.

Large sample sizes
The complete null distribution of U for the one-sided test with sample sizes $n_A=3$ and $n_B=6$ is sketched in Figure 5.2. You will see immediately (as in the similar example for the Wilcoxon signed-rank test) that not only is it symmetric but its shape is very reminiscent of the normal distribution. Indeed, as sample sizes increase, it becomes ever closer to the normal distribution. The mean of the

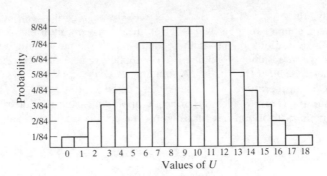

Figure 5.2

distribution is $\mu=\frac{1}{2}n_An_B$ (obviously, since the distribution is symmetric and ranges from 0 to n_An_B) and the standard deviation is $\sigma=\sqrt{n_An_B(N+1)/12}$.

To illustrate the use of the resulting normal approximation we consider the final case given in Table G, namely $n_A=n_B=20$. The value of μ is then $\frac{1}{2}n_An_B=200$ and σ is 36.97. To find what the approximation produces at $\alpha_1=2\frac{1}{2}\%$ (equivalent to $\alpha_2=5\%$ significance level), we calculate $X=\mu-1.96\sigma-\frac{1}{2} = 200-1.96\times36.97-\frac{1}{2}$ $= 127.04$ (the '$-\frac{1}{2}$' is the continuity correction) and then round down; this gives 127, which agrees with the tabulated value.

Strictly speaking, the above formula for the standard deviation is inaccurate if the data include tied observations. Usually this is not troublesome unless there are a lot of ties. However, here are the details of the necessary correction in case you ever need it.

Denote the number of observations tied at a particular value by t (so $t=2$ or 3 or 4 or . . .), and calculate $t^*=t^3-t$ (i.e. 6 or 24 or 60 or . . .). Add up the t^* values for all groups of tied observations, and denote the sum by T. For example, if there are four pairs of tied observations, two sets of three tied observations and one set of four tied observations, then $T=4\times6+2\times24+1\times60=132$. The standard deviation of the null distribution is then calculated using

$$\sqrt{\frac{n_An_B(N^3-N-T)}{12N(N-1)}}$$

(You might like to check that, if you put $T=0$ in this formula, you do of course get the simpler expression for the standard deviation quoted above.)

Relationship between the rank sums and U^*

We have stated that the two possible values of U^* (U_A and U_b) are given respectively by $R_A-n_A(n_A+1)$ and $R_B-n_B(n_B+1)$. To see why these relationships hold, let us compare the calculation of R_A from our data with the corresponding computation of U_A:

U_A		0	0	0	0	0	0		1		3										(U_A=4)
Letter sequence		A	A	A	A	A	A	B	A	B	B	A	B	B	B	B	B	B	B	B	B
R_A		1	2	3	4	5	6		8		11										(R_A=40)

If you compare the ranks included in the computation of R_A with the corresponding contributions to U_A, you will see that they differ respectively by 1, 2, 3, ... , 7 and 8; i.e.

$$U_A = \quad 0 \ + \ 0 \ + \ 0 \ + \ 0 \ + \ 0 \ + \ 0 \ + \ 1 \ + \ 3$$

$$= (1-1)+(2-2)+(3-3)+(4-4)+(5-5)+(6-6)+(8-7)+(11-8)$$

$$= 1+2+3+4+5+6+8+11 \ - \ (1+2+3+4+5+6+7+8)$$

$$= R_A - \tfrac{1}{2} \times 8 \times 9$$

$$= R_A - \tfrac{1}{2} n_A(n_A+1)$$

as stated above. We have used here the well known mathematical result that, for any positive integer n, $1+2+3+ \ldots +n=\tfrac{1}{2}n(n+1)$.

Having seen this pattern in a numerical example, it is then easy to generalize the argument. It depends on the fact that the rank of the ith smallest A is equal to i plus the number of 'B's less than that A (for all i from 1 to n_A). You may check that precisely the same pattern holds even if there are tied observations.

TUKEY'S QUICK TEST

Introduction

The years after World War II saw considerable development of distribution-free statistical methods. Nevertheless, at a meeting of the Industrial Applications Section of the Royal Statistical Society held in Nottingham in 1956, a Mr W. E. Duckworth was reputed as speaking 'vigorously' of the need for a further procedure that would be easier both to use and to teach than those so far available. Less than three years later, Professor John W. Tukey (1959) published, in the very first issue of the journal *Technometrics*, a paper entitled 'A quick, compact, two-sample test to Duckworth's specifications'! The 'quick' in the title is justified by the fact that the statistic is extremely simple to calculate, irrespective of the sample size, and in particular usually requires the ordering of only a few of the observations rather than all of them as in the

Mann–Whitney test. The 'compact' refers to the unusual property that, in most applications, no tables of critical values are needed!

PRACTICAL PROBLEMS, HYPOTHESES AND DATA

These are just the same as those used to illustrate the Mann–Whitney test.

STATISTIC

When H_0 is true we would expect the 'A's and 'B's in the letter sequence to be well mixed, i.e. with no patterns or trends of any kind being discernible (except by occasional, unlucky coincidence).

The most obvious effect on the letter sequence when there is a real difference in location is a tendency for 'A's to accumulate at one end of the sequence, with 'B's in the majority at the other end. So, for example, if the true average (median) in population B is higher than the average in population A, we would expect to see mostly 'A's at the left-hand end and 'B's at the right-hand end. Recall that this is just the type of letter sequence resulting from the car breakdowns survey; in this case, the truth of H_1 would lead us to expect the sequence to begin with an A and end with a B, as did indeed happen.

Tukey's test begins, and sometimes ends, with a simple step motivated by this fact. If we are testing H_0 against the one-sided alternative H_1 that the median of population B is higher than the median of population A, we first check to see whether the overall maximum value is from sample B and the overall minimum value is from sample A. If this is not true, then the test ends then and there with the decision not to reject H_0 in favour of H_1. We could say that the Tukey statistic, denoted by Ty, is zero in these circumstances.

On the other hand, when the overall minimum and maximum observations do come from the 'correct' samples according to H_1, the statistic Ty is simply defined as:

the number of 'A's that are less than the smallest value in sample B

plus

the number of 'B's that are greater than the largest value in sample A

In other words, referring to the letter sequence, Ty is the sum of the lengths of the two extreme runs – the initial run of 'A's and the final run of 'B's.

If the alternative hypothesis H_1 were that the median of population B is *less* than the median of population A, the letters A and B should be interchanged throughout the last two paragraphs.

It should be easy to see that the computation of Ty may easily be carried out without needing to order all the data, i.e. without deriving the complete letter sequence. We shall illustrate this in the 'Solution' section below.

CRITICAL VALUES

The remarkable feature of this test is not so much the simplicity in calculating Ty but the simple form of the critical values (at least for most practical purposes). It turns out that, as long as the sample sizes are not very small nor very different from each other, the $\alpha_1 = 5\%$ and 1% critical regions may be taken as $Ty \geqslant 6$ and $Ty \geqslant 9$ respectively, regardless of the actual sample sizes! Thus you need only commit these two numbers to memory, and you then have a test that is indeed 'compact' in the sense described above.

These simple critical values work very well for ratios of sample sizes from 1 up to $1\frac{1}{2}$ or a little higher. For example, they are valid for the numerical example being studied where $n_A = 8$, $n_B = 12$ and the ratio is $1\frac{1}{2}$. If the sample sizes differ more substantially, some simple amendments to the critical values are available and are mentioned in the 'Null distributions' section below. However, to be on the safe side, we have included a full table of critical values in Table H, which may be consulted if you do not trust these easy guides!

SOLUTION

As already stated, the overall minimum and maximum observations in the car breakdowns data are from samples A and B respectively, consistent with what is to be expected under the one-sided H_1 that Japanese cars have the greater reliability. Thus Ty is given by the sum of the lengths of the two extreme runs in the letter sequence. Now recall that the letter sequence was

A A A A A A B A B B A B B B B B B B B B

We therefore see that the initial run of 'A's has six members and the end run of 'B's contains nine members. Thus $Ty = 6 + 9 = 15$. Recalling that the $\alpha_1 = 5\%$ and 1% critical regions are $Ty \geqslant 6$ and $Ty \geqslant 9$ we see that, as with the Mann–Whitney test, this result is extremely significant; it is so far into the $\alpha_1 = 1\%$ critical region that it would clearly still be significant at much smaller values of α_1. Thus again, even using this very quick-and-easy test, we have quite conclusive evidence of the truth of H_1.

We have mentioned earlier the distinct advantage of Tukey's test that the complete letter sequence is usually not needed. Let us pretend therefore that we only have the original unordered data and see how to calculate Ty quickly *without* ordering them. (You will then realize that this method is easy to apply even with large samples, where otherwise it would take a long time to produce the complete ordering.)

Step 1. Check through the two samples separately, noting the maximum and minimum observations in each sample (say A_{min}, A_{max}, B_{min} and B_{max}).

Step 2. Immediately we may check whether the overall minimum and maximum observations come from the 'correct' samples as expected under H_1; if not, the test ends right here with the decision not to reject H_0 in favour of H_1.

Step 3. Suppose now that H_1 is as in our example, so that we proceed only if the overall minimum and maximum observations are A_{min} and B_{max} respectively. (Note that, if the problem had involved the opposite H_1, i.e. that the median of population A were greater than the median of population B ($\phi_A > \phi_B$), then A and B need interchanging throughout this step.) Trace through sample A, noting all values (we know there is at least one) that are less than B_{min}; similarly trace through sample B, noting *all* values that exceed A_{max}. Ty is then the sum of these two counts.

Illustrating this procedure with the car breakdowns data, we find:

Step 1. $A_{min}=3$, $A_{max}=15$, $B_{min}=8$ and $B_{max}=41$.

Step 2. The overall minimum and maximum observations are $3=A_{min}$ and $41=B_{max}$; as these are expected under H_1, we proceed to step 3.

Step 3. Tracing through sample A we find six observations less than $B_{min}=8$, namely 3, 7, 4, 6, 4 and 7; and in sample B we find nine observations that exceed $A_{max}=15$; these are 19, 36, 25, 23, 38, 17, 41, 25 and 21. Thus $Ty=6+9$, as before.

Discussion

Do not be misled into thinking that because Tukey's test is so easy to execute, then it cannot really be a serious statistical procedure! It is an entirely valid distribution-free test and, while its power is usually not up to that of such sophisticated tests as the Mann–Whitney, it does perform quite well in this respect compared with some other tests that have been proposed elsewhere. Of course, if sample sizes are small, the Mann–Whitney test is quite quick to execute also, and so would probably then be preferred. Otherwise, Tukey's test is an attractive alternative technique, particularly if you come across some data to analyse when you do not have this book or any statistical tables easily to hand!

One-sided and two-sided tests

If we are testing H_0 against the two-sided H_1: $\phi_A \neq \phi_B$ (i.e. that the population medians are unequal, without specifying the direction of the difference), then this

H_1 will be supported by letter sequences that have a preponderance of 'A's at the left-hand end and 'B's at the right-hand end, or vice versa. Thus Ty should now be taken as zero *only* if the overall minimum and maximum observations come from the same sample. If they come from different samples, then Ty is calculated as the sum of the lengths of extreme runs in the letter sequence as before (or again it is easy to see that this computation may be carried out without forming the letter sequence, as described in the 'Solution' section above).

Under the terms described previously, the critical values 6 and 9 now correspond to significance levels $\alpha_2=10\%$ and 2%. Under similar terms, the critical values corresponding to $\alpha_2=5\%$, 1% and $\frac{1}{2}\%$ may be taken as 7, 10 and 13 respectively, which are also very easy to remember and are often referred to as the '7–10–13' rule. However, as shown in the 'Null distributions' section below, for large sample sizes 7 is not strictly conservative at the $\alpha_2=5\%$ level, although it certainly is the nearest critical value if the sample sizes are exactly or approximately equal. Of course, critical values may also be obtained from Table H as usual.

How do we deal with ties?
It is easiest to discuss ties with reference to the letter sequence in spite of the fact that, in practice, it is not usually necessary to form the complete letter sequence to carry out Tukey's test.

First, it is apparent that ties will only affect the test if they occur at or near the extremes of the letter sequence. In fact, the computation of Ty proceeds as above unless there are 'A's tied with B_{min} or B_{max}, or 'B's tied with A_{min} or A_{max}; any ties more central in the letter sequence do not affect the value of Ty. Consequently it is usually very easy to deal with any relevant ties by the process mentioned earlier – breaking them in all possible ways and averaging the resulting values of the statistic. We therefore merely demonstrate the principle with a few examples, rather than producing any complicated general rules. In these examples, ties are indicated by boxed letters, and it is presumed that the sample sizes satisfy the conditions for using the easily remembered critical values.

(a) A A A A $\boxed{\text{A A B}}$ ... A B B

Here the tie could be ordered as AAB, ABA or BAA, resulting in Ty values of 8, 7 or 6 respectively (unless H_1 is $\phi_A>\phi_B$ in which case $Ty=0$, of course). As the average of these is 7, we can just reject H_0 at the $\alpha_2=5\%$ level in favour of H_1: $\phi_A\neq\phi_B$ or at the $\alpha_1=2\frac{1}{2}\%$ level in favour of the alternative H_1: $\phi_A<\phi_B$.

(b) A A A A $\boxed{\text{A A B}}$ ... $\boxed{\text{A B}}$ B B

The first tie can be ordered in three ways as before, so the initial run of 'A's is of length 4, 5 or 6. The tie near the right-hand end makes the run of 'B's either 2 or 3, according as it is ordered BA or AB; the average rank is $2\frac{1}{2}$, yielding $Ty=5+2\frac{1}{2}=\frac{1}{2}$, a slightly more significant result than before.

(c) A A A A A A A A B ... $\boxed{\text{A B}}$

A tie at either extreme usually results in a non-significant result, even if there is a very long run at the other end. The reason is of course that at least one ordering of the tie must give $Ty=0$. Here we obtain $Ty=8+1=9$ if the tie is ordered AB, but $Ty=0$ if it is ordered BA; the average of these values is only $4\frac{1}{2}$, which is not significant.

Null distributions (including large samples)
Although we are usually avoiding presenting much mathematical detail about null distributions, it seems worth making an exception in this case, because the asymptotic null distribution of Ty (i.e. the null distribution as the sample sizes tend to infinity) is easy to establish.

Mathematical statisticians speak of 'asymptotic' probabilities and probability distributions when considering what happens to probabilities as sample sizes 'tend to infinity', for which their notation is $\rightarrow \infty$. If you are unfamiliar with such ideas and language, simply think of the sample sizes being very large (say, a few million!), and you will see that the results to be derived are not absolutely exactly accurate, but are very close indeed to being true.

Suppose that the sample sizes n_A, $n_B \rightarrow \infty$ with $n_A/N \rightarrow p$ and $n_B/N \rightarrow q=1-p$ where, as before, $N=n_A+n_B$. (Of course, $p=q=\frac{1}{2}$ gives the case of equal sample sizes.) Consider the one-sided test where only letter sequences beginning with an A and ending with a B are considered. For any $h\geqslant 2$, we now compute the symptotic value of Prob$(Ty\geqslant h)$ as n_A, $n_B \rightarrow \infty$ in the following manner. The letter sequences giving rise to the event $Ty\geqslant h$ may be partitioned into h types:

Type	Letter sequence	
1	A B . . .	. . . (at least $h-1$ 'B's)
2	A A B . . .	. . . (at least $h-2$ 'B's)
3	A A A B . . .	. . . (at least $h-3$ 'B's)
$\vdots$	$\vdots$	$\vdots$
$h-2$	$(h-2$ 'A's) b . .	. . . (at least 2 'B's)
$h-1$	$(h-1$ 'A's) B . .	. . . (at least 1 'B')
h	(at least h 'A's) . .	. . . (at least 1 'B')

Now, if n_A and n_B are large compared with h, the probability of an A or B being in any prescribed position in the letter sequence will be approximately p or q respectively, almost independently of any other prescribed placings. So the probabilities of occurrence of these types of letter sequence are given approximately by the simple multiplication rule of probability (see Ch. 1) as:

Type of sequence	Asymptotic probability
1	pq^h
2	p^2q^{h-1}
3	p^3q^{h-2}
$\vdots$	$\vdots$
$h-2$	$p^{h-2}q^3$
$h-1$	$p^{h-1}p^2$
h	p^hq

Thus, asymptotically,

$$\text{Prob}(Ty \geqslant h) = pq(q^{h-1}+pq^{h-1}+p^2q^{h-3}+\ldots+p^{h-3}q^2+p^{h-2}q+p^{h-1})$$

By using a well known formula* for the sum of a finite geometric series, this gives, for any $h \geqslant 2$,

$$\text{Prob}(Ty \geqslant h) = \frac{pq(q^h-p^h)}{q-p}$$

as long as $p \neq q$. When $p = q = \frac{1}{2}$, it is easily seen that the probability of each of the h types of letter sequence is $2^{-(h+1)}$, giving $h2^{-(h+1)}$ altogether. In the case of the two-sided Tukey test, all of these sequences may also be reversed (beginning with a B and ending with an A), so that all the probabilities are then doubled.

Let us look at the case $p = q = \frac{1}{2}$, which corresponds to equal sample sizes, in more detail. Here is a table giving some of the probabilities for a one-sided test:

h	5	6	7	8	9	10
$h2^{-(h+1)}$	0.078125	0.046875	0.027344	0.015625	0.008789	0.004883

We therefore confirm that, for large equal-sized samples, 6 and 9 are indeed the best conservative critical values for $\alpha_1 = 5\%$ and 1% respectively. Also, 10 is the best conservative value for $\alpha_1 = \frac{1}{2}\%$ (corresponding also to $\alpha_2 = 1\%$), but $\text{Prob}(Ty \geqslant 7)$ is just over 0.025, and so is not quite the best conservative region for $\alpha_1 = 2\frac{1}{2}\%$ (corresponding also to $\alpha_2 = 5\%$). However, it turns out that, for finite sample sizes, the true probabilities are less than these asymptotic ones, and $\text{Prob}(Ty \geqslant 7)$ is actually less than 0.025 for equal sample sizes up to 24. Even for larger sample sizes, $\text{Prob}(Ty \geqslant 7)$ is a lot closer to 0.025 than is $\text{Prob}(Ty \geqslant 8)$, and this is why Tukey recommended that 7 be used as the most appropriate critical value at this level.

For unequal sample sizes, the probabilities $\text{Prob}(Ty \geqslant h)$ are generally larger than when the sizes are equal, so the critical values may need increasing in these circumstances. A study of the tables of critical values and of the approximate probabilities when $p \neq q$ can yield some approximate amendments. Let us denote by r the larger sample size divided by the smaller, and consider first $1 \leqslant r \leqslant 3$; it is fairly unusual to have one sample more than three times as big as the other. Then the following rules give good approximations to the critical values:

$\alpha_1 = 5\%$, $\alpha_2 = 10\%$	6 for $1 \leqslant r < 7/4$ 7 for $7/4 \leqslant r \leqslant 3$	$\alpha_1 = 1\%$, $\alpha_2 = 2\%$	9 for $1 \leqslant r < 5/3$ 10 for $5/3 \leqslant r < 9/4$ 11 for $9/4 \leqslant r < 11/4$ 12 for $11/4 \leqslant r \leqslant 3$
$\alpha_1 = 2\frac{1}{2}\%$, $\alpha_2 = 5\%$	7 for $1 \leqslant r < 4/3$ 8 for $4/3 \leqslant r < 13/6$ 9 for $13/6 \leqslant r \leqslant 3$	$\alpha_1 = \frac{1}{2}\%$, $\alpha_2 = 1\%$	10 for $1 \leqslant r < 3/2$ 11 for $3/2 < r \leqslant 2$ 12 for $2 < r < 5/2$ 13 for $5/2 \leqslant r \leqslant 3$

* $1 + x + x^2 + \ldots + x^{k-1} = (1-x^k)/(1-x)$.

We do not recommend you to try to commit these to memory! However, they are brief enough for you to note them down in your diary, so that you can carry out this test even in the absence of detailed tables. The rules give best conservative critical values in most cases and usually the nearest critical values otherwise. (Tukey did suggest rather simpler rules than these, but unfortunately they do not seem to be very accurate.)

If required, asymptotic probabilities for unequal sample sizes may easily be found on a calculator using the above formula for Prob($Ty \geqslant h$) with $p = n_A/N$ and $q = n_B/N$.

Assignments

1 Lung functions
In 1984, Burghuber, Bergmann *et al.* (*Respiration* **45** (2)) reported the results of an experiment which investigated various lung functions in two groups of patients. Group 1 contained patients whose pulmonary artery pressure was less than 20 mmHg; group 2 contained patients with a pathologically elevated mean pulmonary artery pressure.

Below we reproduce the data for four lung functions, namely vital capacity (VC), forced expiratory volume (FEV), total lung capacity (TLC) and intrathoric gas volume (IGV). All the results are in litres.

	VC	FEV	TLC	IGV
Group 1	2.87	0.53	7.26	5.56
	2.26	1.53	4.87	3.01
	4.98	2.67	8.09	5.74
	3.91	0.73	9.61	7.42
	3.58	2.10	6.22	3.92
	4.33	3.50	6.41	3.18
	3.91	1.13	7.74	5.41
Group 2	4.68	1.51	7.75	5.38
	3.76	1.43	7.28	5.55
	1.51	0.40	8.46	7.48
	2.87	1.67	4.80	2.27
	3.60	2.53	6.68	3.98
	2.94	0.43	9.11	7.80
	2.08	1.60	4.42	2.69

Task: Perform appropriate two-sample tests to examine the differences between the two groups for each of the four lung functions.

2 Vibration measurements
Two machines (X and Y) are used to measure a vibration property of a particular rubber product. The data below give the vibrational force (kg) of samples from each machine.

Machine X	9.6	11.3	14.2	17.0	17.8	18.6	19.3	20.2	22.1	23.0	23.2
	27.3	31.7	34.0	34.8	36.0	43.3	44.3	53.9	59.1	63.5	
Machine Y	19.5	25.6	27.0	33.5	37.6	38.4	39.4	40.3	42.7	45.2	48.3
	48.9	50.1	51.3	51.6	52.2	55.5	86.2				

Task: The items entering each machine are assumed to have equal characteristics so that any differences apparent in the data are due to the machines. Is there any evidence of the two machines producing different results?

3 Children's diet

A dietician is conducting a study on the effect on children's growth of different diets. Part of the study is investigating two religious sects, A and B. Although both sects are vegetarians, A eat only vegetables from below the ground while B only eat vegetables from above the ground. Samples of young boys are selected from each sect. The height and weight of the boys are measured at regular intervals over a number of years.

The heights (cm) of the boys at the age of 12 are as follows:

Sect A	140	140	140	143	135	144	156	149	146	148	144	153
Sect B	151	154	139	159	159	148	140	157	145			

Task: Is there any evidence of a difference in average height between 12-year-old boys from the sect A and the sect B?

Program 5.1   Mann–Whitney two-sample location test

```
100 REM MANN-WHITNEY TEST

110 REM ** INPUT SAMPLES **
120 INPUT "SIZE OF FIRST SAMPLE ";NA
130 INPUT "SIZE OF SECOND SAMPLE ";NB
140 PRINT
150 DIM A(NA),B(NB)
160 PRINT "INPUT FIRST SAMPLE "
170 FOR I=1 TO NA
180 INPUT A(I);"  ";
190 NEXT I
200 PRINT
210 PRINT "INPUT SECOND SAMPLE "
220 FOR I=1 TO NB
230 INPUT B(I);"  ";
240 NEXT I
250 PRINT
```

Continued overleaf

Program 5.1 Continued

```
260 REM ** CALCULATION OF THE TEST STATISTIC **
270 U=0
280 FOR I=1 TO NA
290 FOR J=1 TO NB
300 IF A(I)<B(J) THEN U=U+1
310 IF A(I)=B(J) THEN U=U+0.5
320 NEXT J
330 NEXT I
340 IF U>NA*NB/2 THEN U=NA*NB-U
350 PRINT "THE VALUE OF THE MANN-WHITNEY STATISTIC FOR NA = ";NA;" AND NB
= ";NB;" IS ";U
360 IF NA<=20 AND NB<=20 THEN STOP

370 REM ** CALCULATION OF APPROXIMATE CRITICAL VALUES **
380 INPUT "PERCENTAGE POINT OF STANDARD NORMAL DISTRIBUTION ";Z
390 LET SD=SQRT(NA*NB*(NA+NB)/12)
400 LET MN=NA*NB/2
410 PRINT "CRITICAL VALUE = ";INT(MN-Z*SD-.5)
```

6

Two independent samples – tests for differences in spread

Introduction

In this chapter we turn our attention to another important kind of difference that may exist between two populations. Tentatively assuming that the two populations being investigated have (at least roughly) equal medians, what now concerns us is whether these populations have differing amounts of *spread* (i.e. dispersion, or variability) about that common median. In many situations, it may be just as important to examine this problem as it was the problem of differences in location (medians) in Chapter 5. For example, consider two machines used for filling the 500 g size of Corn Flakes packets. There are bound to be controls on the machines that can alter the average contents of the packets, and these may be set to ensure that the median is a little over 500 g, say around 505 g. But if this results in one machine producing packets whose contents generally vary between 500 g and 510 g, and the other producing packets whose contents vary between 475 g and 535 g, it is fairly obvious which machine is to be preferred! In classical statistics, such variability is usually measured by the standard deviation; however, in distribution-free statistics there is no such clearly preferred measure, and so we shall just use the qualitative term 'spread' when referring to such variability in populations.

As in most other chapters we shall present two tests – a reasonably sophisticated one and a quick-and-easy one. Indeed there are very strong links here with Chapter 5, since the two tests in this chapter are very closely associated, both in philosophy and execution, with the Mann–Whitney and Tukey tests respectively. Because of this connection, in the unlikely event that you have come to this chapter before reading Chapter 5, we would ask you now to go back and read that chapter before continuing with this one. Further, if you have only read the normal-sized type of Chapter 5, please also in addition read the 'One-sided and two-sided tests' section, since the practical problem to be used in this chapter will require a two-sided test, as opposed to the problem in Chapter 5 which involved a one-sided test.

It is worth mentioning at this point that we are not restricted to testing *just* for location differences (as in Ch. 5) nor *just* for differences in spread (as in this chapter). We might be interested in differences in *both* of these features simultaneously or in *more general* differences that affect the overall shape of the population distributions. Appropriate tests for these more general problems are presented in Chapter 7. (Nevertheless, it is advantageous to isolate the more specific kind of difference of interest if possible, and then use the tests of this chapter or Chapter 5, since they will usually be better able to detect differences of these particular types than will the tests of Chapter 7.)

THE SIEGEL–TUKEY TEST

Introduction

In Chapter 5 we saw that, when there is a location difference between the two populations being compared, the natural effect on the letter sequence is to have 'A's monopolizing one end of the sequence and 'B's monopolizing the other end. Let us now consider what the effect on the letter sequence will be if there is a difference in spread. Consider the two population distributions sketched in Figure 6.1, which clearly differ considerably in spread.

It is easy to visualize how this difference will be reflected in the letter sequence; one of the letters (corresponding to the population having the 'wider' spread) will tend to monopolize both ends of the sequence, while the majority of occurrences of the other letter will be towards the centre. So for the situation illustrated in Figure 6.1, the letter sequence might look something like:

B B B A B B A A B A A A A B B B B B

Now recall that in the Wilcoxon version of the Mann–Whitney test, we simply rank the observations from 1 to $N = n_A + n_B$, from the smallest to the largest, and then sum the ranks of one of the two samples. This rank sum is then unusually small or large if the sample concerned occurs mainly to the left-hand or right-hand end of the letter sequence (i.e. when there is evidence of a location difference), and tends to be between these

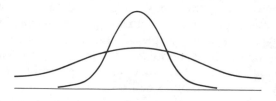

Figure 6.1

two extremes otherwise. What we now need for detecting differences in spread is some alternative ranking or scoring system which will assign, say, large values at *both* extremes of the letter sequence and small values towards the centre (or vice versa). Then if any one of the two letters, say B, does predominate in both extremes, thus indicating a wider spread, the sum of the scores for that sample will be particularly large. Such a sum can therefore form the basis of a useful test for differences in spread.

A number of ingenious ways of applying this principle have been devised. A. M. Mood (1954) published a test where the observations in the letter sequence are ranked as usual from 1 at the left to N at the right, but where each such rank r is then converted to a 'score' of $[r-\frac{1}{2}(N+1)]^2$. With $\frac{1}{2}(N+1)$ being halfway between 1 and N, it is clear that these scores are indeed small in the centre of the letter sequence and large in both extremes. A. R. Ansari and R. A. Bradley (1960) introduced a test involving simpler arithmetic; the positions in the letter sequence are ranked from 1 *at each end* to N or $(N+1)$ (according as N is even or odd) in the middle – these 'ranks' are therefore small in the extremes and large in the middle. Again the test statistic is formed by summing these ranks for either sample.

Unfortunately, both of these tests need special tables of critical values. However, at the same time S. Siegel and J. W. Tukey (1960) produced a test that is very similar in spirit to the Ansari–Bradley test but which has the added convenience of using the Mann–Whitney tables to provide the critical values. Indeed, apart from one vital aspect, the computation of the statistic follows a very similar pattern to that of the Wilcoxon rank-sum version of the Mann–Whitney test. It is mainly because of this rather neat tie-up with previous work that we have selected the Siegel–Tukey test as the most appropriate rank method to present here.

PRACTICAL PROBLEM

Three methods used by investment advisors for analysing and forecasting movements in the stock market are 'fundamental analysis', 'technical analysis' and 'beta analysis'. Beta analysis concentrates on the 'riskiness' of a share, seeking to identify *aggressive* shares and *defensive* shares which are suitable for adventurous and cautious investors respectively. A stockbroker is interested in studying the other two methods of analysis, essentially from a similar point of view. He is satisfied that, 'on the average', or 'in the long run', there is not much to choose between fundamental and technical analysis. What he wants to investigate is whether the methods tend to advise different proportions of aggressive and defensive shares, i.e. whether one method produces more risky advice than the other. (It should be emphasized that 'risky' in this context may not be altogether a bad thing, for although the chances of substantial losses are greater, so are the chances of substantial profits.)

In order to investigate this matter, the stockbroker obtains advice from all his investment advisors on a particular day, telling them that the investments are to be made for a fixed term of six months and then sold. There are 27 advisors in all, 12 favouring fundamental analysis and 15 technical analysis. True to his word, he then monitors the resulting portfolios and six months later calculates the percentage profit or loss in each case.

HYPOTHESES

If one type of advice is more risky than the other, the corresponding percentages will tend to be spread relatively widely. The stockbroker is open-minded about which, if either, type of analysis is likely to prove the more risky. He thus tests the null hypothesis of equality of the percentage spreads against the two-sided alternative that there is some difference in the spreads. So we have:

H_0: There is no difference in 'riskiness', i.e. spread, between the two methods.

H_1: There is some difference in spread between the two methods.

DATA

The percentage gains and losses were as follows:

Fundamental	+5	+20	−24	−9	+50	+32		
(sample A)	+15	−34	−19	+28	+41	+11		
Technical	−4	+19	+21	+13	+2	−7	+24	+10
(sample B)	+26	+14	+6	−10	−21	+36	+7	

STATISTIC

The tie-up with the Wilcoxon rank-sum calculation stems from the fact that the same set of ranks, 1, 2, 3, . . . , $N-1$, N, is used; but the test is converted to a test for differences in spread rather than location simply by reordering these ranks in such a way as to reflect the above argument. The ordered data and corresponding letter sequence, along with the reordered ranks, are as follows:

Data	−34	−24	−21	−19	−10	−9	−7	−4	2	5	6	7	10	11
Sequence	A	A	B	A	B	A	B	B	B	A	B	B	B	A
Ranks	1	4	5	8	9	12	13	16	17	20	21	24	25	27

Data	13	14	15	19	20	21	24	26	28	32	36	41	50
Sequence	B	B	A	B	A	B	B	B	A	A	B	A	A
Ranks	26	23	22	19	18	15	14	11	10	7	6	3	2

You will see that the reordering scheme is to rank the smallest value as 1, then the largest value as 2 and the one next to it as 3, then the next two values at the left-hand end as 4 and 5, then the next two at the right-hand end as 6 and 7, and so on, progressing in pairs towards the middle of the sequence. (The reason for *not* ranking *one* at a time alternatively at the ends to produce

$$1 \quad 3 \quad 5 \quad 7 \quad \ldots \quad \ldots \quad 8 \quad 6 \quad 4 \quad 2$$

is that this makes observations at the left-hand end 'more important' than the corresponding observations at the right-hand end. The Siegel–Tukey scheme is not exactly symmetric, but is the 'fairest' possible share-out of the ranks.)

A rank-sum statistic is then calculated in the usual way, i.e. by summing the ranks for one of the two samples at your choice. This is then converted to a U^* value, and finally to U precisely as was done with the two-sided version of the Mann–Whitney test.

CRITICAL REGIONS

As in the Mann–Whitney test, critical regions are of the form

$$U \leqslant \text{critical value}$$

where the critical values are read from the same table as for the Mann–Whitney test, i.e. Table G (or page 30 in *EST*). From this table, we find that for our problem the $\alpha_2 = 5\%$ and 1% critical regions are $U \leqslant 49$ and $U \leqslant 37$ respectively.

SOLUTION

We note that the rank sum for sample A will probably be the easier to calculate, since it is the smaller sample and also it has several values near the ends of the letter sequence. We therefore compute:

$$R_A = 1+4+8+12+20+27+22+18+10+7+3+2 = 134$$

Then, as in Chapter 5, we convert R_A to a U^* value by subtracting $\frac{1}{2}n_A(n_A+1)$:

$$U^* = R_A - \tfrac{1}{2}n_A(n_A+1)$$
$$= 134 - \tfrac{1}{2} \times 12 \times 13 = 56$$

Had we computed R_B instead, and then subtracted $\frac{1}{2}n_B(n_B+1)$, we would have obtained the other possible value of U^*. As in the (two-sided) Mann–Whitney test, the required final statistic U is the smaller of these two possible values of U^*. To check whether our U^* value (i.e. 56) is the required smaller one, remember that the two values add up to $n_A n_B = 180$, implying that the required value is less than (or, exceptionally, equal to) $\frac{1}{2} n_A n_B = 90$. Therefore, as expected, we have obtained the smaller value, and so the value of U is 56. (You might like to confirm that $R_B = 244$, which gives a U^* value of 124, verifying that the two possible U^* values do indeed sum to $n_A n_B = 180$.)

Checking our value of $U = 56$ against the details of critical regions, we find that it is some distance from the $\alpha_2 = 5\%$ critical region. Indeed, from the table of critical values on page 30 of *EST*, we see that $U = 56$ is just outside the $\alpha_2 = 10\%$ critical region ($U \leq 55$). This is interpreted as either no evidence or, at best, a very low level of evidence in favour of H_1.

Discussion

The Siegel–Tukey test has a couple of disadvantages compared with the other two tests (Mood's and Ansari–Bradley's) mentioned in the introduction. First, it is not exactly symmetric with respect to the letter sequence; thus, if the letter sequence were reversed, it is quite likely that the resulting value of U would not be quite the same. Secondly, the power of the Siegel–Tukey test is a little less than that of Mood's test.

However, both of these 'drawbacks' have only minor effects on the test in practice, and are effectively outweighed in importance by the convenience of being able to use the familiar Mann–Whitney tables to obtain the critical values.

One-sided and two-sided tests

In the case of a one-sided alternative hypothesis H_1, such as 'technical analysis is more risky than fundamental analysis', we proceed as in the Mann–Whitney test to choose a specific calculation for U^* which will tend to give *small* values if this H_1 is true, and to allocate this value to U directly *without* going through the intermediate step of comparing it with $\frac{1}{2} n_A n_B$. If this particular H_1 is true in our particular problem, then the 'B's will tend to predominate in the extremes of the letter sequence. Consequently, we would calculate U specifically using R_B in this case, i.e. $U = R_B - \frac{1}{2} n_B (n_B + 1)$. Its value is then checked against the α_1 critical values in the Mann–Whitney table (Table G) to see if it is significantly small. In the above case we obtain $U = 124$, which would of course furnish no evidence at all for rejecting H_0 against *this* one-sided H_1 since critical regions are of the form $U \leq$ critical value.

Note that, as always, the choice of statistic in this one-sided test is made purely *on the basis of what H_1 suggests*, preferably before the data are inspected (in order to prevent any possibility of the data influencing the choice of hypotheses). Recall from Chapter 2 that H_1 is chosen to interpret properly the practical question being asked, and should therefore not be influenced by the data, which, after all, are being used to judge the truth or otherwise of the hypothesis.

How do we deal with ties?
As previously, the 'ranks' of tied values are simply averaged. In this case, of course, this may well involve averaging ranks such as 1 and 4 to give $2\frac{1}{2}$, which would occur if the two smallest observations were equal.

Null distributions
The particularly clever feature of the Siegel–Tukey statistic is that the null distribution, and hence the critical values, are identical to the Mann–Whitney test. The reason is as follows.

As we know, the principle under which null distributions for two-sample statistics are computed is that, under H_0, all of the possible $\binom{N}{n_A} = \binom{N}{n_B}$ letter sequences are equally likely to occur. In terms of ranks in the Wilcoxon version of the test, this means that (for example) all of the $\binom{N}{n_B}$ possible selections of n_B ranks for sample B out of 1, 2, ..., N occur with equal probability. In the Siegel–Tukey test, the only difference is that the N ranks are laid out in a different order. So it will still happen that, when all of the $\binom{N}{n_B}$ possible letter sequences are generated, each possible allocation of n_B ranks to sample B occurs once and once only – and thus again each occurs with equal probability. Consequently we obtain the same frequency distribution for values of R_B as before, and hence of U^* and U, so we finish up with precisely the same (null) probability distribution and critical values.

Exercise To convince yourself of this, write out the $\binom{7}{3} = 35$ possible letter sequences for $n_A=3$ and $n_B=4$, and find the frequency distributions of R_A and R_B using first the ordinary Wilcoxon ranks and then the Siegel–Tukey ranks.

Large sample sizes
The related comments for the Mann–Whitney test in Chapter 5 apply here also.

A weakness of distribution-free dispersion tests
Although the Kolmogorov–Smirnov and Rosenbaum tests in Chapter 7 deal with situations where there may be differences in both location and dispersion, there is one particular kind of problem that we have not mentioned and which in fact does not seem to have any good distribution-free solution. This is the problem of detecting a dispersion difference *irrespective* of whether there is a location difference. In classical statistics, this problem is solved very neatly by the F-test since the F-statistic remains completely unchanged if either or both samples have constants added or subtracted from them (representing changes in location). Frustratingly, there is, as yet, no such neat equivalent distribution-free method. Several attempts have been made to solve the problem, but all resulting tests suffer from being rather unpowerful or not truly distribution-free, or both. A naively obvious thing to try is to shift one of the samples so that the resulting two samples both have the same median. But, because that would make letter sequences such as AA. . .AABB. . .BB completely impossible, clearly the basic theory of null distributions is violated, and so any resulting tests are not distribution-free.

It is particularly unfortunate that there appears to be no good distribution-free solution to this problem since several researchers have shown that non-normality can upset the behaviour of the F-statistic to a very considerable extent. The best attempt at such a distribution-free method appears to be Moses' 'rank-like' tests, and the interested reader should consult *Nonparametric statistical methods* by M. Hollander and D. A. Wolfe (Wiley, 1973) for details.

A TUKEY-TYPE TEST FOR DIFFERENCE IN SPREAD

Introduction

Having read in Chapter 5 about Tukey's quick test for location differences, you may well be able to anticipate what statistic is going to be used here. We need a statistic of similar nature to that used in Chapter 5, but amended so as to be relevant to differences in spread rather than location. Make a guess as to what it is, and then check in the 'Statistic' section below to see whether you are right.

Unfortunately, only one of the two big advantages of Tukey's location test is retained here. The relevant statistic is still extremely easy to compute (if anything, it is even quicker than the location statistic), and again it does not require the production of the complete letter sequence. However the feature of easily memorable critical values does not hold in this case, at least not to any useful extent. It is true that for large equal-sized samples, the values used in Chapter 5 apply, i.e. 6 for $\alpha_1 = 5\%$ and $\alpha_2 = 10\%$, 7 for $\alpha_1 = 2\frac{1}{2}\%$ and $\alpha_2 = 5\%$, etc. However, the samples need to be larger than in the location tests for these values to apply, and also the critical values are now much more sensitive to the ratio of sample sizes.

One cannot, therefore, usually apply these tests without recourse to tables of critical values, and accordingly these are provided in Table I. (These tables have been specially computed for this book and, to our knowledge, are not available elsewhere.)

PRACTICAL PROBLEM, HYPOTHESES AND DATA

We shall use the same problem and data here as for the Siegel–Tukey test.

STATISTIC

Referring to the letter sequence, the phenomenon that would most obviously indicate a difference in spread is the predominance of one of the samples in *both* extremes. (This is opposite to the location case where, if you remember, the effect we looked for was the predominance of one sample in one extreme and the other sample in the other extreme.) Consequently, in this case the appropriate statistic, Ts say, is the sum of the lengths of the extreme runs in the letter sequence, *as long as these are from the same sample*; otherwise $Ts = 0$.

You can therefore immediately find the value of Ts by referring to the letter sequence produced earlier. However, Ts may be found without deriving the whole letter sequence, and we shall therefore calculate Ts in the 'Solution' section below directly from the original data, imagining that we have not previously gone to the trouble of ordering all the data.

CRITICAL REGIONS

There is a crucial aspect in which the tables of critical values (Table I) for Ts differ from those of other tests. When the sample sizes are unequal, it should be apparent that the values of Ts needed for significance will depend very much on whether it is the larger or smaller sample that is found in the extremes. For example, suppose $n_A=5$ and $n_B=20$; then if the overall minimum and maximum observations come from sample A, so that Ts is being calculated from the 'A's, only a small value of Ts is needed to achieve significance since large values (greater than $n_A=5$) are impossible under any circumstances. In fact, with such a discrepancy in sample sizes, to have the overall minimum and maximum coming from sample A is quite significant by itself: in this case $Ts=2$ is actually significant at the $\alpha_2=10\%$ level! On the other hand, if H_0 is true, it is very likely not only that the overall minimum and maximum will come from the larger sample B but that the extreme runs of 'B's will be quite long – simply because there are far more 'B's than 'A's in the sequence. We shall see from the table that Ts needs to be as large as 15 for significance at the $\alpha_2=10\%$ level if being calculated from the 'B's.

Accordingly, unlike other tests, we do not enter Table I with n_1 and n_2 representing the smaller and larger sample sizes. Instead, n_1 represents the size of that sample *from which Ts is calculated*, i.e. which contains the overall minimum and maximum observations in the data. (Remember that if one sample provides the overall minimum and the other the overall maximum, then Ts is defined as 0 and H_0 cannot be rejected in favour of a difference in spread.)

In our practical problem, Ts is calculated from sample A (see the 'Solution' section below) and so $n_1=12$ and $n_2=15$. From Table I, we then see that the critical regions for $\alpha_2=10\%$, 5% and 1% are respectively $Ts\geqslant5$, $Ts\geqslant6$ and $Ts\geqslant7$.

SOLUTION

The method for calculating Ts directly from the data and without producing the letter sequence may be summarized as follows:

Step 1 Find the minimum and maximum observations in each sample, denoted by A_{min}, A_{max}, B_{min} and B_{max}.

Step 2 Immediately we may check whether the overall minimum and maximum observations are from the same sample or not. If they are not, the test ends at this step with the decision not to reject H_0 in favour of a difference in spread.

Step 3 Suppose that the overall minimum and maximum come from sample B (i.e. $B_{min}<A_{min}$ and $B_{max}>A_{max}$). Trace through sample B, noting every observation that is less than A_{min} and every observation that exceeds A_{max}. The value of the test statistic Ts is the total number of observations thus noted.

Applying this procedure to the investments data from earlier in the chapter gives:

Step 1 $A_{min} = -34$, $A_{max} = +50$, $B_{min} = -21$ and $B_{max} = +36$.

Step 2 The overall minimum and maximum observations both come from sample A, so we proceed to step 3.

Step 3 We find just two observations (-24 and -34) in sample A that are less than $B_{min}=-21$, and there are also two ($+50$ and $+41$) that exceed $B_{max}=+36$. Thus $Ts=2+2=4$.

A quick glance at the critical regions above shows that we have obtained a very similar result to that using the Siegel–Tukey test; i.e. just failing to reject H_0 at the $\alpha_2=10\%$ significance level.

Discussion

Apart from definitely needing tables of critical values, this test has similar attractive properties to Tukey's location test. As one would expect, its power is not so good as the Siegel–Tukey test. However, if anything, the gap between its power and that of the Siegel–Tukey test is smaller than that between Tukey's location test and the Mann–Whitney test. It is therefore a very worthwhile alternative technique for testing for differences in spread.

One-sided and two-sided tests

A one-sided H_1 specifies which population is to have the greater variability if H_0 is untrue. In this case, Ts will only be taken as non-zero if the overall minimum and maximum observations come from the corresponding sample. Thus, with the practical problem used in this chapter, the H_1 specifying fundamental analysis as having the greater riskiness would result in $Ts=4$ again, and this now only just fails to be significant at the $\alpha_1=5\%$ level. Had H_1 specified technical analysis as having the greater riskiness, we would have stopped the test at step 2 with no evidence to reject H_0 in favour of this H_1.

Tied observations

The problem of ties is treated similarly as in the location test, so we will just give three examples for you to check. We assume that we are carrying out either a two-sided test or a one-sided test where we are looking for 'A's in the extremes. Again, boxes show the ties.

(a) A A A A $\boxed{\text{A}\;\;\text{A}\;\;\text{B}}$ . . .   B   A   A $Ts = 7$
(b) A A A A $\boxed{\text{A}\;\;\text{A}\;\;\text{B}}$ . . . $\boxed{\text{A}\;\;\text{B}}$ A   A $Ts = 7\frac{1}{2}$
(c) A A A A B A A A A B . . . $\boxed{\text{A}\;\;\text{B}}$ $Ts = 4\frac{1}{2}$

Null distributions (including large samples)

The theory for asymptotic null distributions is even easier than for the location test. As before, let n_A, $n_B \to \infty$ with $n_A/N \to q$. Now consider the one-sided test, which looks for evidence of population A being the more widely spread. Then, the event $Ts \geq h$ may be partitioned into the following types of letter sequence:

Type	Letter sequence	
1	A B . . .	. . . (at least $h-1$ 'A's)
2	A A B . . .	. . . (at least $h-2$ 'A's)
3	A A A B . . .	. . . (at least $h-3$ 'A's)
⋮	⋮	⋮
$h-2$	$(h-2$ 'A's) B . . .	. . . (at least 2 'A's)
$h-1$	$(h-1$ 'A's) B . . .	. . . (at least 1 'A')
h	(at least h 'A's) . . .	. . . (at least 1'A')

Letter sequences of types 1 to $h-1$ each prescribe the positions of h 'A's and a B, whereas letter sequences of type h prescribe $h+1$ 'A's and no 'B's.

Thus, asymptotically, $\text{Prob}(Ts \geq h) = (h-1)p^h q + p^{h+1}$, for $h \geq 2$,

$$\text{i.e. Prob}(Ts \geq h) = p^h[1 + (h-2)q]$$

If $p = q = \frac{1}{2}$, this gives $h2^{-(h+1)}$ as in the location test, but the formula is quite different otherwise, as might be expected from the completely different tables of critical values. Also, as mentioned earlier, even in the case of equal-sized samples, the samples need to be quite large for the asymptotic values to be appropriate; for example, with samples of size 20, the $\alpha_2 = 10\%$ and 5% values are 6 and 7 as expected, but the 2% and 1% values are 8 and 9 instead of the asymptotic 9 and 10 respectively.

Assignments

1 Soil analysis

In 1979, Wright and Wilson ('On the analysis of soil variability, with an example from Spain' *Geoderma* **22**, 297–313) conducted a study into soil composition in the province of Murcia, Spain. Eight sites were selected and 11 samples from each site were analysed for their silt and clay content. The table below gives the percentage contents of silt (s) and clay (c) for each sample.

Site		Percentage contents from 11 samples										
1	s	46.2	36.0	47.3	40.8	30.9	34.9	39.8	48.1	35.6	48.8	45.2
	c	30.3	27.6	40.9	32.2	33.7	26.6	26.1	34.2	25.4	35.4	48.7
2	s	40.0	48.9	48.7	44.5	30.3	40.1	46.4	42.3	34.0	41.9	34.1
	c	35.9	32.8	36.5	37.7	34.3	35.1	36.2	37.7	28.4	28.4	39.8
3	s	41.9	40.7	44.0	40.7	32.3	37.0	44.3	41.8	41.4	41.5	29.7
	c	34.0	36.6	40.0	30.1	38.6	30.0	28.7	34.5	34.6	34.7	32.8
4	s	41.1	40.4	39.9	41.1	31.9	43.0	42.0	40.3	42.2	50.7	33.4
	c	48.3	49.6	40.4	43.0	49.0	49.1	39.6	44.5	42.2	38.2	59.6
5	s	48.6	50.2	51.2	47.0	42.8	46.6	46.7	48.3	47.1	48.8	38.3
	c	44.3	45.1	44.4	44.7	52.1	42.0	41.8	46.0	46.3	37.1	54.9
6	s	43.7	41.0	44.4	44.6	35.7	50.3	44.5	42.5	48.6	48.5	35.8
	c	37.0	31.3	34.1	29.7	39.1	36.1	32.4	33.4	38.3	36.7	39.9
7	s	47.0	46.4	46.3	47.1	36.8	54.6	43.0	43.7	43.7	45.1	36.1
	c	38.3	35.4	42.6	38.3	45.4	34.0	44.6	38.6	41.9	44.0	54.3
8	s	48.0	47.9	49.9	48.2	40.6	49.5	46.4	47.7	48.9	47.0	37.1
	c	40.1	38.6	38.1	39.8	46.0	39.4	41.6	41.4	39.2	39.5	52.2

Tasks: Is there evidence of differences in spread between the silt and clay contents of soil in this region of Spain? Perform an analysis to see for which sites there is strong evidence of the average contents of silt and clay being different.

2 Swimming ability

Twenty children who enrolled in a swimming class for the handicapped were randomly assigned to one of two groups. Group A, the control group, were taught by traditional methods while group B, the experimental group, were taught by the new method. At the end of the course, each child's swimming ability was assessed by a judge who was unaware of the method by which the child was taught. The results were as follows:

Group A	66	86	80	78	77	63	62	87	75	84
Group B	95	85	56	46	91	79	45	41	54	94

Task: Is there any evidence to suggest that one method produces more erratic results than the other?

Program 6.1   Siegel–Tukey two-sample test for spread

```
100 REM *** SIEGEL-TUKEY TEST FOR SPREAD DIFFERENCES ***

110 REM ** INPUT DATA **
120 INPUT "SAMPLE SIZE FOR A: ";NA
130 INPUT "SAMPLE SIZE FOR B: ";NB
140 LET N=NA+NB
150 DIM D(N),RK(N),B(NB),F(N)
160 PRINT "INPUT THE FIRST SAMPLE:"
170 FOR I=1 TO NA
180 INPUT D(I)
190 LET F(I)=1
200 NEXT I
210 PRINT "INPUT THE SECOND SAMPLE:"
220 FOR I=1 TO NB
230 INPUT B(I)
240 LET F(I)=2
250 NEXT I

260 REM ** MERGE SAMPLES  AND SORT **
270 FOR I=1 TO NB
280 LET D(NA+I)=B(I)
290 NEXT I
300 GO SUB 1000

310 REM ** ASSIGNMENT OF THE RANKS **
320 LET K=INT(N/2)
330 LET R=1
340 LET L=2
350 FOR I=1 TO K STEP 2
360 LET RK(I)=R
370 LET RK(N-I+1)=L
375 IF I=K THEN GO TO 430
380 LET RK(I+1)=R+3
390 LET RK(N-I)=L+1
400 LET R=R+4
410 LET L=L+4
420 NEXT I
430 IF INT(N/2)*2-N<>0 THEN LET RK((N+1)/2)=N

440 REM ** ADJUSTMENT FOR TIES **
450 LET I=1
460 LET B=I
470 LET S=I
480 IF D(I)<>D(I+1) THEN GO TO 530
490 LET S=S+1
500 LET I=I+1
510 IF I=N THEN GO TO 530
520 GO TO 480
530 LET RS=0
540 LET NT=S-B+1
550 FOR J=B TO S
560 LET RS=RK(J)+RS
570 NEXT J
580 FOR J=B TO S
590 LET D(J)=RS/NT
600 NEXT J
610 LET I=I+1
```

Continued overleaf

Program 6.1   Continued

```
615 IF NT=1 AND I=N THEN LET A(N,1)=2
620 IF I>=N THEN GO TO 640
630 GO TO 460

640 REM ** CALCULATION OF THE RANK SUMS **
650 LET RX=0
660 LET RY=0
670 FOR I=1 TO N
680 IF F(I)=1 THEN LET RX=RX+D(I)
690 IF F(I)=2 THEN LET RY=RY+D(I)
700 NEXT I
710 PRINT
720 PRINT "RANK-SUM FOR THE FIRST SAMPLE = ";RX
730 PRINT "RANK-SUM FOR THE SECOND SAMPLE = ";RY
740 STOP

750 REM ** FOR APPROXIMATE CRITICAL VALUES SEE LINES 370-410 OF PROGRAM
   5.1 **

1000 REM ** SORT DATA - USE LINES 1000-1190 OF PROGRAM 4.2  **
```

7
Two independent samples – tests for general differences

Introduction

In the previous two chapters, we have presented tests designed to detect differences in location and spread respectively. It has been assumed (explicitly or implicitly) that if the two populations being sampled *are* different then they differ solely, or at least primarily, in the specified manner, i.e. either in location or in spread but *not* in both, and *not* in any other manner, such as in the shape of distributions. In general, all the tests in Chapters 5 and 6 suffer a reduction in power when used in these latter cases.

But it is quite common for populations to differ in more general ways. Therefore, we need tests that can cope with more general alternative hypotheses than we have so far used. In particular, it is very common for the *spread* (variability) in a population to be directly related to the location (the median, say) of the population.

Consider, for example, two production processes, A and B, from which samples are taken periodically to check for defective items. In order to make the point, assume for the moment that process A is much better than process B so that, for instance, the average number of defectives found in samples from process A is about 2 and in samples from process B is about 10. Under some reasonable assumptions it turns out that the numbers of defectives from process B might typically range between about 3 and 18, with less than a 1% chance of being outside this range. The corresponding range from process A would be from 0 to about 6. (The source of these details is explained in the 'Discussion' section for Rosenbaum's test below.) *Automatically*, the difference in average numbers for defectives implies a difference in variability or spread of the numbers of defectives. Now admittedly, with such a huge difference between the processes, the tests of Chapter 5 would still be highly likely to give significant results. But note the effect of a change in spread. If the spread in the results from process B around the average of 10 had been the same as that from process A about its average of 2, the range of results from process B would have been from about 8 to 14 (rather than the much wider 3 to 18 previously stated). Then, if this were so, *all* the results from process B would probably have exceeded *all* the results from process A, giving rise to the most extreme letter sequence:

$$A \quad A \quad A \quad \dots \quad A \quad A \quad A \quad B \quad B \quad \dots \quad B \quad B \quad B$$

However, because of B's greater spread, there is instead almost bound to be a fair amount of overlap between the 'A's and 'B's, so that the level of significance will be nowhere near as good as if B's spread had stayed as small as A's. If the processes differ, but not by as much as in the discussion so far, the result may well be to deny a rejection of H_0 at all. In other words, the power of the Mann–Whitney and Tukey tests would have been reduced because of the change in spread. It is also worth mentioning that the tests of Chapter 6 have virtually *no* power at all in such situations. In spite of the spread of process B's results being well over double those of process A, which in ordinary circumstances would make the Siegel–Tukey and Tukey-type tests of Chapter 6 very likely to reject H_0, the difference in *averages* renders these tests virtually powerless – they will be almost completely unable to reject H_0 in favour of a difference in spread.

If there were also other differences between the populations, this could exacerbate the problem still further. We therefore present two tests in this chapter which are effective in more general situations. We reverse the order used previously and present a quick-and-easy test first. This test, due to Rosenbaum (1965), is very effective in situations where an increased average implies increased spread, as in the above illustration. But if differences may be of a yet more general nature, then use of the second test to be described, the Kolmogorov–Smirnov test, is recommended instead.

ROSENBAUM'S TEST

Introduction

Let us think more carefully about the effect of the letter sequence when an increase in average is accompanied by an increase in spread. The story can be told via three simple sketches. In Figure 7.1 the horizontal lines indicate the 'effective ranges' of three pairs of populations, which might be defined, say, as ranges in which 99% of the observations in the population lie. The medians of the pair of populations are unchanged in the three cases, but the variations do change.

In case (a), both populations have relatively small spread, in case (b) both have larger spread, and in case (c) A has the smaller spread and B the larger spread. What are we likely to see in the letter sequence for the three cases? In case (a) we get the usual effect described in Chapter 5, i.e. mostly 'A's at the left-hand end and mostly 'B's at the right, so that

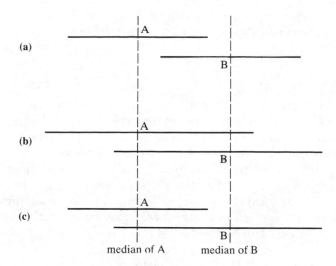

Figure 7.1

both the Mann–Whitney and Tukey tests will perform well. The situation is similar in case (b), though the larger spreads reduce the effect somewhat, so that the tests will not be quite so powerful. However, case (c) is rather different; there is less tendency for 'A's to predominate at the left-hand end than for either of the first two cases. But, at the other end, 'B's predominance is *much greater* than in either of the other two cases.

So, bearing in mind that Rosenbaum's test is of the quick-and-easy type, and is based on the length of extreme runs in the letter sequence, what do you think the test statistic will be?

PRACTICAL PROBLEM

A well known television commercial demonstrates the superiority of a certain make (A) of long-life batteries over ordinary batteries by showing how much longer mechanical toys powered by the long-life batteries keep working compared with those powered by conventional batteries. Another company (B) also starts manufacturing long-life batteries. A consumer organization decides to compare the two types of long-life batteries by carrying out a similar test. Its researchers purchase 20 of the toys and equip 10 of them with A's long-life batteries and the other 10 with B's. The toys are set running and their total operating times are recorded.

During the experiment, it is observed that six of the toys, two in the A sample and four in the B sample, operate *much* longer than the other toys. On subsequent examination it is found that these six toys, though externally similar to the others, are differently designed and in particular are lighter, thus causing less strain on the batteries. It was therefore decided to eliminate these six readings from the test.

HYPOTHESES

The researchers are examining whether there are any systematic differences in performance between the two types of batteries. Their prime interest is to check for a difference in average running time of the toys powered by the two types. However, it is common for the spread of operating times and 'times to failure', etc., to depend upon average times, so they fully expect that if one type of battery is superior, then this may be accompanied by a wider spread of operating times. The researchers have no idea as to which type may be the better, so the test must be two-sided with hypotheses of the form:

H_0: Batteries A and B perform equally on average.
H_1: Batteries A and B do not perform equally on average.

DATA

The 14 observed operating times retained for analysis were as follows:

Batteries A

| 110 h 35 min | 120 h 25 min | 136 h 20 min |
| 129 h 05 min | 139 h 10 min | 99 h 25 min |

Batteries B

| 100 h 55 min | 116 h 00 min | 119 h 35 min | 94 h 40 min |
| 105 h 10 min | 114 h 40 min | 102 h 55 min | 110 h 40 min |

STATISTIC

Recall the discussion on case (c) in the 'Introduction'. When the spread is related to the average, it seems sensible that the test statistic should concentrate on the *right*-hand end of the letter sequence and ignore the left-hand end. So Rosenbaum's test statistic R is therefore simply the length of the extreme run (either of 'A's or 'B's) at the right-hand end of the letter sequence.

As with the previous quick tests, it is of course unnecessary to derive the complete letter sequence. All that is needed is the following procedure. Identify the largest observation in each sample. Then if the largest overall observation is from A, R is the number of 'A's greater than the largest B. Or if the largest overall observation is from B, then R is the number of 'B's greater than the largest A.

CRITICAL REGIONS

Since large values of R support H_1, critical regions are of the form

$$R \geq \text{critical value}$$

Critical values for the usual significance levels are given in Table J. As in the Tukey-type spread test in Chapter 6, it is important to enter the tables with n_1 representing the size of the sample from which R is calculated, with n_2 representing the other sample size.

In the above example, R is in fact calculated from the 'A's (see the 'Solution' section below), so with $n_1=6$ and $n_2=8$ the critical regions are $R \geq 4$ for $\alpha_2=10\%$ or 5% and $R \geq 5$ for $\alpha_2=2\%$ or 1%.

SOLUTION

The largest running time is the 139 h 10 min from sample A; so R is the number of 'A's greater than the largest B, which is 119 h 35 min. All we now do is to count the number of times in sample A that exceed 119 h 35 min; there are four (120 h 25 min, 136 h 20 min, 129 h 05 min and 139 h 10 min). Hence $R=4$ and this result is significant at the $\alpha_2=5\%$ significance level. The researchers have therefore found reasonable evidence of a difference between average performances of the two makes of batteries.

Discussion

If you care to form the letter sequence for the above data and carry out the tests of the previous two chapters, you will find the Mann–Whitney U to be equal to 11, Tukey's Ty to be 5, the Siegel–Tukey U to be 13 and Ts to be 0. *None* of these four results are significant, even at the 10% level. Rosenbaum's test is therefore seen to be very effective when spread increases with average. It also has some power when the spread of a population does not depend on the average, but in this case the tests of Chapter 6 are to be preferred.

If you are familiar with Poisson and exponential distributions, you will know that these are important examples where the standard deviation is very dependent on the mean of the distribution. In fact, in the exponential distribution the standard deviation is *equal* to the mean, and in the Poisson distribution the standard deviation is the square root of the mean. Data likely to come from these distributions are therefore very appropriate for analysis by Rosenbaum's test.

Poisson distributions are well known to model counts accurately in many kinds of random processes (e.g. numbers of shoppers arriving at check-out points) and to approximate many binomial distributions. The illustration in the 'Introduction' concerning numbers of defectives is a case in point, and you may check the statements concerning the likely ranges of these numbers with the details of the Poisson distributions having means equal to 2 and 10 with *EST* pages 14 and 15. Exponential distributions, and other associated distributions such as gamma and Erlang distributions, are often used to model lifetimes, times to failure, times between arrivals of shoppers, etc. Thus, situations for which Rosenbaum's test is relevant are very common.

It is interesting to note that Rosenbaum first presented this test as a test for differences in spread! Of course, it does have some power when differences between populations are purely in spread, but it certainly seems much more appropriate for the context in which it is presented here.

One-sided and two-sided tests
There are no prizes for guessing what the one-sided version of Rosenbaum's test consists of! If H_1 specifies the population that is to have the larger average (and spread), rejection of H_0 is only considered if the corresponding sample contains the overall maximum – so that R is computed from observations in that sample. In this case, α_1 significance levels should be used.

Thus, for example, if the researchers in our practical problem had *suspected* that A was superior to B (perhaps because it is the more expensive of the two), then the hypotheses would have read:

H_0: Batteries A and B have equal performance on the average.
H_1: On the average, battery A has superior performance to battery B.

Then if the overall maximum is from A, we proceed to calculate R as the number of 'A's greater than the largest B. But if the overall maximum is from B, the value of R is taken as 0 and we are unable to reject H_0 in favour of this H_1.

Treatment of ties
In the unlikely event that both samples have the same maximum value, one would not normally consider rejecting H_0. This is perhaps not universally true, but the only exceptions would be when there is a huge disparity between sample sizes, and this should only rarely apply in practice. Otherwise, only a tie that occurs at the lower end of the extreme run need be considered, and this would be dealt with as in the Tukey tests by considering all orderings of those tied observations and averaging the resulting values of R.

As a rather unlikely example, suppose that the right-hand end of the letter sequence appears thus:

$$\dots \boxed{\text{A} \quad \text{A} \quad \text{B} \quad \text{B} \quad \text{B}} \quad \text{A} \quad \text{A} \quad \text{A}$$

with the box, as usual, denoting tied observations. Considering all 10 possible permutations of the tied observations, six give $R=3$, three give $R=4$ and just one gives $R=5$. Thus we would calculate R as $(6\times3+3\times4+1\times5)/10=3.5$.

Null distributions (including large samples)
The theory of Rosenbaum's R statistic is extremely easy, for any size samples. If the sample sizes are n_A and n_B, with $N=n_A+n_B$, the probability that R is formed from 'A's and takes a value of at least h is the probability of there being (at least) h 'A's at the right-hand end of the letter sequence, and this is

$$\frac{n_A}{N} \times \frac{n_A-1}{N-1} \times \dots \times \frac{n_A-h+1}{N-h+1} = \frac{n_A!(N-h)!}{N!(n_A-h)!}$$

Asymptotically, if n_A, $n_B \to \infty$ with $n_A/N \to p$, this expression simply approaches p^h. And this simple expression is extremely convenient to use if we need to derive critical values for sample sizes not included in Table J; in the large majority of cases, it will produce the 'correct' best conservative value.

As an example, suppose $n_A=20$ and $n_B=60$ and the overall maximum observation is an A. The following table compares the exact values of $\text{Prob}(R \geqslant h)$ with the asymptotic approximation (which is just 4^{-h}):

h	1	2	3	4
Exact probability	0.2500	0.0601	0.0139	0.00306
Asymptotic probability	0.2500	0.0625	0.0156	0.00391

Note that, apart from $h=1$, the exact probabilities are all less than the asymptotic probabilities. This is always the case, and so use of the p^h approximation will give critical values erring, if at all, on the conservative side.

THE KOLMOGOROV–SMIRNOV TEST

Introduction

The Kolmogorov–Smirnov test is the best known of several distribution-free procedures which compare two sample cdfs in order to test for differences of *any kind* between the distributions of the populations from which the samples have been taken.

As we saw in Chapter 1, the sample cdf is an approximation of the true cdf of the corresponding population – though, admittedly, a rather crude one if the sample size is small. This fact has already been used in the Kolmogorov–Smirnov goodness-of-fit test in Chapter 4. Any kind of substantial difference between the two distributions will result in a corresponding difference between their cdfs, which should in turn show up as a significantly large difference between the sample cdfs. Such differences may be in location and/or spread or may be more general differences in shape of the distributions.

Various ways of comparing two sample cdfs have been suggested, and the Kolmogorov–Smirnov method is almost certainly the simplest – it uses the *maximum vertical difference* between them as the test statistic (compare the Kolmogorov–Smirnov goodness-of-fit statistic in Chapter 4). The goodness-of-fit test was introduced by A. N. Kolmogorov (1933), and this particular two-sample application was devised by N. V. Smirnov (1939).

PRACTICAL PROBLEM, HYPOTHESES AND DATA

We shall illustrate the Kolmogorov–Smirnov test with the comparison of the two makes of long-life batteries. As is often the case with applications of this test, the prime interest is probably to see if there is a difference in average. There may be a subsidiary interest in other types of difference and/or the realization that other types of difference may reduce the effectiveness of pure location difference tests such as those in Chapter 5. However, it will be of interest also to see how this test deals with the practical problems studied in Chapters 5 and 6, and we shall do this in the 'Discussion' section below.

STATISTIC

As stated in the introduction, the Kolmogorov–Smirnov test statistic is simply the maximum vertical difference between the two sample cdfs. Recall that the cdf for a sample of size n is the step function that rises by $1/n$ at each observation, always starting at 0 and finishing up at 1. The cdf for sample A thus rises in steps of 1/6 and that of sample B in steps of 1/8. The two cdfs are given below:

Sample A			
99 h 25 min	110 h 35 min	120 h 25 min	
1/6	2/6	3/6	
129 h 05 min	136 h 20 min	139 h 10 min	
4/6	5/6	6/6=1	

Sample B			
94 h 40 min	100 h 55 min	102 h 55 min	105 h 10 min
1/8	2/8	3/8	4/8
110 h 40 min	114 h 40 min	116 h 00 min	119 h 35 min
5/8	6/8	7/8	8/8=1

In Figure 7.2, we have drawn the two sample cdfs and have indicated the maximum difference D; it turns out to be equal to 2/3. Actually there is no real need to draw these cdfs. Since D depends only on the order of the 'A's and 'B's, and not on their exact values, it can be computed directly from the letter sequence. Study Figure 7.2 and imagine changing some of the values slightly, but not enough to alter the letter sequence; then you should soon be able to convince yourself that this is true. So, having written down the letter sequence, one could write in the values of the cdfs of samples A and B, respectively, above and below the sequence as follows:

Sample A cdf	0	1/6	1/6	1/6	1/6	2/6	2/6	2/6	2/6	2/6	3/6	4/6	5/6	1
	B	A	B	B	B	A	B	B	B	B	A	A	A	A
Sample B cdf	1/8	1/8	2/8	3/8	4/8	4/8	5/8	6/8	7/8	1	1	1	1	1

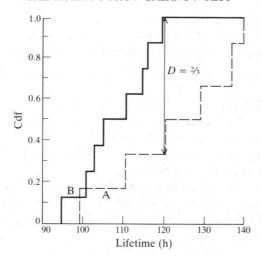

Figure 7.2

Then we compare the two rows of fractions to locate the maximum difference between them, which gives $D = 1-2/6 = 2/3$, as before.

It can sometimes be a little tricky to pinpoint the maximum difference in this latter method when the sample sizes (n_A and n_B), i.e. the denominators of the fractions, are different. But note that, if we multiply all the fractions by $n_A n_B$, the effect is to change them all into integers; and obviously it is a lot easier to find the maximum difference between two rows of integers rather than between two rows of fractions. In practice, the production of the two rows of integers is more easily described as follows. Above the letter sequence, increase the 'score' by n_B (=8 here) at each occurrence of an A; whereas below the letter sequence increase the 'score' by n_A (=6 here) at each occurrence of a B. To check the accuracy, make sure that the final 'score' in both rows is $n_A n_B$ (=6×8 = 48 here):

48 × cdf of sample A	0	8	8	8	8	16	16	16	16	16	24	32	40	48

	B	A	B	B	B	A	B	B	B	B	A	A	A	A
48 × cdf of sample B	6	6	12	18	24	24	30	36	42	48	48	48	48	48

The maximum difference, say D^*, between these rows of integers is now easily located where marked, with $D^*=48-16=32$. Clearly, $D^*=n_A n_B D$, so we can then evaluate D as $D^*/n_A n_B = 32/48 = 2/3$.

However, in practice, because of the form of the tables of critical values, it is not even necessary to convert D^* into D in order to carry out the test.

CRITICAL REGIONS

Because $D^* = n_A n_B D$ must take integer values only, it is simpler to print tables of critical values directly in terms of D^*, as this avoids the messy fractions or decimals that would be involved in tables for D. Thus, if you have evaluated D by the graphical method or by the fractions calculation using the letter sequence, you will need to multiply D by the product of the sample sizes, $n_A n_B$, to obtain D^* before using the tables. Clearly, large values of D^* will cause H_0 to be rejected and so the critical regions are of the form

$$D^* \geq \text{critical value}$$

Critical values for D^* are given in Table K (and on page 31 of *EST*). With $n_1=6$ and $n_2=8$ the $\alpha_2=10\%$, 5%, 2% and 1% critical regions are, respectively, $D^* \geq 30$, $D^* \geq 34$, $D^* \geq 40$ and $D^* \geq 40$ (corresponding to $D \geq 5/8$, $D \geq 17/24$, $D \geq 5/6$ and $D \geq 5/6$).

SOLUTION

We have already calculated the value of D^* (and D) above and obtained $D^*=32$, which we see is significant at a level somewhere between 5% and 10%.

Discussion

Despite its more sophisticated nature, the Kolmogorov–Smirnov test has not achieved quite as good a significance level as Rosenbaum's quick test on these data. This should not be too much of a surprise, bearing in mind the design and purpose of the two tests – and indeed this is an opportune place to survey all the tests of the last three chapters.

The tests of Chapter 5 are appropriate when the difference between the populations is wholly or mainly in location. The tests in Chapter 6 are appropriate when the difference is wholly or mainly in spread. Rosenbaum's test is designed for cases where an upward move in location is accompanied by an increase in spread. Although there is some overlap in sensitivity between these various tests, by and large none of them work well except in the specific situations for which they were designed. The Kolmogorov–Smirnov test is a 'catch-all' test. It has some power in all of the three situations for which the other tests are relevant, and also has power for other kinds of differences. However, it is in the nature of things that such a general-purpose test could not be expected to have such high power in a *specific* situation as other tests that are designed especially for that situation. This is not an inviolable rule, but it is certainly true more often than not. (If it were not, then presumably we would find ourselves using the

Kolmogorov–Smirnov test universally in preference to the other tests.) So the real place of the Kolmogorov–Smirnov test is in situations where it is perhaps unclear what kind of differences to expect between the populations, or where expected differences do not fit into the usual categories of location or spread.

You might care to try out the Kolmogorov–Smirnov test on the problems in Chapters 5 and 6. For the Japanese vs. British car breakdowns data, $D^*=76$ with $n_1=8$ and $n_2=12$; this is extremely significant of a difference between the two, as would be expected with these data. Using the data in Chapter 6 we obtain $D^*=48$ with $n_1=12$ and $n_2=15$; this is not a significant result. Again this is what we might have anticipated since even the two tests of Chapter 6 found only very slight evidence of a difference in spread (which in this case was the kind of difference most expected).

It is worth mentioning that D^* (or D) is much easier to compute if the samples happen to be equal-sized, say $n_A=n_B=n$. For then both sample cdfs rise in steps of $1/n$ and so, even using the fractional calculation above, it is simple to spot where the maximum difference D occurs. However, it is even simpler to take advantage of the common step size by working in steps of 1 (instead of $1/n$ or n) and then finally dividing the maximum difference thus found by n to obtain D or multiplying by n to obtain D^*. Indeed, having derived the letter sequence, the statistic can easily be calculated 'in the head' in this case. To illustrate this, let us ignore the final two operating times in sample B, so that we then have two samples of size 6. The resulting letter sequence, along with the calculation using a step size of 1 is as follows:

$$0 \quad 1 \quad 1 \quad 1 \quad 2 \quad 2 \quad 2 \quad 2 \quad 3 \quad 4 \quad 5 \quad 6$$
$$B \quad A \quad B \quad B \quad A \quad B \quad B \quad B \quad A \quad A \quad A \quad A$$
$$1 \quad 1 \quad 2 \quad 3 \quad 3 \quad 4 \quad 5 \quad 6 \quad 6 \quad 6 \quad 6 \quad 6$$

It can be immediately seen that the maximum difference here is $6-2=4$, so that $D=4/6=2/3$ (coincidentally, exactly the same as with the original data) and $D^*=24$ (which, with sample sizes both equal to 6, is not significant at the 10% level). The quick form of calculation, which can be carried out without writing anything down except for the letter sequence, is to trace through the letter sequence, keeping a mental tally of, say, 'number of 'B's minus number of 'A's', and noting the maximum value of this tally, irrespective of sign. We write it down here to demonstrate the idea, but you will see that this is indeed an operation which can easily be done in your head:

	B	A	B	B	A	B	B	B	A	A	A	A
Number of 'B's − number of 'A's	+1	0	+1	+2	+1	+2	+3	+4	+3	+2	+1	0

The maximum size of this tally is 4, which can then be simply converted to D or D^* as above.

Finally, apart from those tests (mentioned in the introduction) that compare sample cdfs by other criteria, there are still further tests designed for recognizing general rather than specific differences. Perhaps the best-known of these is the Wald–Wolfowitz number-of-runs test, and this test is described in Chapter 17.

One-sided and two-sided tests

Seeing that the Kolmogorov–Smirnov test is deliberately designed to have power for diagnosing differences of all types, it may seem a contradiction in terms to refer to a one-sided Kolmogorov–Smirnov test. However, sometimes one does use an alternative hypothesis to the effect that, say, 'population A is *stochastically greater* than population B'. This is a generalization of the concept of A being located above B, or of the median of A being greater than the median of B – there being now no implication that the distributions are the same except for a location difference. If this alternative hypothesis is true, the effect is that the true cdf of B will rise earlier than that of A, and of course the hope is that this phenomenon will be reflected in the sample cdfs. Therefore the appropriate statistic is now D_{BA}, defined as the maximum non-negative value of $F_B - F_A$, where F_A and F_B are the cdfs of samples A and B. Equivalently, this is the maximum vertical difference between the graphs over that section (if any) where $F_B > F_A$. The value of D_{BA} needs multiplying by $n_A n_B$ to compare with the tabulated values or, as above, it is easiest in practice to work with an integer calculation which produces $n_A n_B D_{BA}$ directly. For this one-sided version of the statistic, α_1 significance levels are appropriate as usual. Such a one-sided test would have been appropriate when analysing the data of Chapter 5; there, in fact, we would have based the test on D_{AB}, the maximum positive value of $F_A - F_B$. You should calculate the value of D_{AB} and compare your conclusion with that in Chapter 5.

Treatment of ties

Tied observations may only cause problems with the Kolmogorov–Smirnov test if they occur in the vicinity of the maximum difference. There are two methods for dealing with ties. One is very easy but has the disadvantage of possibly giving the statistic a slightly lower value than it should have; however, the error is not usually of a size to make any substantial difference to the conclusion. Graphically, the method amounts simply to *ignoring* the points where ties occur for the purposes of locating the maximum difference. Arithmetically, the method amounts to considering differences only at the *end* of ties.

To illustrate the idea, suppose that the operating times of the toys had only been measured to the nearest hour. The data would then have been:

A	111	120	136	129	139	99	
B	101	116	120	95	105	115	103	111

The corresponding letter sequence is:

B   A   B   B   B $\boxed{A \quad B}$ B   B $\boxed{A \quad B}$ A   A   A,

where boxed letters indicate ties. Using the integer calculation for D^* we proceed thus:

0	8	8	8	8		16	16	16		24	32	40	48
B	A	B	B	B	$\boxed{A \quad B}$	B	B	$\boxed{A \quad B}$	A	A	A		
6	6	12	18	24		30	36	42		48	48	48	48

Because there is a tie at the point that previously gave the maximum difference, D^* is in fact now reduced; it is now given by the difference $42-16=26$, and this value is no longer significant at the $\alpha_2=10\%$ level. You might like to check that the above rule concerning the graphical method yields the same result.

The alternative method (which can be tricky to apply if there are a lot of ties) is to go back to the basic principle of ordering ties in all possible ways and averaging the values of the statistic thus obtained. Ties that occur other than in regions where the difference is relatively large may be ignored for this purpose. In the above case, we may therefore ignore the first tie (at 111 h). Ordering the second tie as AB leaves D^* at 26 as above, but ordering it as BA gives $D^*=32$, as we obtained when the data were recorded more accurately. Here we now average these two possible values for D^*, giving $D^*=29$. This value is only just outside the $\alpha_2=10\%$ critical region of $D^*\geqslant30$.

Null distributions

As usual, null distributions may be found by considering all possible letter sequences. For illustration, let us use the same sampling situation as in the Mann–Whitney test, i.e. $n_A=3$ and $n_B=6$. First, consider one of the one-sided statistics, say $D_{AB}=\max(F_A-F_B)$. This statistic can only take on the seven values 0, 1/6, 2/6, 3/6, 4/6, 5/6 and 1 with respective frequencies of 12, 18, 25, 15, 10, 3 and 1. Since the total frequency is $\binom{9}{3}=84$, this gives

$$\text{Prob}(D_{AB}=1) \quad = 1/84 \quad = 0.0119$$

$$\text{Prob}(D_{AB}\geqslant5/6) \quad = 4/84 \quad = 0.04762$$

$$\text{Prob}(D_{AB}\geqslant4/6) \quad = 14/84 = 0.1667$$

You may confirm that these results agree with the critical values for these sample sizes given in Table K, remembering that the values tabulated relate to $D^*=n_A n_B D=18D$ and that α_1 significance levels are appropriate.

You might like to check through the 84 letter sequences again, but this time calculating $D_{BA}=\max(F_B-F_A)$. You should obtain precisely the same distribution as before. (Can you see why?)

Finally you can obtain the distribution of the two-sided D, which may be defined as $\max(D_{AB}, D_{BA})$. You will find that this takes the values 1/6, 2/6, 3/6, 4/6, 5/6 and 1 with frequencies 1, 26, 29, 20, 6 and 2 respectively.

If you have worked through all the null distribution exercises, you will notice some differences here compared with previous distributions, such as those for the sign, Wilcoxon signed-rank and Mann–Whitney statistics. In particular, the null distribution of the one-sided Kolmogorov–Smirnov statistic is *not* symmetric. This has two important ramifications. First, the relationship between the one-sided and two-sided statistics is no longer straightforward. Previously it has always been the case that the value of a two-sided statistic has always been immediately derivable from the value of either of the one-sided statistics; this is no longer true here. So whereas previously the two-sided statistic has taken only half the values of the related one-sided statistic, but accordingly with twice the probability, this relationship also does not now hold. Fortunately, however, this probability relationship *does* hold where it matters, i.e. in the right-hand tail, and usually to such an extent that it *does* remain true that $\alpha_2=2\alpha_1$ for significance levels of interest. So, writing D_1 to indicate either of the one-sided statistics, D_{AB} or D_{BA}, we have

$$\text{Prob}(D=1) \quad \doteq 2\times\text{Prob}(D_1=1) \quad = 2/84$$

and

$$\text{Prob}(D\geqslant5/6) \;= 2\times\text{Prob}(D_1\geqslant5/6) \;= 8/84$$

and even

$$\text{Prob}(D\geqslant4/6) \;= 2\times\text{Prob}(D_1\geqslant4/6) \;= 28/84$$

However, $\text{Prob}(D\geqslant3/6) = 57/84$, whereas $2\times\text{Prob}(D_1\geqslant3/6) = 58/84$.

The second effect of the non-symmetry affects the asymptotic distribution, which we discuss in the next section.

Large sample sizes

It can be shown that the non-symmetry of the null distribution does not diminish as sample sizes increase (as might have been hoped!), so that certainly the asymptotic distribution cannot be normal. In fact it was shown by L. A. Goodman (1954) that the distribution of $4n_An_BD_1^2/N$ is approximately chi-squared with two degrees of freedom, where again D_1 is either of D_{AB} or D_{BA}. As an example, we find from Table B that the $\alpha_1=5\%$ critical value of the chi-squared distribution with two degrees of freedom is 5.991. Hence the approximate $\alpha_1=5\%$ critical value of D_1 is

$$\tfrac{1}{2}\sqrt{5.991N/n_An_B} = 1.2238\sqrt{N/n_An_B}$$

In the table below (which we presented in Chapter 4 for the Kolmogorov–Smirnov goodness-of-fit test), we give the multipliers of $\sqrt{N/n_An_B}$ required for the usual levels of significance:

α_1	5%	$2\tfrac{1}{2}$%	1%	$\tfrac{1}{2}$%
α_2	10%	5%	2%	1%
	1.2238	1.3581	1.5174	1.6276

As usual, let us illustrate this approximation with $n_A=n_B=25$ (the largest sample sizes in Table K). The approximation gives the $\alpha_1=5\%$ critical value as $1.2238\sqrt{50/(25\times25)}=0.3461$. Remembering that Table K refers to $D^*=n_An_BD$, we multiply this value by 625 to obtain 216 (to the nearest integer). Now the entry in Table K is 225, which at first sight looks a long way from 216. But recall that D_1 (or D) must be a multiple of 1/25 (since $n_A=n_B=25$) and so 25^2D_1 must be a multiple of 25. Therefore the next larger critical value to the approximate one we calculated must be 225, which is the same as the value given in Table K. In other words, the critical region $D^*\geqslant216$ is actually the same as $D^*\geqslant225$.

Assignments

1 Soil analysis
Analyse the soil data given in Assignment 1 of Chapter 6.

2 Football results
J. R. Gillett and D. J. Colwell (*Mathematical Gazette*, 1983) investigated data provided by 100 football matches between England and Scotland. The data are:

Number of goals per match	0	1	2	3	4	5	6	7	8	9
Frequency for England	17	39	22	6	7	7	0	1	0	1
Frequency for Scotland	20	32	27	13	3	3	1	1	0	0

Task: Use the Kolmogorov–Smirnov test to see whether there is any significant difference between the results for the two teams.

3 Shopping habits
A nationwide supermarket store commissioned a survey on the shopping habits of its customers. Part of this survey investigated the rate at which customers arrived at the stores. The data below give the times between consecutive arrivals at two stores commening at 0900 h (in fact, these results are from a particular Saturday morning and are just part of total data collected on that day):

Store A

0 min 3 s	0 min 19 s	1 min 53 s	0 min 28 s	0 min 9 s
0 min 20 s	2 min 24 s	0 min 34 s	1 min 46 s	0 min 15 s
0 min 37 s	0 min 16 s	0 min 19 s	1 min 3 s	1 min 30 s
1 min 10 s	0 min 12 s	0 min 12 s	0 min 55 s	0 min 32 s

Store B

0 min 55 s	3 min 47 s	0 min 26 s	1 min 20 s	1 min 35 s
1 min 5 s	1 min 0 s	0 min 2 s	0 min 24 s	2 min 10 s
0 min 17 s	1 min 10 s	1 min 28 s	1 min 40 s	2 min 24 s
0 min 22 s	2 min 46 s			

Task: Construct a dot diagram and/or a histogram for each set of data. Hence choose an appropriate test to see whether there is evidence to suggest that one store is busier than the other.

Program 7.1   The Kolmogorov–Smirnov two-sample test for general differences

```
100 REM *** KOLMOGOROV-SMIRNOV TWO-SAMPLE TEST ***

110 REM ** INPUT THE SAMPLES SIZES **
120 INPUT "SIZE OF THE FIRST SAMPLE: ";NA
130 INPUT "SIZE OF THE SECOND SAMPLE: ";NB
140 LET N=NA+NB
150 DIM D(N),B(NB),FA(N),FB(N),CA(NA),CB(NB),F(N)

160 REM ** INPUT THE DATA **
170 PRINT "INPUT THE OBSERVATIONS (IN ASCENDING ORDER) & FREQUENCIES FOR
    THE FIRST SAMPLE"
180 LET CF=0
190 FOR I=1 TO NA
200 INPUT D(I),FQ
210 LET F(I)=1
220 LET CF=CF+FQ
230 LET CA(I)=CF
240 NEXT I
250 PRINT
260 PRINT "INPUT THE OBSERVATIONS (IN ASCENDING ORDER) & FRQUENCIES FOR
    THE SECOND SAMPLE"
270 LET CF=0
280 FOR I=1 TO NB
290 INPUT B(I),FQ
300 LET F(I+NA)=2
310 LET CF=CF+FQ
320 LET CB(I)=CF
330 NEXT I

340 REM ** MERGE SAMPLES AND SORT **
350 FOR I=1 TO NB
360 LET D(NA+I)=B(I)
370 NEXT I
380 GO SUB 1000

390 REM ** CALCULATION OF TEST STATISTIC **
400 LET Y=0
410 LET Z=0
420 LET CA(0)=Y
430 LET CB(0)=Z
440 FOR I=1 TO N
450 IF F(I)<>1 THEN GO TO 500
460 LET Y=Y+1
470 LET FA(I)=CA(Y)*CB(NB)
480 LET FB(I)=CB(Z)*CA(NA)
490 GO TO 530
500 LET Z=Z+1
510 LET FA(I)=CA(Y)*CB(NB)
520 LET FB(I)=CB(Z)*CA(NA)
530 NEXT I
540 LET ND=0
550 LET PD=0
560 LET DS=0
570 FOR I=1 TO N
580 LET DF=FA(I)-FB(I)
590 IF DF<ND THEN LET ND=DF
600 IF DF>PD THEN LET PD=DF
610 IF ABS(DF)>DS THEN LET DS=ABS(DF)
```

```
620 NEXT I

630 REM ** OUTPUT FOR THE TWO-SIDED ALTERNATIVE **
640 PRINT "VALUE OF TEST STATISTIC FOR TWO-SIDED ALT. = ";DS
650 PRINT

660 REM ** OUTPUT FOR ONE-SIDED ALTERNATIVE **
670 PRINT "VALUE OF TEST STATISTIC FOR A>B IS ";PD," AND FOR A<B IS
";ABS(ND)

1000 REM ** SORT DATA  - USE LINES 1000-1190 OF PROGRAM 4.2 **
```

8
Two related samples

Introduction

We come now to a rather paradoxical situation. We shall have two samples to analyse, but it will turn out that ordinary two-sample methods are invalid and we shall need to have recourse to *one-sample* methods instead. This, of course, has the distinct advantage that, presuming you have already read Chapter 3, you will find virtually nothing new to learn in this chapter!

The particular two-sample situation now under discussion is where the data are in the form of so-called 'matched pairs'. So far in the book, we have always been assuming that all the observations available for analysis are 'statistically independent' of each other, i.e. there is no relationship or connection between any of them apart from the fact that items in any sample originate from the same source or population. We are now going to consider the situation where there is some kind of pairing, natural or otherwise, between observations in the two samples. For example, the two samples might consist of readings of blood pressure, or weight, or reaction time, etc., on the same group of patients before and after some medical treatment. In this situation the data might be:

			Patient			
Response	A	B	C	D	E	F
Before treatment	86	83	78	90	92	77
After treatment	82	81	92	79	92	82

Or on the other hand, an educational researcher might carry out an experiment on pairs of twins (or at least siblings, if it proves too difficult to find enough twins!), teaching some material to one member of each pair by traditional methods and to the other member of each pair by microcomputer. You will see that the resulting form of the data is essentially the same as above – there is a definite pairing between observations in the two samples. Thus the two samples are not truly *random* samples (which implies that *all* the observations are statistically independent of each other) because of such pairwise dependence between them. Consequently, ordinary two-sample tests, such as the Mann–

Whitney and Tukey tests, are inappropriate for analysing such data. Indeed, not only are they invalid for use with matched-pairs data but, even if they were mistakenly applied in this context, they would have little power.

WILCOXON'S SIGNED-RANK TEST FOR MATCHED PAIRS

Introduction

The only valid way to deal with data that are in the form of matched pairs is to regard each matched pair as a single 'sampling unit', and to represent it by an appropriate summary of its original pair of values. Then the data will indeed consist of just *one* sample. It will follow that both the tests in Chapter 3 are immediately applicable. In particular, under the null hypothesis H_0 that the two population distributions are identical, it turns out that this 'summary' value automatically has a *symmetric* null distribution, so that Wilcoxon's signed-rank test may always be used for this kind of application. Because of this, some books introduce the signed-rank test in this context rather than in the single-sample situation. We shall therefore concentrate on Wilcoxon's test here, though bearing in mind that the sign test is also available as a quick-and-easy alternative method.

PRACTICAL PROBLEM

A regional water authority has been carrying out some new pollution-control measures on one of the main rivers under its control. One way of measuring pollution levels is by 'biochemical oxygen demand' (BOD). BOD was measured at 12 sites before the new controls were implemented, and then again four years later at the same sites. Some parts of the river tend to be more heavily polluted than others because of the positions of waste discharge stations and of confluent tributaries of varying pollution.

HYPOTHESES

The water authority is seeking definite evidence that its new controls have been effective, i.e. that average pollution levels have fallen. This therefore defines H_1, with H_0 being that there has been no average change in pollution levels. So we have:

H_0: There is no difference in the average pollution levels before and after implementation of the controls.

H_1: Average pollution levels are greater before implementation of controls than afterwards.

DATA

The BOD values at the 12 sites before and subsequent to implementation of the pollution controls were as follows:

Site	1	2	3	4	5	6	7	8	9	10	11	12
Before controls	17.4	15.7	12.9	9.8	13.4	18.7	13.9	11.0	5.4	10.4	16.4	5.6
Four years later	13.6	10.1	10.3	9.2	11.1	20.4	10.4	11.4	4.9	8.9	11.2	4.8

STATISTIC

Because of the differing environments of the various sites, the BOD readings from different sites are not directly comparable with each other. However, we may certainly compare the two readings at individual sites to see whether there is evidence of improvement after implementation of the controls. So we calculate the *differences* between each pair of readings by subtracting the later reading from the earlier one. Under H_0, the true average (i.e. median) of these differences will be zero, but if H_1 is true then the true average difference will be *positive*. Treating the 12 differences as a single sample, therefore, we may test H_0 against H_1 using the Wilcoxon signed-rank statistic as in Chapter 3.

You will recall that, since H_1 is one-sided, we define the statistic T as *either* the sum of ranks of positive differences *or* the sum of ranks of negative differences, according as which choice would be *expected* to be the *smaller* if H_1 were true. The appropriate choice in this problem is the rank sum of the negative differences.

Note that, in the two-sided case, we would simply choose T to be whichever of the two sums turned out to be the smaller, as opposed to the one-sided case in which the choice is governed by the alternative hypothesis and not by the actual data.

CRITICAL REGIONS

Critical values are obtained from Table D (or page 29 of *EST*) as before, with α_1 significance levels referring to one-sided tests as usual.

In this example with $n=12$, the $\alpha_1=5\%$, 1% and $\frac{1}{2}\%$ critical regions are $T \leqslant 17$, $T \leqslant 9$ and $T \leqslant 7$ respectively.

SOLUTION

The differences (before minus after) in BOD readings at the 12 sites, and their ranks (ignoring signs), are:

Sites	1	2	3	4	5	6	7	8	9	10	11	12
Differences	3.8	5.6	2.6	0.6	2.3	−1.7	3.5	−0.4	0.5	1.5	5.2	0.8
Ranks	10	12	8	3	7	6	9	1	2	5	11	4
Signs of differences	+	+	+	+	+	−	+	−	+	+	+	+

The rank sum of the negative differences is $T=6+1=7$. This value is in fact the boundary of the critical region for $\alpha_1=\frac{1}{2}\%$, and so we have found very strong evidence of a reduction in average pollution levels along the river.

Discussion
Although we have stated that ordinary two-sample tests such as the Mann–Whitney and Tukey tests arc invalid when the data are in the form of matched pairs, you might nevertheless find it instructive to try them out on the BOD data. You will discover that neither test rejects H_0 at even the $\alpha_1=5\%$ level. Compare the details, and in particular think carefully about *why* the Mann–Whitney test fails to reject H_0 whereas the Wilcoxon signed-rank test has found almost conclusive evidence of an improvement.

The reason for the invalidity of ordinary two-sample tests is mentioned again in the 'Null distributions' section below. It is shown in the same section why the Wilcoxon test may *always* be used with matched-pairs data, whereas it has limited applicability to one-sample situations.

One-sided and two-sided tests
See the 'Statistic' section above.

Treatment of zero or tied differences
As in Chapter 3.

Null distributions
The reason for the invalidity of ordinary two-sample tests in the present context is simply that the statistical dependence between the members of each matched pair results in the various possible letter sequences not now being equally likely even when H_0 is true. This is because of the tendency for the A and B corresponding to the members of any matched pair to be relatively close together in the letter sequence.

More importantly, let us examine why the Wilcoxon test *is* always valid when analysing matched pairs, unlike ·when the test is applied to a single sample. As with ordinary two-sample situations, we will take the null hypothesis H_0 to imply that the two components (X_A and Y_B, say) of any matched pair have the same distribution as each other. (It is quite conceivable, however, that each matched pair may have a different such distribution.) We will first prove that, for any given matched pair, the distribution of the difference X_A-Y_B is symmetric about zero if H_0 is true. Such symmetry could be expressed, for example, by requiring $\text{Prob}(X_A-Y_B>d)$ to be equal to $\text{Prob}(X_A-Y_B<-d)$ for all d (see Fig. 8.1). Now,

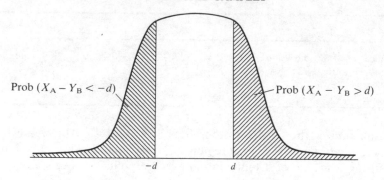

Figure 8.1

$\text{Prob}(X_A - Y_B > d) = \text{Prob}[-(X_A - Y_B) < -d] = \text{Prob}(Y_B - Y_A < -d)$. The crux of the argument is that, since X_A and Y_B have identical distributions, $X_A - Y_B$ and $Y_B - X_A$ must have the same distribution as each other. Consequently, $\text{Prob}(Y_B - X_A < -d) = \text{Prob}(X_A - Y_B < -d)$, and the symmetry condition is thus proved.

Now although the distributions of differences need not be the same for all matched pairs, it follows that they must always be symmetric. Consequently, the basic criterion required for the computation of the null distribution in Chapter 3 is satisfied, i.e. that the probability behaviour of positive and negative differences are identical. Thus (ignoring zero differences) there is a 50–50 chance of the largest difference being positive or negative; and there is a 50–50 chance of the second largest difference being positive or negative; and so on for each and every difference. The null distribution of T is therefore computable as in Chapter 3, and so the tables of critical values (Table D and *EST* page 29) are valid quite generally for matched-pairs data.

Large sample sizes
Exactly as in Chapter 3 for the Wilcoxon signed-rank test.

THE SIGN TEST FOR MATCHED PAIRS

The sign test can of course be applied to the single sample of differences instead of Wilcoxon's test. This provides us with a quicker and simpler test, but one which is not generally as powerful as the signed-rank test for the same reasons as discussed in chapter 3. In the BOD data there are two negative differences out of 12 and, checking with the table of critical values for the sign test (Table C), we see that this is significant at the $\alpha_1 = 2\frac{1}{2}\%$ level but not at the $\alpha_1 = 1\%$ level. The sign test does therefore also find evidence of an improvement in average pollution levels, but the evidence is not as strong as that found by using Wilcoxon's signed-rank test.

Assignments

1 Calf feeding

An experiment was carried out to compare two schemes, A and B, of calf feeding. Scheme A was a new and untried method that was expected to produce better results (in terms of gain in weight) than scheme B, which was a more traditional method of calf feeding. Thirteen pairs of identical twin calves were used in the experiment. One of each pair was fed according to scheme A and the other according to scheme B. The gains in weight (kg) of the calves are given in the following table.

Pair	1	2	3	4	5	6	7	8
Scheme A	20.1	19.5	19.0	21.1	23.1	22.6	18.9	22.8
Scheme B	21.2	18.7	19.0	20.8	19.9	21.4	17.9	23.1

Continued

Pair	9	10	11	12	13			
Scheme A	27.1	19.8	21.7	18.9	20.4			
Scheme B	24.3	18.5	20.3	18.7	19.4			

Task: Use a matched-pairs test to see whether these data support the claim that scheme B is better than A.

2 Distribution of soil particles

In 1973, D. R. Nielsen *et al.* ('Spatial variability of field-measured soilwater properties' *Hilgardia* **42**, 215–59) published the results of a survey on the distribution of particle size in soil. Part of their data is given below, showing percentage of sand and silt at 12 depths:

Depth	Sand	Silt	Depth	Sand	Silt
1	27.3	25.3	7	25.2	28.4
2	31.2	25.4	8	23.6	31.4
3	25.0	26.6	9	33.4	30.3
4	30.1	27.4	10	36.4	28.3
5	33.6	25.1	11	36.4	29.4
6	34.9	24.2	12	20.7	36.7

Task: Use an appropriate procedure to test the null hypothesis that there is no difference in the average percentages of sand and silt.

Program 8.1 Wilcoxon's matched pairs test

```
100 REM *** WILCOXON SIGNED-RANK MATCHED-PAIRS TEST ***

110 REM ** INPUT DATA **
120 INPUT "SAMPLE SIZE  ";N
130 DIM A(N),B(N),D(N),RK(N)
140 PRINT "INPUT THE OBSERVATIONS FOR SAMPLE A & B:"
150 FOR I=1 TO N
160 INPUT A(I),B(I)
170 NEXT I

180 REM ** DIFFERENCES CALCULATED **
190 FOR I=1 TO N
200 LET A(I)=A(I)-B(I)
210 NEXT I

220 REM ** REMOVE ZERO DIFFERENCES **
230 LET NC=0
240 FOR I=1 TO N
250 IF A(I)=0 THEN GO TO 280
260 LET NC=NC+1
270 LET A(NC)=A(I)
280 NEXT I
290 LET N=NC
300 FOR I=1 TO N
310 LET D(I)=ABS(A(I))
320 NEXT I
330 GO SUB 1000

340 REM ** CALCULATION OF RANKS SUMS **
350 LET SN=0
360 LET SP=0
370 FOR I=1 TO N
380 IF A(I)<0 THEN LET SN=SN+RK(I)
390 IF A(I)>0 THEN LET SP=SP+RK(I)
400 NEXT I
410 PRINT
420 PRINT "SUM OF THE POSITIVE RANKS =";SP
430 PRINT "SUM OF THE NEGATIVE RANKS = ";SN
440 PRINT
450 IF N<=50 THEN STOP

460 REM ** CALCULATION OF APPROXIMATE CRITICAL VALUES (N > 50) **
470 INPUT "PERCENTAGE POINT OF STANDARD NORMAL DISTRIBUTION ";Z
480 LET SD=SQRT(N*(N+1)*(2*N+1)/24)
490 LET MN=N*(N+1)/4
500 PRINT "CRITICAL VALUE = ";INT(MN-Z*SD-.5)

1000 REM ** RANK SAMPLE - USE LINES 1000-1140 OF PROGRAM 3.1 **
```

PART IV

Correlation and regression

Chapter 8 dealt with the situation where data occur in the form of 'matched pairs'. This is where we have two samples of equal size but, instead of all the observations being statistically independent of each other, there is some kind of link or connection between corresponding members of the samples. Thus ordinary two-sample methods, which assume the samples are truly *random*, do not apply.

The situation of matched pairs is not far removed from the problems to be studied in this part of the book. In the next three chapters, we cover distribution-free approaches to correlation and regression, topics for which again there exists a considerable non-distribution-free literature. In brief, when we have some data from an ostensibly matched-pairs situation, there are two things to investigate. First, *is* there a matching at all, i.e. is there a pairwise dependence between the samples? Secondly, if there is such a dependence, how can we use it to predict or forecast the value of one member of a matched pair if we know the value of the other one? These two problems are respectively the problems of *correlation* and *regression*.

Although both correlation and regression techniques can be extended to three or more variables, in this book we discuss only the problems arising with two variables. In Chapters 9 and 10, we present some standard distribution-free procedures for dealing respectively with the problems of correlation and regression, while in Chapter 11 we discuss some quick methods for these problems. Chapter 12 deals with correlation between non-numeric variables or, as it is commonly known, the analysis of contingency tables.

9
Correlation

Introduction

The classical approach to correlation is very 'model-dependent'. That is, if a particular kind of formula is proposed to represent the relationship between two components of the matched pairs, then the methods examine the likely validity or otherwise of this type of formula. The methods of *rank correlation* described here are rather less restrictive. They examine simply whether there is a tendency for the two components of the matched pairs to increase and decrease together (*positive* correlation) or, alternatively, for one to decrease as the other increases and vice versa (*negative* correlation); either kind of effect is known as *monotonicity*. The tests to be introduced can be either two-sided (testing for either kind of correlation) or one-sided (testing for *either* positive *or* negative correlation as specified in the alternative hypothesis).

We cannot really refer to the distribution-free and non-distribution-free approaches to correlation as 'modern' and 'traditional' respectively, since both techniques covered in this chapter have a very long history. Spearman's version of rank correlation was published long ago (Spearman, 1904); and the other method, usually attributed to a paper by Kendall (1938), can in fact also be traced back to the turn of the century.

SPEARMAN'S RANK CORRELATION COEFFICIENT

Introduction

Several ways of measuring correlation have been devised. The resulting 'correlation coefficients' are conventionally defined so that they must lie between -1 and $+1$; $+1$ represents extreme evidence of positive correlation (perfect agreement), -1 represents extreme evidence of negative correlation (perfect disagreement), while values near 0 tend to occur if there is little or no such correlation between the two variables.

Spearman's correlation coefficient r_S is of this type. Denoting the data by (X_1,Y_1), (X_2,Y_2), . . . , (X_n,Y_n), r_S will equal $+1$ if and only if it is *strictly* true that 'the larger X is, then the larger Y is' throughout the sample. Conversely, if it is strictly true that 'the larger X is, the *smaller* Y is', then r_S will equal -1. It is unusual to obtain data where such relationships hold exactly (if so, the reality of the situation is often so obvious that a formal test is unnecessary!). But, as you would expect, a tendency towards either of these extremes will produce relatively large positive or negative values of r_S (i.e. close to $+1$ or -1), and otherwise r_S will be closer to 0. Such behaviour thus provides an obvious basis for a test for correlation.

PRACTICAL PROBLEM

A business organization specializes in selling (or renting) copying machines. The managing director is analysing a full year's records of the 15 salesmen employed by a certain branch of the company. The records include details of the number of machines placed by each salesman, and the number of calls or visits made by each salesman to various potential customers during the year. The managing director is an advocate of high activity on the part of the salesmen, i.e. he is keen on them increasing their number of visits! A brave member of the sales team suggests that it is not really the number of visits that matters but rather the *type* of visit. Effectively, there are two types of visit: simple visits and demonstrations ('demos'). In a simple visit, the salesman is armed with brochures, advertising and other literature; whereas, as the name implies, a demo consists of an actual on-site demonstration of one of the copying machines. To an extent, the salesmen are given freedom of choice as regards the number and type of visits that they make. However, the managing director favours simple visits, as they are more flexible and cost less.

The salesmen's records include not only the total numbers of visits but also the numbers of demos made. The data are given below. We want to know: what conclusions should the managing director draw?

HYPOTHESES

Assuming that it is unlikely for sales to *fall* if either the total number of simple visits or the number of demos increase, we could test for positive correlation between *either* of these numbers and the number of sales, i.e. the tests will be one-sided.

In the illustration of Spearman's test we shall consider whether there is evidence of positive correlation between the number of simple visits and the number of sales (the second problem of correlation between the number of demos and the number of sales we leave as an exercise). So the hypotheses of concern to us are:

H_0: There is no correlation between the number of simple visits and the number of sales.
H_1: There is some positive correlation between the number of simple visits and the number of sales.

DATA

The relevant extract from the records is as follows:

Salesman	Demos	Simple visits	Total visits	Sales
1	104	265	369	25
2	161	380	541	47
3	156	270	426	40
4	96	224	320	17
5	149	343	492	49
6	143	359	502	39
7	113	216	329	33
8	142	324	466	30
9	115	381	496	31
10	175	242	417	44
11	135	233	368	34
12	145	350	495	43
13	137	276	413	35
14	151	391	542	42
15	126	290	416	36

Before proceeding with a formal analysis of any such data, it is usually fruitful to depict the values graphically on what is commonly called a *scatterplot*. The scatterplots for our data are shown in Figures 9.1 and 9.2. Such plots often give us a 'feel' for whether there is any correlation between the variables – and, if there is, what type it is (e.g. linear, curved, etc.). Figure 9.1 appears to indicate little, if any, correlation between the number of simple visits and sales. But Figure 9.2 reveals the

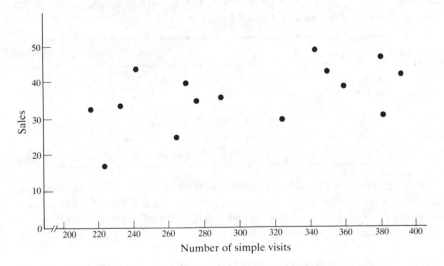

Figure 9.1 Scatterplot of simple visits vs. sales.

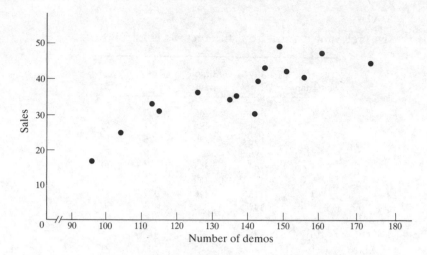

Figure 9.2 Scatterplot of demos vs. sales.

presence of quite strong correlation between the number of demos and sales. It will be interesting to see if the test statistics reflect these indications from the scatterplots.

STATISTIC

Let X_i and Y_i denote the two variables whose correlation coefficient we wish to calculate; so here X_i represents the number of simple visits and Y_i the number of sales by the ith salesman. We first rank both the X_i and Y_i from 1 (for the lowest value) to n (for the highest), where n is the number of pairs of observations; $n=15$ in this example. We shall denote these ranks by $r(X_i)$ and $r(Y_i)$ respectively. The *difference* between the ranks for each pair is then calculated as follows:

Salesman,	i	1	2	3	4	5	6	7	8	9	10	11	12	13	14	15
Visits rank,	$r(X_i)$	5	13	6	2	10	12	1	9	14	4	3	11	7	15	8
Sales rank,	$r(Y_i)$	2	14	10	1	15	9	5	3	4	13	6	12	7	11	8
Difference,	d_i	+3	−1	−4	+1	−5	+3	−4	+6	+10	−9	−3	−1	0	+4	0

Now if the two variables are positively correlated, then the rankings will be rather similar and the rank differences $d_i=r(X_i)-r(Y_i)$ will tend to be small in size. Indeed the strongest indication of positive correlation is when the two sets of ranks are identical, in which case all the rank differences will be zero. Perhaps your first thoughts about trying to summarize these differences would be to average them; but, as you can easily check, the sum of the differences (presuming their signs are taken into account) is always equal to zero, so their mean is not very informative! However, as seen in Chapter 1 when we introduced the sample variance, a common method in statistics of combining a set of numbers that sum to zero is to form the *sum of their squares*:

$$d_1^2 + d_2^2 + \ldots + d_n^2 = \sum_{i=1}^{n} d_i^2 = D^2 \quad \text{(say)}$$

This is obviously 0 when the two sets of ranks are identical. D^2 takes its maximum possible value when the ranks are completely in the 'wrong' order (i.e. the observation whose X rank is 1 has Y rank n, the one whose X rank is 2 has Y rank $n-1$, and so on); it can be shown that this maximum value of D^2 is $(n^3-n)/3$.

Exercise   Confirm for $n=15$ that this formula does indeed give the value of D^2, when the ranks are completely opposite to each other, and then confirm this formula for some even value of n of your own choice.

D^2 could be used directly as a statistic for the current problem. However, bearing in mind what was said in the introduction about correlaton coefficients usually being constructed to have values between -1 and $+1$, Spearman's rank correlation cocfficient is in fact defined by:

$$r_S = 1 - \frac{6D^2}{n^3-n}$$

Obviously, when $D^2 = 0$ (the strongest evidence of positive correlation) then $r_S = +1$; and when $D^2 = (n^3-n)/3$ (its largest value and the strongest evidence of negative correlation) then $r_S = -1$; otherwise r_S lies between -1 and $+1$.

CRITICAL REGIONS

Since the one-sided alternative of positive correlation is supported by values of r_S near $+1$, the required critical regions are of the form

$$r_S \geq \text{critical value}$$

Table L (or the first table on page 40 in *EST*) gives the critical values for r_S, as always, α_1 significance levels relate to one-sided tests.
   In fact, in the tables the significance levels are denoted by α_1^R; the superscript R refers to the one-sided test having a critical region in the right-hand tail of the distribution of r_S. Had we been testing the opposite one-sided alternative, that of *negative* correlation, critical regions would

have consisted of large negative values, i.e. in the left-hand tail and would be of the form

$$r_S \leq -\text{tabulated value}$$

So, in our current problem (with $n=15$), the critical regions corresponding to significance levels $\alpha_1 = 5\%$, $2\frac{1}{2}\%$, 1% and $\frac{1}{2}\%$ are respectively $r_s \geq 0.4464$, $r_s \geq 0.5214$, $r_s \geq 0.6036$ and $r_s \geq 0.6536$.

SOLUTION

Using the table of rank differences constructed earlier, we obtain:

$$
\begin{aligned}
D^2 = \sum_{i=1}^{15} d_i^2 &= (+3)^2 + (-1)^2 + (-4)^2 + (+1)^2 + (-5)^2 + (+3)^2 \\
&\quad + (-4)^2 + (+6)^2 + (+10)^2 + (-9)^2 \\
&\quad + (-3)^2 + (-1)^2 + 0^2 + (+4)^2 + 0^2 \\
&= 320
\end{aligned}
$$

Then

$$r_S = 1 - \frac{6 \times 320}{15^3 - 15} = 1 - \frac{1920}{3360} = 0.4286$$

This is just outside the $\alpha_1 = 5\%$ critical region. So there is only a little evidence of positive correlation between the number of simple visits and the number of sales. This conclusion agrees with the initial view we had of the scatterplot in Figure 9.1.

Exercise Now calculate Spearman's correlation coefficient using the number of demos as the X variable and with the number of sales still as the Y variable.

Discussion
You should have found the value of r_S for the number of demos and number of sales in the exercise to be 0.8714, which is well into the $\alpha_1 = \frac{1}{2}\%$ critical region; so much so that it would clearly be significant for much more stringent values of α_1 (also, this result truly confirms the visual evidence in the scatterplot in Figure 9.2). Thus the salesman's claim that the *type* of visit (i.e. demo as opposed to simple visit) affects sales is well supported by these results. The managing director will hopefully be convinced by the above results that sales are increased more predictably by increasing the number of demos than by increasing the number of simple visits. However, the point remains that demos are expensive to arrange; to increase their number would mean increasing the number of machines to be set aside for demonstration purposes, thereby severely reducing the potential income from those machines and considerably increasing transport, insurance and other costs. To examine whether the increased cost would be worth while, he needs to ascertain how the sales are likely to increase for a certain

increased number of demos. This is the kind of problem tackled by the *regression* techniques in Chapter 10. Thus correlation and regression are somewhat complementary techniques: regression methods can be carried out whatever the data look like, but correlation methods indicate whether they are likely to be of much value.

There are a number of quite tricky points of interpretation concerning correlation, and we shall review these in the 'Discussion' section at the end of the chapter.

Alternative derivation of r_S

This section will be of main interest to readers who are familiar with the standard 'parametric' approach to correlation, which uses Pearson's product-moment coefficient of linear correlation, r. This measures the tendency for the X and Y variables to be not just monotonically related (as with Spearman's coefficient) but for that monotonic relationship to be specifically *linear*. The formula for r can be written in various ways; here are two of the most important forms:

$$r = \frac{\Sigma(X_i - \bar{X})\,(Y_i - \bar{Y})}{\Sigma(X_i - \bar{X})^2 \Sigma(Y_i - \bar{Y})^2} = \frac{\Sigma X_i Y_i - n\bar{X}\bar{Y}}{(\Sigma X_i^2 - n\bar{X}^2)\,(\Sigma Y_i^2 - n\bar{Y}^2)}$$

In these formulae, Σ represents the sum for i going from 1 to n, i.e. $\sum\limits_{i=1}^{n}$, and $\bar{X}$ and $\bar{Y}$ are the sample means, $\bar{X} = \Sigma X_i/n$ and $\bar{Y} = \Sigma Y_i/n$. Since r is a measure of *linear* correlation, it only takes the value +1 if the data lie exactly on some *line* of positive slope, and −1 if they lie on a *line* of negative slope. Unlike r_S, any other monotonic relationship will give a value of r that lies between, rather than at, these extremes. Nevertheless, r_S can be defined in a way that is very closely related to r. In brief, r_S can be computed from exactly the same formula as r, *but using the ranks* $r(X_i)$ *and* $r(Y_i)$ *instead of the actual values* X_i *and* Y_i.

We will first confirm this numerically for the copier salesmen's data and then give a general proof. Using the second form of the formulae for r, we are therefore claiming that

$$r_s = \frac{\Sigma r(X_i)r(Y_i) - nr(\bar{X})r(\bar{Y})}{[\Sigma(X_i)^2 - nr(\bar{X})^2]\,[\Sigma r(Y_i)^2 - nr(\bar{Y})^2]}$$

where $r(X_i)$ and $r(Y_i)$ are the ranks tabulated in the 'Statistic' section earlier in this chapter. Now both the $r(X_i)$ and the $r(Y_i)$ consist of permutations of 1,2,3, ..., 14,15 (=n), so immediately we know that $r(\bar{X}) = r(\bar{Y}) = 8$; you may also check that $\Sigma r(X_i)^2 = \Sigma r(Y_i)^2 = 1^2 + 2^2 + 3^2 + \ldots + 14^2 + 15^2 = 1240$. All that needs working out from the actual arrangement of ranks is

$$\Sigma r(X_i)r(Y_i) = (5 \times 2) + (13 \times 14) + (6 \times 10) + \ldots + (15 \times 11) + (8 \times 8) = 1080$$

(again refer to the table in the 'Statistic' section). Substituting all these figures into the above formula gives

$$\frac{1080 - 15(8)^2}{1240 - 15(8)^2} - \frac{120}{280} - 0.4286$$

as above. As an exercise, you might like to try using this alternative method for calculating r_S using the number of demos as the X variable instead of the number of simple visits.

For the general proof, we first quote two well known mathematical results:

$$r(\bar{X}) = r(\bar{Y}) = (1+2+3+\ldots+n)/n = \tfrac{1}{2}(n+1)$$

and

$$\Sigma r(X_i)^2 = \Sigma r(Y_i)^2 = 1^2+2^2+\ldots+n^2 = n(n+1)\,(2n+1)/6$$

Then, the denominator is

$$n(n+1)\,(2n+1)/6 - n(n+1)^2/4 = (n^3-n)/12 \tag{1}$$

Now consider

$$D^2 = \Sigma d_i^2 = \Sigma[r(X_i)-r(Y_i)]^2 = \Sigma r(X_i)^2 + \Sigma r(Y_i)^2 - 2\Sigma r(X_i)r(Y_i)$$

Again, because

$$\Sigma r(X_i)^2 = \Sigma r(Y_i)^2 = n(n+1)\,(2n+1)/6$$

this gives

$$\Sigma r(X_i)r(Y_i) = n(n+1)\,(2n+1)/6 - D^2/2 \tag{2}$$

Dividing (2) by (1) gives the formula quoted earlier for r_S.

We have previously stated (rather than proved) that r_S lies between -1 and $+1$, and is only equal to -1 when the X_i and Y_i are ranked completely oppositely. That $-1 \leqslant r_S \leqslant +1$ now follows immediately, for this inequality is always true for r, and r_S has been seen to be a particular calculation of r. Also, it is obvious that identical rankings give $D^2 = 0$, and hence $r_S = +1$. Moreover, a plot of the points corresponding to completely opposite rankings, $(1,n)$, $(2,n-1)$, $(3,n-2),\ldots,(n,1)$, gives a line of negative slope (having equation $x+y=n+1$), and therefore immediately this has to be the case where $r_S=-1$.

One-sided and two-sided tests
The null distribution of r_S is symmetric, so critical regions appropriate to tests for negative correlation are

$$r_S \leqslant -\text{tabulated value}$$

where the tabulated value is found from Table L using the α_1^R significance levels.

For two-sided tests, where H_1 includes both negative and positive correlation, critical regions are of the form

$$|r_S| \geqslant \text{critical value}$$

corresponding to α_2 significance levels.

Treatment of ties

Tied observations are given average ranks as usual. Thus, for example, if salesman 8 had made 31 sales instead of 30, he would then be tied with salesman 9, and instead of these two having ranks 3 and 4 respectively, they would now both be ranked as $3\frac{1}{2}$. Or, further, suppose that salesman 7 had also managed only 31 sales instead of 33; then salesmen 7, 8 and 9 would all be ranked at 4. You might like to check that r_S becomes 0.4205 and 0.4607 respectively in these two cases.

Null distributions

If H_0 were true then all rank orderings of the sales figures Y_i would be equally likely, irrespective of the numbers X_i of simple visits.

For illustration, take $n=5$, so that $(r(Y_1), r(Y_2), r(Y_3), r(Y_4), r(Y_5))$ takes on one of the $5!=120$ permutations (orderings) of (1,2,3,4,5). Without loss of generality, let the X values be in natural order, i.e. $r(X_1)=1$, $r(X_2)=2$, $r(X_3)=3$, $r(X_4)=4$ and $r(X_5)=5$. Then clearly the only arrangement of the Y ranks to give $D^2=0$ (and hence $r_S=1$) is also (1,2,3,4,5).

Next you may check that there are four cases yielding $D^2=2$, i.e. $r_S=0.9$; these are (2,1,3,4,5), (1,3,2,4,5), (1,2,4,3,5) and (1,2,3,5,4). There are three cases yielding $D^2=4$, i.e. $r_S=0.8$; these are (2,1,4,3,5), (2,1,3,5,4) and (1,3,2,5,4). Since small values of D^2 (i.e. large positive values of r_S) constitute one-sided critical regions, and Prob($r_S=1.0$)$=1/120=0.83\%$, Prob($r_S \geqslant 0.9$)$=5/120=4.17\%$ and Prob($r_S \geqslant 0.8$)$=8/120=6.67\%$, we have to take $r_S=1.0$ as the best conservative critical region for both $\alpha_1=1\%$ and $2\frac{1}{2}\%$, and $r_S \geqslant 0.9$ for $\alpha_1=5\%$; there is no suitable region for $\alpha_1=\frac{1}{2}\%$. These regions are consistent with the results in Table L.

Large sample sizes

If H_0 is true and n is large, the distribution of r_S is approximately normal with mean 0 and standard deviation $1/\sqrt{(n-1)}$. So, if z is the appropriate percentage point of the standard normal distribution (see Table A) for a particular significance level, the approximate critical value for r_S is given by $z/\sqrt{(n-1)}$. Thus, for example, taking $n=50$ (the largest sample size in Table L), and recalling that $z=1.96$ if $\alpha_2=5\%$, the corresponding approximate critical region is given by $r_S \geqslant 1.96/\sqrt{49} =0.2800$, which is very close to 0.2791, the value given in Table L.

Convergence to normality for r_S is somewhat slower than with some other distribution-free statistics, but the approximation is certainly satisfactory for $n>50$, which is all we need.

KENDALL'S RANK CORRELATION COEFFICIENT

Introduction

This alternative approach to rank correlation seems to have neither any great advantages nor disadvantages compared with Spearman's, although the latter is perhaps the slightly better known and is said by some to be easier to compute for large samples. On the other hand, Kendall's

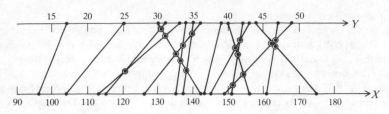

Figure 9.3

coefficient can be computed by a simple graphical, rather than arithmetical, process and also has some theoretical points in its favour.

PRACTICAL PROBLEM, HYPOTHESES AND DATA

We shall use the same situation and data as for the test based on Spearman's coefficient. However, for the detailed illustration we shall take the X variable here to be the number of demos.

STATISTIC

We first present the simple graphical method. The X_i and Y_i values are plotted on two parallel axes and then a line is drawn joining each X_i to its corresponding Y_i. This operation need not be carried out with great accuracy; a freehand sketch will do, particularly if n is fairly small. Similarly, the scales do not have to be chosen according to any particular criterion – anything convenient will do. Figure 9.3 shows our drawing for the data. Now we count the number of times that pairs of lines intersect in the drawing, i.e the points marked by a circle; you will see that there are 16. Note that all points of intersection are considered distinct from each other; if some such points are going to coincide, then this should be avoided by slightly curving the relevant lines in the diagram.

Kendall's approach to rank correlation is based on a comparison of all possible pairs of (X,Y) values with each other. Consider comparing (X_1,Y_1) with (X_2,Y_2), i.e. (104,25) with (161,47). We note that the first of these pairs has both the smaller X value and the smaller Y value; this is an example of a so-called *concordant* pair. Similarly, (X_1,Y_1) is concordant with (X_3,Y_3). When comparing (X_1,Y_1) with (X_4,Y_4), i.e. (104,25) with (96,17), we see that the first pair now has both the *larger* X value and the *larger* Y value; such a pair is also called concordant. In fact all the pairs turn out to be concordant with (X_1,Y_1), which, as we shall see, is reflected by the fact that there are no points of intersection on the line joining $Y_1=25$ to $X_1=104$ in Figure 9.3. Now, if we start comparing $(X_2,Y_2)=(161,47)$ with all the other pairs, we find it to be concordant with both (X_3,Y_3) and (X_4,Y_4). However, when comparing (X_2,Y_2) with (X_5,Y_5), i.e. (161,47) with (149,49), it is now the case that the first pair has the lower Y value but the higher X value. When this occurs (or vice versa) the pair is said to be *discordant*. Notice in Figure 9.3 that the line joining 47 to 161 does intersect with the line joining 49 to 149. It is then easy to generalize this argument to show that each discordant pair results in a (circled) crossing point in the figure, but that concordant pairs do not.

Kendall's rank correlation coefficient is based on the difference between the total number of concordant (N_C) and discordant (N_D) pairs. N_D is given by the number of crossings in Figure 9.3, while $N_C + N_D$ is equal to the total number of pairs compared, and it can be shown that this number is $\frac{1}{2}n(n-1)$ (check it with some small values of n if you cannot see why this should be so). Hence,

$$N_C = \frac{1}{2}n(n-1) - N_D$$

In order to be consistent with the general properties of correlation coefficients (i.e. that they lie between -1 and $+1$, with exceptional cases -1 and $+1$ having the same interpretation as with r_S), Kendall's coefficient, usually denoted by the Greek letter (tau) τ (pronounced taw or tow, as in towel), is defined as

$$\tau = \frac{N_C - N_D}{\frac{1}{2}n(n-1)}$$

The reasoning is as follows. If the X_i and Y_i have the same rank order (the strongest evidence for positive correlation), then there will be no crossings in the drawing, i.e. $N_D = 0$, $N_C = \frac{1}{2}n(n-1)$ and so $\tau = +1$. If the X and Y values are ranked completely opposite to each other, then all pairs will be discordant, so that $N_D = \frac{1}{2}n(n-1)$, $N_C = 0$ and $\tau = -1$.

Since $N_C = \frac{1}{2}n(n-1) - N_D$, it is easy to show that τ may also be written as

$$\tau = 1 - \frac{4N_D}{n(n-1)}$$

This is a particularly convenient form to use after having calculated N_D as the number of crossings in the drawing.

You may now see why no great accuracy is needed when drawing the diagram. The actual values in the data do not matter, just the *order* in which they occur – as with all distribution-free methods.

Exercise It follows that we shall get the same value of N_D, and hence of τ, for any data (X_i, Y_i) giving the arrangement of ranks $(r(X_i), r(Y_i))$ as in our example. In particular, the ranks themselves can be used for this purpose! Just to check, form a table of ranks $(r(X_i), r(Y_i))$ and join corresponding points in this diagram; confirm that we do get the same answer as before.

CRITICAL REGIONS

As with Spearman's r_S statistic, large values indicate positive correlation, and so, for a one-sided alternative hypothesis of positive correlation, critical regions are of the form:

$$\tau \geq \text{critical value}$$

Table M gives critical values for τ, and a fuller table is available on page 40 of *EST*; the layout of these tables is precisely as for r_S.

With $n=15$, the required one-sided critical regions are $\tau \geq 0.3333$, $\tau \geq 0.3905$, $\tau \geq 0.4667$ and $\tau \geq 0.5048$ for $\alpha_1 = 5\%$, $2\frac{1}{2}\%$, 1% and $\frac{1}{2}\%$ respectively.

SOLUTION

Since we have found from the diagram in Figure 9.3 that $N_D = 16$, we can calculate τ as

$$\tau = 1 - \frac{4N_D}{n(n-1)} = 1 - \frac{4 \times 16}{15 \times 14} = 0.6952$$

Since this value of τ lies well inside even the $\alpha_1 = \frac{1}{2}\%$ critical region, we conclude with virtual certainty that there is a positive correlation between numbers of demos and sales; this was also the conclusion arrived at using Spearman's coefficient.

Exercise Calculate τ now using the number of simple visits as the X variable. You should obtain $\tau = 0.3143$, which is just outside the $\alpha_1 = 5\%$ critical region; so the conclusion is essentially the same as that obtained using r_S.

If the sample size is at all large, the graphical method becomes messy and the arithmetical technique shown below is then preferable; and indeed, you may wish to use this method for small values of n also.

Discussion

Both Spearman's and Kendall's approaches to rank correlation are well known and widely used. So it is natural to ask which of the two is preferable. As indicated in the introduction, there seems to be no easy choice between them. For sample sizes less than about 20, Spearman's r_s may have a slight edge over Kendall's τ (see the 'Null distributions' section below). The coefficients involve similar amounts of computation; Kendall's τ is slightly quicker to compute for small to moderate sample sizes, but Spearman's r_S is probably quicker for larger samples. Kendall's coefficient has some rather nice theoretical aspects not shared by Spearman's. For example, (a) its null distribution converges to normality faster than that of r_S (see the 'Large samples' section below); (b) τ is an estimator of an easily identifiable characteristic of the populations, namely the difference between the probabilities of concordance and discordance; and (c) there is a quite well known version of τ that can be used in more complex (multivariate) situations (in fact, a similar extension to so-called partial correlation can also be applied to r_S, but this does not seem to be often used).

It is therefore very much a case of taste and/or tradition as to which of the coefficients is used. However, in Chapter 11 we offer an alternative approach to distribution-free correlation which is rather quicker to execute than either of those described in this chapter.

Arithmetical calculation of τ
We rearrange the data so that the values of one of the variables, say X, are in ascending order (particularly for large n, this may be the major part of the whole operation). Then take each Y value in turn, and count how many of the 'Y's to its right are smaller. You will see that the sum of these counts gives N_D; you can then proceed to calculate τ as before.

This arithmetical method is illustrated on the same data as before.

Salesman,	i	4	1	7	9	15	11	13	8	6
Demos,	X_i	96	104	113	115	126	135	137	142	143
Sales,	Y_i	17	25	33	31	36	34	35	30	39
Count		0	0	2	1	3	1	1	0	0

Salesman,	i	12	5	14	3	2	10
Demos.	X_i	145	149	151	156	161	175
Sales,	Y_i	43	49	42	40	47	44
Count		2	4	1	0	1	–

For the counts on the final row we first check $Y_1=17$ against *all* the other 'Y's (as they all lie to the right of of the 17); in fact they are all greater than 17, resulting in the first count of 0 on the bottom row. Then we check the next Y, i.e. $Y_2=25$, against all the 'Y's lying to its right; again they are all greater than 25, resulting in the second count of 0 in the bottom row. Then we check $Y_3=33$ with all the 'Y's to its right; in this case there are two (31 and 30) less than 33, and this produces the count of 2 as printed in the table. Carrying on in this way, all the counts may be confirmed; and adding them gives $N_D=16$, as above.

Note that there is some similarity between this counting method and that for the Mann–Whitney U (Ch. 5). Note also that this arithmetical calculation may, if preferred, be carried out on the ranks $r(X_i)$ and $r(Y_i)$ in place of the original numbers X_i and Y_i. (As an exercise, try it and see!)

One-sided and two-sided tests
Reread the corresponding paragraph for r_S, earlier in the chapter, replacing r_S by τ throughout.

Treatment of ties

Simple ties are dealt with in the graphical method easily enough by counting $\frac{1}{2}$ for any crossing that lies on the X or the Y 'axes', but multiple ties can cause difficulties. With the arithmetical calculation, however, there is an easy rule: count $\frac{1}{2}$ for any pair whose X values and/or Y values are tied.

Exercise   Given the following data, verify that $\tau=17/21=0.8095$.

X	1	3	3	6	7	7	10
Y	2	4	5	5	10	11	11

(If you get $N_D=\frac{1}{2}+\frac{1}{2}$, giving $\tau=19/21=0.9048$, you have probably not allowed for the ties in the X values.)

Null distributions

Again, the principle is essentially the same as for r_S. You may like to confirm that, when $n=5$, we obtain $\text{Prob}(\tau=1)=1/120$, $\text{Prob}(\tau\geqslant0.8)=5/120$ and $\text{Prob}(\tau\geqslant0.6)=4/120$, and that the critical values in Table M are in accord with these results.

It is worth pointing out that there are just 11 possible values of τ with $n=5$ ($-1, -0.8, -0.6, \ldots, 0.8, 1$) whereas there were 21 possible values of r_S ($-1, -0.9, -0.8, \ldots, 0.9, 1$). This difference between the number of possible values of the two test statistics increases markedly with n, so that τ is in fact a cruder representation of the data than is r_S. This may well explain, at least in part, the apparent slight superiority in power of Spearman's test over Kendall's.

Large sample sizes

The null distribution of τ when n is large is approximately normal with mean $\mu=0$ and standard deviation $\sigma=\sqrt{2(2n+5)/9n(n-1)}$, and the convergence to this asymptotic distribution is faster than was the case with r_S. Thus approximate critical values may be obtained using $z\sigma$, where z is the appropriate percentage point of the standard normal distribution.

So, for example, with $n=50$ and $\alpha_2=5\%$ (for which $z=1.96$), we obtain an approximate critical value of $1.96\sqrt{2\times105/(9\times50\times49)} = 0.1913$, which compares very favourably with the critical value 0.1918 given in Table M. This is of similar accuracy to the Spearman example, but if you go further out into the tails of the distribution (i.e. take smaller values of α) you will find the Kendall approximation to be the more accurate.

Further discussion on correlation

There are a number of matters concerning correlation that sometimes tend to trap the unwary into misinterpreting the data and the results of the significance tests. This section is an attempt to make the unwary less so.

(a) It is perhaps natural to imagine that a strongly significant result from either of the two tests in this chapter implies, and is implied by, a high correlation between the X and Y variables. Neither implication is correct! The test simply judges whether or not the null hypothesis of zero correlation is consistent with the

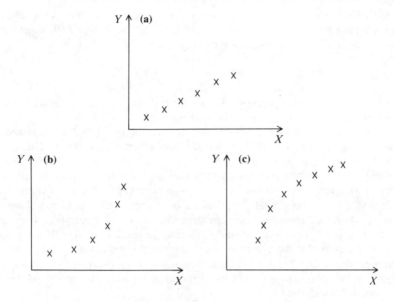

Figure 9.4

data. Thus, if n is large, a pretty small value of r_S or τ may be highly significant. If you check the tables you will see, for example, that with $n=50$ a value of 0.4 for either coefficient is extraordinarily significant. Such a value indicates nothing more than a rather loose relationship between X and Y; but, on the other hand, it is high enough virtually to ensure that some such relationship does exist. However, if n is small, quite high values of r_S or τ may not be significant; for example, if $n=6$, a value of around 0.7 fails to reject H_0. Similar difficulties can arise with hypotheses tests in other areas of statistics, but somehow in practice they seem to cause most problems with correlation.

(b) Even if r_S or τ turn out to be zero or very small, that does not necessarily imply that X and Y are unrelated; in fact, they can still be very strongly related. Remember that r_S and τ are measuring the extent of a monotonic relationship between X and Y (and the traditional correlation coefficient r is even more specific as it measures the extent of *linear* relationship). Thus if the data are exactly related but in a *non*-monotonic way, it is quite conceivable for any or all of the three coefficients to be close to zero.

(c) As mentioned in (b), r_S and τ measure the tendency towards *monotonicity*, not just linearity. This is an automatic consequence of the distribution-free philosophy. As with other distribution-free statistics, neither r_S nor τ relates directly to the precise numerical values in the data, but only indirectly via their ranks. This has to imply that the rank correlation coefficients measure the tendency for X and Y to increase together (or for one to decrease as the other increases), *irrespective of whether the relationship is linear or not*. Thus r_S and τ will both equal $+1$ in all three scatterplots shown in Figure 9.4, whereas r would be less than 1 in (b) and (c). Whether this is good or bad depends on context. When exploring the possibility of two variables being related, it is probably better not to be too specific, so that the rank correlation methods will then be preferable. However, the simplest useful method of predicting the Y that will result from a given value of X is by a linear equation (see Ch. 10):

$$\text{predicted } Y = a + bX$$

So r would be the more appropriate measure if we wished to examine whether such a prediction equation might be appropriate.

　(d) A very common error is to assume that high correlation between two variables implies that one of them has a *causal* effect on the other. This error is possibly encouraged by some of the standard terminology in the subject; for example, in the prediction equation above, Y is often referred to as the *dependent* variable. However, even if the X and Y variables are well related numerically, there may still be no causal, physical or other connection between them. For example, there are some well known data that show extremely high correlation between electricity consumption and birth rate! In this and many other situations, the real reason is that there are *other* variables or factors having a direct effect on both variables being considered and, without such extraneous influences, there might well be no relationship of any importance between the two variables with which we are concerned.

RANK CORRELATION WITH NON-NUMERIC DATA

Both r_S and τ essentially measure the correlation between two variables through their ranks. A useful consequence of this feature is that we can measure the correlation between variables that are not measured or counted – all we need to be able to do is *rank* the data. We illustrate this idea by applying Spearman's r_s to a rather interesting problem.

PRACTICAL PROBLEM

A colleague of ours has two teenage daughters who, naturally, have quite a number of suitors. Just for fun, he asked us to devise a simple test to see whether his daughters are likely to compete for the same type of suitor. We drew up a list of attributes of males (trying to cast ourselves as females!) and then told the girls to rank these attributes from 1 (for the most important) to 10 (the least important). Of course, no conferring was allowed.

HYPOTHESES

Since our colleague is particularly interested in whether his daughters are likely to compete with each other (i.e. have highly correlated attitudes as measured by these attributes), a one-sided alternative hypothesis of positive correlation is appropriate. Thus the hypotheses may be stated as follows:

H_0: There is no correlation between the two girls' attitudes to the given attributes.

H_1: There is some positive correlation between the girls.

DATA

The list of the attributes and the ranks given by the two girls, Kathryn and Fiona, are shown below.

	Ranks	
Attribute	Fiona	Kathryn
personality	2	1
sense of humour	1	2
wealth	4	6
personal hygiene	5	5
good cook	10	7
good looks	8	9
height	7	8
age/maturity	6	3
sex appeal	9	10
dependability	3	4

CRITICAL REGIONS

Consulting Table L with $n=10$ gives the $\alpha_1=5\%$ and 1% critical regions as $r_S \geqslant 0.5636$ and $r_S \geqslant 0.7455$ respectively.

CALCULATION OF THE STATISTIC

Since we already have the ranks, the calculation of r_S is easily performed as in the following table:

	Ranks			
Attribute	Fiona	Kathryn	d_i	d_i^2
personality	2	1	1	1
sense of humour	1	2	−1	1
wealth	4	6	−2	4
personal hygiene	5	5	0	0
good cook	10	7	3	9
good looks	8	9	−1	1
height	7	8	−1	1
age/maturity	6	3	3	9
sex appeal	9	10	−1	1
dependability	3	4	−1	1

Summing the d_i^2 values gives $D^2 = 28$, and so r_s is:

$$r_S = 1 - \frac{6D^2}{n^3 - n} = 1 - \frac{6 \times 28}{990} = 0.8303$$

CONCLUSION

This result is well into the $\alpha_1 = 1\%$ critical region, and so it seems that our colleague is in for an interesting time watching his daughters compete for the same males!

This example illustrates very well the effectiveness of rank correlation on problems where the data are 'non-numeric'; and this, of course, is a definite advantage over Pearson's classical measure of correlation.

Assignments

1   Diabetes

In 1979, G. M. Reaven and R. G. Miller ('An attempt to define the nature of chemical diabetes using a multidimensional analysis' *Diabetologia* **16**, 17–24) presented the results of an experiment concerning diabetes in non-obese adults. Part of the information collected was the relative weight and the insulin resistance of each subject. These data for the first 20 subjects are given below.

Patient	Relative weight	Insulin resistance	Patient	Relative weight	Insulin resistance
1	0.81	55	11	0.90	53
2	0.95	76	12	0.73	66
3	0.94	105	13	0.96	142
4	1.04	108	14	0.84	93
5	1.00	143	15	0.74	68
6	0.76	165	16	0.98	102
7	0.91	119	17	1.10	76
8	1.10	105	18	0.85	37
9	0.99	98	19	0.83	60
10	0.78	94	20	0.93	50

Task: Investigate whether these data provide evidence of positive correlation between relative weight and insulin resistance.

2   Strange correlation

The table below gives the number of postgraduate awards in medical sciences and the death rate per million from tuberculosis for the years 1959–69 (source: *Annual Abstract of Statistics* 1970).

Year	Number of awards	Tuberculosis death rate
1959	277	83
1960	318	74
1961	382	71
1962	441	65
1963	486	62
1964	597	52
1965	750	47
1966	738	48
1967	849	42
1968	932	43
1969	976	38

Task: Show that these data provide strong evidence of negative correlation between the number of awards and the tuberculosis death rate. Explain this 'strange' result.

Program 9.1 Spearman's rank correlation coefficient

```
100 REM *** SPEARMAN'S RANK CORRELATION COEFFICIENT ***

110 REM ** INPUT NUMBER OF PAIRS OF OBSERVATIONS **
120 INPUT "HOW MANY PAIRS OF OBSERVATIONS ? ";N
130 DIM X(N),Y(N),D(N),RX(N),RY(N),RK(N)
140 PRINT

150 REM ** INPUT OBSERVATIONS **
160 PRINT "INPUT THE PAIRS OF OBSERVATIONS "
170 FOR I=1 TO N
180 INPUT X(I),Y(I)
190 LET D(I)=X(I)
200 NEXT I

210 REM ** RANK  THE X-SAMPLE **
220 GO SUB 1000
230 FOR I=1 TO N
240 LET RX(I)=RK(I)
250 LET D(I)=Y(I)
260 NEXT I

270 REM ** RANK  THE Y-SAMPLE **
280 GO SUB 1000
290 FOR I=1 TO N
300 LET RY(I)=RK(I)
310 NEXT I

320 REM ** CALCULATION OF SPEARMAN'S RHO **
330 LET P=0
340 FOR I=1 TO N
350 P=P+(RX(I)-RY(I))^2
360 NEXT I
370 LET R=1-6*P/N/(N*N-1)
380 PRINT "VALUE OF SPEARMAN'S RHO = ";R
390 IF N<=50 THEN STOP
```

Continued overleaf

Program 9.1   Continued

```
400 REM ** CRITICAL VALUES FOR LARGE SAMPLE SIZES (N > 50) **
410 INPUT "PERCENTAGE POINT OF STANDARD NORMAL DISTRIBUTION ? ";Z
420 LET SD=1/SQRT(N-1)
430 PRINT "APPROXIMATE CRITICAL VALUE = ";INT(10000*Z*SD+.5)/10000

1000 REM ** RANK SUBROUTINE - USE LINES 1000-1140 OF PROGRAM 3.1 **
```

Program 9.2   Kendall's rank correlation coefficient

```
100 REM *** KENDALL'S RANK CORRELATION COEFFICIENT ***

110 REM ** INPUT NUMBER OF PAIRS OF OBSERVATIONS **
120 INPUT "HOW MANY PAIRS OF OBSERVATIONS ? ";N
130 DIM X(N),Y(N)
140 PRINT

150 REM ** INPUT OBSERVATIONS **
160 PRINT "INPUT THE PAIRS OF OBSERVATIONS "
170 FOR I=1 TO N180 INPUT X(I),Y(I)
190 NEXT I

200 REM ** CALCULATION OF KENDALL'S TOR **
210 LET ND=0
220 FOR I=1 TO N-1
230 FOR J=I+1 TO N
240 IF X(I)<X(J) AND Y(I)>Y(J) THEN LET ND=ND+1
250 IF X(I)>X(J) AND Y(I)<Y(J) THEN LET ND=ND+1
260 IF X(I)=X(J) OR Y(I)=Y(J) THEN LET ND=ND+0.5
270 NEXT J
280 NEXT I
290 LET T=1-4*ND/(N*(N-1))
300 PRINT
310 PRINT "VALUE OF KENDALL'S TAU = ";T
320 PRINT

330 REM ** APPROXIMATE CRITICAL VALUES FOR LARGE SAMPLES **
340 LET SD=SQRT(2*(2*N+5)/(9*N*(N-1)))
350 INPUT "PERCENTAGE POINT OF STANDARD NORMAL DISTRIBUTION ? ";Z
360 PRINT "APPROXIMATE CRITICAL VALUE = ";INT(10000*Z*SD+.5)/10000
```

10
Regression

Introduction

In our discussion of correlation in Chapter 9, we tested for the existence of some kind of relationship between two variables. Within our distribution-free environment, the most natural type of correlation of interest is monotonicity, whereas in the classical approach one tests for linearity or some other more detailed mathematical interdependence.

A significant result from such a test is evidence that a relationship of the relevant type is present. It rarely indicates a *perfect* relationship in the sense that the value of one variable, say Y, can be exactly predicted if the value of the other variable, say X, is known. The relationship is rather between X and the *average* value of Y; the *actual* value of Y is made up of this average value plus some random variation. The best we can do, therefore, after having established that X and Y are correlated, is to attempt to *estimate* the average value of Y in terms of the value of X. This is the problem of **regression**.

We should point out that, in general, one can always go through the motions of calculating a detailed regression relationship; but it is the corresponding correlation test that tells us whether the regression is likely to be useful or not (according as to whether or not the test gives a significant result).

The origins of the use of the word 'regression' in this context go back some 100 years to the geneticist, Francis Galton. In studying the relationship between the heights of parents and their offspring, he noticed two rather unsurprising things. One was that parents' and offsprings' heights are positively correlated (tall parents tend to have tall children, and short parents short children). His other observation was a little more subtle. Let us consider, say, a child of tall parents. Then, although from what we have just said, this child would be expected to grow up to have an above-average height, the fact is that, on average, the child would *not* reach the height of the corresponding parent. In other words, he or she would tend to be closer to the population mean than that parent. Similarly, a child of short parents, though likely to be below-average height, tends to be taller than the corresponding parent, being again closer to the population mean. Galton referred to this tendency of offsprings' heights to revert towards the population mean as '*regression* towards the mean', that is 'moving back towards the mean'.

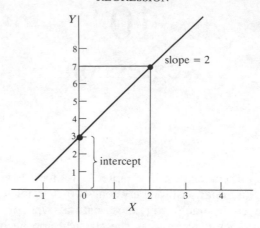

Figure 10.1

Practical applications of regression are common. For example, an economist may be interested in the relationship between share prices and the level of investment; a biologist may wish to establish a relationship between an animal's body weight and its food consumption; or a keep-fit instructor may want to know the relationship between a person's time to run a fixed distance and his heart-rate recovery. In each case, the idea is to establish a relationship either graphically or in the form of an equation which can be used to predict values of one variable, conventionally denoted Y and often called the *dependent* variable, given values of the other variable X, the so-called *independent* variable. For example, if the relation between them is believed to be $Y=4+3X$, then the predicted value of Y (or rather of its average) when $X=6$ is $Y=4+18=22$.

The nature of these relationships could be of many forms or *models*. For instance, one might presume that the data are best modelled by the following:

(a) A *linear* relationship, represented by the equation

$$Y = a + bX$$

where a and b are respectively the *intercept* and the *slope* of the line. For example, $Y=3+2X$ has the graphical form shown in Figure 10.1.

(b) An *exponential* relationship, represented by an equation of the type

$$Y = ab^X$$

For example, $Y=3(2^X)$ has the graphical form shown in Figure 10.2.

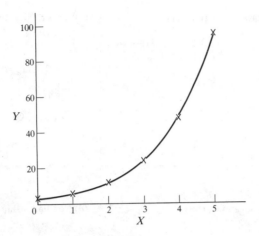

Figure 10.2

It is important to realize that we do not usually expect the value of Y itself to be given by such equations, but it is feasible for the *average* value of Y, for some given value of X, to be represented in this way. Whatever relationship is appropriate to the data, some technique needs to be used to *estimate* the values of a and b from the observed data.

It is obviously necessary to have some idea about which type of relationship best models the data. A simple, but effective, method of doing this is to construct a scatterplot, a technique that we met in Chapter 9. Figure 10.3 gives some indications of the kind of thing to expect.

In the first part of this chapter, we look at a method of estimating a and b when the underlying model is assumed to be linear (see Fig. 10.3a); the so-called *linear regression model*. We will also discuss hypothesis tests for inferences regarding the unknown parameter b (the slope of the regression line). After this, we examine a method for *monotonic* regression, i.e. which requires only the assumption of monotonicity rather than any more specific form of relationship – in other words, the technique is substantially *model-free*.

Before looking at these methods, it is worth while to mention something about the classical approach to linear regression. This is based on the 'least-squares' method, so-called because it is based on minimizing the sum of the squares of errors (or *residuals*) between the actual values of Y and the values of Y predicted by the regression. Figure 10.4 shows these residuals for a 'reasonable-looking' line.

The least-squares method is widely used and, as long as the underlying model is valid, it is without doubt a sound technique *provided there are no* 'rogue' points (or outliers) in the data. Unfortunately, outliers are often present; they can be caused by a number of reasons, for instance human

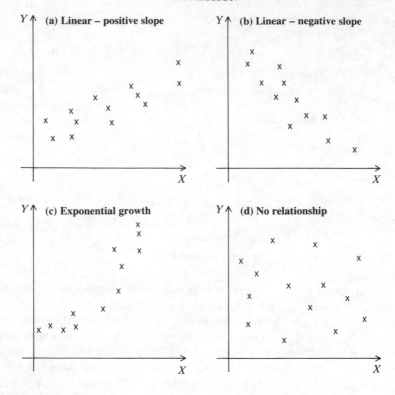

Figure 10.3

error, machine error, untypical conditions and so on. Any such problem points can seriously disturb the least-squares regression line and thus cause it to be quite unrepresentative of the actual relationship between the two variables. Figure 10.5 illustrates what can happen when there are just two rogue points in the data. Common sense indicates that the freehand line drawn in Figure 10.5 is far more representative of the underlying process than is the least-squares line. Fortunately, the regression methods in this chapter, and the next one, are relatively 'robust' in the sense that they are nowhere as susceptible to rogue values as is the traditional least-squares method.

THEIL'S 'INCOMPLETE' METHOD

Introduction

Theil's original method for estimating the unknown parameters a and b dates back to 1950 (Theil 1950). However, the amount of calculation required in this method can be quite substantial. With n data points, the

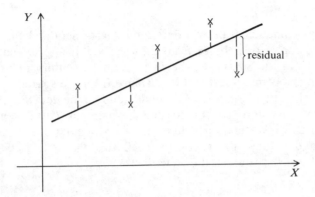

Figure 10.4

number of computations needed is $\frac{1}{2}n(n-1)$; for example, with only 10 data points there are 45 calculations, while with 20 points there are 190. Although the calculations involved are fairly simple, the fact that there can be so many of them makes Theil's original technique rather unappealing. It is for this reason that his method was later modified in order to substantially reduce the number of calculations whilst still maintaining most of the effectiveness of the original technique. This modification, which we discuss below, is often called Theil's 'incomplete' method; the effect of the modification is such that, for example, with 10 or 11 data points only five simple calculations are needed, and only 10 calculations are needed with 20 or 21 points.

Following our usual pattern, we will present this technique through a practical problem, and later we will consider tests for the intercept a and slope b.

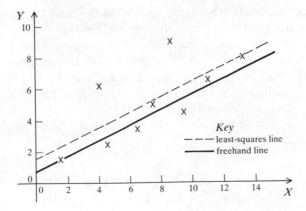

Figure 10.5

PRACTICAL PROBLEM

A geologist conducted an experiment on one of Scotland's largest rivers. He took samples of pebbles from the riverbed at approximately 0.5 km intervals from the source to the first (major) tributary. The volume of each pebble was measured and its distance from the source recorded. He reasoned that the larger stones would tend to be located close to the source, with the stone size decreasing downstream. If this were the case, he hoped this investigation would lead to a linear relationship between the average volume of stones (we call this the Y variable) and the distance from the source (the X variable).

DATA

Fifteen samples were taken along a 7 km stretch of the river from the source. The results obtained were:

Distance, X	0.2	0.5	0.9	1.4	2.1	2.7	3.0	3.6
Volume, Y	50	48	42	36	34	32	29	31

Distance, X	4.1	4.4	5.0	5.6	6.2	6.6	7.1
Volume, Y	28	24	19	17	10	12	9.5

PROCEDURE

Before looking at the rationale of Theil's method, let us review the notion of a *slope* or *gradient* of a line. The slope measures the steepness of the line and, for example, the slope of the line joining points (X_1, Y_1) and (X_2, Y_2) is measured by

$$B_{12} = \frac{Y_2 - Y_1}{X_2 - X_1}$$

In practical problems, there are usually more than two points, which, because of random variation, do not all lie on one line. Our basic assumption in regression is that without the random variation the points *would* all lie on a line $Y = a + bX$ – and it is these constants a and b we wish to estimate. For example, the situation may be like that shown in Figure 10.6, where the line drawn represents the theoretical line $Y = a + bX$ which we seek to estimate.

Suppose we were to calculate the slopes of the three lines joining:

(X_1, Y_1) and (X_4, Y_4), i.e.

$$B_{1,4} = \frac{Y_4 - Y_1}{X_4 - X_1}$$

(X_2, Y_2) and (X_5, Y_5), i.e.

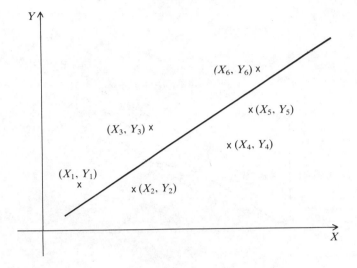

Figure 10.6

$$B_{2,5} = \frac{Y_5 - Y_2}{X_5 - X_2}$$

(X_3, Y_3) and (X_6, Y_6), i.e.

$$B_{3,6} = \frac{Y_6 - Y_3}{X_6 - X_3}$$

These are shown as broken lines in Figure 10.7. Of course, we could have considered other possibilities, say (X_2, Y_2) joining (X_3, Y_3); but we have chosen those particular lines used in Theil's incomplete method.

Clearly, each of these slopes are different; but if we take an average, in particular the *median*, of these slopes then we should obtain a value that is not too far from the true value of b. This is Theil's incomplete method, and it can be summarized as follows:

Step 1 Suppose we have n data points (X_1, Y_1), (X_2, Y_2), . . . , (X_n, Y_n). Arrange these points in ascending order of the X values. (Note: this step is automatic for our data since X represents the increasing distance from the source.)

Step 2 Divide the ordered data at the halfway mark to give two equal groups; if there is an odd number of points then simply ignore the middle point.

Step 3 Calculate the values of the slopes of the lines joining

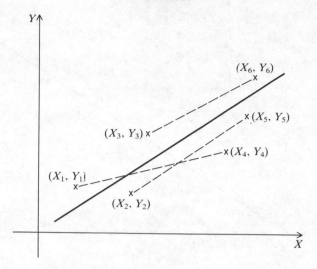

Figure 10.7

(a) thé first points of the two groups,
(b) the second points of the two groups,
and so on to the last points of the two groups.

Step 4 Calculate the median of these slopes as the estimate B of the unknown slope b.

The application of this method to our practical problem is quite simple. Since step 1 is already done we proceed immediately to step 2:

Step 2 The two groups of data points are as follows (note that the middle point (3.6,31) is discarded to give two equal groups of points):

Group 1	X	0.2	0.5	0.9	1.4	2.1	2.7	3.0
	Y	50	48	42	36	34	32	29
Point number		1	2	3	4	5	6	7
Group 2	X	4.1	4.4	5.0	5.6	6.2	6.6	7.1
	Y	28	24	19	17	10	12	9.5
Point number		8	9	10	11	12	13	14

Step 3 The individual slopes are

$$B_{1,8} = \frac{28 - 50}{4.1 - 0.2} = -5.64$$

$$B_{2,9} = \frac{24 - 48}{4.4 - 0.5} = -6.15$$

$$B_{3,10} = \frac{19 - 42}{5.0 - 0.9} = -5.61$$

$$B_{4,11} = \frac{17 - 36}{5.6 - 1.4} = -4.52$$

$$B_{5,12} = \frac{10 - 34}{6.2 - 2.1} = -5.85$$

$$B_{7,14} = \frac{9.5 - 29}{7.1 - 3.0} = -4.76$$

Step 4 Arranging these seven values in ascending order gives the sequence:

$$
\begin{array}{ccccc}
-6.15 & -5.85 & -5.64 & -5.61 & -5.12 \\
-4.76 & -4.52 & & &
\end{array}
$$

from which we immediately find the median slope to be -5.61. This is our estimate B for the unknown slope b.

Now recall that we are attempting to fit an equation of the form $Y=a+bX$ to the observed data. We have just obtained the estimate $B = -5.61$ of b. To estimate the value of a, Theil proposed that, for each data point (all 15 in our problem), the quantity $A_i=Y_i-BX_i$ $(i=1,2,\ldots,n=15)$ should be calculated. The required estimate A of a is then taken to be the median of the A_i values. For our data we obtain:

$$
\begin{aligned}
A_1 &= 50 + 5.61 \times 0.2 = 51.12 \\
A_2 &= 48 + 5.61 \times 0.5 = 50.81 \\
A_3 &= 42 + 5.61 \times 0.9 = 47.05 \\
A_4 &= 36 + 5.61 \times 1.4 = 43.85 \\
A_5 &= 34 + 5.61 \times 2.1 = 45.78 \\
A_6 &= 32 + 5.61 \times 2.7 = 47.15 \\
A_7 &= 29 + 5.61 \times 3.0 = 45.83 \\
A_8 &= 31 + 5.61 \times 3.6 = 51.20 \\
A_9 &= 28 + 5.61 \times 4.1 = 51.00 \\
A_{10} &= 24 + 5.61 \times 4.4 = 48.68 \\
A_{11} &= 19 + 5.61 \times 5.0 = 47.05 \\
A_{12} &= 17 + 5.61 \times 5.6 = 48.42 \\
A_{13} &= 10 + 5.61 \times 6.2 = 44.78
\end{aligned}
$$

$$A_{14} = 12 + 5.61 \times 6.6 = 49.03$$
$$A_{15} = 9.5 + 5.61 \times 7.1 = 49.33$$

You may easily verify that the median of the A_i values is 48.42 and so, finally, our estimated regression line is $Y = 48.42 - 5.61X$.

(You should note that this model implies there are no stones at distances greater than $48.47/5.61 = 8.64$ km from the source. If this is unrealistic, then the assumption of a linear model is probably wrong, and perhaps the method appropriate to the general monotonic model, described later, should be used instead.)

Figure 10.8 shows the data points and this estimated regression line.

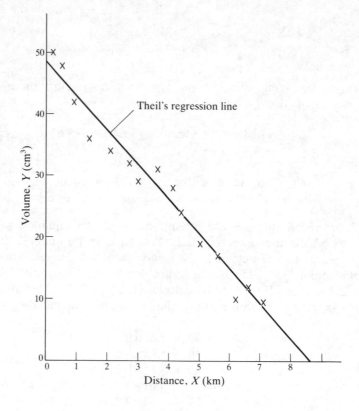

Figure 10.8

Hypothesis test for the slope, b

Perhaps the most frequent type of hypothesis test in linear regression problems has the null hypothesis H_0: $b=0$. Now, *if b is equal to 0* then the regression line reduces to just $Y=A$, i.e. the prediction of Y is constant for all values of X. So a rejection of this H_0 effectively constitutes evidence that useful predictions can be made from the regression line, subject of course to the linear model being appropriate. Sometimes, a look at the scatterplot is sufficient to judge whether B, the estimate of b, is significantly different from zero. However, we may also wish to see whether there is evidence that b is different from some other particular value of interest. Thus for example, in our practical problem we may wish to test the null hypothesis H_0: $b=-4$, i.e. that the volume of stones decreases by a factor of 4 as the distance from the source increases, against the alternative hypothesis of H_1 that the factor is different from 4. We already know that our estimated value of b is $B = -5.61$; but there is almost bound to be some error in this estimate, and more formal work needs to be carried out to ascertain whether our estimate is reasonable under the H_0 of $b=-4$, or whether the difference is sufficient to constitute evidence against this H_0.

Fortunately there is a simple test for such a hypothesis. It is based on Spearman's rank correlation coefficient, which we met in the previous chapter.

PRACTICAL PROBLEM

We shall use the scenario based on the geology experiment introduced earlier in the chapter.

HYPOTHESES

For the purpose of illustrating the test procedure, we will suppose that the geologist's initial thoughts (which were based on previous experiments on similar rivers) led him to believe that the volume of stones would decrease by a factor of 4 with increasing distance from the river's source; thus the null hypothesis is that the slope b of the regression line is -4. Since he has no reason to suspect that the slope should be substantially less than -4 on the one hand or greater than -4 on the other, it seems best to select a two-sided alternative hypothesis to the effect that the slope is not equal to -4. Thus we have:

$$H_0: b = -4.$$

$$H_1: b \neq -4.$$

DATA

The data are as before.

TEST PROCEDURE

For each data pair (X_i, Y_i) for $i=1,2,\ldots,n$, we calculate the difference $T_i=Y_i-bX_i$, which in our example is $T_i=Y_i+4X_i$ for $i=1,2,\ldots,15$. Now if H_0 is true there will be no strong pattern (i.e. no significant correlation) between the X_i and the T_i values. But if H_0 is false, there will be correlation (either negative or positive) between these two quantities. So all we need to do is to perform Spearman's rank correlation test on the X and the T values. For our data, the 15 differences are given by

$$T_1 = 50+4\times0.2 = 50.8$$

$$T_2 = 48+4\times0.5 = 50.0$$

. . . and so on

The following table gives the results of these calculations and those required for Spearman's correlation coefficient.

			Ranks			
Point	X_i	T_i	$r(X_i)$	$r(T_i)$	d_i	d_i^2
1	0.2	50.8	1	15	−14	196
2	0.5	50.0	2	14	−12	144
3	0.9	45.6	3	12	−9	81
4	1.4	41.6	4	6½	−2.5	6.25
5	2.1	42.1	5	8	−3	9
6	2.7	42.8	6	9	−3	9
7	3.0	41.0	7	5	2	4
8	3.6	45.4	8	11	−3	9
9	4.1	44.4	9	10	−1	1
10	4.4	41.6	10	6½	3.5	12.25
11	5.0	39.0	11	4	7	49
12	5.6	49.4	12	13	−1	1
13	6.2	34.8	13	1	12	144
14	6.6	38.4	14	3	11	121
15	7.1	37.9	15	2	13	169

Using Spearman's rank correlation formula

$$r_S = 1 - \frac{6D^2}{n^3-n}$$

where in this case $D^2=955.5$, we obtain

$$r_S = 1 - \frac{6\times955.5}{15^3-15} = -0.706$$

CRITICAL REGIONS

Consulting the table of critical values for Spearman's rank correlation coefficient (Table L) with $n=15$, we obtain the $\alpha_2=5\%$ and 1% critical regions as $|r_S|\geqslant0.5214$ and $|r_S|\geqslant0.6536$ respectively.

SOLUTION

The calculated value of $r_S = -0.706$ falls in the $\alpha_2 = 1\%$ critical region, giving us very strong evidence to support H_1. It would appear that the geologist's hunch, at least with regard to the stones in this river is wrong; the true factor of decrease would appear to be greater than he surmised.

THE IMAN–CONOVER METHOD FOR MONOTONIC REGRESSION

Theil's regression method is particularly robust in the sense that it is not unduly influenced by outliers, whether they be caused by the underlying distribution of one of the variables or are just rogue points. This is a substantial advantage over the standard regression methods based on the least-squares principle. However, it is still a *linear* regression method in that it assumes the underlying relationship between the values of X and Y is linear, i.e. $Y = a + bX$.

In regression work, this assumption can be generalized for, as we have previously mentioned, instead of a linear relationship an exponential model might be assumed. There are other possibilities, such as a quadratic relationship ($Y = a + bX + cX^2$), or a cubic, or a higher-powered polynomial.

It seems more in the spirit of the development of distribution-free methods to seek regression techniques that are not only distribution-free but *model-free* also, i.e. techniques that do not require much in the way of assumptions about the particular form of the regression relationship. Such methods only began to be developed in the 1970s, and the particular technique described here was published by Iman and Conover (1979) quite recently. The only assumption required for this technique is that the underlying relationship between X and Y be *monotonic*, which is exactly the kind of general relationship measured and tested by the rank correlation methods in Chapter 9. In fact, as we shall see, there is a strong link between this regression method and Spearman's r_S, and this is entirely analogous to the link between classical regression and Pearson's correlation coefficient.

PRACTICAL PROBLEM AND DATA

We return to the dependence of sales on 'demos' and 'simple visits' used throughout Chapter 9. In particular, since the tests in Chapter 9 strongly indicated some positive correlation between demos and sales, let us focus our attention on predicting the number of sales in terms of the number of demos made by a typical salesman. For convenience we repeat the relevant data below.

Salesman	Demos	Sales
1	104	25
2	161	47
3	156	40
4	96	17
5	149	49
6	143	39
7	113	33
8	142	30
9	115	31
10	175	44
11	135	34
12	145	43
13	137	35
14	151	42
15	126	36

The Iman–Conover method produces a *graph* (rather than an equation) from which the (average) number Y of sales can be estimated from the number X of demos. No assumption is made about the relationship except that it is monotonic, which, in effect, means that the average number of sales does increase with the number of demos, and, of course, we already have strong evidence for this from our work in Chapter 9. Note that, while this assumption is eminently reasonable, the assumption required by Theil's method that the relationship is *linear* might not be so reasonable since, for example, if a salesman substantially increases his number of demos, the length, quality and effectiveness of those demos might deteriorate so that 'sales per demo' might be expected to suffer. This method deals quite *automatically* with such effects.

METHOD

In this section we demonstrate the mechanics of the method, leaving the justification to the 'Theory' section below. The operation may seem a little involved, but remember that it is tackling the rather ambitious task of predicting Y from X using very few assumptions about the underlying relationships.

Step 1   We work with a regression equation that relates the ranks $r(X)$ and $r(Y)$ of X and Y respectively; this equation is

$$1r(Y) = r_S r(X) + \tfrac{1}{2}(n+1)(1-r_S)$$

where r_S is the appropriate value of Spearman's rank correlation coeffficient. From Chapter 9, the value of r_S in this problem is 0.8714 and so with $n=15$, the above rank *regression* equation becomes

$$r(Y) = 0.8714r(X) + 1.0288$$

Step 2 Now we construct a graph of the Y_i (number of sales) against their ranks $r(Y_i)$. The table below shows the Y_i and their corresponding $r(Y_i)$, arranged in ascending order, from which the graph in Figure 10.9 can be easily formed.

Salesman, i	4	1	8	9	7	11	13	15	6	3	14	12	10	2	5
Y_i	17	25	30	31	33	34	35	36	39	40	42	43	44	47	49
$r(Y_i)$	1	2	3	4	5	6	7	8	9	10	11	12	13	14	15

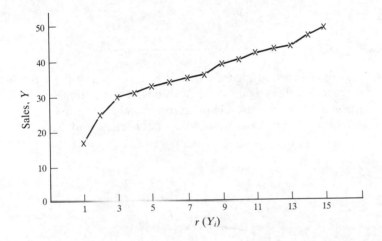

Figure 10.9

Step 3 We now establish a relationship between the original X values and the predicted average Y values (under the assumption of monotonicity) as follows:

(a) Relate each X value to its rank $r(X)$.

(b) For each $r(X)=1,2,3,\ldots,n$ ($n=15$ here), compute $r(Y)$ from the rank regression equation.

(c) For each $r(Y)$ thus found, use Figure 10.9 to obtain the corresponding estimated average Y value.

The numerical details are as follows, where the points have been rearranged for convenience according to ascending X values.

X	r(X)	r(Y)	Y
96	1	1.90	24.20
104	2	2.77	28.86
113	3	3.64	30.64
115	4	4.51	32.02
126	5	5.39	33.39
135	6	7.13	35.13
137	7	7.13	35.13
142	8	8.00	36.00
143	9	8.87	38.61
145	10	9.74	39.74
149	11	10.61	41.22
151	12	11.49	42.49
156	13	12.36	43.36
161	14	13.23	44.69
175	15	14.10	47.20

Step 4   A graph, shown in Figure 10.10, is now plotted of these predicted average Y values against the X values. The figure also shows the original data points. This graph is the required estimated monotonic regression relationship between Y and X.

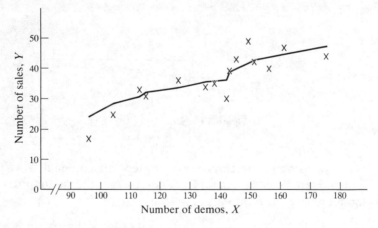

Figure 10.10

Thus, for example, the estimated average sales Y for a salesman carrying out 120 demos can be read off Figure 10.10 as about 32.6. Note that estimates of Y are *only* available for 'X's within the range of X values contained in the data; extrapolation outside this range is not possible. Even with other methods, which do not have this restriction, extrapolation is often a very dangerous exercise since there is no evidence available in the data that the model being assumed is valid outside this range. In a sense, therefore, this restriction might be a blessing in disguise!

Discussion

As stated earlier, this regression method is tackling a somewhat ambitious task in estimating a completely general monotonic relationship, especially with only 15 data points. With rather more data, and especially if the X values are more equally spaced than here (which is often the case), the method can be very powerful and accurate. Indeed, even in this illustration the result has much to commend it. A particularly interesting feature here is the abrupt change at around $X=142$ which, incidentally, indicates that a linear model would probably be invalid. This might indicate an actual change in the underlying relationship, which perhaps could be caused by the existence of two different types or groups of salesmen in the data. Of course, the effect might be spurious, but the method does at least enable such possibilities to be recognized. The best way to further the investigation is, if possible, to obtain more data and see whether or not the phenomenon is reinforced.

As a general comment, the ability of this method to work with any monotonic relationship is both unusual and useful. It is perhaps unfortunate that the final graph used for predicting Y from X is not more smooth, but that is a somewhat cosmetic problem and is a virtually necessary consequence of the wide generality of the method. Hand calculation becomes more tedious if n is at all large, but the procedure is easily computerized (see Program 10.2).

Theory

The theory of the Iman–Conover method involves several ideas from standard least-squares regression. So, if you are not familiar with this, you might be well advised to give this section a miss!

Recall that r_S may be found by calculating the ordinary linear correlation coefficient r from the *ranks* of the observations. Similarly, the rank regression equation is obtained by applying the standard least-squares principle to the *ranks*. When predicting Y from the simple linear equation $Y=A+BX$, the least-squares theory produces the coefficients:

$$B = \frac{\sum X_i Y_i - n\bar{X}\bar{Y}}{\sum X_i^2 - n\bar{X}^2}$$

$$A = \bar{Y} - B\bar{X}$$

where $\bar{X}$ and $\bar{Y}$ are the sample means $\sum X_i/n$ and $\sum Y_i/n$ respectively, and all the sums $\sum$ run from 1 to n. Using the ranks $r(X_i)$ and $r(Y_i)$ therefore, we predict the average $r(Y)$ for a given $r(X)$ by $r(Y) = a + br(X)$, where

$$b = \frac{\sum r(X_i)r(Y_i) - n\overline{r(X)}\,\overline{r(Y)}}{\sum r(X_i)^2 - n\overline{r(X)}^2}$$

$$a = \overline{r(Y)} - b\overline{r(X)}$$

In Chapter 9 we saw that $\overline{r(X)}=\overline{r(Y)}=\tfrac{1}{2}(n+1)$ and $\sum r(X)^2 = \sum r(Y)^2$ $=n(n+1)(2n+1)/6$. In particular, since $\overline{r(X)}=\overline{r(Y)}$ and $\sum r(X)^2=\sum r(Y)^2$, it follows that $b=r_S$; and then immediately $a=\frac{1}{2}(n+1)(1-r_S)$, from which the rank regression equation follows.

An obvious consequence is that if the data do not contain convincing evidence of a monotonic relationship, the slope b will be small; this is in complete analogy to the way the slope in standard regression analysis is proportional to Pearson's linear correlation coefficient, r. On the other hand, if $r_S=+1$ or -1, i.e. the data are completely monotonic, this method then reduces simply to plotting and joining the actual (X_i, Y_i); this is analogous to the fact that if $r=+1$ or -1 (so that the data points all lie on a line) then this line *is* the regression line. In this exceptional situation, our distribution-free method also produces this very same line.

The motivation for the procedure lies in the fact that, if the two variables (X, Y) have a completely monotonic relationship, their ranks $(r(X), r(Y))$ will also have a linear relationship with $r(X)=r(Y)$ or $r(X)+r(Y)=n+1$ in the case of increasing or decreasing relationships respectively. Also, scatter around the monotonic pattern results in corresponding scatter in the ranks. It is common practice in traditional regression methods to deal with, for example, a double-logarithmic model $\log Y=a+b \log X$ by transforming to new variables $W=\log Y$ and $Z=\log X$ in order to give the linear prediction model $W=a+bZ$, and then using the standard least-squares formulae on these new variables. Having obtained the prediction equation, one then simply transforms back to the original variables X and Y using $X=e^Z$ and $Y=e^W$. Here we are similarly using ranks for a transformation to linearity. Again, as in the logarithmic example, having carried out the linear regression on the transformed variables (the ranks), we finally transform back to the original (X, Y) variables. This is all that the procedure of this section amounts to.

Assignments

1 Wind chill

In 1975, J. J. Wiorkowski ('The wind chill index – a case study in table sleuthing', *Am. Statist.* **29**, 154–7) investigated the relationship between wind speed and the chilling effect of wind. The table opposite below presents the National Oceanic and Atmospheric Administration's wind chill equivalent temperatures.

The wind chill equivalent temperature attempts to combine the joint cooling effects of actual temperature (°F) and wind speed (mph) into one 'equivalent' temperature, which indicates the actual cooling effect on human flesh. For example, if the actual temperature is 20°F and the wind speed is 15 mph, then the human body would 'sense' a temperature of −6°F.

Task: For each wind speed (5 to 50 mph), obtain the equation of the regression line of chill index (Y) on actual temperature (X).

2 Weights and heights

The table gives the weights (kg) and heights (cm) of 42 male students who enrolled on a business studies course in a certain college in 1978.

Wind speed (mph)	Wind chill equivalent temperatures (°F)																
	35	30	25	20	15	10	5	0	-5	-10	-15	-20	-25	-30	-35	-40	-45
calm																	
5	33	27	21	16	12	7	1	-6	-11	-15	-20	-26	-31	-35	-41	-47	-54
10	21	16	9	2	-2	-9	-15	-22	-27	-31	-38	-45	-52	-58	-64	-70	-77
15	16	11	1	-6	-11	-18	-25	-33	-40	-45	-51	-60	-65	-70	-78	-85	-90
20	12	3	-4	-9	-17	-24	-32	-40	-46	-52	-60	-68	-76	-81	-88	-96	-103
25	7	0	-7	-15	-22	-29	-37	-45	-52	-58	-67	-75	-83	-89	-96	-104	-112
30	5	-2	-11	-18	-26	-33	-41	-49	-56	-63	-70	-78	-87	-94	-101	-109	-117
35	3	-4	-13	-20	-27	-35	-43	-52	-60	-67	-72	-83	-90	-98	-105	-113	-123
40	1	-4	-15	-22	-29	-36	-45	-54	-62	-69	-76	-87	-94	-101	-107	-116	-128
45	1	-6	-17	-24	-31	-38	-46	-54	-63	-70	-78	-87	-94	-101	-108	-118	-128
50	0	-7	-17	-24	-31	-38	-47	-56	-63	-70	-79	-88	-96	-103	-110	-120	-128

Source: 1973 Associated Press Almanac, p. 171.

Weight	Height	Weight	Height	Weight	Height
74.8	189.0	70.0	188.0	63.6	181.0
61.4	170.0	73.2	188.0	73.6	178.0
70.0	189.0	70.0	180.0	76.4	177.0
68.0	182.0	63.6	178.0	60.3	179.5
108.0	180.0	63.6	178.0	60.3	172.0
67.0	187.0	66.8	175.0	60.3	176.0
70.0	180.0	79.5	185.0	70.0	167.0
70.0	173.0	79.5	182.0	66.7	177.0
90.9	170.0	60.0	170.0	70.0	177.0
66.8	183.0	73.6	167.0	66.2	165.0
89.0	188.0	71.6	178.0	63.2	179.0
58.6	179.0	67.3	178.0	62.0	167.0
66.8	174.0	63.6	171.0	72.0	184.0
68.4	187.5	65.5	172.0	70.0	176.0

Task: Use Theil's incomplete method to obtain a regression line for predicting the weight of a student from his height.

3   Vehicle tyres

A laboratory test of vehicle tyres is designed to investigate the effect of speed on the heat produced in the tyre material. Tyres are run on a test rig at chosen speeds under controlled conditions of load, inflation pressure and ambient temperature. The table below gives the average temperature (°C) at speeds ranging from 10 to 70 mph.

Speed	10	15	20	25	30	35	40	45	50	55	60	65	70
Temp	46	53	56	68	65	79	77	85	107	106	124	131	137

Task: Fit a monotonic regression relationship to these results and hence predict the temperature at speeds of (a) 28 mph, (b) 38 mph and (c) 68 mph.

Program 10.1   Theil's incomplete regression method

```
100 REM *** THEIL'S INCOMPLETE REGRESSION METHOD ***

110 REM ** INPUT DATA **
120 INPUT "NUMBER OF DATA-PAIRS: ";ND
130 LET NL=INT(ND/2)
140 IF 2*NL-ND<>0 THEN L=NL+1
150 IF 2*NL-ND=0 THEN L=NL
160 DIM X(ND),Y(ND),A(ND),D(ND)
170 PRINT "INPUT THE DATA, X-VALUE THEN Y-VALUE"
180 FOR I=1 TO ND
190 INPUT X(I),Y(I)
200 NEXT I
```

```
210 REM ** SORT THE X-VALUES TAKING THE Y'S **
220 LET N=ND
230 GO SUB 1000

240 REM ** CALCULATE THE GRADIENTS **
250 FOR I=1 TO NL
260 LET D(I)=(Y(L+I)-Y(I))/(X(L+I)-X(I))
270 NEXT I

280 REM ** CALCULATE MEDIAN OF THE GRADIENTS **
290 LET N=NL
300 GO SUB 2000
310 LET J1=INT(NL/2)+1
320 LET J2=NL-INT(NL/2)
330 LET M=(D(J1)+D(J2))/2

340 REM ** CALCULATION OF THE INTERCEPT **
350 FOR I=1 TO ND
360 LET D(I)=Y(I)-M*X(I)
370 NEXT I
380 LET N=ND
390 GO SUB 2000
400 LET J1=INT(ND/2)+1
410 LET J2=ND-INT(ND/2)
420 LET C=(D(J1)+D(J2))/2

430 REM ** OUTPUT OF THE REGRESSION LINE **
440 PRINT "GRADIENT = ";M
450 PRINT "INTERCEPT = ";C
460 STOP

1000 REM ** SORT THE X-VALUES WITH THE Y'S: USE LINES 1000-1190 OF **
1010 REM ** PROGRAM 4.2, REPLACING D(*) WITH X(*) AND F(*) WITH YO(*) **

2000 REM ** SORT **
2010 LET N1=N
2020 LET N1=INT(N1/2)
2030 IF N1=0 THEN GO TO 2160
2040 FOR I=1 TO N-N1
2050 FOR J=I TO 1 STEP -N1
2060 LET J1=J+N1
2070 IF D(J)>D(J1) THEN GO TO 2100
2080 LET J=0
2090 GO TO 2130

2100 LET T=D(J)
2110 LET D(J)=D(J1)
2120 LET D(J1)=T
2130 NEXT J
2140 NEXT I
2150 GO TO 2020
2160 RETURN
```

Program 10.2   The Iman–Conover monotonic regression method

```
100 REM ** IMAN-CONOVER MONOTONIC REGRESSION METHOD **

110 REM ** INPUT THE DATA **
120 INPUT "THE NUMBER OF PAIRS ";N
130 DIM D(N),X(N),Y(N),RX(N),YP(N),PRY(N),YO(N)
140 PRINT "INPUT THE DATA, X-VALUE THEN Y-VALUE "
150 FOR I=1 TO N
160 INPUT X(I),Y(I)
170 LET YO(I)=Y(I)
180 NEXT I

190 REM ** RANK SAMPLE **
200 FOR I=1 TO N
210 LET T=0
220 LET S=0
230 LET C=X(I)
235 FOR J=1 TO N
240 NEXT I
250 IF X(J)>C THEN GO TO 300
260 IF X(J)<C THEN GO TO 290
270 LET S=S+1
280 GO TO 300
290 LET T=T+1
300 NEXT J
310 LET RX(I)=T+(S+1)/2
320 NEXT I
330 REM ** END OF RANKING **

340 REM ** SORT THE X-VALUES WITH THE Y'S **
350 GO SUB 1000

360 REM ** SORT THE Y-VALUES **
370 FOR I=1 TO N
380 LET D(I)=Y(I)390 NEXT I
400 GO SUB 2000
410 FOR I=1 TO N
420 LET Y(I)=D(I)
430 NEXT I

440 REM ** CALCULATE RANK REGRESSION EQUATION **
450 INPUT "SPEARMAN'S COEFFICIENT: ";RS
460 FOR I=1 TO N
470 LET PRY(I)=RS*I+(N+1)*(1-RS)/2
480 NEXT I

490 REM ** SORT THE PREDICTED Y-RANKS **
500 FOR I=1 TO N
510 LET D(I)=PRY(I)
520 NEXT I
530 GO SUB 2000
540 FOR I=1 TO N
550 LET PRY(I)=D(I)
560 NEXT I

570 REM ** OUTPUT OF PREDICTED Y FOR THE GIVEN X-VALUES **
580 FOR I=1 TO N
590 LET L=INT(PRY(I))
600 LET U=L+1
```

```
610 IF RS>0 THEN LET YP(I)=Y(L)+(Y(U)-Y(L))*(PRY(I)-L)
620 IF RS<0 THEN LET YP(N-I+1)=Y(L)+(Y(U)-Y(L))*(PRY(I)-L)
630 NEXT I
640 PRINT "X","Y","PRED. Y"
650 FOR I=1 TO N
660 PRINT X(I),YO(I),YP(I)
670 NEXT I

680 REM ** PREDICTED VALUE OF Y FOR A GIVEN X-VALUE **
690 INPUT "DO YOU WISH TO PREDICT A Y-VALUE? ";A$
700 IF A$="N" THEN STOP
710 INPUT "VALUE OF X: ";NX
720 FOR I=1 TO N
730 IF NX>X(I) THEN GO TO 750
740 GO TO 760
750 NEXT I
760 LET C=I-1
770 LET PY=YP(C)+(YP(C+1)-YP(C))*(NX-X(C))/(X(C+1)-X(C))
780 PRINT "PREDICTED VALUE OF Y GIVEN X=";NX;" IS ";PY
790 GO TO 690
800 STOP

1000 REM ** SORT THE X-VALUES : USE LINES 1000-1140 OF PROGRAM 4.2 **

2000 REM ** SORT - USE LINES 2000-2160 OF PROGRAM 10.1 **
```

11

Quick methods for correlation and regression

Introduction

All the methods presented in the previous two chapters involve fairly substantial computations, and become tedious to execute with more than moderate-sized samples. In this chapter we present alternative methods for both correlation and regression, which are rather quicker and easier.

We begin the chapter with a test for correlation, which is another example of a 'Tukey-type' test in the sense that it only considers observations in the extremes of the samples and completely ignores the rest. This is followed by a regression method, which was introduced by Brown and Mood (1951). It is essentially a graphical procedure that produces a good prediction line very quickly. We complete the chapter with 'quick' tests for the slope and intercept of the regression line, which again use Tukey-type ideas.

THE OLMSTEAD–TUKEY 'CORNER' TEST

Introduction

This very interesting test was published by Olmstead and Tukey (1947) and, in our opinion, deserves wider usage than it has so far enjoyed. Unless the sample size n is very small, it is quicker to carry out than Spearman's or Kendall's tests of Chapter 9. Also, it has reasonable power properties, often quite comparable with those of previous tests. Furthermore, it has critical values that are largely independent of n; thus it is easy to memorize sufficient information to permit the test usually to be carried out without needing full tables of critical values (as is the case with Tukey's quick test for location differences given in Chapter 5).

PRACTICAL PROBLEM, HYPOTHESES AND DATA

We return to studying the relationship between sales and simple visits and demos used in Chapter 9. For the moment, we concentrate on the connection between the numbers of simple visits and sales. Recall from

Chapter 9 that the alternative hypothesis was of positive correlation between these two quantities.

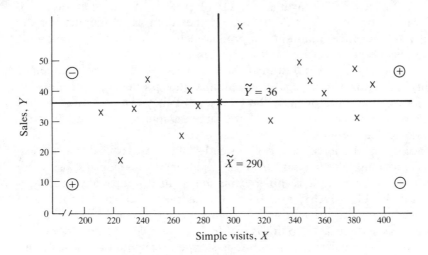

Figure 11.1

STATISTIC

It is easiest to introduce the test statistic with reference to a scatterplot, although in practice the diagram may not be necessary.

After drawing the scatterplot of the data, we compute the medians $\tilde{X}$ and $\tilde{Y}$ of the X_i and Y_i respectively. If n is large, this can be the most time-consuming part of the whole operation, and so we discuss later in this chapter how to speed up the computation of the medians. Once $\tilde{X}$ and $\tilde{Y}$ have been found, we draw the lines $X=\tilde{X}$ and $Y=\tilde{Y}$ on the diagram. (It may or may not happen that the point of intersection $(\tilde{X},\tilde{Y})$ is one of the data points; in the current case, this does happen.) These are, of course, vertical and horizontal lines respectively, which divide the picture into four regions called *quadrants*. Figure 11.1 shows the scatterplot together with these median lines.

The top-right and bottom-left quadrants are termed *positive* (+) quadrants and the other two are called *negative* (−) quadrants. The quadrants are referred to in this way because, if there is positive correlation between the X and Y variables, there will tend to be more points in the + quadrants than in the − quadrants, and vice versa. This follows since positive correlation implies that relatively large values of X and Y will occur together and also that relatively small values of X and Y will occur together; and such points will lie respectively in the top-right and bottom-left quadrants, i.e. the two + quadrants. Similarly, negative correlation increases the proportion of points lying in the negative quadrants. On the other hand, if H_0 is true, every point should have equal probabilities of falling in a $+$ or $-$ quadrant. Therefore a suitable statistic for testing H_0 against an H_1 of positive correlation, negative correlation, or either, should reflect whether there is a tendency for the positive or negative quadrants to predominate, as opposed to the points being fairly equally divided between them.

Therefore, one obvious statistic would be a count of the number of points in the positive or negative quadrants, thus producing a form of sign test for correlation. However, the Olmstead–Tukey test presented here is quicker to carry out, particularly for large samples, and seems to have superior power properties over this sign test.

To develop the ideas of the Olmstead–Tukey test, consider a vertical line approaching the diagram from the right-hand side (Fig. 11.2a). Note that the first point that is 'hit' by this line is in the top-right quadrants (point A in Fig. 11.2b), i.e. in a $+$ quadrant. Let the vertical line continue moving to the left, noting any further '$+$' points hit (if any), and stopping as soon as a '$-$' point is hit. In our example, the next point (B) hit is in the $-$ quadrant, so the line is stopped straightaway at this point (Fig. 11.2c). We record the number, C_1 say, of '$+$' points crossed by the line; in this example, $C_1 = 1$.

If, instead, the line had first met a '$-$' point, we would then have continued its progress until it was stopped by a '$+$' point; C_1 would then have been given by *minus* the number of '$-$' points encountered by the line before it is stopped by the '$+$' point.

We now repeat the operation, first with a vertical line approaching from the *left*, then with a *horizontal* line approaching from *above* the diagram, and finally with a horizontal line approaching from *below*. Let the counts obtained in these three cases be C_2, $C3$ and C_4 respectively. (In practice, the order in which the four operations are carried out is unimportant.) In our example, a '$+$' point is encountered first in each one of the four operations, so all of C_1, C_2, C_3 and C_4 are positive. But *do not forget* that when and if a '$-$' point is the first point hit, the corresponding count must be taken as *negative*.

The test statistic C is given by the sum of these counts:

$$C = C_1 + C_2 + C_3 + C_4$$

Minor difficulties may occur if the data contain ties; as usual, we discuss this possibility in a later section. An associated difficulty may occur if n is an *odd* number. In this case there is bound to be a point lying on the median line $X = \tilde{X}$, and similarly there must be a point lying on $Y = \tilde{Y}$. Sometimes, as in the current example, these may be the *same* point, i.e. $(\tilde{X}, \tilde{Y})$, which is the intersection of the two median lines, though more usually they will be two separate points. The easiest thing to do with such points as regards the calculation of C is to ignore their

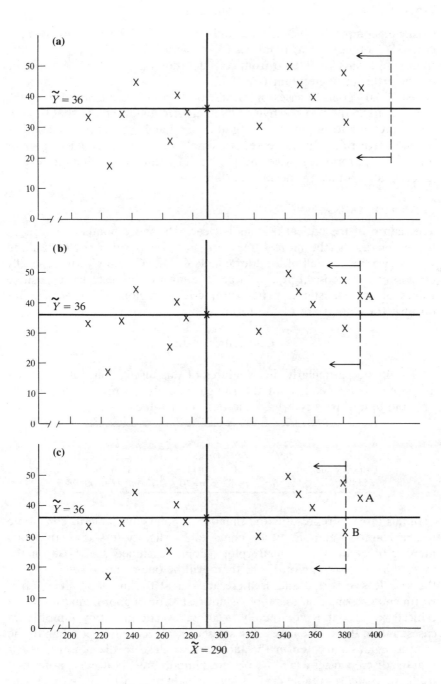

Figure 11.2

existence completely. (Olmstead and Tukey's advice was more compli-
cated. Denoting the two points as $(\tilde{X}, Y_0)$ and $(X_0, \tilde{Y})$, they also required
that these points be deleted from consideration but that they be replaced
by the artificial single point (X_0, Y_0).)

As a final detail, in cases of strong correlation it is possible for all the
points to lie in the two positive or two negative quadrants, so that there is
never anything to stop our moving horizontal and vertical lines according
to the above rules. In this case, we simply define C as equal to plus or
minus (as appropriate) twice the number of points in the diagram (again
ignoring any points on the median lines).

CRITICAL REGIONS

The nature of the critical regions is clear. The more points occurring in
the + quadrants, the more support there is for positive correlation. In
such a case, most or all of the four counts C_1, C_2, C_3 and C_4 will generally
be positive and possibly quite large, leading to relatively large positive
values of the statistic C. Therefore, critical regions when testing for
positive correlation are of the form:

$$C \geq \text{critical value}$$

One of the particularly nice features of this test is that critical values
are virtually independent of the sample size. It is sufficient to provide
only the following very brief table of critical values.

α_1	5%	$2\frac{1}{2}$%	1%	$\frac{1}{2}$%
α_2	10%	5%	2%	1%
Critical value	9	11	13	15 or 14
Valid for	$n \geq 6$	$n \geq 8$	$n \geq 10$	$10 \leq n \leq 47$ or $n \geq 48$

In this table, n represents the number of points available to contribute
to the counts, i.e. it is either equal to or slightly less than the total
number of points in the scatterplot. (Points excluded are those on the
median lines $X = \tilde{X}$ and/or $Y = \tilde{Y}$; there will be one or more such points if
the sample size is odd and/or there are ties at the median values.) It is
worth emphasizing that this table is not just a rough approximation to the
critical values – it is completely accurate except in a tiny minority of
cases; and in those rare cases, the significance levels corresponding to the
critical regions indicated in the table are so close to the nominal levels
that the discrepancies are of no practical importance. However, note that,
if n is very small, suitable critical regions may not exist (see the final row
of the table).

It follows from the table that, since our practical problem involves a
one-sided test, the 5% and 1% critical regions are $C \geq 9$ and $C \geq 13$

respectively (n is equal to 14 in this example, and so there are no validity problems).

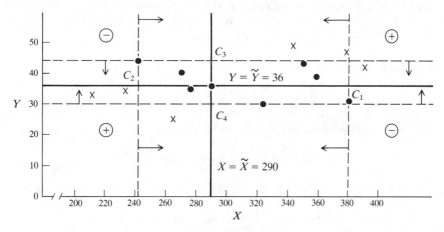

Figure 11.3

SOLUTION

Figure 11.3 shows the scatterplot again, but this time with the finishing positions of the two vertical and horizontal lines. To clarify matters, only those points which contribute to one or more of the counts C_1, C_2, C_3 and C_4 are indicated by a '$\times$'; the others are indicated by dots. We have $C_1=+1$, $C_2=+3$, $C_3=+2$ and $C_4=+2$, giving $C=1+3+2+2=8$. This point is just outside the $\alpha_1=5\%$ critical region $C\geqslant9$, which is wholly consistent with the results obtained from the other correlation tests in Chapter 9. Note that it is quite usual for some points to contribute to two of the four counts.

Exercise Carry out the corner test using the number of demos as the X variable. You will find the more usual situation here concerning points on the median lines, i.e. there are two different points involved. Also, you will find that, except for the two points on the median lines, all the remaining 13 points are in the positive quadrants; thus the statistic C, by virtue of the special rule for this extreme case, takes the value $2\times13=26$, which of course is virtually conclusive evidence of there being positive correlation between the two variables.

Discussion

For a relatively quick test, the Olmstead–Tukey test has good power properties, often being very comparable with Spearman's and Kendall's tests. Of course, it is not a *very* quick test to perform, since it still involves finding the sample medians; however, as we have mentioned, a method is shown later to help with this operation. Also, when n is large, it would be quite a lengthy matter to form the complete scatterplot; but in fact it is not necessary to do this. One could, for example, select from the data a few points (say, six each) having the largest and smallest X and Y values. If just these points are plotted, this is usually sufficient to find the values of C_1, C_2, C_3 and C_4 immediately (unless any of these counts are particularly large, in which case we will need to select a few more appropriate points from the data). Adopting this approach will generally make the calculation quite speedy, however large n happens to be.

One-sided and two-sided tests

We have been dealing with the version of the test appropriate for when H_1 stipulates positive correlation. If H_1 had stipulated negative correlation, this alternative hypothesis would be supported by large negative values of C. Therefore appropriate critical regions would then be

$$C \leq -\text{tabulated value}$$

Thus for example, $C \leq -9$ is the appropriate critical region for the $\alpha_1 = 5\%$ significance level.

For testing against the two-sided alternative hypothesis of correlation of either type, critical regions are of the form:

$$|C| \geq \text{critical value}$$

using α_2 significance levels.

Treatment of ties and median values

The discussion has so far ignored the possibility of tied observations, except in the case of ties occurring at median values; in this special case we ignore all such points, and reduce the value of n accordingly.

The kind of tie that can cause difficulties is where one (or more) of the moving horizontal or vertical lines used to evaluate the counts C_1, C_2, C_3 and C_4 encounters two or more points simultaneously. If these points all lie in the same quadrant there is no difficulty. However, consider the first five points met by the vertical line approaching from the right in Figure 11.4. The line meets two '+' points first, and then finds three points, two above and one below the X axis, all of which have the same X coordinate. Olmstead and Tukey's suggestion for this situation was the following: In the tie, call those points in the 'correct' quadrant, i.e. the quadrant that is contributing to the count (the + quadrant in this case), 'favourable' and the others 'unfavourable'. Then the tied points are regarded as contributing

$$\frac{\text{number of favourable points}}{1 + \text{number of unfavourable points}}$$

to the score (either + or − according as 'favourable' means + or − respectively).

In the above example, there are two favourable and one unfavourable, so the contribution is $2/(1+1) = 1$, giving $C_1 = 3$ altogether.

Finally, should the moving horizontal or vertical line hit both + and − points at

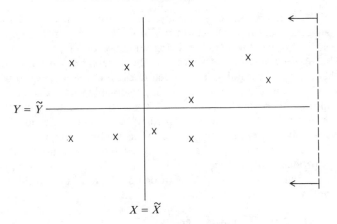

Figure 11.4

its first impact with the scatterplot (as with the vertical line approaching from the left in Figure 11.4), the corresponding count (C_2 in this case) is taken to be 0.

Null distributions
As usual, the values of the individual counts C_1, C_2, C_3 and C_4 and the overall C do not depend on the actual values of the observations (X_1,Y_1), (X_2,Y_2), . . . , (X_n,Y_n) only on their ranks $(r(X_1),r(Y_1))$, $(r(X_2),r(Y_2))$, . . . , $(r(X_n),r(Y_n))$, using the notation of the previous two chapters. Without loss of generality, we may reorder the data according to their X values so that $r(X_1)=1$, $r(X_2)=2$, . . . , $r(X_n)=n$. For the purpose of calculating null distributions we assume, as usual, that there are no ties. Then under H_0 all the $n!$ possible permutations of $r(Y_1)$, $r(Y_2)$, . . . , $r(Y_n)$ are equally likely. The null distribution may be obtained in the familiar way by writing down these $n!$ permutations, calculating C in each case, and building up a frequency distribution. As a simple example, if $n=4$, you might like to confirm that the $4!=24$ permutations give four cases of $C=+8$, one of $C=+4$, four of $C=+2$, six of $C=0$, four of $C=-2$, one of $C=-4$ and four of $C=-8$. (You will need to sketch 24 four-point scatterplots to do this!) Thus, in the one-sided case relative to the 'Practical problem', the smallest critical region is $C=+8$, but as the probability of this is $4/24=16.67\%$, there is certainly no $\alpha_1=5\%$ (or smaller) critical region, and this is as indicated by the final 'validity' row in the above table.

Large samples
The above table is appropriate for all sample sizes.

Quick calculation of medians

In Chapter 5, we suggested a way of speeding up the operation of ordering (ranking) the observations in a sample. In particular, this method can of course be used to find the median. However, the method does a lot more than just find the median so if the median is really all that we want, we should be able to reduce the work involved. One obvious way of doing this is first to look briefly through the data and suggest some interval within which we are fairly sure the median lies. Then we scan through the data, ordering all those observations that lie in the interval, but merely tallying (i.e. counting) the observations lying to the left and right of the interval. Presuming the median does lie in the interval, it will now be very easy to locate it. Even if it does not, it presumably will not lie far outside the interval, and a further quick scan through the data to identify a few values just outside the interval should enable the median to be quickly found.

Even with only 15 points, as in our current example, this method should be noticeably quicker than completely ordering all the observations, and for large samples it produces a very considerable improvement. Let us illustrate the method by finding the median number of demos. Here again are the numbers of demos done by the 15 salesmen:

104	161	156	96	149	143	113	142
115	175	135	145	137	151	126	

A quick glance through the data shows that the number of demos ranges between 96 and 175, with no noticeable asymmetry, so it would seem reasonable to guess that the median lies between, say, 130 and 140. Scanning through the 15 values, we place numbers in the interval on a roughly linear scale, and simply tally the others. Doing this we obtain the following picture:

$$\text{卌} \qquad | \qquad\qquad 135 \qquad 137 \qquad\qquad | \quad \text{卌} $$
$$\qquad\quad (130) \qquad\qquad\qquad\qquad\qquad\qquad (140) \;\; ||| $$

This shows we have just missed trapping the median value. We want the 8th (= the 8th smallest) value, and this lies just to the right of 140; for we have five values less than 130, two between 130 and 140 and eight greater than 140. So, we simply rescan the data, now looking for the smallest value larger than 140, and this is almost immediately seen to be 142. Of course, had we chosen the interval as, say (130,145), this second scan would have been unnecessary as we would then have had:

$$\text{卌} \quad | \qquad\qquad 135 \quad 137 \qquad\qquad 142 \;\; 143 \qquad \overset{145}{|} \;\; \text{卌}$$
$$\quad (130) \qquad\qquad\qquad\qquad\qquad\qquad\qquad\qquad (145)$$

from which the median value of 142 is immediately obtained.

BROWN AND MOOD'S QUICK REGRESSION METHOD

Introduction

G. W. Brown and A. M. Mood (1951) introduced a simple but effective technique for quickly fitting a straight line $Y = a + bX$ to a set of points. Although they presented it as a numerical procedure, the technique seems best suited to a graphical approach; this makes it even faster to carry out and reduces computation to a minimum. Also, as it is based on medians, the method is quite robust against the occurrence of 'rogue values' in the data. After presenting their regression method, we shall take a look at a simple method for testing hypotheses concerning the slope b and the intercept a.

PRACTICAL PROBLEM AND DATA

To illustrate Brown and Mood's regression method, we will use the geology problem discussed in the previous chapter. For convenience, we reproduce the data of that problem below.

Distance, X (km)	0.2	0.5	0.9	1.4	2.1	2.7	3.0	3.6
Volume, Y (cm³)	50	48	42	36	34	32	29	31
Distance, X (km)	4.1	4.4	5.0	5.6	6.2	6.6	7.1	
Volume, Y (cm³)	28	24	19	17	10	12	9.5	

PROCEDURE

Brown and Mood's procedure is best described by the following steps.

Step 1   Construct the scatterplot of the data.
Step 2   Draw a vertical line through $\tilde{X}$, the median of the 'X's; in our example, we have $\tilde{X}=3.6$ (see Fig. 11.5).
Step 3   Find the X median and the Y median of the points lying to the left of the median line just drawn (i.e. $\tilde{X}=3.6$, in this example); we will call these medians $\tilde{X}_1$ and $\tilde{Y}_1$. In our case, $\tilde{X}_1=1.4$ and $\tilde{Y}_1=36$.
Step 4   Now find the X median and the Y median of. the points lying to the right of the median line; call them $\tilde{X}_2$ and $\tilde{Y}_2$. In our case, $\tilde{X}_2=5.6$ and $\tilde{Y}_2=17$.

(It so happens here that both $(\tilde{X}_1,\tilde{Y}_1)$ and $(\tilde{X}_2,\tilde{Y}_2)$ are actual data points. This tends to happen if there is a strong monotonic relationship in the data but, in general, this does not happen.) We can now use the line defined by $(\tilde{X}_1,\tilde{Y}_1)$ and $(\tilde{X}_2,\tilde{Y}_2)$ as a very quick and simple regression line – this is the broken line in Figure 11.6. More usually it is regarded as the *first approximation* to the final regression line.

To improve on this first approximation, we consider the *deviations* or differences between the actual Y values and those Y values predicted from the regression line (i.e. the vertical distance from the actual data point to the line). Brown and Mood reasoned that for a particularly good regression line, the *median* of these deviations in both groups of points (those lying to the left and right of the median line $X=\tilde{X}$) should be zero.

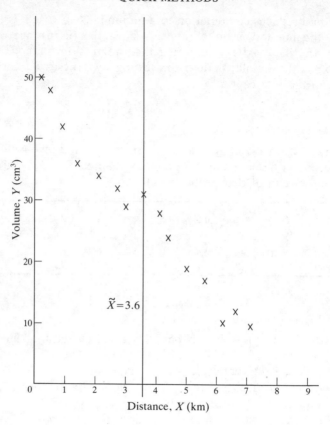

Figure 11.5

However, using the above first approximation to the regression line, we find the deviations to be:

| Left-hand group | 8.50 | 8.00 | 3.75 | 0 | 1.00 | 2.00 | 0.25 | (median=2) |
| Right-hand group | 4.00 | 1.50 | −0.75 | 0 | −4.25 | −2.50 | −0.75 | (median=−0.75) |

This confirms what we see in Figure 11.6; the first approximation is not too good for this case since, in particular, all six points in the left-hand group (apart from the one point on the line) lie *above* the line, corresponding to positive deviations.

The final version of the regression line (which is most easily obtained using a transparent ruler) is found by shifting the line around until, as suggested above, the median of the deviations in both groups is equal to 0. This needs some experimenting but, with practice, it is quickly achieved. Basically, it is a matter of ensuring that, in each group, there are as many points above the line as below; if there are an odd number of

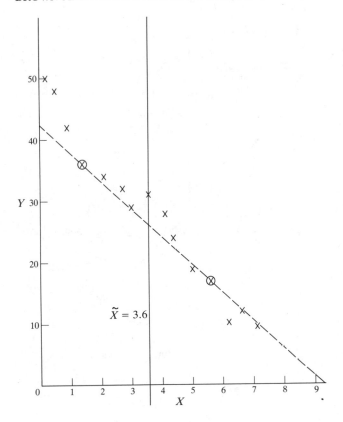

Figure 11.6

points in the group, the line will go through one of them but if the number of points is even, then a little judgement is needed to make the middle two deviations the same size (one above and one below the line).

In our case, the required line goes through the points (2.7,32) and (6.6,12), as drawn in Figure 11.7. Predictions for Y given an X value can now be directly obtained from this line.

If preferred, one can carry out a little algebra to discover that the equation of the line going through the points (2.7,32) and (6.6,12) is $Y=45.846-5.128X$. The deviations in the two groups may then be calculated as:

Left-hand group	5.18	4.75	0.77	−2.67	−1.08	0	1.46
Right-hand group	3.18	0.72	−1.21	−0.13	−4.05	0	0.06

Note that the median deviation in each group is zero, as required.

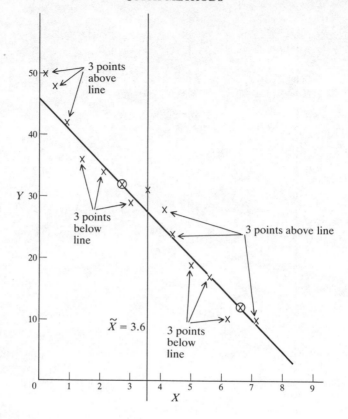

Figure 11.7

A QUICK HYPOTHESIS TEST FOR THE SLOPE

Introduction

We now present an interesting procedure for a quick and easy hypothesis test on the slope b of a regression line. A similar test may also be designed for testing a hypothesis about the intercept a and this is presented at the end of the chapter. After drawing the scatterplot, plus a simple construction on this diagram, the test is really just a simple applicaton of Tukey's quick test of Chapter 5.

PROBLEM AND DATA

We shall study a familiar situation, namely the relationship between the volumes of stones and their distances from the river source.

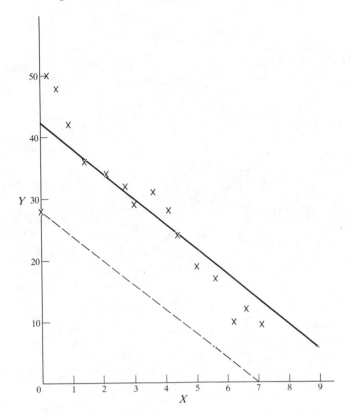

Figure 11.8

HYPOTHESES

When analysing the same problem in Chapter 10 we used the hypotheses:

H_0: $b = -4$.

H_1: $b \neq -4$.

We shall use the same hypotheses here, and it will be interesting to see how this quick test compares with the more powerful test in the previous chapter.

STATISTIC

On the scatterplot (Fig. 11.8), we first draw a 'guide line', which is any line having the hypothesized slope ($b=-4$ in this example); this is the broken line in this figure. Then, retaining this slope, we move the line up or down *until there are as many points above it as below* – this line is also

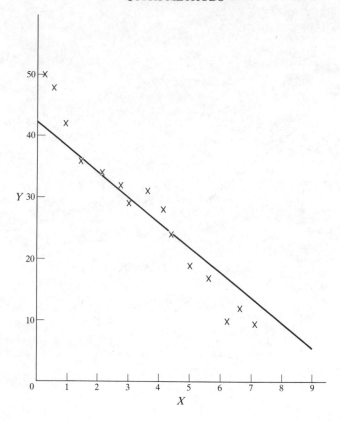

Figure 11.9

drawn in Figure 11.8. Sometimes, as *in this example*, this cannot be achieved exactly, but we get as close to equality as possible. Here, the best we can do is to have seven points above and eight points below. This line is shown in Figure 11.9. Now denote each point above the line as a '+', and each point below the line as '−'. We write down the appropriate sequence of '+'s and '−'s going from left to right in Figure 11.9. By this process, we obtain the following sequence of signs:

$$+ \quad + \quad + \quad - \quad + \quad + \quad - \quad + \quad + \quad - \quad - \quad - \quad - \quad - \quad -$$

Regarding the '+'s and '−'s as two samples, we then carry out the usual Tukey quick test.

CRITICAL REGIONS

These are exactly as referred to previously in Chapter 5, with the critical values being obtained from Table H. Thus with $n_1 = 7$ and $n_2 = 8$, we reject

H_0 in favour of H_1 at the $\alpha_2=5\%$ and 1% significance levels if $Ty\geqslant7$ and $Ty\geqslant9$ respectively.

SOLUTION

There is a run of three '+'s at the left-hand end and six '−'s at the right-hand end, giving a value of the test statistic of $Ty=3+6=9$. This result therefore is just significant at the $\alpha_2=1\%$ level.

Discussion
The result just obtained is not quite as conclusive as that in Chapter 10, but it is clearly not far behind. In view of the very quick and easy nature of this procedure, we seem to be getting good power relative to the effort required to carry out the test.

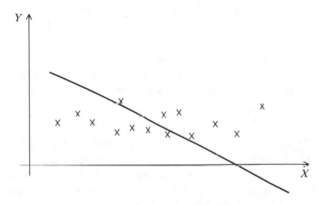

Figure 11.10

One-sided and two-sided tests
The test is based on the fact that if the hypothesized slope is seriously in error then there will be a tendency for deviations at the left side of the diagram to be negative and those on the right to be positive, or vice versa. A one-sided test, such as for H_0: $b=-4$ against H_1: $b>4$ will be based on the appropriate selection from these two alternatives. For this example, $b>-4$ implies the line is *less* steep than implied by H_0 (or even of positive slope). Imagine the situation if the true value of b were substantially greater than -4, say $b=0$. We would then obtain a diagram something like Figure 11.10, where most of the deviations on the left of the diagram are negative (−) and those on the right are positive (+).

Consequently, we would only allow the Tukey statistic to count for this one-sided test if there is a '−' at the left of the sequence and a '+' at the right. Subject to this, α_1 significance levels should be used (i.e. 7 for $\alpha_1=2\frac{1}{2}\%$, 10 for $\alpha_1=\frac{1}{2}\%$, etc., unless n is small). In the current case, the signs are the opposite way round and so, unsurprisingly, there is no evidence in our data for rejecting H_0: $b=-4$ in favour of the alternative H_1: $b>-4$; the evidence in fact points the other way.

Null distributions and large samples

There is virtually nothing to add to the information given in Chapter 5. Note that the procedure automatically provides equal, or nearly equal, numbers of '+'s and '−'s, which is the situation when the '7–10–13' rule applies best for critical values, as long as the samples sizes are not too small. So, if the number n of data points available is, say, at least 20, we also have the advantage that we do not need to refer to Table H for the critical values.

A QUICK HYPOTHESIS TEST FOR THE INTERCEPT

Introduction

We now conclude this chapter with a quick-and-easy test on the intercept ($=a$) of the regression line. This test is very similar to that just given for the slope (b), and so we really have two tests for the price of one!

PRACTICAL PROBLEM AND DATA

As before, we shall use the geologist's problem, i.e. the relationship between the volume of stones and distance from the river source.

HYPOTHESES

Using his previous experience with similar rivers, the geologist believes that, near the river source, the average volume of stones should be about 42 cm^3, i.e. the intercept a of the regression line should be 42. It is certainly of interest to him to see whether or not this is a reasonable value for this particular river, and so appropriate hypotheses are:

H_0: $a = 42$.
H_1: $a \neq 42$.

STATISTIC

On the scatterplot (Fig. 1.11), we draw a reference line through the point $(0,a)=(0,42)$ (this is shown as a broken line in the figure). We then simply rotate this line about the point (0,42) until there are an equal number of points above as below the line (as with the previous test, this process is easily done with the aid of a transparent ruler). This line is drawn in Figure 11.11; notice that it passes through the point (4.4,24) to give seven points above and seven below the line.

As with the previous test, we denote each point above the line as a '+' and each point below as a '−'. Writing down the sequence of '+'s and '−'s obtained when going from left to right in Figure 11.11 gives:

+ + + − + + − + + − − − − −

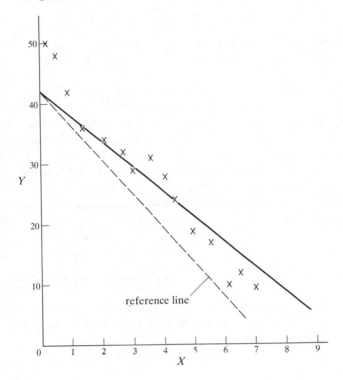

Figure 11.11

As before, we regard the '+'s and '−'s as two samples and carry out the usual Tukey two-sample test.

CRITICAL REGIONS

With $n_1=7$ and $n_2=7$, Table H gives the $\alpha_2=5\%$ and 1% critical regions as $Ty \geqslant 7$ and $Ty \geqslant 9$ respectively.

SOLUTION

There is a run of three '+'s at the left-hand end and five '−'s at the right-hand end, giving $Ty=3+5=8$. So this result is significant at the $\alpha_2=5\%$ level but not at the 1% level, i.e. we have some (but not strong) evidence in support of the alternative hypothesis that the volume of stones near (or at) the source is not equal to 42 cm^3.

One-sided and two-sided tests and large samples
The same comments apply here as with the previous test.

Assignments

In addition to the assignments of Chapters 9 and 10, we include the following for this chapter.

1 Medical data

In 1957, W. H. Gibson and G. H. Jowett ('"Three group" regression analysis. Part I. Simple regression analysis', *Appl. Statist.* **6**, 114–22) presented a regression analysis of some medical data. In fact, the data are ideal for the techniques presented in this chapter. In the table below, X is the diastolic blood pressue (mmHg) and Y is the heart weight (g) of men dying from cerebral haemorrhage.

X	121	120	95	123	140	112	92	100	102	91
Y	521	465	352	455	490	388	301	395	375	418
X	143	94	108	78	170	80	179	110	120	163
Y	567	264	503	320	458	399	524	465	432	602

Task: Use the Olmstead-Tukey method to test for positive correlation in these data. Apply Brown and Mood's regression technique to obtain a suitable regression line.

12
Association between two variables

Introduction

In this chapter we are concerned with a problem that is similar to testing for correlation, i.e. whether two variables, or quantities, are related to each other. The essential difference from our previous investigations into correlation is that the 'quantities' of interest may not be numerical; indeed, even if they are numerical then they are usually measured on a relatively crude scale so that we may expect several of the data to take on the same recorded values as each other. In this situation, we refer to 'association' between quantities rather than 'correlation'.

Problems of association occur in many disciplines, such as educational studies, social sciences, pure sciences, medical research and so on. For instance, a sociologist may be concerned as to whether the type of crime a person commits is associated with his social background; medical researchers ask 'is there any association between food colourings and stomach cancer?'; a market researcher may be interested in whether a person's sex or age is associated with preferences in packaging colours.

The most common statistical technique for analysing such problems is attributed to Karl Pearson's (1900) work around the turn of the century. He used what is essentially a chi-squared goodness-of-fit test since, as we shall see, the method involves comparing a set of observed frequencies with a set of 'expected' frequencies calculated under the null hypothesis of no association between the two quantities.

At this point, it will be useful for you to see a typical set of data on which Pearson's association test may be used. In fact, the data we give below were quoted by Pearson in 1909 and concern the drinking habits of criminals and the type of crime committed.

Offence	Drinker	Abstainer
arson	50	43
rape	88	62
violence	155	110
stealing	379	300
coining	18	14
fraud	63	144

Clearly, these data comprise 'observed frequencies'; for example, 144 people who committed fraud were abstainers. These data were collected in an attempt to answer the question 'Is the type of crime committed associated with drinking habits?'.

It is usual to refer to such a tabular layout of frequencies as an $r \times c$ *contingency table*,* where r represents the number of rows and c the number of columns in the table. Thus the above data are said to be in a 6×2 contingency table. In view of this terminology, many authors refer to the 'analysis of contingency tables' when dealing with this kind of situation.

THE CHI-SQUARED TEST

PRACTICAL PROBLEM

In the early 1980s, a household survey was conducted on the inhabitants of four regions of South Wales (Rhiubina, Cyn Coed, Splott/Adamstown and Canton/Riverside). There were many aspects to this survey, and the one we have chosen to investigate is that arising from the question 'How satisfied are you with the level of facilities for sport activities in your region?'.

As we work through the practical problem, you will see the resemblance between the techniques of this chapter and the χ^2 test of Chapter 4.

HYPOTHESES

The above question was posed to see whether people's opinion on sporting facilities depends on where they live. The alternative hypothesis is then a statement to this effect, with the null hypothesis saying that a person's opinion on sporting facilities is *independent* of where they live. Thus the hypotheses may be stated as:

H_0: Opinion on sporting facilities in South Wales is independent of the region.

H_1: There is some association between regions in South Wales and opinions on sporting facilities.

DATA

The table below shows the number of people in each of the four regions who were 'very satisfied', 'satisfied', 'not very satisfied' or 'dissatisfied' with the level of sporting facilities in their area.

---

* The term contingency means 'depending on chance'.

Opinion	Rhiubina	Cyn Coed	Splott	Canton
very satisfied	7	7	7	3
satisfied	18	37	24	30
not very satisfied	19	19	10	19
dissatisfied	15	8	4	21

Notice that the data form a 4×4 contingency table.

STATISTIC

As we mentioned earlier, Pearson's test for independence (no association) between two variables is essentially the same as his goodness-of-fit test; therefore, the test statistic is of the form

$$\chi^2 = \frac{\Sigma(\text{Ob.} - \text{Ex.})^2}{\text{Ex.}}$$

the sum being taken over all the $r \times c$ positions in the table. However, for contingency tables, the frequencies expected (Ex.) under H_0 are obtained in a different way from those for the goodness-of-fit test in Chapter 4. In order to explain how these expected frequencies are calculated, we now reproduce the data together with the *marginal* row and column totals and also the *grand* total.

Opinion	Rhiubina	Cyn Coed	Splott	Canton	Row totals
very satisfied	7	7	7	3	24
satisfied	18	37	24	30	109
not very satisfied	19	19	10	19	67
dissatisfied	15	8	4	21	48
Column totals	59	71	45	73	248

Now, what we would 'expect' of these frequencies if the null hypothesis of independence between the row and column factors were true? First, the pattern (i.e. proportions) of responses 'very satisfied', 'satisfied', 'not very satisfied' and 'dissatisfied' should be the same in each of the four regions; as in Chapter 4, we would not expect this to be *exactly* true in our sample, but we would expect it 'on the average' or 'in the long term'. Also, there is no reason for us to 'expect' different row and column totals from those in the observed data. Therefore we need to calculate expected frequencies that (i) satisfy the above rule concerning proportions, and (ii) retain the row and column marginal totals in the table.

Fortunately, there is a very simple rule which gives such expected frequencies. To find the expected frequency for any position in the table, i.e. for any given row and column, the rule is to multiply together the corresponding row and column marginal totals and then divide by the grand total, or more concisely:

$$\text{expected frequency} = \frac{\text{row total} \times \text{column total}}{\text{grand total}}$$

This formula can be derived by the following argument. Consider the category 'very satisfied *and* in Rhiubina'. If H_0 *is true* and so 'opinion' is independent of 'region', we can calculate the probability of someone being in this category by using the multiplication law given in Chapter 1: if events A and B are independent then

$$\text{Prob(A } and \text{ B)} = \text{Prob(A) Prob(B)}$$

so that

$$\text{Prob(very satisfied } and \text{ in Rhiubina)}$$
$$= \text{Prob(very satisfied) Prob(in Rhiubina)}$$

Now, since 24 out of the grand total of 248 are 'very satisfied' we estimate that

$$\text{Prob(very satisfied)} = 24/248$$

and, likewise,

$$\text{Prob(in Rhiubina)} = 59/248$$

Thus, if H_0 is true we have

$$\text{Prob(very satisfied } and \text{ in Rhiubina)} = (24/248 \times 59/248)$$
$$= \frac{\text{row total}}{\text{grand total}} \times \frac{\text{column total}}{\text{grand total}}$$

Hence the number 'expected' in this category if H_0 is true is found by multiplying this probability by the grand total, which gives the formula quoted above.

Below are the tables of expected frequencies, before and after the arithmetic is carried out. Before the actual calculations are performed the table is as follows:

Opinion	Rhiubina	Cyn Coed	Splott	Canton	Row totals
very satisfied	$\dfrac{24\times59}{248}$	$\dfrac{24\times71}{248}$	$\dfrac{24\times45}{248}$	$\dfrac{24\times73}{248}$	24
satisfied	$\dfrac{109\times59}{248}$	$\dfrac{109\times71}{248}$	$\dfrac{109\times45}{248}$	$\dfrac{109\times73}{248}$	109
not very satisfied	$\dfrac{67\times59}{248}$	$\dfrac{67\times71}{248}$	$\dfrac{67\times45}{248}$	$\dfrac{67\times73}{248}$	67
dissatisfied	$\dfrac{48\times59}{248}$	$\dfrac{48\times71}{248}$	$\dfrac{48\times45}{248}$	$\dfrac{48\times73}{248}$	48
Column totals	59	71	45	73	248

After the calculations are carried out, we have:

Opinion	Rhiubina	Cyn Coed	Splott	Canton	Row totals
very satisfied	5.7	6.9	4.4	7.1	24
satisfied	25.9	31.2	19.8	32.1	109
not very satisfied	15.9	19.2	12.2	19.7	67
dissatisfied	11.5	13.7	8.6	14.1	48
Column totals	59	71	45	73	248

By examining the first of these tables, you should see that the desired conditions are exactly satisfied; they are only approximately satisfied in the second table because of rounding. (Note that there is no reason to round the expected frequencies to integers; to do so would only result in the test being less accurate.)

It is worth noting that, because of the retention of marginal totals, some of the arithmetic could be shortened. For example, suppose we have computed the first three entries, 5.7, 25.9 and 15.9 in the first column; then, since we know the four entries in this column should add up to 59, we could simply calculate the final entry as

$$59 - 5.7 - 25.9 - 15.9 = 11.5.$$

We could do the same in the second and third columns. *All* of the entries in the final column could be computed by a similar 'indirect' method, using the knowledge about the row totals. The details might differ slightly in practice because of rounding errors.

The minimum number of 'direct' calculations (nine in our problem) is called the *number of degrees of freedom*. In the general case of a contingency table having r rows and c columns, there are $(r-1)(c-1)$ degrees of freedom (df).

CRITICAL REGIONS

Since large discrepancies between Ob. and Ex. support the alternative hypothesis and give a large value of χ^2, we reject H_0 in favour of H_1 if

$$\chi^2 \geq \text{critical value}$$

As we saw in Chapter 4, χ^2 does not have a precise null distribution – it varies according to circumstances (even for a fixed sample size). Fortunately, under certain provisos, it does not vary to any great extent, and it can be well approximated by the chi-squared distribution having $(r-1)(c-1)$ degrees of freedom.

Using this approximation, Table B gives the 5% and 1% critical regions for our problem with 9 df as $\chi^2 \geq 16.919$ and $\chi^2 \geq 21.666$ respectively.

SOLUTION

The calculation of $\chi^2 = \Sigma(\text{Ob.}-\text{Ex.})^2/\text{Ex.}$ is quite straightforward once the expected frequencies (Ex.) have been found. The details of the calculation are shown in the following table.

Ob.	Ex.	Ob.−Ex.	(Ob.−Ex.)^2	(Ob.−Ex.)^2/Ex.
7	5.7	1.3	1.69	0.30
18	25.9	−7.9	62.41	0.41
19	15.9	3.1	9.61	0.60
15	11.5	3.5	12.25	1.07
7	6.9	0.1	0.01	0.00
37	31.2	5.8	33.64	1.08
19	19.2	−0.2	0.04	0.00
8	13.7	−5.7	32.49	2.37
7	4.4	2.6	6.76	1.54
24	19.8	4.2	17.64	0.89
10	12.2	−2.2	4.84	0.40
4	8.6	−4.6	21.16	2.46
3	7.1	−4.1	16.81	2.37
30	32.1	−2.1	4.41	0.14
19	19.7	−0.7	0.49	0.02
21	14.1	6.9	47.61	3.38
			total =	19.03

The value of $\chi^2=19.03$ is certainly significant at the 5% level; in fact, consulting the more detailed tables in *EST* reveals that this value is just significant at the $2\frac{1}{2}$% level (the critical value for which is 19.023). So it seems that the data contain fairly strong evidence to support the alternative hypothesis that a person's opinion on the level of sporting facilities in South Wales does depend on where that person lives.

DISCUSSION

Since H_0 has been rejected, we might wish to examine the data further to find out more about this dependence. However, this is not an easy job! An exploratory method is simply to look at the column of values for $(\text{Ob.}-\text{Ex.})^2/\text{Ex.}$ to see which contribute most to the value of χ^2. If we do this and select those categories for which $(\text{Ob.}-\text{Ex.})^2/\text{Ex.}>2$ (say) we obtain:

Rhiubina *and* satisfied
Cyn Coed *and* dissatisfied
Splott   *and* dissatisfied
Riverside *and* very satisfied
Riverside *and* dissatisfied

So, on this fairly subjective basis, the lack of independence shows up most in just these five categories. Since three of these (including the final one which corresponds to the largest value of $(\text{Ob.}-\text{Ex.})^2/\text{Ex.}$) involve the factor 'dissatisfied', in particular, we might conclude that dissatisfaction depends upon region.

A note on small expected frequencies

As with Pearson's 'chi-squared' goodness-of-fit test, small expected frequencies can invalidate the critical values obtained from the chi-squared distribution. A generally accepted guideline is the following:

(a) no more than one-fifth of the expected frequencies should be less than 5, and

(b) no expected frequency should be less than 1.

If these conditions are not satisfied then we usually combine categories to ensure that the conditions are fulfilled. In our practical problem only one expected frequency, the 4.4, was less than 5 and so we were quite justified in proceeding with the usual calculation of χ^2. However, another question on the same survey was 'How important do you think that hobbies and leisure pursuits are?'. The data resulting from this question are given below, where the figures in brackets denote the corresponding expected frequencies.

Opinion	Rhiubina	Cyn Coed	Splott	Canton	
very important	36 (29.2)	41 (37.0)	17 (29.2)	37 (35.6)	131
important	18 (19.9)	27 (25.1)	24 (19.9)	20 (24.1)	89
quite important	4 (8.7)	8 (11.0)	15 (8.7)	12 (10.6)	39
not very important	2 (2.2)	0 (2.9)	4 (2.2)	4 (2.7)	10
	60	76	60	73	269

In this case, all four of the expected frequencies for 'not very important' are less than 5 and this, of course, represents 25% of all the expected frequencies. The remedy in this instance is to combine 'not very important' with 'quite important' (let us call the combined class 'less important') to give the following table:

Opinion	Rhiubina	Cyn Coed	Splott	Canton	
very important	36 (29.2)	41 (37.0)	17 (29.2)	37 (35.6)	131
important	18 (19.9)	27 (25.1)	24 (19.9)	20 (24.1)	89
less important	6 (10.9)	8 (13.0)	19 (10.9)	16 (13.3)	49
	60	76	60	73	269

The analysis of this 3×4 contingency table would then proceed as before.

Of course, we might have had the low frequencies all in one column, in which case we would have combined that column with another; in this example the choice of column to combine with might be quite arbitrary unless it is possible to relate the regions by geographical or some other factor. But, in the case of the 'not very important' row it was certainly more meaningful to combine it with the 'quite important' row than with any other since it was the closest in meaning.

Yates' correction

In an attempt to improve the accuracy of the chi-squared approximation, especially in the case of 2×2 contingency tables, the following amended version of the statistic was once recommended:

$$\chi^2 = \sum \frac{(|\text{Ob.} - \text{Ex.}| - \frac{1}{2})^2}{\text{Ex.}}$$

the $\frac{1}{2}$ representing a continuity correction. You may still find this modified version in some books. However, research carried out in the 1960s showed that this alteration was just as likely to worsen the approximation as to improve it in standard contingency table applications, and therefore we do not recommend its use except in the particular situations covered in Chapter 18.

Assignments

1 Recreation habits

Three other questions and their responses from the survey on recreation habits in South Wales are given below.

(i)   How important do you consider physical recreation to be?

	Rhiubina	Cyn Coed	Splott/ Adamstown	Canton/ Riverside
very important	36	37	18	37
important	19	26	21	20
quite important	5	9	15	10
not important	3	4	7	6

(ii) How satisfied are you with the level of facilities for leisure activities in your area?

	Rhiubina	Cyn Coed	Splot/ Adamstown	Canton/ Riverside
very satisfied	5	7	4	5
satisfied	24	42	24	32
not very satisfied	11	19	16	15
dissatisfied	11	18	1	21

(iii) Do you think that participation in leisure and recreation improves your health?

	Rhiubina	Cyn Coed	Splott/ Adamstown	Canton/ Riverside
yes	38	62	51	70
no	0	4	2	0
don't know	7	10	6	3

Task: Analyse these contingency tables using the technique given in the chapter.

Program 12.1   Chi-squared test for association

```
100 REM *** CHI-SQUARED TEST FOR ASSOCIATION ***

110 REM ** INPUT SIZE OF CONTINGENCY TABLE **
120 INPUT "NUMBER OF ROWS & COLUMNS ? ";NR,NC
130 PRINT
140 DIM R(NR),C(NC),OB(NR,NC),EX(NR,NC)
150 FOR I=1 TO NR
160 LET R(I)=0
170 NEXT I
180 FOR I=1 TO NC
190 LET C(I)=0
200 NEXT I
210 LET GT=0

220 REM ** INPUT OBSERVED FREQUENCIES **
230 PRINT "INPUT THE OBSERVED FREQUENCIES FOR :"
240 FOR I=1 TO NR
250 PRINT "ROW ";I
260 FOR J=1 TO NC
270 INPUT OB(I,J)
280 LET R(I)=R(I)+OB(I,J)
290 LET C(J)=C(J)+OB(I,J)
300 NEXT J
310 LET GT=GT+R(I)
320 NEXT I

330 REM ** CALCULATION OF EXPECTED FREQUENCIES **
340 LET F=0
350 FOR I=1 TO NR
360 FOR J=1 TO NC
370 LET EX(I,J)=R(I)*C(J)/GT
380 IF EX(I,J) < 5 THEN LET F=F+1
390 NEXT J
400 NEXT I
410 PRINT

420 REM ** LOW-FREQUENCIES WARNING **
430 IF F=0 THEN GO TO 460
440 PRINT "WARNING ... THERE ARE ";F;" EXPECTED FREQUENCIES LESS THAN 5"
450 PRINT

460 REM ** CALCULATION OF THE TEST STATISTIC **
470 LET Q=0
480 FOR I=1 TO NR
490 FOR J=1 TO NC
500 LET Q=Q+(OB(I,J)-EX(I,J))^2/EX(I,J)
510 NEXT J
520 NEXT I
530 PRINT "VALUE OF THE TEST STATISTIC = ";Q
```

PART V

Tests involving more than two samples

This part of the book is concerned with comparisons between *more than two* populations on the basis of samples drawn from them.

In Chapter 13, 14 and 15 we present tests for detecting differences in location between k (>2) populations. In Chapter 13, the situation is an extension of the two-independent-samples situation of Chapter 5, while Chapters 14 and 15 are an extension to k (>2) samples of the matched-pairs concept of Chapter 8.

The essential difference between Chapters 14 and 15 lies with the alternative hypotheses. In Chapter 15, the alternative hypothesis is quite specific about which populations are 'better' than which, that is, the populations are 'ordered'; however, Chapter 14 deals with the more general style of alternative hypothesis which simply states that there are *some* differences between the averages of the k populations without attempting to say which averages are larger or smaller.

The first part of Chapter 16 tackles a different sort of problem. Rather than simply looking for differences in average between the populations, we look for evidence of more complicated kinds of behaviour between the populations known as *interactions*. A typical example is where we are interested in the speed of a chemical reaction as related to the heat and pressure at which the reaction takes place. Since, for example, 10°C increase in temperature will have a greater effect at a high pressure than at a low pressure, such a situation cannot be dealt with in terms of average speed of reaction at a particular temperature nor at a particular pressure – the 'interactive' effect of temperature and pressure must be taken into account.

In the second part of Chapter 16, we use distribution-free methods to analyse the so-called latin squares design.

13

More than two (k) independent samples

Introduction

In Chapter 5, we used the information in two independent samples to look for evidence that the two populations from which the samples were taken had different averages (medians, usually). In this chapter, we deal with similar investigations, but now we have independent samples from three, four, five or even more populations. For example, suppose the consumer magazine in Chapter 5 had conducted its survey on cars from *four* countries, say Britain, Japan, West Germany and Italy. Then we would be looking for evidence of differences in reliability in cars from these four countries.

In classical statistics, this type of problem is called *one-way analysis of variance*. The analyses involve *F*-tests which rely for their validity on the observations being from normal distributions. The term 'analysis of variance' is not appropriate in distribution-free statistics since 'variance' is not relevant in this more general context. We shall simply refer to the problem of *k independent samples*. As usual, our procedures will not depend on any normality assumptions.

An early distribution-free test for *k* independent samples was an extension to Mood's (1950) median test; this is just a chi-squared test (see Ch. 12) based on the numbers of observations in each sample lying above and below the overall median. Then in 1952, W. H. Kruskal and W. A. Wallis (Kruskal 1952, Kruskal & Wallis (1952) introduced a test that is now by far the best-known distribution-free procedure for this situation. Both of these procedures for *k* independent samples are described in this chapter.

We also deal with another important issue in this chapter. Whenever we have evidence to support the alternative hypothesis that the averages of the *k* populations are differernt, we naturally want to know which populations are 'better' and which are 'worse'. To deal with this, we shall use O. J. Dunn's (1964) *multiple comparisons* procedure.

THE KRUSKAL–WALLIS TEST

Introduction

This popular test for the k-independent-samples problem is effectively an extension of the Mann–Whitney test (see Ch. 5). As you might deduce, therefore, it has very good power and is reasonably easy to execute unless the sample sizes are large (then you could always use the computer program – Program 13.1). The only requirements for the validity of the test are that the samples are independent of each other (meaning that the observations in any sample are not related to the observations in any other sample in any way) and, at least for theoretical purposes, that the populations are continuously distributed so that we are not troubled with ties.

It is interesting to note that the Kruskal–Wallis test was derived from the F-test (which is the classical test under normality for this situation) by replacing the actual observations by their ranks; this is analogous to the way that Spearman's rank correlation coefficient r_S was derived from the classical product-moment correlation coefficient r.

PRACTICAL PROBLEM

A survey was conducted by a consumer organization (in fact, the same organization we first mentioned in Chapter 5) on cars from Britain, Japan, West Germany and Italy. As before, they published a table giving the percentages of new cars that broke down in their first year. Our concern here is whether the published data suggest differences in reliability in cars from these different countries.

HYPOTHESES

The null hypothesis H_0 is that cars from the four countries are equally reliable with respect to breakdowns. In other words, H_0 says that the average percentage breakdowns is the same for all four countries. The alternative hypothesis H_1 is that there are some differences between the average percentage breakdowns. If it turns out that there is evidence to support H_1, then a further investigation would be useful to ascertain the relative performance of each country's cars – such a *multiple comparisons* investigation will be considered in a later section.

A summary of the hypotheses is:

H_0: There is no difference in the average reliability between cars from the four countries.

H_1: There are some differences in average reliabilities between cars from the four countries.

As with distribution-free procedures, the theory of the Kruskal–Wallis test is based on a more specific null hypothesis, namely that the populations are identically distributed (that is, identical in all respects, rather than just having the same average). Effectively, we assume that the populations are identical in *all* respects except, possibly, location. Thus it is usual to describe the hypotheses as something like:

H_0: The k populations have the same average (median).
H_1: There are some differences in average (median) between the k populations.

DATA

The survey gave breakdown information on 13 British models, seven Japanese, eight West German and four Italian. The percentages of cars of each type breaking down during their first year were:

Britain	21	33	12	28	41	39	24	29	30	19	27	38	23
Japan	9	13	6	3	5	10	4						
West Germany	18	35	8	17	22	20	37	11					
Italy	41	41	48	34									

As with the two-sample case, the conclusion seems apparent from a cursory glance at the data! Nevertheless, let us see if the test supports our intuition.

STATISTIC

The general idea behind the Kruskal–Wallis test is quite simple. Consider, for the moment, all the samples combined into one sample of size $N=n_1+n_2+\ldots+n_k$, where n_i is the size of the ith sample $(i=1,2,\ldots,k)$; in our example $N=32$, with $k=4$ and $n_1=13$, $n_2=7$, $n_3=8$ and $n_4=4$. These N observations are then ranked from 1 to N. Now, if H_0 is true, then the $N=32$ ranks should be randomly distributed between the four groups; in other words, each group should have its fair share of low, medium and high ranks. But if H_1 is true, then we would perhaps expect one group to have mainly low ranks, another group to have medium-sized ranks and so on. Thus, if H_0 is true, the mean of the ranks assigned to one group would not differ much from the mean of the ranks for any other group. The Kruskal–Wallis statistic is based on comparing each group's mean rank with the mean of all the ranks. In practice, this is achieved by calculating the sum of the squares of the differences

group mean rank − overall mean rank

with these squares being weighted by the appropriate sample size to compensate for the effect of unequal sample sizes.

Let us put this idea into practice with the car breakdown data. First we need to rank the combined samples, yet at the same time keep track of which ranks belong to which sample. This is effectively achieved by a technique similar to that used for the Mann–Whitney test: the observations are roughly placed on a linear scale and then the assignment of ranks is a trivial matter. In Table 13.1, the ranks are shown in brackets (note that, as usual, tied values are assigned average ranks).

From this table it is easy to obtain R_i, the sum of the ranks for sample i ($i=1,2,3,4$) and hence $\overline{R}_i$, the mean of the ranks for sample i. We obtain

R_i	33	261.5	117	116.5
$\overline{R}_i = R_i/n_i$	4.71	20.12	14.63	29.13

The overall mean rank, $\overline{R}$, is $(1+2+...+32)/32 = 16.5$. The weighted sum of the squared deviations is then given by:

$$\sum_{i=1}^{4} n_i(\overline{R}_i - \overline{R})^2 = n_1(R_1 - \overline{R})^2 + n_2(R_2 - \overline{R})^2 + n_3(R_3 - \overline{R})^2 + n_4(R_4 - \overline{R})^2$$

$$= 7(4.71 - 16.5)^2 + 13(20.12 - 16.5)^2 + 8(14.63 - 16.5)^2 + 4(29.13 - 16.5)^2$$
$$= 1809.43$$

To produce the Kruskal–Wallis statistic, we multiply this result by

$$\frac{12}{N(N+1)} = \frac{12}{32 \times 33}$$

So we obtain the statistic:

$$H = \frac{12}{N(N+1)} \sum_{i=1}^{k} n_i(R_i - \overline{R})^2$$

$$= \frac{12}{32 \times 33} \times 1809.43$$

$$= 20.56$$

In practice, it is more convenient to use an alternative, but equivalent, formula for H, namely:

$$H = \frac{12}{N(N+1)} \sum_{i=1}^{k} \frac{R_i^2}{n_i} - 3(N+1)$$

Table 13.1

	1 (Japan)	2 (Britain)	3 (W. Germany)	4 (Italy)
0 →				
	3 (1)			
	4 (2)			
	5 (3)			
	6 (4)			
			8 (5)	
	9 (6)			
10 →	10 (7)			
			11 (8)	
		12 (9)		
	13 (10)			
			17 (11)	
			18 (12)	
		19 (13)		
20 →			20 (14)	
		21 (15)		
			22 (16)	
		23 (17)		
		24 (18)		
		27 (19)		
		28 (20)		
		29 (21)		
30 →		30 (22)		
		33 (23)		34 (24)
			35 (25)	
			37 (26)	
		38 (27)		
		39 (28)		
40 →				
		41 (29.5)		41 (29.5)
				46 (31)
				48 (32)
50 →				

where again R_i is the sum of the ranks in the ith group. Performing the calculation with this formula gives

$$H = \frac{12}{32 \times 33}\left(\frac{33^2}{7} + \frac{261.5^2}{13} + \frac{117^2}{8} + \frac{116.5^2}{4}\right) - 3 \times 33$$

$$= 20.56$$

as before.

CRITICAL REGIONS

Our discussion in the previous section clearly indicates that the alternative hypothesis is supported by large values of H, arising from an uneven distribution of ranks among the groups, which leads to relatively large differences between the mean ranks. Thus H_0 will be rejected in favour of H_1 if

$$H \geqslant \text{critical value}$$

Critical values of H are tabulated on pages 32 to 34 of *EST* for a large range of cases; Table N is an abbreviated version of this table. For values of k or for sample sizes not included in either table, approximate critical values are obtained from the chi-squared distribution (Table B) using $k-1$ degrees of freedom.

The sample sizes in our example are beyond the range of Table N, and therefore we need to obtain approximate critical values from Table B. The number of degrees of freedom for our problem is $k-1=4-1=3$. Hence, the appropriate approximate critical regions for $\alpha=5\%$ and 1% are given by $H \geqslant 7.815$ and $H \geqslant 11.345$ respectively.

Note that, since the terms 'one-sided' and 'two-sided' have no meaning in the k-sample context, we simply use α without any suffices to denote the significance level.

SOLUTION

Given these particular data, we should not be too surprised to discover that $H=20.56$ is well into the 1% critical region. Indeed it should be clear that the result is significant at very stringent levels (the detailed chi-squared tables in *EST* show the result to be in the 0.1% critical region), yielding essentially conclusive evidence of differences. So the Kruskal–Wallis test has firmly supported our intuitive feelings on these data.

Discussion
In the 'Discussion' section for the Mann–Whitney test, we remarked that the consensus of practical considerations seems to favour its use above all other appropriate distribution-free tests for two independent samples. The same is true

of the Kruskal–Wallis test when considering k independent samples; when sampling from a normal distribution its power is almost equal to that of the classical F-test. Also, it is interesting to note that the Kurskal–Wallis test is much more reliable than the F-test when outliers are present in the data.

It is a pity that, unless the sample sizes are small, the Kruskal–Wallis test is rather tedious to calculate by hand, although our systematic layout of the data certainly helps, as does the computer program (Program 13.1). Having said this, it should be observed that the F-test is, if anything, even more tedious and, of course, it does not have the distribution-free features of the Kruskal–Wallis test.

Ties
One of the underlying assumptions of the Kruskal–Wallis test is that the samples are taken from continuous populations so as to avoid the problem of tied observations. However, ties in data do occur, perhaps because of rounding errors in recording the observations or because the data were in fact taken from discrete distributions. When they do occur, they are dealt with by using average ranks, as with the two observations of 41 in the numerical example above. Whatever the cause of ties, their presence affects the null distribution of H and so, strictly speaking, the usual critical values are not valid. If the number of ties is small then H is calculated and used in the usual way (which is just what we did in analysing the car breakdowns data).

However, should there be a large number of ties, then it is as well to incorporate a correction factor. The value of H calculated from

$$H = \frac{12}{N(N+1)} \sum_{i=1}^{k} \frac{R_i^2}{n_i} - 3(N+1)$$

is divided by

$$C = 1 - \frac{\sum(t^3 - t)}{N(N^2 - 1)} = 1 - \frac{\sum t^3 - \sum t}{N(N^2 - 1)}$$

to give the statistic $H^* = H/C$, which is approximately chi-squared distributed with $k-1$ degrees of freedom. In this formula, t is the number of ties for a given (tied) value and the summation is taken over all sets of tied values. An example will clarify the procedure, with which we are already familiar from Chapter 5. Consider the following three samples A, B and C:

A	B	C
4	14	10
9	10	14
10	9	14
	12	8

The rank sums are easily obtained from the usual layout:

	A	B	C
0 →			
	4 (1)		
			8 (2)
	9 (3.5)	9 (3.5)	
10 →	10 (6)	10 (6)	10 (6)
		12 (8)	
		14 (10)	14 (10)
			14 (10)
20 →			

They are as follows:

i	1	2	3
Rank sums R_i	10.5	27.5	28
n_i	3	4	4

Using

$$H = \frac{12}{N(N+1)} \sum_{i=1}^{3} \frac{R_i}{n_i} - 3(N+1) \text{ gives } H = 2.346.$$

However, as there are three different tied values, namely 9, 10 and 14, it may be worth using the refinement recommended above. Now, 9 occurs twice, giving $t=2$; 10 and 14 each occur three times, giving $t=3$ for each. To calculate the correction C it is helpful to construct the following table:

Observations	t	t^3
9	2	8
10	3	27
14	3	27

Then summing over the three ties, we have $\sum t=8$ and $\sum t^3=62$, from which

$$C = 1 - \frac{(\Sigma t^3 - \Sigma t)}{N(N^2 - 1)} = 1 - \frac{(62 - 8)}{11 \times 120}$$

i.e.

$$C = 0.959$$

Hence the 'corrected' value H^* of the Kruskal–Wallis statistic is

$$H^* = \frac{H}{C} = \frac{2.346}{0.959} = 2.446$$

which, as you can see, is not very different from H.

Incidentally, recalling that the car breakdown data contained a few ties, you might like to confirm that the correction for these data is $C=0.9998$, which gives $H^* = H/C = 20.43/0.9998 = 20.43$ (i.e. unchanged to two decimal places). Clearly we were justified in ignoring the correction in this case!

Null distributions
The null hypothesis for the k-independent-sample problem states that the populations from which the samples are drawn have identical, continuous distributions (although as we stated previously, the hypotheses are usually worded in terms of differences in averages, everything else being assumed equal). In other words, under H_0 the k samples can be regarded as all coming from the same population, and so all arrangements of the $N=n_1+n_2+\ldots+n_k$ observations are equally likely; it is on this principle that the null distributions of H are derived. Correspondingly, all the arrangements of the N ranks into groups of sizes n_1, $n_2, \ldots, n_k$ are equally likely under H_0. There are

$$\frac{N!}{n_1! n_2! \ldots n_k!}$$

such arrangements and, in order to obtain the distribution of H, we need to compute H for each of these arrangements. Even for moderate values of N, this is not only tedious but even beyond the limits of many computers. The size of the problem can be envisaged if we just look at a small-scale problem; with $k=4$ and $n_1=n_2=n_3=n_4=4$ there are 63 063 000 such arrangements! Even the existence of recurrence relations for the distributions of H (see Kruskal & Wallis 1952) does not greatly help matters, although they do permit some progress. However, we can easily demonstrate how to derive a null distribution of H for a small value of N. Consider $k=3$, $n_1=n_2=2$ and $n_3=1$, giving $N=5$. For this case there are 30 arrangements to consider. These are given below, together with the corresponding values of H. (In fact, we need to list only 15 arrangements since, for example, (1,2), (3,4), 5 and (3,4), (1,2), 5 obviously give the same value of H.)

Ranks of sample			
1	2	3	H
1,2	3,4	5	3.6
1,2	3,5	4	3.0
1,2	4,5	3	3.6
1,3	2,4	5	2.4
1,3	2,5	4	1.4
1,3	2,5	4	3.0
1,4	2,3	5	2.0
1,4	2,5	3	0.4
1,4	3,5	2	1.4
1,5	2,3	4	0.6
1,5	3,4	2	0.6
1,5	2,4	3	0
2,3	4,5	1	3.6
2,4	3,5	1	2.4
2,5	3,4	1	2.0

Thus,

$$\text{Prob}(H=0) \quad = 1/15$$
$$\text{Prob}(H=0.4) = 1/15$$
$$\text{Prob}(H=0.6) = 2/15$$
$$\text{Prob}(H=1.4) = 2/15$$
$$\text{Prob}(H=2.0) = 2/15$$
$$\text{Prob}(H=2.4) = 2/15$$
$$\text{Prob}(H=3.0) = 2/15$$
$$\text{Prob}(H=3.6) = 3/15$$

From these probabilities, we construct a table of 'upper-tail' probabilities $\text{Prob}(H \geqslant h)$ from which critical values would normally be obtained:

h	$\text{Prob}(H \geqslant h)$
0	1
0.4	0.9333
0.6	0.8667
1.4	0.7333
2.0	0.6000
2.4	0.4667
3.0	0.3333
3.6	0.2000

In fact, in this case, because of the high probabilities associated with the high values of H, no meaningful critical values can be obtained; the smallest 'round figure' significance level for which a critical region exists is $\alpha=20\%$! This explains the blank entry for $k=3$, $n_1=n_2=2$ and $n_3=1$ on page 32 of *EST*.

THE MEDIAN TEST

Mood (1950) introduced his *median test* for two independent samples, and this has since been extended to deal with k independent samples. It is much quicker to use than the Kruskal–Wallis test, since all that is necessary is to count the number of observations that are above and below the median of the combined sample. However, it obviously uses the data more crudely than does the Kruskal–Wallis procedure, and so it will generally be somewhat less powerful. As usual, therefore, we are giving you the choice of a test that is particularly easy to carry out or one that is a little more demanding but has greater sensitivity. A drawback of the median test is that, strictly speaking, it should not be used unless the sample sizes are at least 10; it is for this reason that we have chosen a different practical problem to illustrate the test.

PRACTICAL PROBLEM

The manager of a local sports club has devised four new training methods suitable for marathon runners. He asks for volunteers to participate in an experiment to determine whether there is any effective difference in the training schemes. Forty-nine members agreed to cooperate with the manager. Four groups of roughly equal sizes were randomly selected from the 49; each group was then randomly assigned to a particular training method. At the end of three months, the volunteers are to be timed on a trial marathon run.

HYPOTHESES

The hypotheses suggested by the nature of the experiment are simply:

H_0: The four training methods produce the same average running times.

H_1: There are some differences in average running times produced by the four training methods.

DATA

For various reasons, not all the volunteers completed their three-month training course. The times to run the trial marathon for the 44 who did complete the course are given below, for training methods A, B, C and D:

A	B	C	D
3 h 32 min	3 h 51 min	4 h 13 min	4 h 39 min
3 h 1 min	2 h 56 min	2 h 54 min	3 h 39 min
3 h 43 min	3 h 6 min	3 h 46 min	4 h 32 min
4 h 59 min	2 h 49 min	3 h 27 min	3 h 11 min
5 h 31 min	2 h 54 min	2 h 58 min	2 h 50 min
4 h 15 min	3 h 11 min	3 h 58 min	4 h 54 min
4 h 27 min	3 h 00 min	4 h 30 min	3 h 11 min
5 h 4 min	3 h 5 min	4 h 21 min	4 h 25 min
3 h 37 min	2 h 55 min	4 h 1 min	4 h 16 min
4 h 6 min	3 h 28 min	3 h 10 min	4 h 46 min
3 h 38 min	2 h 58 min		4 h 58 min
4 h 16 min			

STATISTIC

The idea behind this test is very simple. We first find the median of the whole set of observations; we shall refer to this as the *overall median*. For each sample we count the number of observations that lie above and below the overall median. If H_0 is true we would expect that each sample should have roughly the same number of observations above and below this median. So, if we construct a $2 \times k$ contingency table from these counts, then we can test H_0 with the usual χ^2 test (see Ch. 12). The form of the table is shown below and the test statistic χ^2 is again $\Sigma(\text{Ob.} - \text{Ex.})^2/\text{Ex.}$ (summed over all $2k$ cells in the table) where the expected frequencies are calculated as before from the formula:

$$\text{Ex.} = \frac{\text{row total} \times \text{column total}}{\text{grand total}}$$

Sample	1	2	3	...	k
Number above overall median	A_1	A_2	A_3	...	A_k
Number below overall median	B_1	B_2	B_3	...	B_k
Totals	n_1	n_2	n_3	...	n_k

Now consider the data in our problem. Since there are $N=44$ observations altogether, the overall median is the average of the 22nd and 23rd values; this is easily found using the quick method given in Chapter 11, and its value is 3 hr 41 min. The contingency table is then as follows:

Training method	A	B	C	D	
Number above 3 h 41 min	8	1	6	7	22
Number below 3 h 41 min	4	10	4	4	22
	12	11	10	10	44

The calculation for χ^2 is:

Ob.	Ex.	$(Ob.-Ex.)^2/Ex.$
8	6	0.667
4	6	0.667
1	5.5	3.682
10	5.5	3.682
6	5	0.200
4	5	0.200
7	5.5	0.409
4	5.5	0.409
		$9.916 = \chi^2$

CRITICAL REGIONS

Approximate critical values are obtained from the chi-squared distribution (Table B) with $k-1$ degrees of freedom. As with the usual contingency table analysis, we reject H_0 in favour of H_1 if

$$\chi^2 \geqslant \text{critical value}$$

Here we have $(r-1)(c-1)=(2-1)(4-1)=3$ degrees of freedom, and so the appropriate (approximate) critical regions for $\alpha=5\%$ and 1% are given by $\chi^2 \geqslant 7.815$ and $\chi^2 \geqslant 11.345$ respectively.

SOLUTION

The calculated value of χ^2 is 9.916, which lies well in the 5% critical region but not in the 1% region. In other words, there is some evidence to support the alternative hypothesis that there are some differences in the average running times produced by the training methods. In fact, if we look at the values of $(Ob.-Ex.)^2/Ex.$, we see that the greatest difference between Ob. and Ex. occurs with method B, and seeing that 10 out of the 11 times with this method are below the median, we are certainly tempted to say that this is a superior training method.

Discussion
Although, as we have said earlier, Mood's median test treats the data rather crudely, it is still quite capable of producing highly significant results. The

desirability of using it only when sample sizes are at least 10 is not a serious restriction, since the Kruskal–Wallis test itself is fairly easy and quick to carry out when sample sizes are small. But when sample sizes are large, the Kruskal–Wallis test becomes very tedious to execute, whereas the median test is still quite quick, particularly if the technique in Chapter 11 is used to find the overall median. The median test is also far more convenient to use if there are a lot of ties in the data, since problems of averaging ranks and associated effects on the null distribution are of little importance in this test.

As an exercise, we suggest you apply Mood's test to the car breakdown data. Although the smallness of the sample sizes implies that the details of the critical regions may be rather inaccurate, you will find that $\chi^2=16.77$, which is a clear indication of very significant evidence in support of H_1, a conclusion that is very similar to that from the Kruskal–Wallis test.

MULTIPLE COMPARISONS

So far in this chapter, our concern has been the search for evidence of *some* differences between the averages (say the medians) of the k populations under investigation. If a test (be it the Kruskal–Wallis or the median test) finds such evidence, then it is natural to follow up by asking: 'Which populations can be most confidently claimed to have different averages from each other?' This query is answered by using a so-called *multiple comparisons* technique.

There are several such techniques available. We have chosen one due to O. J. Dunn (1964), mainly because of its simplicity and effectiveness, although its conclusions do tend to be on the 'conservative' side. In this procedure $\frac{1}{2}k(k-1)=p$ comparisons are made in order to judge the level of evidence for pairs of populations differing. Thus we have p sets of hypotheses of the form:

$H_0^{(ij)}$: There is no difference between the ith and jth populations.
$H_1^{(ij)}$: There is some difference between the ith and jth populations.

with $i, j=1,2, \ldots ,k$ and $i<j$.

It is usual to use one overall level of significance α for all of these statements rather than considering there to be a separate level for each. In this case, α is interpreted as the overall probability of making at least one error (i.e. saying there is a difference) in the p comparisons when in fact no differences exist among the k populations. Dunn argues for α to be taken greater than the 'usual' maximum value of 5% so that any differences among the comparisons can be easily detected. The reason why we dare think of using what would otherwise be such unrealistically high significance levels here is that we agree at the outset only to invoke this multiple comparisons procedure when we have already had a significant result from the Kruskal–Wallis or the median test. Since this automatically provides us with a high degree of protection from even entering the procedure when the 'overall H_0' is true (i.e. when the whole set of p pairwise comparison H_0's are true or, in other words, when there are no differences in averages between the k populations), there is no harm caused by using Dunn's suggested high α levels. Significance levels of 10%, 15%, 20% or even 25% are therefore recommended. As a general rule, the higher the value of k the larger the value of α that should be used, for there are then larger numbers of pairwise comparisons amongst which to share out the risk of making an error of the type mentioned above. (In the problem discussed below, $k=4$ and we shall use $\alpha=20\%$.)

PRACTICAL PROBLEM

We use the car breakdowns data again; this situation is very suitable for Dunn's procedure since the Kruskal–Wallis test gave very strong evidence of some differences between the four populations, i.e. between the average reliabilities of cars from the four countries involved in the survey.

HYPOTHESES

The six $(-\frac{1}{2}k(k-1)=\frac{1}{2}\times4\times3)$ sets of hypotheses for this multiple comparison test are:

$H_0^{(ij)}$: The ith and jth country's cars have the same average number of breakdowns.

$H_1^{(ij)}$: The ith and jth country's cars have different average number of breakdowns.

with $(i,j)=(1,2)$, $(1,3)$, $(1,4)$, $(2,3)$, $(2,4)$ and $(3,4)$ and where, for convenience, we have attached the numerical labels 1,2,3 and 4 to Japan, Britain, West Germany and Italy respectively.

STATISTIC

An obvious way to attempt to identify differences in the averages is to compare the means of the ranks assigned to the samples. Dunn's procedure does just this. The $p=\frac{1}{2}k(k-1)=\frac{1}{2}\times4\times3=6$ absolute differences

$$|D_{ij}| = \left| \frac{R_i}{n_i} - \frac{R_j}{n_j} \right|$$

are first calculated for each of the six pairs of values of (i,j), where R_i and R_j are the sums of the ranks in the ith and jth samples. Clearly if there is a real difference between the ith and jth populations, then D_{ij} will tend to be large. The six differences for our problem are calculated below; recall from earlier in the chapter that $R_1=33$, $R_2=261.5$, $R_3=117$ and $R_4=116.5$ with $n_1=7$, $n_2=13$, $n_3=8$ and $n_4=4$.

Pair (i,j)	$\|D_{ij}\| = \left\| \dfrac{R_i}{n_i} - \dfrac{R_j}{n_j} \right\|$	
(1,2)	$\|D_{12}\| = \left\| \dfrac{33}{7} - \dfrac{261.5}{13} \right\|$	$= 15.40$
(1,3)	$\|D_{13}\| = \left\| \dfrac{33}{7} - \dfrac{117}{8} \right\|$	$= 9.91$
(1,4)	$\|D_{14}\| = \left\| \dfrac{33}{7} - \dfrac{116.5}{4} \right\|$	$= 24.41$
(2,3)	$\|D_{23}\| = \left\| \dfrac{261.5}{13} - \dfrac{117}{8} \right\|$	$= 5.49$
(2,4)	$\|D_{24}\| = \left\| \dfrac{261.5}{13} - \dfrac{116.5}{4} \right\|$	$= 9.01$
(3,4)	$\|D_{34}\| = \left\| \dfrac{117}{8} - \dfrac{116.5}{4} \right\|$	$= 14.50$

Now it can be shown that, under H_0, the standard deviation of any difference D_{ij} is given by

$$\sigma_{ij} = \sqrt{\frac{N(N+1)}{12}\left(\frac{1}{n_i} + \frac{1}{n_j}\right)}$$

and that the mean of D_{ij} is 0. It is also the case that D_{ij} is approximately normally distributed, and so if we divide D_{ij} by σ_{ij} we obtain a statistic T_{ij} which, under H_0, has approximately the standard normal distribution. Recalling that $N=32$, we obtain:

i,j	$\|D_{ij}\|$	σ_{ij}	$\|T_{ij}\|$
1,2	15.40	$\sqrt{\dfrac{32\times33}{12}\left(\dfrac{1}{7} + \dfrac{1}{13}\right)} = 4.40$	3.50
1,3	9.91	$\sqrt{\dfrac{32\times33}{12}\left(\dfrac{1}{7} + \dfrac{1}{8}\right)} = 4.86$	2.04
1,4	24.41	$\sqrt{\dfrac{32\times33}{12}\left(\dfrac{1}{7} + \dfrac{1}{4}\right)} = 5.88$	4.15

Continued

i,j	$|D_{ij}|$	σ_{ij}	$|T_{ij}|$
2,3	5.49	$\sqrt{\dfrac{32\times33}{12}\left(\dfrac{1}{13}+\dfrac{1}{8}\right)}=4.22$	1.30
2,4	9.01	$\sqrt{\dfrac{32\times33}{12}\left(\dfrac{1}{13}+\dfrac{1}{4}\right)}=5.36$	1.68
3.4	14.50	$\sqrt{\dfrac{32\times33}{12}\left(\dfrac{1}{8}+\dfrac{1}{4}\right)}=5.74$	2.53

CRITICAL REGIONS

As we mentioned in the previous section, the statistic T_{ij} is approximately distributed as a standard normal variable. So, since large values of T_{ij} will tend to support the two-sided alternative hypothesis, H_0 will be rejected if

$$|T_{ij}| \geqslant z$$

where z is the percentage point corresponding to some prescribed probability in the standard normal distribution. Let us think how we should choose this probability. If we were only carrying out a single test, this probability would be $\frac{1}{2}\alpha$ (since the test is two-sided). However, in fact we are carrying out six tests here (and in general $\frac{1}{2}k(k-1)$ tests will be performed). Sharing out the risk equally between these tests, the appropriate probability is thus $\frac{1}{2}\alpha/\frac{1}{2}k(k-1) = \alpha/k(k-1)$.

So, taking $\alpha=20\%$ and remembering that $k=4$, we seek that value of z corresponding to an upper probability of $\alpha/k(k-1) = 0.20/12 = 0.0167$. From Table A, we obtain $z=2.128$. Therefore, the H_0 corresponding to ith and jth populations will be rejected if $|T_{ij}|\geqslant2.128$.

To save you the trouble of carrying out this kind of calculation, we give below a table of such critical values of z for $k=3$ to 10 and $\alpha=5\%$ to 30%. From this, you can immediately check that for $\alpha=20\%$ and $k=4$, the critical value is indeed 2.128.

	Significance level					
k	5%	10%	15%	20%	25%	30%
3	2.394	2.128	1.960	1.834	1.731	1.645
4	2.638	2.394	2.241	2.128	2.037	1.960
5	2.807	2.576	2.432	2.326	2.241	2.170
6	2.935	2.713	2.576	2.475	2.394	2.326
7	3.038	2.823	2.690	2.593	2.515	2.450
8	3.125	2.913	2.785	2.690	2.615	2.552
9	3.200	2.990	2.823	2.772	2.700	2.658
10	3.260	3.060	2.933	2.844	2.764	2.713

SOLUTION

Comparing the successive values of $|T_{ij}|$ with the critical value of 2.128, we find significant differences between the following pairs:

(a)   1 and 2, i.e. Japan and Britain;
(b)   1 and 4, i.e. Japan and Italy;
(c)   3 and 4, i.e. West Germany and Italy.

Furthermore, from the direction of the differences, we have evidence that the likelihood of breakdowns is higher for British cars than Japanese, and for Italian cars than Japanese and for Italian cars than West German.

   Results from such a multiple comparisons investigation are often presented in a diagram like the one in Figure 13.1. The populations are written down according to the order of the mean ranks, and lines are drawn to join together any populations that the procedure has failed to separate. These results confirm our previous feelings on these data, and this should give us confidence in the ability of Dunn's procedure to provide a valid analysis of other data, which may not be so easy to interpret at first sight.

Figure 13.1

Ties

We have ignored ties in applying Dunn's procedure to our problem. However, a correction for ties exists and consists of a familiar type of modification to the standard deviation σ_{ij}. The corrected standard deviation σ_{ij}^* is given by:

$$\sigma_{ij}^* = \sqrt{\left(\frac{N(N+1)}{12} - \frac{\Sigma t^3 - \Sigma t}{12(N-1)}\right)\left(\frac{1}{n_i} + \frac{1}{n_j}\right)}$$

where t is the number of ties for a given (tied) value and the summation is taken over all sets of tied values in the data. With our practical problem, the correction is slight; the difference between:

$N(N+1)/12$ and $N(N+1)/12 - (\Sigma t^3 - \Sigma t)/12(N-1)$ being only 0.01.

Assignments

1   Water pollution

In a study of the pollution of English inland waterways, five pike were caught at each of seven locations. The amount of pollution present was assessed by measuring the concentration of copper in the livers of the fish. The table below gives the logarithm of the copper concentration.

Windermere	0.187	0.836	0.704	0.938	0.124
Grasmere	0.449	0.769	0.301	0.045	0.846
River Stour	0.628	0.193	0.810	0.000	0.855
Wimbourne St Giles	0.412	0.286	0.497	0.417	0.337
River Avon	0.243	0.258	−0.276	−0.538	0.041
River Leam	0.134	0.281	0.529	0.305	0.459
River Kennet	0.471	0.371	0.297	0.691	0.535

Task: Investigate these data to examine differences in average copper concentrations between the seven locations. Should there be evidence to suggest such differences, investigate further using Dunn's multiple comparisons procedure.

2 Baby food

A paediatrician conducted an experiment to investigate the claim that three different brands of milk powder (designated A, B and C for anonymity) produce different average weight increases in babies. A sample of 35 babies, all born at a local maternity hospital, were randomly assigned to be fed from birth on one of the brands of milk powder. Their increases in weight (kg) over a fixed period of time are recorded in the following table.

A	B	C
3.24	3.42	3.73
2.22	2.37	3.56
2.40	2.59	3.27
2.58	3.57	2.51
2.40	2.36	3.30
3.49	3.61	3.12
2.68	2.94	3.11
2.15	3.86	3.05
2.30	2.43	3.78
3.21	2.76	2.40
2.86	2.36	2.65
	2.86	3.21

Task: Use an appropriate procedure to test the null hypothesis that the average increases in weight are the same for the three brands of milk powder.

Program 13.1   The Kruskal–Wallis test

```
100 REM *** KRUSKAL-WALLIS TEST ***

110 REM ** INPUT THE NUMBER OF SAMPLES **
120 INPUT "NUMBER OF SAMPLES ( >2 ) ";K
130 DIM M(K),R(K)
140 LET N=0

150 REM ** INPUT SIZE OF SAMPLES & OBSERVATIONS **
160 FOR I=1 TO K
170 PRINT "INPUT SIZE OF SAMPLE ";I
180 INPUT M(I)
190 LET N=N+M(I)
200 NEXT I
210 PRINT
220 PRINT
230 DIM D(N),RK(N)
240 LET L=0
250 FOR I=1 TO K
260 PRINT "INPUT OBSERVATIONS FOR SAMPLE ";I
270 FOR J=1 TO M(I)
280 LET L=L+1
290 INPUT D(L)
300 NEXT J
310 NEXT I
320 GO SUB 1000

330 REM ** CALCULATION OF THE TEST STATISTIC **
340 LET S=0
350 LET L=0
360 FOR I=1 TO K
370 FOR J=1 TO M(I)
380 LET L=L+1
390 LET R(I)=R(I)+RK(L)
400 NEXT J
410 NEXT I
420 FOR I=1 TO K
430 LET S=S +R(I)^2/M(I)
440 NEXT I
450 LET H=12*S/N/(N+1)-3*(N+1)
460 PRINT
470 PRINT "VALUE OF KRUSKAL-WALLIS STATISTIC = ";H

480 REM *** DUNN'S MULTIPLE COMPARISONS ***
490 PRINT
500 PRINT "DIFFERENCES IN MEAN RANKS FOR DUNN'S MULTIPLE COMPARISONS :"
510 PRINT
520 PRINT
530 FOR I=1 TO K
540 LET R(I)=R(I)/M(I)
550 NEXT I
560 FOR I=1 TO K-1
570 FOR J=I+1 TO K
580 LET DF=ABS(R(I)-R(J))/SQRT(N*(N+1)*(1/M(I)+1/M(J))/12)
590 PRINT "DIFFERENCE BETWEEN ";I;" & ";J;" IS ";DF
600 NEXT J
610 NEXT I

1000 REM ** RANK SAMPLE - USE LINES 1000-1140 OF PROGRAM 3.1 **
```

14

More than two (k) related samples

Introduction

The main practical problem we looked at in Chapter 13 was the following: on the basis of samples of cars from Italy, West Germany, Britain and Japan, is there evidence to suggest that these four countries (i.e. populations) produce cars of differing average reliability?

In this chapter we are still asking the same type of question, i.e. is there evidence of real differences between populations? The essential change between this and the last chapter is in the way the populations are sampled. Previously the samples have been independent of each other, i.e. there has been absolutely no connection between the observations in the different samples. In practice, though, it is often the case that observations are related in some way across the samples. For example, suppose a nurse took four readings of the pulses of three patients, these readings being taken at specific times of the day. Typically we might have:

	Patient		
Time (h)	Kathryn	Fiona	Richard
0600	60	62	55
1000	65	66	65
1800	70	80	75
2200	65	72	68

The observations in the $k=3$ samples of pulse readings are not independent, but are related by a common feature: the time of day. It looks as if the time of day has an important influence on the readings – the pulse rates are relatively low first thing in the morning and high in the early evening. Therefore, the effectiveness of our analysis of these data will be reduced unless we take the time of day into account.

The idea of samples being related is not new to us. In Chapter 8 we dealt with the 'matched-pairs' situation, i.e. where the data in two samples were 'matched' or related in pairs. This led to a substantially different analysis from that of two independent samples in Chapter 5. So our topic in this chapter of 'k related samples' is an extension of the matched-pairs concept to more than two samples.

Let us consider another example of k related samples. A seed producer wishes to compare the yields of five ($5=k$) varieties of wheat. Four areas or 'blocks' of land were selected for the experiment and each seed variety was sown on equal-sized plots in each block. The table shows the yields (in kg/plot) of the five varieties:

Block of land	Variety of seed				
	Early Cropper	Wet Resistant	Big Cropper	Prairie Special	New Standard
1	46.7	48.2	50.6	45.6	45.2
2	42.8	43.7	45.7	47.3	39.8
3	50.1	49.1	51.9	48.1	44.6
4	49.2	50.6	52.3	47.6	42.7

Naturally, the producer is interested in finding out if there are any systematic differences between the yields of the five varieties.

Readers who have been trained in 'orthodox' statistical methods will recognize that both of the above examples could be analysed using the classical F-test for two-way analysis of variance, provided of course that the user is willing and able to take the big step of assuming that the samples were taken from normal distributions. However, consider the following situation: the five finalists in a seaside beauty contest were placed in order of beauty by three judges. The results were:

Judge	Contestant				
	A	B	C	D	E
Mayor	4	2	1	5	3
Local celebrity	3	1	2	4	5
Last year's winner	5	1	2	3	2

We see that the data consist simply of ranks and there is no way that they can be considered normally distributed! So, use of the classical F-test is out of the question in this case and we *must* use a distribution-free procedure to deal with such data. Even if, as previously, we do have numerical data available (rather than ranks), but the normality assumption is unjustified, the numbers can of course be converted to ranks and the same distribution-free procedure is still appropriate and valid.

One of the earliest distribution-free tests was designed for the problems we have just seen. Milton Friedman (1937), the renowned economist, introduced a test which now bears his name. This has become well known and widely used, for not only are the required computations fairly easy, but also the test has good performance over a wide range of conditions. We shall examine Freidman's test in detail in this chapter.

Not surprisingly, since 1937 a number of distribution-free competitors to Friedman's test have been devised. However, not many can compete with regard to both power and ease of computation. Nevertheless, we present later in the chapter two very simple procedures – one is particularly easy to apply but has only moderate power, while the other is slightly more involved but yields greater power (sometimes exceeding the power of Friedman's test). Both of these tests are based on the so-called matching principle, which was first investigated by Montemort in 1708, but has only recently been applied in the current context. One reason for introducing these 'match tests' is that they can be applied to quite a wide range of k-sample problems for which it is otherwise difficult to obtain distribution-free procedures.

A note on terminology

A characteristic feature of the k-related-samples problem is that the data may be presented in a tableau of k columns and n rows (say). Many authors refer to the columns as 'treatments' and the rows as 'blocks'; this jargon stems from one of the first main areas of application of the k-related-samples problem, which was in agricultural experiments. It is also for this reason that the term 'randomized block design' is sometimes used (often incorrectly) to describe the situations of this chapter.

FRIEDMAN'S TEST

Introduction

Friedman's test is arithmetically easier than the Kruskal–Wallis test as one has now only to rank the observations within each row rather than ranking all the observations in the (often large) combined sample. As usual with distribution-free procedures, the main theory assumes there are no ties in the data, implying that the samples are drawn from populations having continuous distributions. However, this assumption is frequently relaxed, particularly as the test can easily tolerate a moderate number of ties.

PRACTICAL PROBLEM

A popular weekly photographic magazine reviewed a 200 mm telephoto lens from each of four top Japanese manufacturers. For each of the four lenses, the resolution (in lines per millimetre) at various apertures was recorded. Our concern here is whether the data suggest differences in performance of lenses from the four manufacturers.

The readings in the four samples are related by the apertures, so we are indeed dealing with a problem of related, rather than independent, samples. The reader might justifiably consider this to be a poor experiment where only one lens from each manufacturer is examined. We agree! It would certainly have been preferable to examine more than one lens from each manufacturer; this would have helped to overcome problems caused by manufacturing variations. However, the staff of the magazine designed the experiment – not us! Had the experiment been improved in this way, the identical procedure to that described below could have been carried out on *averages* of the results.

HYPOTHESES

The null hypothesis H_0 is that the four manufacturers produce 200 mm lenses of equal average performance. The alternative hypothesis H_1 is that there are some differences between the average performances of the lenses. Clearly, if evidence is found to support this alternative hypothesis, then a further multiple comparisons investigation may be needed in order to ascertain which of the differences between lenses are significantly large.

A summary of the hypotheses is:

H_0: There is no difference in the average performances of 200 mm lenses from the four manufacturers.

H_1: There are some differences in the average quality of 200 mm lenses from the four manufacturers.

DATA

The table shows the resolutions recorded for the lenses from the four manufacturers (which we shall refer to as A, B, C and D to preserve anonymity) at apertures of $f/2.8$, 4, 5.6, 8 and 11.

Aperture	Manufacturer			
	A	B	C	D
2.8	83	77	88	87
4	92	96	110	109
5.6	124	119	129	125
8	127	123	132	129
11	124	117	122	123

A quick glance at these data might well immediately make you doubt the truth of H_0 – but we shall see!

STATISTIC

The observations *within each row* are ranked from 1 to k (where $k=4$ in this problem). Now, if H_0 is true, we would expect the ranks 1, 2, 3 and 4 to be fairly evenly distributed among the four manufacturers. On the other hand, if there are substantial differences then we would expect to find at least one manufacturer getting consistently high or low ranks. In other words, if H_0 is true then there should be little difference between the average ranks assigned to the four manufacturers, whereas if H_1 is true we would expect to see some relatively large differences between these average ranks.

We will denote the mean of the ranks in columns 1 to k by $\overline{R}_1$, $\overline{R}_2, \ldots, \overline{R}_k$. Observe also that since the k 'treatments' (lenses, in our problem) are ranked from 1 to k for each row (i.e. for each aperture), the average overall rank $\overline{R}$, say, must be equal to $\frac{1}{2}(k+1)$ since this is the average of the numbers $1, 2, \ldots, k$. In Friedman's test we compare each of the average ranks $\overline{R}_1, \overline{R}_2, \ldots, \overline{R}_k$ with the overall average rank $\overline{R}$ by forming the differences $\overline{R}_1-\overline{R}, \overline{R}_2-\overline{R}, \ldots, \overline{R}_k-\overline{R}$. Friedman's statistic is then based on the sum of the squares of these differences, namely

$$S = \sum_{j=1}^{k} (\overline{R}_j-\overline{R})^2$$

If H_0 is true, this statistic should be fairly small, for then the $\overline{R}_j$ values will generally be close to $\overline{R}$. But if there are sizeable differences between the column mean ranks, thus indicating the truth of H_1, then S will be relatively large.

Let us put this idea into practice with the lenses data. Although we shall evolve Friedman's statistic by following the above idea, we shall later give an alternative formula, which most people find more convenient to use.

Ranking the observations within each row gives the following table of ranks. (Notice how these ranks immediately reveal a clearer picture about the relative performance of the lenses even before we embark on the test itself.)

	A	B	C	D
	2	1	4	3
	1	2	4	3
	2	1	4	3
	2	1	4	3
	4	1	2	3
sum of ranks	11	6	18	15
mean, $\overline{R}_j$	2.2	1.2	3.6	3.0

The overall mean $\overline{R}$ of the ranks is $\frac{1}{2}(k+1) = \frac{1}{2}(4+1) = 2\frac{1}{2}$. So we calculate S as follows:

$$S = \sum_{j=1}^{4} (\overline{R}_j - \overline{R})^2 = (2.2-2.5)^2 + (1.2-2.5)^2 + (3.6-2.5)^2 + (3.0-2.5)^2$$

$$= 3.24$$

Friedman's statistic M is not actually S itself but the following multiple of S:

$$M = \frac{12n}{k(k+1)} S$$

In our example, $k=4$ and $n=5$, and so we have

$$M = \frac{12 \times 5}{4 \times 5} S = 3S = 3 \times 3.24 = 9.72$$

The reason we use this particular multiple of S is that the resulting statistic M then behaves, when H_0 is true, approximately like a chi-squared variable. This allows us to use chi-squared tables to obtain approximate critical values for cases not covered by Table O (or the table on page 34 in *EST*).

The alternative version of Friedman's statistic mentioned above, which often shortens the computation, is

$$M = \frac{12}{nk(k+1)} \sum_{j=1}^{k} R_j^2 - 3n(k+1)$$

where R_j is the sum of the ranks in column j. Referring back to the table of ranks we see that $R_1=11$, $R_2=6$, $R_3=18$ and $R_4=15$. Hence the alternative formula gives

$$M = \frac{12}{5 \times 4 \times 5} (11^2 + 6^2 + 18^2 + 15^2) - 3 \times 5 \times 5 = 9.72$$

just as before.

CRITICAL REGIONS

In the previous section, we observed that large values of the sum of squares, and hence M, would support the claim of the alternative hypothesis that there are differences in average performance between the manufacturers. Thus H_0 will be rejected in favour of H_1 if

$$M \geq \text{critical value}$$

Critical values of M are tabulated on page 34 of *EST* for $k=3$ to 6 and n up to 25. Table O is an abbreviated version of this table.

For values of k or n not included in either table, approximate critical values are obtainable from the chi-squared distribution (Table B) using $k-1$ degrees of freedom and α_1 significance levels (for k between 3 and 6, they are also given in Table O).

In our particular problem, $k=4$ and $n=5$, and so we are able to use Table O. The critical regions for $\alpha=5\%$ and 1% are $M \geq 7.800$ and $M \geq 9.960$ respectively.

SOLUTION

A cursory glance at the ranked data suggests that a rejection of H_0 might be appropriate, and indeed this turns out to be so. The value $M=9.72$ is in the 5% critical region, though it does not quite make the 1% region. (In fact, the more detailed tables in *EST* show that the result is significant at the 2% level.) So we have quite strong evidence to support the claim that there are some differences in the quality of lenses from the four manufacturers.

Discussion

In our particular problem, we applied Friedman's statistic to the lenses data to see whether there is evidence of differences in average quality between the four manufacturers. However, one of the advantages of organizing the data so that the samples are related is that we can check for significant differences between the rows (apertures) as well as between the columns (manufacturers). In other words, for our problem we could also test the null hypothesis that there are no average differences in the lens performances throughout the aperture range against the alternative hypothesis that the average performance does differ according to the aperture used. In this case we would rank the data within each column, giving the following table of ranks:

	Manufacturer			
Aperture	A	B	C	D
2.8	1	1	1	1
4	2	2	2	2
5.6	3.5	4	4	4
8	5	5	5	5
11	3.5	3	3	3

Friedman's test would then be applied with $k=5$ and $n=4$. Most photographers would agree with this alternative hypothesis, and you may like to verify that Friedman's test does indeed find strong evidence to support it.

Null distributions

As in the previous chapter, the null hypothesis claims that there are no differences between the averages of the k populations. As usual, we further assume there to be no other differences either – except here, for differences caused by the 'rows' factor. Since we are only ranking the observations within the rows, we may argue that, under H_0, in every row, each of the $k!$ possible arrangements of the ranks $1, 2, \ldots, k$ is equally likely to occur. Since we have n rows each with k ranks, there are altogether $(k!)^n$ possible configurations of ranks. By calculating the value of M for each of these configurations we can build up the frequency distribution for M; the null distribution is then obtained by dividing these frequencies by the total number of configurations (i.e. by $(k!)^n$).

We illustrate this procedure with the case of $k=3$ and $n=3$. Although there are $(k!)^n=(3!)^3=216$ configurations of three rows of three ranks, we need only consider the $(k!)^{n-1}=6^2=36$ of them obtained by fixing the first row as 1 2 3. (Can you see why? Note that, if you swap the columns around in any given configuration, the value of M remains unchanged.) To save space, rather than listing all 36 distinct possibilities, we present just a few to give you the idea. So a partial table of ranks for $k=3$, $n=3$ is as follows:

	1 2 3	1 2 3	1 2 3	1 2 3	1 2 3	1 2 3
	1 2 3	1 2 3	1 2 3	1 2 3	1 2 3	1 2 3
	1 2 3	1 3 2	2 1 3	2 3 1	3 1 2	3 2 1
$R_j = 369$	378	459	477	558	567	
$M = 6$	4.667	4.667	2	2	0.667	

	1 2 3	1 2 3	1 2 3	1 2 3	1 2 3	1 2 3
	1 3 2	1 3 2	1 3 2	1 3 2	1 3 2	1 3 2
	1 2 3	1 3 2	2 1 3	2 3 1	3 1 2	3 2 1
$R_j = 378$	387	468	486	567	576	
$M = 4.667$	4.667	2.667	2.667	0.667	0.667	

Continuing in this way until all 36 configurations have been recorded, we eventually obtain the following frequency distribution of M:

Value of M	Frequency
6	1
4.667	6
2.667	6
2	6
0.667	15
0	2

From this table we can deduce that, under H_0,

$$\text{Prob}(M=0) \quad = \quad 2/36$$
$$\text{Prob}(M=0.667) = 15/36$$
$$\text{Prob}(M=2) \quad = \quad 6/36$$
$$\text{Prob}(M=2.667) = \quad 6/36$$
$$\text{Prob}(M=4.667) = \quad 6/36$$
$$\text{Prob}(M=6) \quad = \quad 1/36$$

Using these probabilities, we are able to construct a table of upper-tail probabilities $\text{Prob}(M \geqslant m)$, which, since the critical regions for this test are of the form $M \geqslant$ constant, can then be used to obtain the critical values. Thus the table of $\text{Prob}(M \geqslant m)$ for $k=3, n=3$ is as follows:

m	$\text{Prob}(M \geqslant m)$
6	0.0278
4.667	0.1945
2.667	0.3612
2	0.5279
0.667	0.9446
0	1

The table on page 34 of *EST* gives $M \geqslant 6$ (i.e. $M=6$) as the best conservative critical region for $\alpha = 10\%$ and 5%, and gives no region for $\alpha = 2\%$ and 1%. The above table confirms these entries; the next larger critical region, $M \geqslant 4.667$, corresponds to a significance level of nearly 20%, and so cannot be considered. The probability that $M=6$ is 0.0278, i.e. 2.78%, which is of course less than 5% and 10% but greater than 2% and 1%. (Table O just gives details for $\alpha = 5\%$ and 1%.)

The above process is obviously very tedious, but recurrence methods may be used to carry out the computations more efficiently. There are also some excellent approximate methods available, and these two approaches have been used to provide Table O and the table in *EST*.

Large sample sizes

As we mentioned in the 'Critical regions' section, for values of k or n not included in Table O, approximate critical values can be obtained from the chi-squared distribution using $k-1$ degrees of freedom. Thus, for example, if $k=7$ then the chi-squared distribution with $k-1=6$ degrees of freedom gives approximate critical values for $\alpha = 5\%$ and 1% as 12.592 and 16.812 respectively.

Treatment of ties

We are not usually troubled much by tied observations when using Friedman's test because of the fact that comparisons are now only being made within rows rather than over the data as a whole as in the Kruskal–Wallis test.

If equal observations are found in the same row, then we assign to them average rank values as usual. With the number of such ties normally being very small, this is usually sufficient to deal with the problem.

However, if, exceptionally, there are a lot of such tied observations, then the null distribution of M is noticeably affected, and we shall need to take this into account. The usual method is to compute a familiar-looking correction factor C and then modify the Friedman statistic to $M^* = M/C$.

The correction factor C is calculated as follows. Denoting by t the number of observations contributing to a tie, we form $t^* = t^3 - t$. (Remember we are now only concerned with ties within rows, and so it will probably be rare for t to exceed 3.) We go through all the rows, adding up such t^* for any ties found, and denote the total of these t^* by T. Then the correction factor C is given by

$$C = 1 - \frac{T}{n(k^3 - k)}$$

To illustrate the procedure, consider the following data, where $k=4$ and $n=3$:

		Treatment		
Row	A	B	C	D
1	8.5	8.9	8.8	8.8
2	8.2	8.4	8.2	8.2
3	8.9	9.1	9.1	8.9

These can be ranked as follows:

		Treatment		
Row	A	B	C	D
1	1	4	$2\frac{1}{2}$	$2\frac{1}{2}$
2	2	4	2	2
3	$1\frac{1}{2}$	$3\frac{1}{2}$	$3\frac{1}{2}$	$1\frac{1}{2}$
rank sums	$4\frac{1}{2}$	$11\frac{1}{2}$	8	6

Then the usual calculation for Friedman's statistic gives $M=5.5$.

Table O shows the 5% critical region to be $M \geqslant 7.4$, so 5.5 is not significant. However, let us now compute the correction factor C in order to evaluate the modified statistic, M^*. In the first row there is just one pair of tied observations, and so $t=2$ and $t^*=6$. In the second row, three observations are tied, giving $t=3$ and $t^*=24$; and in the final row, there are two pairs of tied observations and so $t^*=6$ twice. Hence $t=6+24+6+6=42$, and so

$$C = 1 - \frac{T}{n(k^3 - k)} = 1 - \frac{42}{3(4^3 - 4)} = \frac{23}{30} = 0.7667$$

This gives $M^* = 5.5/0.7667 = 7.17$. This is close to, but does not quite reach, the 5% critical region. However, from page 34 of EST, we see that the 10% critical region is $M \geqslant 6.6$ (or rather $M^* \geqslant 6.6$), and so the modified statistic is well inside this region indicating that, perhaps there is after all, some significant evidence here.

THE MATCH TESTS

The authors have developed two simple tests for k related samples; the tests are based on a well known 'matching' principle. To begin, let us take a look at the general ideas on which the match statistics (which we shall call M_1 and M_2) are founded. Consider the following set of ranks from data arranged in five columns and two rows (which corresponds to $k=5$ treatments and $n=2$ rows in the current context):

$$
\begin{array}{ccccc}
1 & 3 & 5 & 4 & 2 \\
2 & 4 & 5 & 1 & 3
\end{array}
$$

We say there is a match between two ranks in the same column if those ranks are identical. In the above table, there is just one match; it occurs between the '5's in the third column. For the M_2 statistic we also use *near-matches*; we have a *near-match* between two corresponding ranks if they differ by *one*. In the above table, there are three near-matches; they occur in columns 1, 2 and 5.

The statistic M_1 uses only matches and not near-matches. The test based on M_1 may be described as 'quick and easy' since, besides involving only very simple computations, it has the added advantage that critical values are almost independent of the number of column (treatments) in the experiment. Not surprisingly, the power of this test is lower than that of the test based on the M_2 statistic, which incorporates the extra information of near-matches. In fact, the power of the M_2 test has been shown to be close to (and sometimes better than) Friedman's test.

Let us see how these ideas can be applied to the practical problem of the camera lens manufacturers.

HYPOTHESES

These are the same as before.

STATISTICS

We recall that the ranks of the data are:

	Manufacturer			
Aperture	A	B	C	D
2.8	2	1	4	3
4	1	2	4	3
5.6	2	1	4	3
8	2	1	4	3
11	4	1	2	3

Now, if the lenses differ markedly, we would expect some of the columns to contain mainly high or low ranks. This would result in a relatively large number of matches and/or near-matches. On the other hand, if H_0 is true, we would expect there to be only a small number of matches and/or near-matches.

Now let us see the details, beginning with the M_1 statistic. We first count the number of matches obtained when rows 2, 3, 4 and 5 are compared in turn with row 1; in other words, we take the top row as a 'reference row', and count the number of times that ranks in this reference row are repeated in the same columns in the remaining rows. Doing this, we find a total of $2+4+4+2=12$ matches. Next, row 2 is used as the reference row and the remaining rows 3, 4 and 5 are compared with it; this gives $2+2+1=5$ matches. Repeating the process with row 3 as the reference row gives $4+2=6$ matches and finally, with row 4 as the reference row we get 2 matches. The value of M_1 is given by the total number of matches from all these comparisons. So we obtain

$$M_1 = 12+5+6+2 = 25$$

Now we consider the second statistic M_2. We follow a similar procedure for doing the comparisons but this time we record the number of near-matches as well as the number of matches. We give these values in the following table.

Reference row	Number of matches	Number of near matches
1	$2 + 4 + 4 + 2 = 12$	$2 + 0 + 0 + 0 = 2$
2	$2 + 2 + 1 = 5$	$2 + 2 + 1 = 5$
3	$4 + 2 = 6$	$0 + 0 = 0$
4	$2 = 2$	$0 = 0$
totals	25	7

M_2 is defined as *the number of matches plus half the number of near-matches* (since near-matches represent 'near-misses' it is only right that they do not contribute the same amount as matches). So we have,

$$M_2 = \text{(number of matches)} + \tfrac{1}{2}\text{(number of near-matches)}$$
$$= 25 + 3\tfrac{1}{2} = 28\tfrac{1}{2}$$

CRITICAL REGIONS

M_1 test
Since it is large values of M_1 that are significant, the null hypothesis is rejected in favour of the alternative hypothesis if

$$M_1 \geqslant \text{critical value}$$

Critical values of M_1 are given in Table P for $k=3$ to 6 and n up to 20.

In our problem, we have $k=4$ and $n=5$ and so we see that the critical regions for $\alpha=5\%$ and 1% are $M_1\geqslant17$ and $M_1\geqslant20$ respectively.

M_2 test

As with M_1, large values of M_2 support the alternative hypothesis, and so H_0 is rejected in favour of H_1 if

$$M_2 \geqslant \text{critical value}$$

Table Q gives critical values of M_2 for $k=3$ to 6 and n up to 20.

In our problem, we have $k=4$ and $n=5$, and so Table Q shows that H_0 is rejected in favour of H_1 if $M_2\geqslant23$ and $M_2\geqslant26.5$ at the 5% and 1% significance levels respectively.

SOLUTION

Both match tests, M_1 and the more powerful M_2, give results that are significant at better than the 1% level. In other words, both tests indicate strong evidence supporting the claim that the lens manufacturers produce lenses of differing average qualities.

Discussion

It is interesting to note that both the match tests give results that are significant at the 1% level whereas Friedman's test only gave significance at about the 2% level. One should not be too surprised by this; after all, the match statistics and Friedman's statistic are using different aspects of the information in the ranks. It is not at all unusual for a good 'quick' test to produce better levels of significance than more 'orthodox' tests.

The match tests, which, at the time of writing, have only recently been developed, appear to have much in their favour. The computations are simple, and approximate critical values are available in a relatively 'compact' form. These are properties shared by some of the quick tests in earlier chapters, e.g. Tukey's test in Chapter 5. As with these other quick tests, therefore, the match tests may prove particularly attractive to less numerately skilled workers.

The matching principle also has a further advantage, of perhaps even more importance. This is that it can be applied to more complex experiments for which, at present, other distribution-free methods currently seem to be either unworkable or even unavailable (for details see Worthington 1982). An illustration of the match tests to more complex situations is given in Chapter 16.

Treatment of ties

We follow the usual procedure of giving tied observations a rank equal to the average of the ranks which would otherwise have been assigned to those tied observations. Then we need to decide how much these average ranks should contribute (if anything) to the values of M_1 and M_2. We shall discuss the two statistics in turn.

Suppose that we are comparing two observations whose ranks are r_1 and r_2. A reasonable assessment of the contributions to M_1 is the following:

$$\text{if} \quad |r_1 - r_2| \begin{cases} = 0 & \text{then contribute 1 (as usual)} \\ = \tfrac{1}{2} & \text{then contribute } \tfrac{1}{2} \\ > \tfrac{1}{2} & \text{then contribute 0} \end{cases}$$

To illustrate this procedure, consider the following data for seven columns and two rows:

Row 1	2.1	9.5	11.0	9.5	5.4	9.5	9.5
Row 2	3.2	6.1	10.3	6.1	4.0	6.1	8.0

These can be ranked as follows:

	Row 1	1	$4\tfrac{1}{2}$	7	$4\tfrac{1}{2}$	2	$4\tfrac{1}{2}$	$4\tfrac{1}{2}$
	Row 2	1	4	7	4	2	4	6
Contribution to M_1		1	$\tfrac{1}{2}$	1	$\tfrac{1}{2}$	1	$\tfrac{1}{2}$	0

which gives $M_1 = 4\tfrac{1}{2}$.

For the M_2 statistic we recommend the following procedure when ties are present:

$$\text{if} \quad |r_1 - r_2| \begin{cases} = 0 & \text{then contribute 1} \\ \left.\begin{array}{l} = \tfrac{1}{2} \\ = 1 \\ = 1\tfrac{1}{2} \end{array}\right\} & \text{then contribute } \tfrac{1}{2} \\ > 1\tfrac{1}{2} & \text{then contribute 0} \end{cases}$$

Let us see what this procedure produces for M_2 using the same data as above. We have the following ranks:

	Row 1	1	$4\tfrac{1}{2}$	7	$4\tfrac{1}{2}$	2	$4\tfrac{1}{2}$	$4\tfrac{1}{2}$
	Row 2	1	·4	7	4	2	4	6
Contribution to M_2		1	$\tfrac{1}{2}$	1	$\tfrac{1}{2}$	1	$\tfrac{1}{2}$	$\tfrac{1}{2}$

which gives $M_2 = 5$.

Null distributions

The argument by which we derive the null distributions of the match statistics is the same as with Friedman's statistic. That is, in each row, any one of the $k!$ possible arrangements of the k ranks is equally likely to occur under H_0. So we may build up a frequency distribution for M_1 and M_2 in the case of n rows of k ranks by calculating the value of M_1 and M_2 for each of the $(k!)^n$ possible configuraions. (Or again, without loss of generality, one may 'fix' the first row, leaving $(k!)^{n-1}$ configurations to examine.) The null probability distribution is then found by dividing the frequencies by the total number of such configurations, $(k!)^{n-1}$. Since this procedure is so like that for Friedman's statistic, we leave the details for you to check. As an example, the null distributions of M_1 and M_2 for $k=3$ and $n=3$ are given below for you to verify:

m	0	2	3	5	9
Prob($M_1=m$)	0.056	0.500	0.167	0.250	0.028
Prob($M_1 \geqslant m$)	1	0.944	0.444	0.278	0.028

m	3	4	5	7	9
Prob($M_2=m$)	0.056	0.333	0.417	0.167	0.028
Prob($M_2 \geqslant m$)	1	0.944	0.611	0.194	0.028

Large sample sizes

M_1 *test* For values of k or n not included in Table P, two useful approximate methods of finding critical values are available:

(a) If $k \geqslant 4$ then approximate critical values can be obtained from the Poisson distribution of mean $\frac{1}{2}n(n-1)$. Clearly, these critical values are not dependent on the number of columns k. Below we present a table of critical values for $n=3$ to 20 at significance levels $\alpha=5\%$ and 1% based on this approximation.

	Significance level			Significance level	
n	5%	1%	n	5%	1%
3	7	9	12	81	87
4	11	13	13	94	100
5	16	19	14	108	115
6	23	26	15	123	131
7	30	33	16	139	147
8	38	42	17	156	165
9	47	52	18	175	183
10	57	62	19	194	203
11	68	74	20	214	224

(b) If n is large then M_1 is approximately normally distributed with mean and variance both equal to $\frac{1}{2}n(n-1)$. So if z denotes the boundary of the right-hand tail area of α in the standard normal distribution, for example $z=1.6449$ if $\alpha=5\%$ (see Table A), then we approximate the 5% critical value for M_1 as

$$1.6449\sqrt{\tfrac{1}{2}n(n-1)} + \tfrac{1}{2}n(n-1) + \tfrac{1}{2}$$

the '$+\frac{1}{2}$' being incorporated as a continuity correction. So, for example, with $n=20$, $\frac{1}{2}n(n-1) = \frac{1}{2}\times20\times19 = 190$ and thus the 5% approximate critical value is

$1.6449\sqrt{190} + 190 + \frac{1}{2} = 213.7 = 214$ effectively, as shown in the table.

M_2 *test* For $k \geqslant 4$, approximate critical values of M_2 may be obtained using the normal distribution. For a significance level α and with z defined as above, the approximate critical value for M_2 is given by

$$z\sigma + \mu + \tfrac{1}{2}$$

where $\mu = \frac{1}{2}n(n-1)(2-1/k)$ and

$$\sigma = \sqrt{\frac{n(n-1)(3k^3-9k^2+6k+22)}{4k^2(k-1)}}$$

So, for example, with $k=4$ and $n=10$, $\mu=78.75$ and $\sigma=6.64$, giving a 5% approximate critical value as $1.6449 \times 6.64 + 78.75 + \frac{1}{2} = 90.2 = 91$ effectively.

MULTIPLE COMPARISONS

Conclusions such as 'there is evidence at a 5% (or 1%) level of significance to support the claim that the k population averages are not all equal' should not be regarded as the end of the story. Again, it is natural to follow such conclusions by looking for evidence of 'which populations are different from which?'. In Chapter 13, we used Dunn's multiple comparison method to answer such a question, and we will use the same method here.

With k populations under scrutiny, there are $\frac{1}{2}k(k-1)$ paired comparisons to be performed. Hence there are $\frac{1}{2}k(k-1)$ sets of hypotheses of the form:

$H_0^{(ij)}$: There is no difference between the ith and jth populations.
$H_1^{(ij)}$: There is a difference between the ith and jth populations.

where $i,j=1,2,\ldots,k$ and $i<j$.

The same comments regarding the overall significance level applies in this situation as in Chapter 13.

PRACTICAL PROBLEM

To illustrate the idea of multiple comparisons with k related samples, we return to the data on the four lens manufacturers. This is an appropriate situation to explore further since we have previously shown there to be evidence of differences in lens quality between the manufacturers.

HYPOTHESES

Appropriate hypotheses for this problem are:

$H_0^{(ij)}$: The ith and jth manufacturers produce lenses of equal average performance.

$H_1^{(ij)}$: Lenses from the ith and jth manufacturers differ in average quality.

where $i,j=1,2,3$ and 4 and $i<j$.

DATA

For convenience, we reproduce the ranked data below:

	A	B	C	D
	2	1	4	3
	1	2	4	3
	2	1	4	3
	2	1	4	3
	4	1	2	3
rank sums	11	6	18	15

STATISTIC

As we are working with a table of ranks, we base our procedure on the absolute differences $|D_{ij}| = |R_i - R_j|$, where R_i and R_j are the rank sums of the ith and jth columns, to examine a possible difference between the ith and jth populations. Unlike the equivalent procedure for k independent samples (see Ch. 13), there is no need to use mean ranks here since the number of ranks in each sample is always the same (namely, n). If there is no real difference between the two populations, $|D_{ij}|$ is likely to be small; on the other hand, a substantial difference between the ith and jth populations will tend to produce a large value of $|D_{ij}|$.

The $\frac{1}{2}k(k-1)=6$ differences for the above data are:

$$|D_{12}| = |R_1 - R_2| = 5$$
$$|D_{13}| = |R_1 - R_3| = 7$$
$$|D_{14}| = |R_1 - R_4| = 4$$
$$|D_{23}| = |R_2 - R_3| = 12$$
$$|D_{24}| = |R_2 - R_4| = 9$$
$$|D_{34}| = |R_3 - R_4| = 3$$

As with the multiple comparison procedure for k independent samples, the differences D_{ij} are approximately normally distributed, now with mean 0 and standard deviation $\sqrt{nk(k+1)/6}$. So if we divide each D_{ij} by the standard deviation $\sqrt{5 \times 4 \times 5/6} = 4.0824$ we obtain a 'standardized' statistic T_{ij}. The values of $|T_{ij}|$ are:

$$|T_{12}| = 1.2247$$
$$|T_{13}| = 1.7146$$
$$|T_{14}| = 0.9798$$
$$|T_{23}| = 2.9394$$
$$|T_{24}| = 2.2045$$
$$|T_{34}| = 0.7348$$

CRITICAL REGIONS

Since we conclude that the ith and jth populations differ if $|D_{ij}|=|R_i-R_j|$ is large, and consequently if $|T_{ij}|$ is large, the critical regions will take the form

$$|T_{ij}| \geqslant z$$

where z is the standard normal value corresponding to a single-tail probability of $\alpha/k(k-1)$. (The argument for this being the probability is identical to that in Chapter 13.)

For our example, taking $\alpha=20\%$, z must correspond to a probability of $\alpha/k(k-1)=0.20/12=0.067$. Table A gives $z=2.128$ and so $H_0^{(ij)}$ is rejected in favour of $H_1^{(ij)}$ if

$$|T_{ij}| \geqslant 2.128$$

SOLUTION

Comparing each of the six values of $|T_{ij}|$ reveals that there are significant differences between manufacturers:

(a) B and C, with the lenses from C having a higher resolution than those from B;
(b) B and D, with the lenses from D having a higher resolution than those from B.

We can represent this result pictorially as in Figure 14.1.

Figure 14.1

Assignments

1 Pulse readings

Consider the situation presented at the beginning of this chapter. A nurse took four readings of the pulses of three patients, the readings being obtained at specific times of the day. The data given were:

	Patient		
Time (h)	Kathryn	Fiona	Richard
0600	60	62	55
1000	65	66	65
1800	70	80	75
2200	65	72	68

Task: Analyse these data to see whether pulse readings differ significantly between (a) the patients and (b) the times of day.

2 Animal diet

In 1968, Koch and Sen ('Some aspects of the statistical analysis of the mixed model', *Biometrics* **24**, 27–48) examined the results of experiments undertaken at the Department of Pathology, Duke University Medical Centre, North Carolina by Dr N. Kaufmann and Dr J. V. Klavins. In one of their experiments, 16 animals were randomly placed into one of two groups – an experimental group which received ethionine in their diets, and a control group. The liver of each animal was divided into two parts, one of which was treated with radioactive iron and oxygen, and the other with radioactive iron and nitrogen. The data consist of the amount of iron absorbed by the variously treated liver portions; in the table the treatments are denoted by EO (ethionine–oxygen), EN (ethionine–nitrogen), CO (control–oxygen) and CN (control–nitrogen).

Pair	EO	EN	CO	CN
1	38.43	31.47	36.09	32.53
2	36.09	29.89	34.01	27.73
3	34.49	34.50	36.54	29.51
4	37.44	38.86	39.87	33.03
5	35.53	32.69	33.38	29.88
6	32.35	32.69	36.07	29.29
7	31.54	31.89	35.88	31.53
8	33.37	33.26	34.17	30.16

Task: Analyse these data to see whether there are significant differences in the amounts of iron absorbed in livers subjected to the four treatments. Should you conclude that differences do exist, then perform Dunn's multiple comparison procedure.

3   Chemical analysis

Four students are each given two samples of four specimens to analyse. The data give the percentage by weight of a certain ingredient.

	Student			
Specimen	A	B	C	D
1	12.0	13.8	16.5	18.0
	16.2	15.8	12.0	15.0
2	18.2	18.5	15.9	14.5
	13.6	15.0	19.7	19.7
3	16.6	16.7	18.0	18.0
	16.8	15.2	18.4	18.1
4	17.0	18.7	17.6	20.2
	17.6	18.3	17.5	19.8

Task: Replace each of the 16 pairs of results with an average (usually the mean or median; here, with just two observations to average, the mean and the median are equal) and then carry out an analysis to see whether there are significant differences in the results between (a) the students and (b) the specimens.

Program 14.1   Friedman's test

```
100 REM *** FRIEDMAN'S  TEST ***

110 REM ** INPUT NUMBER OF TREATMENTS AND BLOCKS **
120 INPUT "NUMBER OF TREATMENTS AND BLOCKS ";K,N
130 DIM A(N,K),RK(N,K),R(K)

140 REM ** INPUT DATA **
150 FOR I=1 TO N
160 PRINT "INPUT THE OBSERVATIONS FOR BLOCK ";I
170 FOR J=1 TO K
180 INPUT A(I,J)
190 NEXT J
200 NEXT I

210 REM ** RANK DATA **
220 GO SUB 1000
```

```
230 REM ** CALCULATION OF TEST STATISTIC **
240 FOR I=1 TO K
250 LET R(I)=0
260 NEXT I
270 LET SUM=0
280 FOR I=1 TO K
290 FOR J=1 TO N
300 LET R(I)=RK(J,I)+R(I)
310 NEXT J
320 LET SUM=SUM+R(I)^2
330 NEXT I
340 LET M=12*SUM/(N*K*(K+1))-3*N*(K+1)
350 PRINT
360 PRINT "VALUE OF FRIEDMAN'S STATISTIC IS ";M

370 REM ** MULTIPLE COMPARISONS **
380 PRINT
390 PRINT "THE RANK DIFFERENCES FOR MULTIPLE COMPARISONS ARE:"
400 FOR I=1 TO K-1
410 FOR J=I+1 TO K
420 PRINT "D";I;J;" = ";ABS(R(I)-R(J))
430 NEXT J
440 NEXT I
450 PRINT
460 INPUT "INPUT THE VALUE OF Z ";Z
470 LET X=Z*SQRT(N*K*(K+1)/6)
480 PRINT "REJECT Ho IF ANY DIFFERENCE IS GREATER THAN ";X
490 STOP

1000 REM ** WITHIN-BLOCK RANKS **
1010 FOR I1 = 1 TO N
1020 FOR I=1 TO K
1030 LET T=0
1040 LET S=0
1050 LET C=A(I1,I)
1060 FOR J=1 TO K
1070 IF A(I1,J) > C THEN GO TO 1120
1080 IF A(I1,J) < C THEN GO TO 1110
1090 LET S=S+1
1100 GO TO 1120
1110 LET T=T+1

1120 NEXT J
1130 LET RK(I1,I)=T + (S + 1)/2
1140 NEXT I
1150 NEXT I1
1160 RETURN
```

Program 14.2   The match tests

```
100 REM *** MATCH TESTS - REPLACE LINES 230-360 OF PROGRAM 14.1 WITH: ***

230 REM ** CALCULATION OF TEST STATISTIC **
240 LET M1=0
250 LET M2=0
260 FOR I=1 TO N-1
270 FOR J=I+1 TO N
280 FOR G=1 TO K
290 IF RK(I,G)=RK(J,G) THEN LET M1=M1+1
300 LET RD=ABS(RK(I,G)-RK(J,G))
310 IF RD=0.5 THEN LET M1=M1+0.5
320 IF RD>0 AND RD<=1.5 THEN LET M2=M2+0.5
330 NEXT G
340 NEXT J
345 NEXT I
350 LET M2=M2+M1
360 PRINT "VALUES OF M1 AND M2 ARE ";M1;" AND ";M2

500 REM ** APPROXIMATE CRITICAL VALUES **
510 IF N<=20 AND K<=6 THEN STOP
520 INPUT "PERCENTAGE POINT OF STANDARD NORMAL DISTRIBUTION ";Z

530 REM ** VALUES FOR M1 **
540 LET B=N*(N-1)/2
550 PRINT "APPROXIMATE CRITICAL VALUE FOR M1 = ";Z*SQRT(B)+B+0.5

560 REM ** VALUES FOR M2 **
570 LET M=B*(2-1/K)
580 LET SD=SQRT(B*(3*K^3-9*K^2+6*K+22)/(4*K^2*(K-1)))
590 PRINT "APPROXIMATE CRITICAL VALUE FOR M2 = ";Z*SD+M+0.5
```

15

More than two (k) samples – ordered alternative hypothesis

Introduction

When discussing two-sample problems in Chapter 5, we saw that the form of the alternative hypothesis could be one of two possibilities:

(a) H_1: $\phi_1 \neq \phi_2$
(b) H_1: $\phi_1 > \phi_2$ (or $\phi_1 < \phi_2$)

where ϕ_1 and ϕ_2 are the two population medians.

The first type, corresponding to a two-sided test, is a general statement that there is some difference between the two population medians. In the k-sample problems of the previous two chapters, the equivalent alternative hypothesis is:

H_1: Not all of $\phi_1, \phi_2, \ldots, \phi_k$ are equal

where $\phi_1, \phi_2, \ldots, \phi_k$ are the k population medians. That is to say, we have a general statement that there are *some* differences among the k population averages.

Now consider the second type of alternative hypothesis, which corresponds to one-sided tests. Here we have a *more specific* statement saying that the median of one population is greater than the median of the other. Is there an equivalent statement for the k-sample problem? The answer is yes; we can have an alternative hypothesis of the form:

H_1: $\phi_1 > \phi_2 > \ldots > \phi_k$ (or $\phi_1 < \phi_2 < \ldots < \phi_k$).

This alternative hypothesis therefore specifies the *order* of any differences which may exist between the population medians. Such a statement is generally known as an *ordered* alternative hypothesis so as to clearly distinguish this situation from that described by the more *general* alternative hypothesis in the previous two chapters. (More accurately, this alternative hypothesis should be written using $\geq$ instead of $>$, with the proviso that at least one of the inequalities should be strict. For convenience, the simpler form of H_1 will be used in the text, but this type of interpretation will always be appropriate. Note also that if the desired H_1 refers to some other ordering of the populations, it can be expressed in the form indicated in the text by simply renaming (renumbering) the populations and samples.)

The decision to have an ordered alternative hypothesis rather than a general alternative is dictated by the circumstances of the situation being examined. For example, the 'treatments' might be a number of increasingly expensive forms of advertising, and a natural alternative hypothesis might be that sales increase according to the advertising costs. Or we might simply want to test our own personal opinions as to the order of differences that exist. Or, in an agricultural experiment, we might want to test the alternative hypothesis that average yields increase according to the amount of a certain nutrient added to the growing compound.

In this chapter, we shall consider procedures for dealing with ordered alternatives for both independent and related samples.

THE TERPSTRA–JONCKHEERE TEST FOR k (>2) INDEPENDENT SAMPLES

Introduction

Although there are quite a few procedures available for the testing k independent samples with an ordered alternative hypothesis, the best (combining both ease and power) is probably T. J. Terpstra's (1952) test. The same test was also developed, quite independently, by A. R. Jonckheere (1954). Jonckheere also pointed out an interesting application of such a test to time series studies where observations on some items are taken at each of k successive time points and evidence is sought of an upward or downward trend.

Before proceeding further, we should remind ourselves just why the Kruskal–Wallis test is inappropriate for testing an ordered H_1 of the form

$$H_1: \phi_1 > \phi_2 > \ldots > \phi_k \quad (\text{or } \phi_1 < \phi_2 < \ldots < \phi_k).$$

The Kruskal–Wallis test will reject H_0 whenever there is sufficient difference between the rank sums, *irrespective* of their order; thus a significant result in the Kruskal–Wallis test cannot be held as evidence for a *particular* ordered H_1.

PRACTICAL PROBLEM

It is often presumed that more expensive brands of goods are of a higher quality than their less expensive counterparts, i.e. quality increases with price. From each of three stores we bought six 'own-brand' light bulbs. The stores were categorized as:

A a national 'low-priced' supermarket
B an international general stores
C a high-class department store

HYPOTHESES

In view of our comment regarding price and quality, we are clearly interested in the claim that the average lifetime of bulbs is in direct proportion to their price. If we denote the average lifetime of bulbs from the three stores by m_A, m_B and m_C respectively, the hypotheses may be concisely written as:

H_0: $m_A = m_B = m_C$
H_1: $m_A < m_B < m_C$

Thus, as usual, H_0 expresses the belief that there are no differences in quality (as measured by average lifetimes) between the three brands. But now H_1 is a much more specific statement about the relative performance of the bulbs, rather than merely saying that H_0 is untrue.

DATA

The lifetimes, in hours, of the three samples of bulbs are given below. Unfortunately, one of brand A's bulbs was broken before it could be tested, so our sample sizes are $n_1=5$, $n_2=6$ and $n_3=6$. We have presented the data so that the order of the samples (A, B, C) corresponds to that postulated in H_1.

A	B	C
619	343	3670
35	2437	2860
126	409	502
2031	267	2008
215	1953	5004
	1804	4782

It is well known that the lifetimes of light bulbs are well modelled by non-symmetric distributions called exponential distributions, and so attempts to analyse such data using classical techniques, which rely on normality, would be untrustworthy.

STATISTIC

The Terpstra–Jonckheere statistic is formed by calculating the Mann–Whitney U statistic for each possible pair of samples and adding all the resulting U values. As in the one-sided version of the Mann–Whitney test in Chapter 5, the particular U statistic to be calculated in each case is the one which should yield *small* values if the alternative hypothesis is true. So, in our particular case where we have three samples and are testing H_0 against the alternative H_1: $m_A<m_B<m_C$, we will have the following three U statistics to add:

(a) U_{BA} = the number of (A,B) pairs with the B less than the A;
(b) U_{CA} = the number of (A,C) pairs with the C less than the A;
(c) U_{CB} = the number of (B,C) pairs with the C less than the B.

Now if H_1 is true, then some or all of these U statistics will tend to be small, and so therefore will their sum $W=U_{BA}+U_{CA}+U_{CB}$; otherwise W will tend to be rather larger. (Actually, Terpstra and Jonckheere used a different, but equivalent, version of W; our definition generally involves simpler arithmetic.)

To ease the calculation of W, we adopt a similar technique to that used for the Mann–Whitney statistic in Chapter 5, which is particularly useful for large samples. On a roughly linear scale we indicate, using the appropriate sample letter, the position of the observations. This is shown below.

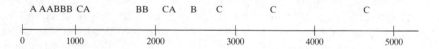

Then

$$U_{BA} = 0 + 0 + 0 + 3 + 5 = 8$$
$$U_{CA} = 0 + 0 + 0 + 1 + 2 = 3$$
$$U_{CB} = 0 + 0 + 0 + 1 + 1 + 2 = 4$$

Hence the value of the test statistic is $W = 8 + 3 + 4 = 15$.

CRITICAL REGIONS

We know that it is small values of W that support H_1, and so the critical regions are of the form

$$W \leqslant \text{critical value}$$

Table R gives critical values of W for various values of k and sample sizes.

In our example, $k=3$, $n_1=5$, $n_2=6$ and $n_3=6$, and so critical regions for significant levels of 5% and 1% are $W \leq 28$ and $W \leq 21$ respectively.

SOLUTION

The value of W obtained above was $W=15$, and this lies well in the 1% critical region. A glance at the data will convince the reader that a result of this sort was to be expected! So the test has given us very strong evidence in this instance to support the claim that the average lifetime of the 'own-brand' bulbs increases with price.

Ties

With the Terpstra–Jonckheere test, tied observations are only troublesome if they occur in different samples; ties within the same sample may be treated as 'ordinary' observations (why?). When ties do occur between observations in different samples, the contribution to the Mann–Whitney count is taken as $\frac{1}{2}$, as in Chapter 5. As an example, consider the following three small samples:

A	B	C
2.6	4.1	2.6
3.2		5.7
3.2		

Again portraying the data on an approximate linear scale we have:

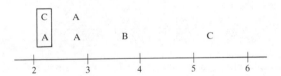

where the tie at 2.6 is indicated by a box. Presuming H_1 is as in our main example, we compute

$$U_{BA} = 0 + 0 + 0 = 0$$
$$U_{CA} = \tfrac{1}{2} + 1 + 1 = 2\tfrac{1}{2}$$
$$U_{CB} = 1 \qquad\quad = 1$$

giving $W = 0 + 2\tfrac{1}{2} + 1 = 3\tfrac{1}{2}$.

Null distributions

The principle for deriving the null distribution of W follows the familiar pattern. Interpreting H_0 as implying that the data come from identical (continuous) distributions, all possible letter sequences are then equally likely to occur. As usual, the principle is that W is computed from each such letter sequence, a frequency distribution is thereby built up, and the null distribution obtained by dividing each frequency by the total frequency. Also as usual, the trouble is that this total frequency gets very large, even for quite small sample sizes; for example, in the above illustration with $k=3$, $n_1=5$ and $n_2=n_3=6$, the number of letter sequences to be considered is

$$\frac{N!}{n_1!n_2!n_3!} = \frac{17!}{5!6!6!} = 5717712$$

Furthermore, although the reasoning behind this null distribution is similar to that for the Kruskal–Wallis statistic, we cannot use a symmetry argument to reduce the work; for example,

A	B	C	and	A	B	C
1,2	3,4	5,6		5,6	1,2	3,4

give the same value for the Kruskal–Wallis statistic but have W values of $0+0+0=0$ and $4+4+0=8$ respectively.

Fortunately, modern computers, aided by a recursion formula given in Jonckheere's paper, have produced a set of critical values for quite a wide range of sample sizes.

Large sample sizes
It can be shown that, as the sample sizes n_i increase, the null distribution of W gets close to normality. The mean of the distribution is

$$\mu=(N^2-\textstyle\sum n_i^2)/4$$

and its standard deviation is

$$\sigma=\sqrt{[N^2(2N+3)-\textstyle\sum n_i^2(2n_i+3)]/72}$$

This can be used to obtain approximate critical values when the n_i are beyond the range of Table R. For a significance level α, we reject H_0 in favour of H_1 if

$$W \leqslant \mu - z\sigma - \tfrac{1}{2}$$

where z is the corresponding (right-hand tail) standard normal value and the $\tfrac{1}{2}$ is the continuity correction.

To see how well this approximation performs, again consider $k=3$, $n_1=5$, $n_2=n_3=6$. We find

$$\mu = [17^2-(25+36+36)]/4=48$$

and

$$\sigma = \sqrt{[17^2\times37-(25\times13+36\times15+36\times15)]/72} = 11.36$$

For $\alpha=5\%$, $z=1.6449$ and so H_0 is rejected if $W\leqslant48-1.6449\times11.36-0.5$ $= 28.82$. The exact (conservative) critical value is 28, which in practice corresponds exactly with this approximate value. Thus, even for sample sizes as low as these, the approximation works well.

k (>2) RELATED SAMPLES

In the previous chapter we used Friedman's test and the match tests to analyse the problem of k related samples. When the nature of the practical problem demands an ordered alternative hypothesis, these tests are inappropriate for exactly the same reason as given earlier in the chapter concerning the Kruskal–Wallis test. Instead, we shall analyse such problems using a test due to E. B. Page (1963) and two tests based on the matching principle used in the previous chapter. The match tests, recently developed by one of the authors, are particularly quick and easy to use.

PAGE'S TEST

Introduction

Page's test is a well known distribution-free test for ordered alternatives in the k-related-samples problem. It is easy to apply and its underlying logic is straightforward. The assumptions of the test are as for Friedman's test, namely that the data be in the form of a 'randomized block design' of, say, k columns (treatments) and n rows (blocks). The theory also assumes the populations have continuous distributions; but, as before, this assumption can be relaxed in practice if it does not result in too many ties.

PRACTICAL PROBLEM

An international company is dissatisfied with the quality of output from six of its subsidiary companies. These companies manufacture various porcelain articles ranging from cups and saucers to toilets. The parent company instigates a four-month training programme for the managers of these subsidiaries. If the programme is effective, the quality should rise over the months. No doubt the parent company will interpret any such rise as validating their training programme.

HYPOTHESES

The null hypothesis is of the same form as for any k-related-samples problem: that is, there is no difference in the average quality of the output over the five-month period (observations were also included for the month immediately preceding the start of the programme so as to have a standard or control with which to compare subsequent observations). Since the company is interested in seeing whether the training programme is effective, the appropriate alternative hypothesis is that the average quality of the output is increasing over time. If we denote the average quality of the output for the five months by m_1, m_2, m_3, m_4 and m_5 respectively, the hypotheses may be written as:

$$H_0: m_1=m_2=m_3=m_4=m_5.$$
$$H_1: m_1<m_2<m_3<m_4<m_5.$$

(Note: It is important for the construction of the test statistic that H_1 be in this particular form, i.e. $m_1<m_2<\ldots<m_k$, rather than $m_1>m_2>\ldots>m_k$ or any other of the possibilities. If the required ordering is not this particular one, then the populations and samples must be renumbered so that it becomes so.)

DATA

The observations record the number of acceptable items as a percentage of the total output for each subsidiary. Month 1 indicates the control month, and months 2 to 5 cover the training period.

	Month				
Subsidiary	1	2	3	4	5
A	62.59	67.11	73.02	92.34	83.48
B	55.75	63.03	63.93	71.61	93.73
C	65.88	69.89	82.53	77.33	84.82
D	66.13	66.79	85.37	76.72	98.88
E	65.73	57.85	63.08	71.75	87.04
F	78.36	76.17	82.97	91.49	89.61

STATISTIC

As with Friedman's statistic, the observations within each block are ranked from 1 to k (1 to 5 in our example). Evidently, if H_0 is true, these ranks should be evenly distributed among the five columns. On the other hand, if H_1 is true (i.e. $m_1<m_2<m_3<m_4<m_5$), we would expect the ranks to tend to increase as we go from column 1 to column 5. Page's test statistic is obtained by summing the ranks in each column to produce the rank sums R_1, R_2, . . . , R_k and then multiplying R_1 by 1, R_2 by 2, R_3 by 3 and so on, and finally adding these k quantities to obtain:

$$L = R_1 + 2R_2 + 3R_3 + \ldots + kR_k$$

or, more concisely,

$$L = \sum_{i=1}^{k} iR_i$$

Thus the rank sums that we expect to be largest when H_1 is true have been multiplied by the biggest constants, while those expected to be the smallest have been multiplied by the smaller constants.

Let us now calculate Page's statistic for the data in our practical problem. The table of ranks for the data is given below; the rank-sums R_i are also shown.

			Month		
Subsidiary	1	2	3	4	5
A	1	2	3	5	4
B	1	2	3	4	5
C	1	2	4	3	5
D	1	2	4	3	5
E	3	1	2	4	5
F	2	1	3	5	4
rank sum, R_i	9	10	19	24	28

Hence

$$L = \sum_{i=1}^{5} iR_i$$

$$= 1\times9 + 2\times20 + 3\times19 + 4\times24 + 5\times28$$
$$= 9 + 20 + 57 + 96 + 140$$
$$= 312$$

CRITICAL REGIONS

Clearly it is large values of L that support H_1. Thus H_0 will be rejected in favour of H_1 if

$$L \geqslant \text{critical value}$$

Table S gives critical values of L for $k=3$ to 6 and n up to 20.

In our practical problem, $k=5$ and $n=6$, and so the critical regions for $\alpha=5\%$ and 1% are $L\geqslant291$ and $L\geqslant299$ respectively.

SOLUTION

The calculated value of $L=312$ certainly falls well into the 1% critical region. It would appear that the company has quite conclusive evidence supporting the effectiveness of their programme.

Null distributions
The argument is almost identical to that for Friedman's statistic in Chapter 14. The only difference is that we cannot reduce the $(k!)^n$ configurations to $(k!)^{n-1}$ by 'fixing' the first block. For example, in the simple case where $k=3$ and $n=2$, the two configurations

$$
\begin{array}{ccc}
1 & 2 & 3 \\
2 & 1 & 3
\end{array}
\quad \text{and} \quad
\begin{array}{ccc}
2 & 3 & 1 \\
1 & 3 & 2
\end{array}
$$

would automatically result in the same value of Friedman's M, but give $L=27$ and $L=24$ respectively.

Large sample sizes
For values of n beyond the range given in Table S, we can use the fact that, for large values of n, L is approximately normally distributed. Under H_0, the mean of L is

$$\mu = nk(k+1)^2/4$$

and its standard deviation is

$$\sigma = \sqrt{nk^2(k+1)(k^2-1)/144}$$

So, for a given significance level α, the approximate critical region is given by

$$L \geqslant \mu + z\alpha + \tfrac{1}{2}$$

where z is the corresponding (right-hand tail) value from the standard normal distribution and the $\tfrac{1}{2}$ is the continuity correction.

To see how well this approximation performs, consider the values $k=5$ and $n=6$ as in our practical problem. The values of μ and σ are 270 and 12.247 respectively. Hence the approximate critical regions are given by

$$L \geqslant 270 + 12.247z + \tfrac{1}{2}$$

For $\alpha=5\%$ and 1%, for which $z=1.6449$ and 2.3263 respectively, we obtain $L \geqslant 290.65$ and $L \geqslant 298.99$ which correspond exactly, in practice, with the exact (conservative) critical regions of $L \geqslant 291$ and $L \geqslant 299$.

THE MATCH TESTS FOR ORDERED ALTERNATIVES

Introduction

The matching principle, introduced in the last chapter, can be applied in an obvious way to the case of ordered alternatives. We shall present two statistics, L_1 and L_2; the first is based solely on matches while the other incorporates the idea of near-matches. Not only are the tests based on these statistics simple to use, but they also possess very respectable power, particularly L_2, which utilizes more information than does L_1. The simple L_1 has the attraction of (approximate) critical values which depend only on n, the number of rows; i.e. these approximate critical values are effectively independent of the number of treatments.

PRACTICAL PROBLEM, HYPOTHESES AND DATA

These are as for Page's test.

STATISTICS

As previously, we shall describe the nature of the statistics with reference to the practical problem.

Both statistics rely on the fact that the strongest evidence for the truth of H_1 is found when column 1 mainly has ranks of 1, column 2 has ranks of 2, column 3 has ranks of 3, and so on. All we do is to compare the ranks in each row in turn with the ranks predicted under H_1 (for example, the predicted ranks could be $1,2,3, \ldots ,k$). In each comparison, we record the number of matches and near-matches. The two statistics, L_1 and L_2 are then defined as:

$$L_1 = \text{total number of matches}$$
$$L_2 = L_1 + \tfrac{1}{2}(\text{number of near-matches})$$

Let us now apply these simple statistics to the practical problem. Below we reproduce the ranked data in addition to the predicted ranks.

Predicted ranks	1	2	3	4	5
Subsidiary			Actual ranks		
A	1	2	3	4	5
B	1	2	3	4	5
C	1	2	4	3	5
D	1	2	4	3	5
E	3	1	2	4	5
F	2	1	3	5	4

Performing the comparisons row by row, we obtain:

$$L_1 = 5 + 5 + 3 + 3 + 2 + 1 = 19$$

and

$$L_2 = 19 + \tfrac{1}{2}(0 + 0 + 2 + 2 + 2 + 4) = 24$$

CRITICAL REGIONS

The L_1 test
Clearly, if the ranks of the observed data follow the predicted order, then this results in a high value of L_1, i.e. it is large values of L_1 that support H_1. Thus we reject H_0 in favour of H_1 if

$$L_1 \geq \text{critical value}$$

Table T gives critical values of L_1 for $k=3$ to 6 and n up to 20.
   In our problem, $k=5$ and $n=6$, and so critical regions corresponding to $\alpha=5\%$ and 1% are $L_1 \geq 11$ and $L_1 \geq 13$ respectively.

The L_2 test
Similarly, large values of L_2 provide evidence in support of H_1. Thus critical regions are of the form

$$L_2 \geq \text{critical value}$$

Table U gives the critical values of L_2 for $k=3$ to 6 and n up to 20.
   For our problem where $k=5$ and $n=6$, the critical regions corresponding to $\alpha=5\%$ and 1% are $L_2 \geq 15$ and $L_2 \geq 17$ respectively.

SOLUTION

Both the L_1 test and the L_2 test give results that lie well into their 1% critical regions. These conclusions are consistent with those obtained using Page's test.

Discussion
It is interesting to note that the process of looking for matches helps to bring our notice to those columns that 'disagree' with the predicted order. For example, there appears to be a slight disagreement in columns 3 and 4. In other words, applying these simple tests brings us 'closer to the data' – which is no bad thing in this age of automation.
   The fact that $L2$ utilizes more information than L_1 is reflected in the relative performances of the corresponding tests. Computer simulation studies have shown that L_2 has consistently higher power than L_1, although even the simple test based on L_1 performs very creditably (see Worthington 1982).

Ties

Tied observations are tackled in a similar manner as with the M_1 and M_2 tests of the previous chapter. As usual, ties are assigned mean ranks. In the following discussion, r_i refers to a rank in the ith column.

When using the L_1 test, the contributions to L_1 are as follows:

$$\text{if} \quad |r_i - i| \begin{cases} = 0 & \text{then contribute } 1 \\ = \tfrac{1}{2} & \text{then contribute } \tfrac{1}{2} \\ > \tfrac{1}{2} & \text{then contribute } 0 \end{cases}$$

To illustrate this rule, consider the following block of ranks:

Predicted	1	2	3	4	5
Observed	1	$2\tfrac{1}{2}$	4	$2\tfrac{1}{2}$	5
Contribution to L_1	1	$\tfrac{1}{2}$	0	0	1

When using the L_2 test, the contributions are as follows:

$$\text{if} \quad |r_i - i| \begin{cases} = 0 & \text{then contribute } 1 \\ \left.\begin{array}{l} = \tfrac{1}{2} \\ = 1 \\ = 1\tfrac{1}{2} \end{array}\right\} & \text{then contribute } \tfrac{1}{2} \\ > 1\tfrac{1}{2} & \text{then contribute } 0 \end{cases}$$

The above ranks give

$$L_2 = 1 + \tfrac{1}{2} + \tfrac{1}{2} + \tfrac{1}{2} + 1 = 3\tfrac{1}{2}$$

Null distributions

If H_0 is true, thus implying that the k populations have identical (continuous) distributions, we would expect the ranks to be fairly evenly spread between the treatments. Thus, for given values of k and n, the null distributions of L_1 or L_2 may be obtained by computing their value for each of the $(k!)^n$ rank configurations.

For example, with $k=3$ and $n=1$ there are $3!=6$ different rank configurations and, with the predicted order under H_1 being 1 2 3, the null distribution of L_2 is derived as follows:

Predicted ranks	1 2 3	1 2 3	1 2 3	1 2 3	1 2 3	1 2 3
Possible ranks	1 2 3	1 3 2	2 1 3	2 3 1	3 1 2	3 2 1
Value of L_2	$1+1+1$	$1+\tfrac{1}{2}+\tfrac{1}{2}$	$\tfrac{1}{2}+\tfrac{1}{2}+1$	$\tfrac{1}{2}+\tfrac{1}{2}+0$	$0+\tfrac{1}{2}+\tfrac{1}{2}$	$0+1+0$
	$=3$	$=2$	$=2$	$=1$	$=1$	$=1$

Hence the null distribution is

$$\text{Prob}(L_2=1) = 3/6$$
$$\text{Prob}(L_2=2) = 2/6$$
$$\text{Prob}(L_2=3) = 1/6$$

Once the null distributions for $n=1$ are found, subsequent distributions for $n>1$ are easily obtained by a process called convolution. This has enabled extensive tables of exact critical values to be produced.

Large samples
The L_1 test If k is large, then it can be shown that the null distribution of L_1 is approximately Poisson with a mean of n. This enables approximate critical values to be obtained for values of k not included in Table T; and indeed these approximate critical values are thus *independent* of k. Below is a table of these approximate critical values for $\alpha=5\%$ and 1%.

| | α | |
n	5%	1%
2	6	7
3	7	9
4	9	10
5	10	12
6	11	13
7	13	15
8	14	16
9	15	18
10	16	19

Incidentally, the exact critical values for our practical problem where $k=5$ and $n=6$ are precisely the same as those obtained from this table of approximate values.

The L_2 test For values of n greater than those included in Table U, we may obtain critical values of L_2 using a normal approximation. The mean and standard deviation of L_2 are given by

$$\mu=n(2-1/k)$$

and

$$\sigma = \sqrt{\frac{n}{k}\left(\frac{3(k-2)}{2} + \frac{1}{k(k-1)}\right)}$$

So, for a given significance level α, the approximate critical region is

$$L_2 \geqslant \mu+z\sigma+\tfrac{1}{2}$$

where z is the corresponding (right-hand tail) percentage point of the standard normal distribution and the $\tfrac{1}{2}$ is the continuity correction. To see how this approximation performs, consider again the case when $k=5$ and $n=6$. With these values we find that $\mu=10.8$ and $\sigma=2.337$. The approximate critical regions are then $L_2 \geqslant 10.8+2.337z+\tfrac{1}{2}$. For $\alpha=5\%$ and 1%, we obtain $L_2 \geqslant 15.14$ and

$L_2 \geqslant 16.74$. The exact (conservative) critical regions are $L_2 \geqslant 15$ and $L_2 \geqslant 17$ respectively; so here the approximation has produced the correct 1% region but is over-conservative as regards the 5% region.

Assignments

1 Light conditions
An experiment was conducted to investigate the effect of different lighting conditions on manual dexterity. Four lighting conditions were chosen for the test:

> A   Light from a window
> B   Fluorescent light
> C   Tungsten bulb light
> D   Candle light

Eighteen people volunteered to take part in the experiment. They were randomly assigned to four groups and each group was subjected to one of the lighting conditions. The time (seconds) taken by each person to complete a simple manual task is given in the following table.

A	B	C	D
29	63	41	41
43	15	19	59
44	27	37	36
46	30	27	36
	31		40

Task: Choose an appropriate test to investigate the claim that the average time to complete the manual task increases with worsening light conditions.

2 Food deprivation
In 1972 G. J. Syme and J. S. Pollard ('The relation between differences in level of food deprivation and dominance in food getting in rats', *Psychon. Sci.* **29**, 297–8) presented the results of their experiment into the effect of food deprivation in rats. The table below gives the amount of food (g) eaten by eight rats under three levels of food deprivation:

	Hours of food deprivation		
Rat	0	24	72
1	3.5	5.9	13.9
2	3.7	8.1	12.6
3	1.6	8.1	8.1
4	2.5	8.6	6.8
5	2.8	8.1	14.3
6	2.0	5.9	4.2
7	5.9	9.5	14.5
8	2.5	7.9	7.9

The second table gives the times (seconds) spent at the food trough by the rats:

	Hours of food deprivation		
Rat	0	24	72
1	570	706	840
2	589	520	781
3	267	784	817
4	425	753	799
5	666	861	849
6	653	816	810
7	746	790	854
8	785	810	797

Task: Investigate the claims that (i) the amount of food eaten tends to increase with length of deprivation, and (ii) the time spent at the trough tends to increase with length of deprivation.

Program 15.1   Terpstra–Jonckheere test for ordered alternatives

```
100 REM *** TERPSTRA-JONCKHEERE TEST ***

110 REM ** INPUT NUMBER OF SAMPLES **
120 INPUT "NUMBER OF SAMPLES (>2) ";K
130 DIM N(K)
140 LET GN=0

150 REM ** INPUT DATA **
160 FOR I=1 TO K
170 PRINT "INPUT SIZE OF SAMPLE ";I
180 INPUT N(I)
190 LET GN=GN+N(I)
200 NEXT I
210 PRINT
220 DIM D(GN,2)
230 LET L=0
```

```
240 FOR I=1 TO K
250 PRINT "INPUT DATA FOR SAMPLE ";I
260 FOR J=1 TO N(I)
270 LET L=L+1
280 INPUT D(L,1)
290 LET D(L,2)=I
300 NEXT J
310 NEXT I

320 REM ** CALCULATION OF TEST STATISTIC **
330 LET U=0
340 FOR I=1 TO K-1
350 FOR I1=I+1 TO K
360 FOR J=1 TO GN
370 IF D(J,2)<>I THEN GO TO 430
380 FOR J1=1 TO GN
390 IF D(J1,2)<>I1 THEN GO TO 420
400 IF D(J,1)>D(J1,1) THEN LET U=U+1
410 IF D(J,1)=D(J1,1) THEN LET U=U+.5
420 NEXT J1
430 NEXT J
440 NEXT I1
450 NEXT I
460 PRINT "VALUE OF THE TEST STATISTIC IS ";U
470 PRINT
480 IF K<=6 AND N<=10 THEN STOP

490 REM ** APPROXIMATE CRITICAL VALUES **
500 LET S1=0
510 LET S2=0
520 FOR I=1 TO K
530 LET S1=S1+N(I)^2
540 LET S2=S2+(2*N(I)+3)*N(I)^2
550 NEXT I
560 LET M=(GN^2-S1)/4
570 LET S=SQRT((GN^2*(2*GN+3)-S2)/72)
580 INPUT "VALUE OF Z: ";Z
590 LET C=M-Z*S+.5
600 PRINT "APPROXIMATE CRITICAL VALUE IS ";C
```

Program 15.2   Page's test for ordered alternatives

```
100 REM *** PAGE'S TEST FOR ORDERED ALTERNATIVES ***

110 REM ** INPUT NUMBER OF TREATMENTS AND BLOCKS **
120 INPUT "NUMBER OF TREATMENTS AND BLOCKS ? ";K,N
130 DIM A(N,K),RK(N,K)

140 REM ** INPUT DATA **
150 FOR I=1 TO N
160 PRINT "INPUT THE OBSERVATIONS FOR BLOCK ";I
170 FOR J=1 TO K
180 INPUT A(I,J)
190 NEXT J
200 NEXT I
210 GO SUB 1000
```

Continued overleaf

Program 15.2   Continued

```
220 REM ** CALCULATION OF TEST STATISTIC **
230 DIM R(K)
240 FOR I = 1 TO K
250 LET R(I) = 0
260 FOR J = 1 TO N
270 LET R(I) = R(I) + RK(J,I)
280 NEXT J
290 NEXT I
300 LET L = 0
310 FOR I=1 TO K
320 LET L = L + I*R(I)
330 NEXT I
340 PRINT "VALUE OF PAGE'S STATISTIC = ";L
350 PRINT
360 IF N <= 20 AND K <= 6 THEN STOP

370 REM ** APPROXIMATE CRITICAL VALUES **
380 INPUT "PERCENTAGE POINT OF STANDARD NORMAL DISTRIBUTION ";Z
390 LET LC = N*(K^3-K)*(Z/SQRT(N*(K-1))+3*(K+1)/(K-1))/12
400 PRINT "APPROXIMATE CRITICAL VALUE = ";LC

1000 REM ** WITHIN-BLOCK RANKS - USE LINES 1000-1160 OF PROGRAM 14.1 **
```

Program 15.3   Match tests for ordered alternatives

```
100 REM *** MATCH TESTS FOR ORDERED ALTERNATIVES ***

110 REM ** INPUT NUMBER OF TREATMENTS AND BLOCKS **
120 INPUT "NUMBER OF TREATMENTS AND BLOCKS ? ";K,N
130 DIM A(N,K),RK(N,K)

140 REM ** INPUT DATA **
150 FOR I=1 TO N
160 PRINT "INPUT THE OBSERVATIONS FOR BLOCK ";I
170 FOR J=1 TO K
180 INPUT A(I,J)
190 NEXT J
200 NEXT I
210 GO SUB 1000

220 REM ** CALCULATION OF TEST STATISTIC **
230 LET L1=0
240 LET L2=0
250 FOR I=1 TO K
260 FOR J=1 TO N
270 LET RD=ABS(RK(J,I)-I)
280 IF RD=0 THEN LET L1=L1+1
290 IF RD=0.5 THEN LET L1=L1+0.5
300 IF RD>0 AND RD<=1.5 THEN LET L2=L2+0.5
310 LET L2=L2+L1
320 NEXT J
330 NEXT I
340 PRINT "VALUE OF MATCH L1 STATISTIC = ";L1
350 PRINT "VALUE OF MATCH L2 STATISTIC = ";L2
360 PRINT
370 IF N<=20 AND K<=6 THEN STOP

380 REM ** APPROXIMATE CRITICAL VALUES **
390 INPUT "PERCENTAGE POINT OF STANDARD NORMAL DISTRIBUTION ";Z
```

```
400 REM ** VALUES FOR L1  **
410 LET LC=SQRT(N)*Z+N+0.5
420 PRINT "APPROXIMATE CRITICAL VALUE FOR L1 = ";LC

430 REM ** VALUES FOR L2 **
440 LET M=N*(2-1/K)
450 LET SD=SQRT(N*(3*(K-2)/2+1/K/(K-1))/K)
460 PRINT "APPROXIMATE CRITICAL VALUE FOR L2 = ";M+Z*SD+0.5

1000 REM ** WITHIN-BLOCK RANKS - USE LINES 1000-1160 OF PROGRAM 14.1 **
```

16

Tests for interaction and latin squares designs

Introduction

In the first part of this chapter, we present procedures for detecting whether two variables or *factors* (such as the dosage of a medicine and the amount of alcohol consumed) *interact* with each other. Naturally, interaction between two variables can indicate erratic behaviour patterns, and so it is important to test for its presence.

As in Chapter 14, the second part of this chapter deals with the *k*-related samples problem. However, here the observations are affected by a third factor and, in the particular situation we consider, the data are arranged according to the so-called latin squares design. As we shall see, with this situation we can examine *three* sets of hypotheses – one for each of the three factors. To analyse such a design we present a procedure in which either Friedman's test or the match tests of Chapter 14 may be used.

INTERACTION

The layman's meaning of the term *interaction* is 'the action of one on another', which suggests that some quantity is involved with another quantity (or quantities) in a possibly complex manner. Interaction has the same kind of interpretation in statistics. For example, in an experiment on the effects of two variables, these two variables in conjunction with each other may lead to dramatically different results than if they are considered singly. For instance, suppose they represent quantities of alcohol and aspirins consumed by a foolish volunteer!

Consider an experiment in which three grades of seed (A=poor, B=medium and C=best-quality) are subjected to four different strengths of fertilizer (I=20, II=30, III=45 and IV=60 kg/acre). The kind of results that common sense might predict, i.e. yield increasing with higher seed quality and also yield increasing with the strength of fertilizer, are shown below, for yields (kg/m^2) obtained:

Fertilizer strength	Seed quality		
	A	B	C
I	2	5	8
II	3	6	9
III	5	8	10
IV	6	11	17

But now compare these responses with those from a similar experiment conducted on a different (though with similar characteristics) plot of land.

Fertilizer strength	Seed quality		
	A	B	C
I	2	7	3
II	4	3	8
III	6	5	4
IV	10	6	9

Although we would have not expected exactly the same yields as before, we would have expected a similar kind of behaviour. Figure 16.1 shows the behavioural patterns for the two experiments. In the second experiment, *something* has caused this interaction between the seed quality and fertilizer.

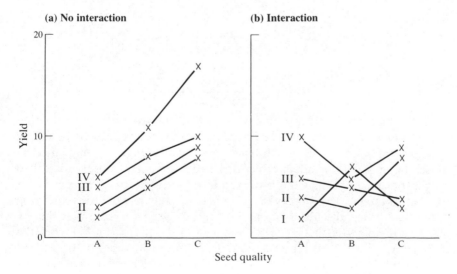

Figure 16.1

Naturally, experiments could involve three, or more, factors (or treatments). Then we could investigate the presence of interaction between any two of the factors, or between any three, and so on. However, in this book we confine our thoughts to experiments with just *two* factors (as in the above illustration). Having said that, even in experiments with only two factors, we do need to distinguish between two types of experiment – those with *linked* observations and those with *unlinked* observations. To see what we mean by these terms, consider the following tables. At first glance, these tables appear to be identical – however, look more closely.

Linked observations		Treatment		
		A	B	C
I	1	7.6	7.2	8.2
	2	6.9	7.3	7.8
II	1	5.6	7.1	7.2
	2	6.8	6.7	8.0
III	1	7.4	8.2	7.4
	2	6.9	7.9	7.5

Unlinked observations	Treatment		
	A	B	C
I	7.6	7.2	8.2
	6.9	7.3	7.8
II	5.6	7.1	7.2
	6.8	6.7	8.0
III	7.4	8.2	7.4
	6.9	7.9	7.5

In the first table, the two observations for each treatment combination have some kind of natural order, which we have indicated by assigning an 'observation number', 1 or 2, to each. This natural ordering may arise by observation 1 relating to day 1 of the experiment and observation 2 to day 2, or it may be that the observation number refers to the particular person obtaining the observation. Whatever the reason, this ordering allows us to link the observations in a certain way; for example, the 7.6 (A,I) is linked with the 7.2 (B,I) and also to the 8.2 (C,I); likewise, the 6.8 (A,II), the 6.7 (B,II) and the 8.0 (C,II) are linked. In the second table, there is no ordering of the observations – the order in which the observations are recorded is immaterial.

It is interesting to note that some authors suggest that it is good enough to impose some arbitrary ordering; this then allows them to use a test like Wilcoxon's interaction test (see below). Clearly, the danger with this practice is that someone else could choose a different ordering and then possibly end up with a quite different conclusion. For situations where the observations are unlinked, we shall present procedures based on the match tests of Chapter 14.

WILCOXON'S INTERACTION TEST

Introduction

Frank Wilcoxon (1949) wrote an interesting booklet introducing a number of supposedly quick statistical methods. One of these was a technique for testing for interaction when the observations are linked. His idea was to reduce the data (by a sequence of subtractions) to leave only the interaction effect (if any). He then applied Friedman's test to these reduced data.

In common with most other tests for interaction, Wilcoxon's procedure becomes tedious when the two factors (treatments) are divided into many components (levels of treatment). For this reason, we shall illustrate this technique using a small-size experiment, and then indicate the necessary extensions for larger experiments.

PRACTICAL PROBLEM

To back up a new advertising campaign, a paint manufacturer tests dyes for their resistance to fading when subjected to ultraviolet (UV) light. Three technicians each perform the test on red and blue paint, those colours being chosen because of their diverse pigment structure.

HYPOTHESES

The main concern is probably with the effect of increasing the intensity of the UV light, and then with the differences in fading between the two colours. However, a sensible move is first to check for the presence of interaction between the colour and the UV light. So our chosen hypotheses are:

H_0: There is no interaction between paint colour and UV light.
H_1: There is interaction between paint colour and UV light.

DATA

The technicians recorded the percentage shift in the wavelength of light reflected from the painted surface. Three levels of UV light intensity were used (low, medium and high), each for 200 h. The data are given in the following table.

Paint	Technician	UV intensity		
		Low	Medium	High
red	1	4.9	7.2	7.3
	2	5.2	7.3	7.1
	3	6.1	6.9	7.4
blue	1	5.2	7.2	6.9
	2	4.8	7.7	7.1
	3	4.6	7.4	6.8

STATISTIC

Since we are interested in testing for interaction between paint colour and UV light, we subtract from each 'red' observation the corresponding 'blue' observation. This gives the following table of R−B (red–blue) differences:

Technician	UV intensity		
	Low	Medium	High
1	−0.3	0	−0.4
2	0.4	−0.4	0
3	1.5	−0.5	0.6

Now, if the null hypothesis is true, the R−B differences should be roughly the same along each row. Thus if the differences within each row are ranked (from 1 to 3, in this example) and then Friedman's statistic calculated, this should result in a small value of M. On the other hand, if H_1 is true, then M will tend to be large, as then the ranks of the R−B differences will tend to exhibit some patterns in the table.

Ranking the above data and proceeding to compute Friedman's statistic, we have:

	Ranks		
	2	3	1
	3	1	2
	3	1	2
rank sums	8	5	5

Hence,

$$M = \frac{12}{nk(k+1)} \sum_{j=1}^{3} R_j^2 - 3n(k+1)$$

$$= \frac{12}{3\times3\times4} (64+25+25) - 3\times3\times4 = 2$$

CRITICAL REGIONS

As we have seen, Wilcoxon's method is to modify the observed data in such a way that Friedman's test becomes a test for interaction. This means that critical values can be obtained from Table O (at least in this size of experiment, see the 'Discussion' section below). Thus critical regions are of the form:

$$M \geqslant \text{critical value}$$

In our problem, $k=3$ and $n=3$, giving the $\alpha=5\%$ critical region as $M \geqslant 6.000$ (with such a small value of n, no 1% critical region is available).

SOLUTION

Since the calculated value of $M=2$ does not lie in the 5% critical region, there is no evidence of interaction between paint colour and UV light.

Discussion

In our example, it was easy enough to apply Wilcoxon's procedure. However, with larger experiments, the test statistic is made up of several components, each of which comes from applying Friedman's procedure to a set of ranks. For example, suppose our practical problem had involved *three* colours, say red, blue and yellow. In this case, Wilcoxon's procedure is as follows:

Step 1 As before, derive the differences R−B and calculate Friedman's statistic (call it m_1).
Step 2 Form a table of differences R+B−2Y and calculate Friedman's statistic (call this one m_2) from the ranks.
Step 3 The final test statistic is $M=m_1+m_2$.

This test statistic is approximately distributed as a chi-squared variable with $2(k-1)$ degrees of freedom, which enables appropriate critical values to be obtained.

If there were *four* colours in the experiment, say red, blue, yellow and green, the final test statistic is then $M=m_1+m_2+m_3$ where m_1 and m_2 are calculated as explained above, and m_3 is calculated from the table of differences R+B+Y−3G.

The statistic M is now approximately distributed as a chi-squared variable with $3(k-1)$ degrees of freedom.

In general, with p colours C_1, C_2, . . . , C_p the test statistic M is given by m_1+m_2+. . .$+m_{p-1}$, where m_i is the Friedman statistic based on differences of the form C_1+C_2+. . .$+C_i-(i-1)C_{i+1}$, for $i=2,3,$. . . ,$p-1$. You will see that the ith set of such differences provide data on the possible interaction between C_{i+1} and the previous colours C_1, C_2, . . . , C_i. Under the null hypothesis of no interactions, M is approximately distributed as chi-squared with $(p-1)(k-1)$ degrees of freedom.

MATCH TESTS FOR INTERACTION

Introduction

As we discussed at the beginning of the chapter, our study of interaction is divided between those experiments with linked observations and those with unlinked observations. Wilcoxon's method just described is probably the simplest of many distribution-free procedures for the former case. Unfortunately, *simple* procedures for dealing with the case of unlinked observations are scarce. However, in this section, we present such a technique, which involves the match ideas. As with the previous match tests, we give two tests; one is based solely on the number of matches, while the other incorporates near-matches.

PRACTICAL PROBLEM

An international cycling team is concerned with the road-holding capabilities of various brands of tyres. It seems that individual members disagree about the optimum tyre pressure for wet conditions; some members argue that certain makes of tyre respond better if the pressure is lower than normal with the opposite being true for the other brands. Other team members scorn this idea and keep the tyre pressure normal regardless of the brand of tyre.

The team manager happened to mention his team's views to a member of the research department of a famous bicycle manufacturer. The researcher, being intrigued, offers to conduct an experiment in the company's test laboratory.

HYPOTHESES

Naturally, the team members are interested in finding out about the differences in performance between the tyres. However, because of the conflicting arguments, the researcher suspects that there may be some interaction between the various makes of tyre and tyre pressures. So his hypotheses for this situation are:

H_0: There is no interaction between tyre pressure and brand of tyre.
H_1: There is some interaction between tyre pressure and brand of tyre.

DATA

Apparently, four different brands of tyre are used by members of the team, and so the researcher selects these brands for the test; we shall denote the brands by A, B, C and D to preserve anonymity. After a discussion with the team about tyre pressures, four tyre pressures were used in the experiment: 20, 40, 50 and 70 lb/sq. in. For each combination of pressure and brand, the experiment was performed three times.

The data record the speed (mph) at which slipping occurred on a standard inclined, wet surface.

	Brand of tyre			
Pressure	A	B	C	D
20	33.16	30.89	35.38	33.88
	30.23	28.38	33.86	32.53
	30.19	30.49	34.77	33.10
40	29.05	31.66	31.64	34.51
	29.72	34.23	30.42	34.89
	31.48	34.44	31.82	34.84
50	32.96	29.00	33.20	32.42
	31.59	32.68	32.36	32.01
	30.98	33.14	35.07	33.29
70	27.84	33.32	31.76	34.07
	29.43	33.15	32.83	35.16
	29.90	32.52	30.76	34.26

STATISTICS

Because of the somewhat intangible nature of interaction, you might suppose that any test procedure would be involved and lengthy. To some extent this is true; the procedure we now present is possibly the simplest available, but even so you will find it tedious to do without a calculator.

The basic idea is to remove the effects of the rows (pressures) and columns (tyres) to leave data that represent just interaction. Before doing this, we replace the group of observations for each combination of pressure and brand by their mean (the observation means). This gives the following data on which we apply further manipulations.

Pressure	Brand of tyre				Row means
	A	B	C	D	
20	31.19	29.92	34.64	33.17	32.23
40	30.08	33.44	31.29	34.75	32.39
50	31.84	31.61	33.54	32.57	32.39
70	29.06	33.00	31.78	34.50	32.08
Column means	30.54	31.99	32.81	33.75	32.27 = overall mean

Notice that we have also calculated the row means, column means and the overall mean in readiness for the next stage.

From this reduced set of data, we obtain the interaction component as:

interaction
= observation mean − row mean − column mean + overall mean

So, for example, taking the top-left observation, we calculate

$$31.19 - 32.23 - 30.54 + 32.27 = 0.69$$

Doing this for all 16 values gives:

Pressure	Brand of tyre			
	A	B	C	D
20	0.69	−2.03	1.87	−0.54
40	−0.58	1.33	−1.64	0.88
50	1.18	−0.50	0.61	−1.30
70	−1.29	1.20	−0.84	0.94

The rest is now easy! The data in this table are ranked by row and by column to give two tables of ranks:

Row ranks					Column ranks			
3	1	4	2		3	1	4	2
2	4	1	3		2	4	1	3
4	2	3	1		4	2	3	1
1	4	2	3		1	3	2	4

To each of these tables we apply one of the match tests of Chapter 14;

either M_1 or M_2. Suppose M_1 is chosen; then we calculate two values of the statistic, M_{1r} and M_{1c} where the r and c denote that the value is obtained from the row ranks and column ranks respectively. The test statistic S_1 is the sum of these two values. For our problem we obtain $M_{1r}=2$ and $M_{1c}=0$, giving $S_1=2$.

Similarly, if M_2 is chosen we calculate two values M_{2r} and M_{2c} giving a test statistic $S_2=M_{2r}+M_{2c}$. Our problem gives $M_{2r}=7$ and $M_{2c}=6$ from which $S_2=13$.

CRITICAL REGIONS

If H_1 is true then the presence of interaction in the form of erratic behaviour patterns will tend to give small values of S_1 and S_2; for example, the no-interaction situation shown in Figure 16.1a would tend to give a high value of S_1 (or S_2) whereas the interaction situation in Figure 16.1b would tend to produce a low value of S_1 (or S_2). Thus critical regions are of the form:

$$\text{test statistic} \leq \text{critical value}$$

Tables V and W give critical values of S_1 and S_2 respectively.

In our problem, $k=4$ and $n=4$ and so the 5% and 1% critical regions for S_1 are $S_1 \leq 6$ and $S_1 \leq 5$ respectively, while the corresponding critical regions for S_2 are $S_2 \leq 16$ and $S_2 \leq 15$ respectively.

CONCLUSION

Our conclusion is the same whether we use S_1 or S_2, as both give values that lie in the 1% critical region. Thus there is strong evidence to support the researcher's suspicion regarding interaction between tyre pressure and make of tyre.

Large experiment sizes

S_1 *test*   Approximate critical values can be obtained using a normal approximation. If we have k columns and n rows in the experiment, then an approximate critical value for an $\alpha\%$ level of significance is the integer part of:

$$\tfrac{1}{2}[n(n-1) + k(k-1)] - z\sqrt{\tfrac{1}{2}[n(n-1)+k(k-1)]} - \tfrac{1}{2}$$

where z is the appropriate percentage point of the standard normal distribution (e.g. for $\alpha=5\%$, $z=1.6449$) and the $\tfrac{1}{2}$ is the continuity correction.

S_2 *test*   Approximate critical values can be obtained using a normal approximation. If the experiment has k columns and n rows, then an approximate critical value for an $\alpha\%$ level of significance is the value of:

$$z \frac{\frac{1}{2}\left[n(n-1)\left(2-\frac{1}{n}\right)+k(k-1)\left(2-\frac{1}{n}\right)\right]-}{\sqrt{\frac{n(n-1)(3k^3-9k^2+6k+22)}{4k^2(k-1)}+\frac{k(k-1)(3n^3-n^2+6n+22)}{4n^2(n-1)}}+\frac{1}{2}}$$

to the nearest 0.5 (since S_2 has values which are multiples of 0.5), and where z is as above.

LATIN SQUARES DESIGNS

Introduction

As in Chapter 14, this part of the chapter deals with the k-related samples problem, but here the observations are related by an extra variable so that now *three* factors are involved. There are many ways of analysing such experiments. The simplest method is to use the so-called latin squares design, which is an extension of the randomized block design we mentioned in Chapter 14. This design allows us to test for differences between the averages of the k populations and also for differences among each of the other two factors; thus we have three sets of hypotheses, some or all of which we may choose to investigate.

The following example illustrates the concept of a latin square design. A company measures productivity on five different jobs (factor 1) during a particular week, the five working days constituting factor 2. Five different working conditions (factor 3) are used, which are:

A   complete silence
B   piped-in popular music
C   piped-in country and western music
D   piped-in classic music
E   'request' music

By constructing a so-called 5×5 latin squares design, each combination of these three factors can be represented. A typical 5×5 design for this problem is given below:

Day	Job type 1		2		3		4		5	
Mon	A	137	B	121	C	118	D	113	E	108
Tues	B	126	C	130	D	135	E	137	A	129
Wed	C	126	D	127	E	147	A	129	B	139
Thurs	D	113	E	118	A	113	B	112	C	104
Fri	E	117	A	115	B	116	C	110	D	118

So, for example, the figure underlined represents the productivity on Friday for job type 4 and under working conditions C. The assignment of letters (which here represent working conditions) to the rows (days) and columns (jobs) is not unique; another valid arrangement of letters is the following:

	Job type				
Day	1	2	3	4	5
Mon	A	C	E	B	D
Tues	B	A	C	D	E
Wed	E	D	B	C	A
Thurs	C	E	D	A	B
Fri	D	B	A	E	C

The essential feature is that each row and column contains no duplication of letters. Thus, for example, the following 5×5 table would not be a valid latin square design.

	Job type				
Day	1	2	3	4	5
Mon	A	C	E	B	D
Tues	B	A	C	D	E
Wed	A	B	B	C	A
Thurs	C	E	E	A	C
Fri	D	B	A	E	C

An obvious restriction of such designs is that each of the three factors must be represented by the same number of different *levels*; in the above example, there were five job types, five days and five working conditions. Another, not so obvious, restriction is that the presence of interactions (say, between day *and* job type or between day and job type *and* working conditions) cannot be detected.

Latin square designs were probably devised for agricultural experiments where the k populations represented k treatments (fertilizers, different varieties of seed, etc.) and the other two factors were simply the coordinates of a plot in a field.

In this section, we present a procedure for analysing latin squares designs by Friedman's test or the match tests of Chapter 14.

PRACTICAL PROBLEM

The R&D section of a well known tyre manufacturer conducted an experiment to find out whether differences existed among the average life of four brands of tyre. The brands are denoted by T_1 (their own leading tyre), T_2, T_3 and T_4. The tyres were tested under four different climatic conditions: C_1=Arctic, C_2=British summer, C_3=British winter and C_4=hot and dry. Four different road conditions were used: R_1=rough, R_2=newly tarmacadamed, R_3=concrete, and R_4=stone-chippings surface.

HYPOTHESES

In this situation with three factors (tyres, climate and road conditions), we have in fact three possible sets of hypotheses to explore. Although the company's main concern is with differences in average life between the tyres, the design of the experiment also makes it possible to test for differences caused by the climatic conditions and by the road surfaces. These hypotheses are:

(I) H_0: There are no differences in average tyre wear between the four brands of tyre.
     H_1: There are differences in average tyre wear between the four brands of tyre.

(II) H_0: There are no differences in average tyre wear between the four climatic conditions.
      H_1: There are differences in average tyre wear between the four climatic conditions.

(III) H_0: There are no differences in average tyre wear between the four road surfaces.
       H_1: There are differences in average tyre wear between the four road surfaces.

DATA

For each of the three factors, the amount of tread wear (mm) over a given mileage was recorded. The data are presented in the following 4×4 latin square design.

Climate	Brand of tyre			
	T_1	T_2	T_3	T_4
C_1	R_1 3.2	R_2 1.4	R_3 0.4	R_4 2.6
C_2	R_2 2.5	R_3 2.3	R_4 2.8	R_1 3.3
C_3	R_3 2.4	R_4 2.7	R_1 2.9	R_2 0.9
C_4	R_4 3.1	R_1 3.7	R_2 0.6	R_3 0.5

METHOD

From the above latin square table, we construct three other tables, one for each of the combinations: (1) brand × climate, (2) brand × road, and (3) climate × road. These tables are given below.

Climate	Brand			
	T_1	T_2	T_3	T_4
C_1	3.2	1.4	0.4	2.6
C_2	2.5	2.3	2.8	3.3
C_3	2.4	2.7	2.9	0.9
C_4	3.1	3.7	0.6	0.5

Road	Brand			
	T_1	T_2	T_3	T_4
R_1	3.2	3.7	2.9	3.3
R_2	2.5	1.4	0.6	0.9
R_3	2.4	2.3	0.4	0.5
R_4	3.1	2.7	2.8	2.6

Road	Climate			
	C_1	C_2	C_3	C_4
R_1	3.2	3.3	2.9	3.7
R_2	1.4	2.5	0.9	0.6
R_3	0.4	2.3	2.4	0.5
R_4	2.6	2.8	2.7	3.1

We shall now test each set of hypotheses using both Friedman's test and the match tests.

Hypotheses (I)
Using the first table, we rank the observations within each row. This produces the following table of ranks.

	Brand			
	T_1	T_2	T_3	T_4
	4	2	1	3
	2	1	3	4
	2	3	4	1
	3	4	2	1
rank sums	11	10	10	9

From this table of ranks we immediately obtain

$$M_1 = 0 + 1 + 1 = 2$$
$$M_2 = 2 + \tfrac{1}{2}(5 + 3 + 2) = 7$$

and Friedman's statistic is

$$M = \frac{12}{nk(k+1)} \sum_{j=1}^{4} R_j^2 - 3n(k+1)$$

$$= \frac{12}{4 \times 4 \times 5}(11^2 + 10^2 + 10^2 + 9^2) - 3 \times 4 \times 5$$

$$= 0.3$$

Alternatively, the test statistics could have been produced from the second table, again by ranking within each row. This time the ranks are:

	Brand			
	T_1	T_2	T_3	T_4
	2	4	1	3
	4	3	1	2
	4	3	1	2
	4	2	3	1
rank sums	14	12	6	8

Hence, $M_1=8$, $M_2=12$ and $M=6$.

Hypotheses (II)
To test these hypotheses we may use either the first table (ranking the columns) or the third table (ranking the rows). The first table gives $M_1=2$, $M_2=7$ and $M=0.3$, while the third table gives $M_1=6$, $M_2=10.5$ and $M=3.0$.

Hypotheses (III)
To test these hypotheses we may use either the second or third table, ranking the columns in each case. Both tables give $M_1=18$, $M_2=21$ and $M=11.1$.

CRITICAL REGIONS

Naturally, critical regions are just as for Friedman's test and the match tests. Hence the 5% and 1% critical regions are respectively:

for Friedman's test (from Table O)

$$M \geqslant 7.800 \quad \text{and} \quad M \geqslant 9.600$$

for the M_1 test (from Table P)

$$M_1 \geqslant 12 \quad \text{and} \quad M_1 \geqslant 15$$

for the M_2 test (from Table Q)

$$M_2 \geqslant 15.0 \quad \text{and} \quad M_2 \geqslant 18.0$$

SOLUTION

Hypotheses (I)
There is no evidence to reject H_0 and so we have no evidence to claim there are differences between the four brands of tyre.

Hypotheses (II)
None of the test values lie in their respective critical regions, and so we have no evidence to support H_1.

Hypotheses (III)
All three tests give results that lie in the 1% critical region, thus providing strong evidence to support the claim that there are differences in the average tyre wear due to different road surfaces.

Discussion
Since the test statistics can be calculated from one of two tables of ranks, it is quite feasible that one value could be significant and the other non-significant. It seems that this conflict arises when interaction exists between the factors and in this case a further investigation would be desirable.

Ties and large sample sizes
The comments made in Chapter 14 apply here.

Program 16.1 Match tests for interaction

```
100 REM *** MATCH TESTS FOR INTERACTION ***

110 REM ** INPUT DATA **
120 INPUT "NUMBER OF ROWS & COLUMNS ? ";N,K
130 INPUT "NUMBER OF REPLICATIONS ?";NR
140 DIM X(N,K,NR),A(N,K),RW(N),CL(K),Y(N,K),RK(N,K)
150 LET S = 0
160 FOR I = 1 TO N
170 FOR J = 1 TO K
```

Continued overleaf

Program 16.1   Continued

```
180 LET A(I,J) = 0
190 NEXT J
200 NEXT I

210 REM ** INPUT OBSERVATIONS **
220 FOR I = 1 TO N
230 FOR J = 1 TO K
240 PRINT "OBSERVATIONS FOR ROW ";I;" & COLUMN ";J
250 FOR L = 1 TO NR
260 INPUT X(I,J,L)
270 LET A(I,J) = A(I,J) + X(I,J,L)/NR
280 LET S = S + X(I,J,L)
290 NEXT L
300 PRINT
310 NEXT J
320 NEXT I

325 REM ** CALCULATION OF TEST STATISTICS **
330 FOR I=1 TO N
340 LET RW(I) = 0
350 NEXT I
360 FOR I = 1 TO K
370 LET CL(I) = 0
380 NEXT I
390 FOR I = 1 TO N
400 FOR J = 1 TO K
410 LET RW(I) = RW(I) + A(I,J)/K
420 LET CL(J) = CL(J) + A(I,J)/N
430 NEXT J
440 NEXT I
450 FOR I = 1 TO N
460 FOR J = 1 TO K
470 A(I,J) = A(I,J) - RW(I) - CL(J) + S/N/K/NR
475 LET Y(I,J)=A(I,J)
480 NEXT J
490 NEXT I
500 GO SUB 1000
510 GO SUB 2300
520 LET S2=M2
530 LET S1=M1
540 FOR I=1 TO N
550 FOR J=1 TO K
560 LET A(J,I)=Y(I,J)
570 NEXT J
580 NEXT I
590 LET F=N
600 LET N=K
610 LET K=N
620 GO SUB 1000
630 GO SUB 2300

635 REM ** OUTPUT OF VALUES OF S1 AND S2 **
640 LET S2=S2+M2
650 LET S1=S1+M1
660 PRINT S2,S1
670 STOP

1000 REM ** WITHIN-BLOCK RANKS  - USE LINES 1000-1160 OF PROGRAM 14.1 **

2300 REM ** CALCULATION OF M1 AND M2 - USE LINES 230-360 OF PROGRAM 14.2 BY **
2305 REM ** ADDING A '0' TO  THE LINE NUMBERS **
```

PART VI
Miscellaneous procedures

The three chapters in this part of the book present a variety of tests and procedures. In Chapter 17, we introduce tests based on what are known as 'runs'; these ideas will not only analyse two-sample situations such as those in Chapters 5 and 6 but will also deal with the problem of 'non-randomness' in a sequence of observations.

Chapter 18 presents more tests using frequency data. First, we discuss Fisher's 'exact test' for analysing 2×2 contingency tables and then we lead into Mood's two-sample median test followed by the Mood–Westenberg two-sample dispersion test.

The final chapter describes some common distribution-free methods for constructing confidence intervals for the population median and for the difference of two population medians.

17
Tests based on runs

Introduction

In this chapter, we describe a number of tests based on numbers of runs. The one-sample version provides an extremely useful check for certain features of non-randomness in a sequence of observations, while the two-sample version has a remarkably wide range of general applications.

The term 'run', in the sense relevant to this chapter, is quite familiar to us, for we have all heard the expression 'a run of good (or bad) luck' applied to someone's fortunes. Indeed, it is likely that the statistical usage of the word 'run' originated in gambling situations.

Suppose that a person tossing a coin 20 times generates the following sequence of heads (H) and tails (T):

T H T T T T T T T T T T T T H H H T T T

We see that this sequence includes a long run of tails (of length 12, from the third to the fourteenth toss inclusive), which, in a gambling game, could well represent a run of good or bad luck according to the rules of the game. Scanning the whole sequence from left to right, we start with a 'run' of just one 'T', which is followed by a run of one 'H', then a run of 12 'T's, followed by a run of three 'H's, and finishing with a run of three 'T's; five runs altogether. Note that a 'run' may consist of only one observation, as is the case with both the first two runs in this example.

In the context of statistical testing, we might ask: can the above sequence of 'H's and 'T's reasonably be regarded as random – or is there evidence of an element of 'luck' (good or bad) or some other non-random influence? The term 'random' here means effectively that there is no tendency for any discernible pattern to emerge.

As we shall see, the number of runs in the sequence can help answer this question and, of course, this technique can also be applied to many situations other than gambling games. For example, it is usually important to check for non-randomness on a quality control chart; perhaps there is a long run of observations above the central line, giving a picture such as that in Figure 17.1.

Representing values above and below the central line by A and B respectively, we have the sequence:

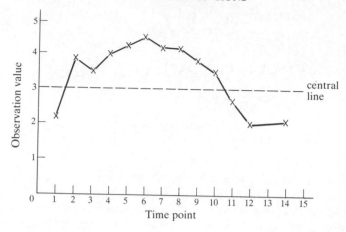

Figure 17.1

B A A A A A A A A A B . . .

Surely we should be suspicious of such a long run (of length 9) of 'A's – perhaps a machine characteristic was wrongly set over this period of time.

In this latter type of example, an alternative 'runs' analysis may be used to check for non-randomness. This is based on the number of 'runs up and/or down' – runs of steadily rising or falling values. We shall see an example of this later in the chapter.

We conclude the chapter with a particularly quick-and-easy two-sample test, again based on runs, designed for detecting general differences between two populations. This is therefore a simple test for the task tackled in Chapter 7 by the Kolmogorov–Smirnov test and, although its power cannot match that of the Kolmogorov–Smirnov test, its simplicity makes it a useful test to have available.

RUNS TEST FOR RANDOMNESS

Introduction

One of the appealing features of the runs test for randomness (or rather, lack of randomness, which is what we want the test to be able to discover) is its 'common sense' nature. Most people would be immediately suspicious of, for example, a sequence of coin tossings which produces too few runs:

H H H H H H H H T T T T T T T T

or too many runs: .

H T H T H T H T H T H T H T H T H T H T

Both of these extremes indicate in an obvious way a complete lack of randomness, for each has a clear pattern. (Although, at first glance, the second sequence may strike you as being random, in fact heads and tails alternate strictly throughout the sequence – and that is actually just as unlikely an occurrence as the first sequence.)

The runs test we discuss here requires a minimum of formal assumptions. All we require is that each observation be capable of classification as one type or the other.

PRACTICAL PROBLEM

A manufacturer of ceramic wash-basins also makes the mixer taps for the basins. An important component of these taps is a brass T-connector which (if water is not to spurt everywhere!) should form a 'perfect' fit with the incoming pipes. Clearly, it is necessary that the diameters of these connectors should be made with minimal variation from some target value determined by the designer. A control chart was set up in order to monitor the machine producing these junctions. Now, in a quality control chart, there are many warning signs of something untoward happening to the process. One such possible sign is a lack of randomness – perhaps a high value is always followed by a low value and vice versa (which might indicate the presence of some self-compensating effect), or there might be correlation between adjacent observations which may result in long sequences above and below the average value.

HYPOTHESES

In this simple test for randomness (or rather lack of randomness), our hypotheses are just:

H_0: The sample values come from a random sequence.
H_1: The sample values do not come from a random sequence.

DATA

To establish a control chart for the sample means, 20 samples of four T-junctions were taken at 15 min intervals. The diameters were measured and the mean of the diameters (mm) for the 'vertical' part of the T-junction are given below.

Sample number	1	2	3	4	5	6	7	8	9	10
Mean	15.0	14.8	14.9	15.0	15.1	15.3	15.0	14.9	14.7	15.1
Sample number	11	12	13	14	15	16	17	18	19	20
Mean	15.2	15.3	14.9	15.2	15.1	15.0	14.9	14.8	14.7	14.8

To apply a runs test for investigating whether there is a lack of randomness about the overall mean value of 14.985, we simply record a '+' for each sample mean above 14.985 and a '−' for each value below 14.985. This gives the following sequence of '+'s and '−'s:

$$+ \quad - \quad - \quad + \quad + \quad + \quad - \quad - \quad + \quad + \quad + \quad - \quad + \quad + \quad + \quad - \quad - \quad - \quad -$$

Now, as we saw in the introductory discussion, a lack of randomness can show itself by the sequence of signs having either too few or too many runs. This immediately suggests that a suitable test statistic is simply:

$$T = \text{total number of runs}$$

In order to use the table of critical values, we must also note the numbers n_1 and n_2 of + and − signs, respectively. In this case we have $n_1=11$ and $n_2=9$.

CRITICAL REGIONS

Since it is very low or very high values of T that lead us to reject H_0, the critical regions are of the form:

$$T \leqslant \text{lower critical value}$$

or

$$T \geqslant \text{upper critical value}$$

These lower and upper critical values are given in Table X for $\alpha_2=5\%$ and 1% and various values of n_1 and n_2.

We have $n_1=11$ and $n_2=9$, and so at $\alpha_2=5\%$ we reject H_0 in favour of H_1 if $T \leqslant 6$ or $T \geqslant 16$.

SOLUTION

The number of runs T is equal to 8, comprising runs of length

1 of +
2 of −
4 of +
2 of −
3 of +
1 of −
3 of +
4 of −

This value, $T=8$, does not fall in the $\alpha_2=5\%$ critical region, and so we have no evidence to support H_1. Of course, this is good news for the company since a contrary decision would presumably result in some investigation on the apparent non-randomness.

Tied values
It might happen that one or more of the observed values is the same as the mean value, in which case we cannot record the usual $+$ or $-$ sign. If the number of such cases is small compared with the total length of the sequence, then it is usual to ignore these cases and proceed as normal with the remaining $+$ and $-$ signs.

(Note: A more sophisticated approach is to consider all possible sequences arising from recording such tied observations as $+$ or $-$ in turn, and averaging the numbers of runs resulting from such sequences.)

One-sided tests
Suppose that the situation under study is such that the only type of non-randomness likely to occur tends to make the sequence alternate too rapidly (a self-compensating effect is an obvious example). In this case our alternative hypothesis may be expressed something like:

H_1: The process's output tends to 'zigzag' more than would be expected under true randomness.

Critical regions are of the form

$$T \geqslant \text{critical value}$$

with α_1 upper critical values being obtained from Table X.

Conversely, it might be that we are only interested in types of non-randomness that tend to produce longer (and therefore fewer) runs than usual; a common cause of this is positive correlation (as opposed to independence) between adjacent observations. In this case the appropriate alternative hypothesis might be:

H_1: The process's output tends to be 'smoother' than would be expected under true randomnesses.

Now the critical regions are of the form:

$$T \leqslant \text{critical value}$$

with the α_1 lower critical values being obtained from Table X.

Large sample sizes
Should either n_1 or n_2 be greater than 20, then approximate critical values may be obtained as follows. It can be shown that, for large values of n_1 and n_2, T is approximately normally distributed with mean

$$\mu = 1 + 2n_1 n_2/N$$

and standard deviation

$$\sigma = \sqrt{2n_1 n_2 (2n_1 n_2 - N)/(N^2(N-1))}$$

So approximate lower and upper critical values (T_L and T_U) are given by

$$T_L = \mu - z\sigma - \tfrac{1}{2}$$

$$T_U = \mu + z\sigma + \tfrac{1}{2}$$

where z is the appropriate percentage point in the standard normal distribution and the '$\tfrac{1}{2}$' is the continuity correction. For example, if $n_1=20$ and $n_2=20$ then $\mu = 21$ and $\sigma = 3.12$ and so, for $\alpha_2=5\%$ (for which $z=1.96$) the critical values are

$$T_L = 21 - 1.96 \times 3.12 - \tfrac{1}{2} = 15$$

$$T_U = 21 + 1.96 \times 3.12 + \tfrac{1}{2} = 27 \qquad \text{(when rounded appropriately)}$$

Table X gives the best conservative critical values as 14 and 28 respectively; so, even with n_1 and n_2 as low as 20, the approximation works well.

Runs up and down

Provided our data are recorded as numerical values rather than just as 'H'/'T', etc., it is possible to examine a sequence of observations for another aspect of non-randomness, namely 'runs up' and 'runs down'. To see what this idea involves, consider the following sequence of values:

5.6   6.2   6.5   7.6   8.0   6.1   7.5   4.8   3.2   2.6

The plot of these values in Figure 17.2 clearly shows the run up (of length 4) from 5.6 to 8.0, the run down (of length 1) to 6.1, and so on. (Note that we do not include the first point in counting the length of the first run up since we cannot tell whether or not it belongs to that run without previous history.)

Of course, we can easily study such runs (up or down) without drawing a graph. All we need to do is to record a + or a − if a value is greater or less than its predecessor, respectively. So, applying this idea to the above sequence gives:

5.6	6.2	6.5	7.6	8.0	6.1	7.5	4.8	3.2	2.6
	+	+	+	+	−	+	−	−	−

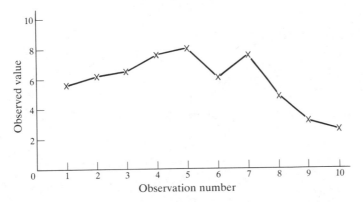

Figure 17.2

where the '+'s and '−'s denote moves up and down respectively.

Intuitively, in a 'random' sequence we would expect moderate numbers of runs up and runs down. But, a sequence that has a general upward trend will tend to have quite a number of long runs up, with only the occasional short run down (and naturally, a sequence with a downward trend will exhibit long runs down). In either case, therefore, the numbers of runs up and runs down will be unusually small. On the other hand, a sequence having particularly erratic behaviour will tend to have many short runs of each type.

As you probably expect, the test statistic used for this feature of randomness is the total number of runs (up or down), or, in other words, just the number of runs of '+'s and '−'s in the above sequence. So it now all looks very much like the previous runs test. But beware! These '+'s and '−'s are different from before, and the corresponding critical values are generally different as well; so we shall need a new table of critical values for this test.

PRACTICAL PROBLEM

The problem of the brass T-connectors for taps (see the previous section) can be examined for this different exhibition of non-randomness, i.e. the tendency for too long or too short runs up and runs down. Too few runs up and runs down might indicate a trend or some broad oscillatory tendency, whereas too many indicates a zigzag effect.

HYPOTHESES

The hypotheses for the situation just discussed may be summarized as:

H_0: The averages occur 'at random'.
H_1: The averages have one or more non-random features, such as trends, oscillations or too much zigzag behaviour.

DATA

The data are as before.

STATISTIC

As we have already seen, a suitable test statistic (U) for this situation is given by

$$U = \text{number of runs (up or down)}$$

CRITICAL REGIONS

Clearly, the alternative hypothesis will be supported if there are unusually few or unusually many runs, and so H_0 will be rejected if

$$U \leq \text{lower critical value}$$

or

$$U \geq \text{upper critical value}$$

Table Y gives critical values for samples up to $n=25$, where n is the length of the sequence of data.

We have $n=20$ in our problem and so we shall reject H_0 at $\alpha_2=5\%$ and 1% if $U\leq 8$ or $U\geq 17$ and $U\leq 7$ or $U\geq 18$ respectively.

SOLUTION

By simply observing whether an observation is greater than or less than its predecessor, we obtain the following sequence of signs:

15.0	14.8	14.9	15.0	15.1	15.3	15.0	14.9	14.7	15.1
	−	+	+	+	+	−	−	−	+

15.2	15.3	14.9	15.2	15.1	15.0	14.9	14.8	14.7	14.8
+	+	−	+	−	−	−	−	−	+

Immediately we see that $U=8$, which is significant at $\alpha_2=5\%$. Thus there is some evidence to support H_1; indeed a glance at the data reveals two 'longish' runs (a run up of length 4 and a run down of length 5), which might warrant some further investigation.

Tied values

Equal values in the sequence only pose a problem if they are consecutive. If a particular observation is equal to its predecessor, we shall indicate this by a zero instead of by + or − (since a zero is neither positive nor negative). Then, if the number of zeros in the sequence of signs is small, we shall simply ignore them and reduce the value of n accordingly. So, for example, consider the following sequence of values:

5.6	6.1	2.8	2.8	2.8	3.4	5.8	6.1	4.8
	+	−	0	0	+	+	+	−

Ignoring the zeros gives the test sequence

$$+ \quad - \quad + \quad + \quad + \quad -$$

with $U=4$ and $n=6$.

One-sided tests

As discussed earlier, some types of non-randomness tend to make the number of runs up and down lower than usual and others make the number larger than usual. These situations result in sequences that might be described as smoother or more erratic, respectively, than expected under the null hypothesis of randomness. If we are only interested in our test diagnosing one of these types of non-randomness, we can of course produce a one-sided version of the test. In the former case, the type of non-randomness of interest tends to produce long runs up or runs down, and therefore relatively few of them.

The appropriate alternative hypothesis might (as earlier in this chapter) be expressed as:

H_1: The process's output tends to be 'smoother' than would be expected under true randomness.

In this case, the α_1 lower critical values from Table Y are used and the critical regions have the form:

$$U \leqslant \text{lower critical region}$$

Likewise, we might be interested in the alternative hypothesis:

H_1: The process's output tends to 'zigzag' more than would be expected under true randomness.

Then the α_1 upper critical values from Table Y are used and the corresponding critical regions are:

$$U \geqslant \text{upper critical value}$$

Large sample sizes

Should the sample size n be greater than 25, then approximate critical values may be obtained using a normal distribution approximation. It can be shown that, for large values of n, U is approximately normally distributed with mean $\mu = (2n-1)/3$ and standard deviation $\sigma = \sqrt{(16n-29)/90}$. Thus, approximate lower and upper critical values U_L and U_U are given by

$$U_L = \mu - z\sigma - \tfrac{1}{2}$$

$$U_U = \mu + z\sigma + \tfrac{1}{2}$$

where z is the appropriate percentage point from the standard normal distribution and the '$\tfrac{1}{2}$' is the continuity correction.

You might like to check that, if we take $n=25$, we obtain $\mu=16.33$ and $\sigma=2.03$. Now for $\alpha_2=5\%$ the value of z is 1.96 and so we obtain

$$\mu - z\sigma - \tfrac{1}{2} = 11.85$$

and

$$\mu + z\sigma + \tfrac{1}{2} = 20.80$$

giving $U_L=11$ and $U_U=21$. These are the same values as those in Table Y.

THE WALD–WOLFOWITZ TWO-SAMPLE RUNS TEST

A. Wald and J. Wolfowitz (1940) proposed a simple two-sample test based on the idea of runs. A very useful feature of their test is that (if the sample sizes are large enough) it can detect differences in averages, or spread, or in any other important aspect between the two populations being studied. However, as might be expected of a test that is both simple and ambitious, its power is not great. Consequently, if one's prime interest is in detecting differences in average, the tests of Chapter 5 are to be preferred. Or, if the main interest is in detecting differences in spread, we would prefer the tests in Chapter 6. However, one problem with these previous tests is that a difference of a type not being catered for can harm their ability to carry out the task for which they are designed; for example, the power of both the Mann–Whitney and Tukey tests for detecting differences in location can be severely reduced if the populations also differ substantially in spread. On the other hand, the Wald–Wolfowitz test might well have greater power in these and other situations of more general differences. The Wald–Wolfowitz test can therefore be regarded as a fairly quick-and-easy alternative to the two-sample Kolmogorov–Smirnov test (see Ch. 7), which also has power for general types of differences.

However, because of this very generality, there could conceivably be difficulties in interpreting significant results from this test. It is easy enough with the 'special-purpose' tests; if we have a significant result from the Mann–Whitney test we know that this indicates a difference in location and, similarly, a significant result from the Siegel–Tukey test definitely indicates a difference in spread. But significant results from the Wald–Wolfowitz test can be caused by any kind of substantial difference. In practice, however, it is usually easy to make an informal judgement of the reason for rejection of the null hypothesis by taking a quick look at the letter sequence. Incidentally, this discussion also implies that the notion of one-sided tests is not relevant to the Wald–Wolfowitz test.

Let us now get an idea of the way the test works. As usual, we will denote observations from our two populations by A and B and consider the letter sequence thus obtained. However, now we concentrate on the number of runs in the letter sequence. Thus, if we have the letter sequence:

A   A   B   B   A   B   B   A   B   A   A

then we find a total of seven runs.

If the two samples are from the same population, then we would expect the 'A's and 'B's in the letter sequence to be 'well mixed', so producing a relatively large number of runs. On the other hand, suppose the two populations differ in location; their distributions might be as shown in Figure 17.3.

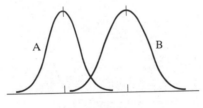

Figure 17.3

A possible letter sequence for this situation could be

A   A   A   A   A   B   A   B   B   B   B

which contains relatively few runs.

Now consider two populations which instead differ with respect to spread. Their distributions might be something like the ones shown in Figure 17.4. A possible letter sequence for this could be

A   A   B   B   B   B   B   A   A   A   A   A

which is again a sequence with few runs.

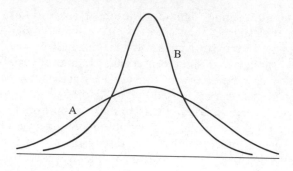

Figure 17.4

Finally suppose the populations differ in both location and spread, as in Figure 17.5. A typical letter sequence is

A   A   A   A   A   B   B   B   B   A   A

yet again a sequence with few runs.

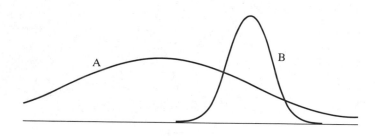

Figure 17.5

PRACTICAL PROBLEM

We will illustrate the Wald–Wolfowitz runs test with the stockbroker's data from Chapter 6, where we were looking for differences in riskiness between fundamental and technical investment methods.

HYPOTHESES

We use the same form of hypotheses as in Chapter 6:

H$_0$: There is no difference in 'riskiness' between the two methods.
H$_1$: There is some difference in 'riskiness' between the two methods.

DATA

The percentage gains and losses were as follows:

Fundamental (sample A)	+5 −19	+20 +28	−24 +41	−9 +11	+50	+32	+15	−34
Technical (sample B)	−4 +26	+19 +14	+21 +6	+13 −10	+2 −21	−7 +36	+24 +7	+10

STATISTIC

As described above, the rationale of the Wald–Wolfowitz test is to count the runs in the combined letter sequence to give a test statistic:

$$T = \text{total number of runs}$$

The combined letter sequence for our data is given below.

−34	−24	−21	−19	−10	−9	−7	−4	2	5	6	7	10
A	A	B	A	B	A	B	B	B	A	B	B	B

11	13	14	15	19	20	21	24	26	28	32	36	41	50
A	B	B	A	B	A	B	B	B	A	A	B	A	A

The number of runs is $T=17$, and the sample sizes are $n_1=12$ and $n_2=15$.

CRITICAL REGIONS

As we have seen, the effect of substantial differences in location and/or spread between the two populations is a tendency to reduce the number of runs. Consequently, critical regions for this test are always of the form

$$T \leq \text{critical value}$$

where the lower critical values for $\alpha=5\%$ are given in Table X. (Note that since the Wald–Wolfowitz test cannot distinguish the direction of a difference, we use α without a subscript to denote the significance level and use the significant levels from the α_2 entries in the table.)

With sample sizes $n_1=12$ and $n_2=15$, the 5% critical region is $T \leq 8$.

SOLUTION

Clearly, the calculated value of $T=17$ lies nowhere near the 5% critical region, and so the Wald–Wolfowitz test provides no evidence of any difference in riskiness between the two investment methods.

Discussion

The Wald–Wolfowitz test is very useful in principle (because it tackles a general and widespread task), but is less so in practice (because of low power). To compensate for its relatively low power, it is probably wise in general not to use it unless sample sizes are moderately large – certainly into double figures.

Large sample sizes

The approximate critical values for large sample sizes are as for the ordinary runs test using the expression for T_L.

Assignments

In addition to trying out the various two-sample procedures given in this chapter on the assignments in Chapters 5 and 6, we give below a problem from quality control to investigate for non-randomness.

1 Quality control

In a particular manufacturing process, items can be classified as being defective or non-defective. Samples of 50 items are taken every 6 h and the percentage number of defectives calculated; the results of 25 such samples are given below.

Sample number	1	2	3	4	5	6	7	8	9	10	11	12	13
Percentage defective	8	12	7	5	12	12	4	11	4	7	5	6	8

Sample number	14	15	16	17	18	19	20	21	22	23	24	25
Percentage defective	6	10	6	8	9	11	6	10	7	5	4	10

Task: Carry out runs tests to check these data for non-randomness.

18

More tests using frequency data

Introduction

The chi-squared test in Chapter 12 was designed to detect association between two variables that were both measured on a relatively crude 'categorized' scale rather than an ordinary numerical scale. Thus the data used for analysis were the frequency counts of the number of observations falling into each combination of the categories. The statistic for this test was

$$\chi^2 = \sum \frac{(\text{observed frequency} - \text{expected frequency})^2}{\text{expected frequency}}$$

where the summation covered all combinations of categories (i.e. all the cells in the contingency table) and the expected frequencies were calculated to reflect the statement in the null hypothesis H_0 of no association between the variables. Evidence to support the alternative hypothesis of association between the variables was indicated by large values of χ^2, caused by large discrepancies between the observed and expected frequencies. Consequently, the appropriate critical regions for rejecting H_0 were of the form

$$\chi^2 \geqslant \text{critical value}$$

However, as we indicated in Chapter 12, there are some unpleasant theoretical difficulties in finding exact critical values; indeed, in most situations, they do not exist! If the sample size is large enough, then the difficulties are effectively removed by the fortunate fact that approximate critical values are obtainable from chi-squared tables. In this chapter, we first study an alternative procedure, which may be used when the sample size is too small for this approximation to be trusted; this procedure is usually known as Fisher's exact test. Unfortunately, it has two drawbacks, namely (a) it is only appropriate for 2×2 contingency tables (i.e. where each variable can only be classified into two categories), and (b) the calculations of critical values depend on an assumption that is not usually met in practice! However, later in the chapter we cover two particular applications where the assumption is satisfied; the first is a particular case of Mood's median test, which we introduced in Chapter 13, and the other is a two-sample test for differences in spread, known as the Mood–Westenberg interquartile test.

FISHER'S EXACT TEST

Introduction

Fisher's exact test is a method of analysing 2×2 contingency tables which may be carried out even when the sample size is too small for the chi-squared approximation to be valid. It is called an 'exact' test because, unlike the analyses we have previously seen, probability distributions are based on exact computations rather than chi-squared approximations. However, as we mentioned above, there is also a validity problem for Fisher's test, which is that the calculations providing the critical values are conditional on both the row and column totals (the marginal totals) being *fixed*. Of course, in most situations they are not fixed (i.e. they are not known prior to the collection of data), so traditional practice has generally been to ignore this fact simply because this is the only technique available for analysing a 2×2 table based on a small sample! However, it should be noted that the two tests that complete this chapter, Mood's median test and the Mood–Westenberg interquartile test, are special cases where the condition on the marginal totals is satisfied.

PRACTICAL PROBLEM

An international drug company is developing a new treatment for leg ulcers. The most commonly used treatment has been to cleanse and then cover the infected area; the response to such treatment is generally slow with, in some cases, several months elapsing before improvement is observed. The company hopes that their new drug will accelerate the healing process.

The company's R&D section were asked to carry out a pilot survey on a prototype of the drug. Depending on the results of the survey, the company may be encouraged either to continue the development of the drug or alternatively to abandon it.

HYPOTHESES

Since the company is interested in seeing whether or not the results of the pilot survey indicate the new treatment to be better than the old, appropriate hypotheses are:

H_0: There is no difference, on average, between responses to the standard treatment and the new drug.

H_1: Response to the new drug is better, on average, than that for the standard treatment.

A more specific statement of the hypotheses, more closely reflecting the sampling experiment being carried out, is:

H_0: The average proportions of people responding in some given time are the same for both types of treatment.

H_1: The average proportion of people responding to the new drug in the given time is higher than that responding to the standard treatment.

It is interesting to note that here we have a one-sided H_1; this is in contrast to the chi-squared test of Chapter 12, where the natural alternative hypothesis is the general, or two-sided, alternative of 'H_0 is not true'. Using Fisher's test, both types of situation may easily be dealt with.

DATA

Eighteen people suffering from leg ulcers were asked to participate in the pilot survey. Ten were randomly chosen for the new treatment; the rest were given the standard treatment. The numbers responding (and not responding) to treatment after two weeks were recorded in the following contingency table.

	Responding	Not responding	
New treatment	8	2	10
Standard treatment	3	5	8
	11	7	18

(Note: although the two row totals can be regarded as 'fixed' by the design of the experiment, the same can certainly not be said of the column totals of 11 and 7. That is to say, another trial of the same experiment – with the same design and sample size – would again be bound to yield row totals of 10 and 8, but the column totals could be any two frequencies that add up to 18. So, as we warned earlier, the precise conditions required by the theory are not always met in practice.)

STATISTIC AND CRITICAL REGIONS

The identification of the statistic for Fisher's test and of the appropriate critical region for the one-sided test is carried out by the simple steps shown below. Be assured that when you are familiar with them, you will find these steps much quicker to execute than to describe!

STATISTIC

Step 1 Examine the four marginal totals (the two row totals and the two column totals) to find the smallest of them; we shall denote this value by m. In the table above, $m=7$; it is the second of the two column totals. (If there is more than one marginal total taking the smallest value, then simply choose any one of them).

Step 2 Think of what is likely to happen to the two frequencies making up the value of m when the alternative hypothesis H_1 is true compared to when the null hypothesis H_0 is true. Under H_1, one of them would be expected to be smaller than under H_0, the other being larger. The required test statistic is simply the former of these, i.e. that frequency which you would expect to be smaller under H_1 than under H_0.

In our example, $m=7$ is the total frequency in the second column, which represents the frequencies of those failing to respond to the new treatment and to the standard treatment respectively. If H_1 is true, i.e. the new drug is better than the standard treatment, we would clearly expect the number failing to respond under the new treatment to be relatively low and the number not responding to the standard treatment to be relatively high compared with the figures we might expect under H_0. The *former* frequency, i.e. the number failing to respond to the new treatment, is therefore our statistic; we will denote it by f. Inspecting the contingency table, we find that $f=2$.

CRITICAL REGIONS

Step 3 Denote the other marginal frequency to which f contributes by M. In our example, f is the frequency in the first row and the second column. We already have m representing the total frequency in the second column ($m=7$), and so M is the total frequency in the first row: $M=10$.

Step 4 Denote the total sample size by N; here $N=18$. Now look in the section of Table Z headed by $N=18$, and find the entry with the relevant values of m and M in the first and second columns of the table, respectively. Remembering that we have $m=7$ and $M=10$, you will find that it is in fact the sixth entry from the end of this section of the table.

Step 5 Read off the values in the third and fourth columns; these are $C=1$ and $\alpha=1.8\%$.

Step 6 Compare the obtained value of f with C. Remembering that the smaller the value of f, the more significant it is, the possible conclusions are as follows (these are relevant to one-sided tests, as in our practical problem).

(a) If $f>C$ then the result is not significant at the 5% significance level, i.e. the test has failed to find evidence against H_0.

(b) If $f<C$ then the result is significant at (better than) the $\frac{1}{2}$% significance level, which means that the test has found very strong evidence in favour of H_1.

(c) If $f=C$ then the result is significant at the $\frac{1}{2}\alpha$% significance level, where α is the percentage read from the fourth column. (The reason for the $\frac{1}{2}\alpha$% rather than α% is that the significance levels in the table apply directly to two-sided rather than one-sided tests; see below for details on two-sided applications.)

SOLUTION

In our example, we have $f=2$ and $C=1$. Thus conclusion (a) is appropriate; the result is not significant at the 5% level, and so we have no evidence to support H_1. Of course, the fact that f is only one greater than C is some indication of the truth of H_1, so the result of the experiment should not be taken as a definite recommendation that the project be abandoned.

Two-sided tests
It is very easy to adapt the above procedure for two-sided tests. In this case, step 1 is as above but, instead of choosing a specific one of the two frequencies contributing to m as the test statistic, we consider *both* of them in turn. Formally, you could say that we carry out steps 3 to 6 above for both the frequencies; usually, however, it is immediately apparent that at least one of these frequencies is too big for consideration, i.e. it will not get anywhere near the corresponding (low) tabulated value of C.

Since the significance levels for two-sided tests are double those of the corresponding one-sided tests, all significance levels mentioned in the above three possible conclusions must be doubled, i.e. replace the 5% by 10% in (a), the $\frac{1}{2}$% by 1% in (b), and of course the $\frac{1}{2}\alpha$% by α% in (c).

An example of the use of this procedure for two-sided tests is given below in the section dealing with the Mood–Westenberg test.

MOOD'S TWO-SAMPLE MEDIAN TEST

Introduction

In Chapter 13, we introduced Mood's median test in a form suitable for any number ($k \geqslant 2$) of samples. It is a quick, convenient test for differences in location; and the fact that it is a straightforward application of a standard technique (i.e. analysing a contingency table using the chi-squared statistic), which is already familiar to many who have attended introductory statistics courses, makes it particularly attractive.

However, as we know, this 'attractive' feature is not so attractive when the samples are small, for then the critical values obtained from the chi-squared tables are less reliable. But, when we have just two samples, we find ourselves in a situation for which Fisher's exact test is appropriate; indeed, as we shall see, it is particularly appropriate because the condition of the marginal totals being fixed, which was not satisfied in the above example, turns out to hold in the case of this two-sample median test. We shall soon see why.

PRACTICAL PROBLEM, HYPOTHESES AND DATA

Let us return to the problem and data used in Chapter 5 involving the proportions of British and Japanese cars breaking down in the first year. The null hypothesis H_0 of equal proportions was being tested against the one-sided alternative hypothesis H_1 that the proportion of British cars breaking down is greater. The data (percentages of different models breaking down) were as follows:

Japanese	3	7	15	10	4	6	4	7				
British	19	11	36	8	25	23	38	14	17	41	25	21

STATISTIC

First we find the overall median of these data. We have 20 observations altogether, so the median is halfway between the 10th and 11th values when arranged in ascending order. The reader may easily confirm that the relevant values are 14 and 15 respectively, giving the median value of $14\frac{1}{2}$. It is then apparent that, of the eight Japanese models, only one of the percentages exceeds $14\frac{1}{2}$, and consequently we arrive at the following contingency table.

	Below overall median	Above overall median	
Japanese	7	1	8
British	3	9	12
	10	10	20

We now proceed as in the previous example. We shall write down the details in terms of the same six steps as before.

Step 1 The smallest marginal total is $m=8$, being the total frequency in the first row (i.e. the number of Japanese models in the survey).

Step 2 If H_1 is true (i.e. Japanese cars are better), we would expect the number of Japanese models with percentages breaking down below and above the overall median to be high and low respectively; the second percentage is therefore the one we want, giving $f=1$.

CRITICAL REGIONS

Step 3 $f=1$ is in the first row (having total frequency $m=8$) and second column, which has total frequency of 10. Thus $M=10$.

Step 4 The total frequency is $N=20$.

Step 5 Entering Table Z at $N=20$, $m=8$ and $M=10$, we read $C=1$ and $\alpha=2.0\%$.

SOLUTION

Step 6 Conclusion (c) is appropriate in this case, i.e. there is evidence in favour of H_1 (that Japanese cars are better, on average, than British cars) at the $\frac{1}{2}\alpha=\frac{1}{2}\times2.0 = 1\%$ significance level, which of course represents strong evidence for the truth of H_1.

Remarks

First, let us check why the condition of fixed marginals holds with Mood's two-sample median test whereas it did not with the first example in this chapter. Clearly the row totals have to be 8 and 12 as these are just the two sample sizes. (For the same reason, the row totals in the previous example were also fixed rather than being variable.) But, in this case, the column totals are also fixed; they have to be 10 each because of the definition of the overall median – half of the observations have to be below the overall median and the other half above. Consequently, the condition of fixed marginals is satisfied with Mood's test.

   The condition of fixed marginals has another interesting consequence. You will recall our mention in Chapter 12 of Yates' correction, which for many years was an adjustment generally made to the chi-squared statistic in 2×2 tables. As we discussed in that chapter, research during the 1960s showed that this correction was not useful in general. The reason was that the theory leading to Yates' correction was again based on the condition of fixed marginal totals. As we have just pointed out, this condition is not met in most situations describable by 2×2 tables. However, we have just shown that this condition is satisfied in the case of Mood's two-sample test. The conclusion is that, when the sample sizes are large enough for the chi-squared (approximate) critical values to be used, which means that in effect both sample sizes should be at least 10, the use of Yates' correction does improve the accuracy of the test. This correction consists of reducing the differences between the observed (Ob.) and expected (Ex.) frequencies in the numerator of the chi-squared statistic before squaring, i.e. the corrected statistic is now

$$\alpha^2 = \sum \frac{(|\text{Ex.} - \text{Ob.}| - \frac{1}{2})^2}{\text{Ex.}}$$

The same is true for the Mood–Westenberg test to follow, so we will wait until then for an illustration.

Finally, a slight problem arises if the total number of observations is odd, for then of course the overall median is an actual observation. The easiest thing to do in such a case is simply to ignore that median observation, and to reduce by one the corresponding sample size.

THE MOOD–WESTENBERG TWO-SAMPLE DISPERSION TEST

J. Westenberg (1948) published a simple procedure for testing whether or not two populations have the same spread. Because the test can be presented in a form similar to Mood's two-sample test, we shall refer to it as the Mood–Westenberg test.

As with the Siegel–Tukey test (see Ch. 6) for this situation, it is assumed that the two populations have roughly the same average. However, unlike the Siegel–Tukey test, the Mood–Westenberg test does not involve a ranking procedure and so is somewhat quicker to perform. We will illustrate the Mood–Westenberg procedure with the investment problem of Chapter 6.

HYPOTHESES

As in Chapter 6, the hypotheses for this problem are as follows:

H_0: There is no difference in 'riskiness' between the two methods.
H_1: There is some difference in spread between the two methods.

DATA

For convenience, we reproduce the data below.

Fundamental	+5	+20	−24	−9	+50	+32		
(sample A)	+15	−34	−19	+28	+41	+11		
Technical	−4	+19	+21	+13	+2	−7	+24	+10
(sample B)	+26	+14	+6	−10	−21	+36	+7	

STATISTIC

The idea is really quite simple. First, we combine the two samples (as we did for the Siegel–Tukey test) and then obtain the lower quartile (Q_L) and the upper quartile (Q_U) of this combined sample. Now, if H_0 is true, i.e. there is no difference in spread between the two populations, then we would expect to have (roughly) equal number of observations from each

A A A A B | A A B B B A B B B A | A B A A A

Q_L Q_U

Difference in spread

A B B A B | A B A A B B A B A A | B B A A B

Q_L Q_U

Equal spread

Figure 18.1

sample between Q_L and Q_U and outside this range. This idea is illustrated in Figure 8.1, which also shows typical letter sequences from the two situations.

So all we have to do is to count the numbers of 'A's and 'B's between Q_L and Q_U, i.e. within and outside the interquartile range; we will denote the numbers between Q_L and Q_U by m_A and m_B respectively. This information is conveniently expressed in the form of a 2×2 contingency table; such a table is shown below, where n_A and n_B are the two sample sizes from the respective populations.

	Sample		
	A	B	
Between Q_L and Q_U	m_A	m_B	$m_A + m_B$
Outside Q_L and Q_U	$n_A - m_A$	$n_B - m_B$	$n_A + n_B - (m_A + m_B)$
	n_A	n_b	$n_A + n_B$

We now follow the procedure given for the previous tests in this chapter, but first we recommend writing down the observations on a rough linear scale (as we have done with other two-sample tests). This we have done in Figure 18.2. The values of Q_L and Q_U are easily calculated using the following rules. If N is the total sample size then

(a) if $N/4$ is not a whole number then Q_L and Q_U are the 'next whole number larger than $N/4$' values from each end of the ordered sample;

(b) if $N/4$ is a whole number then Q_L and Q_U are taken to be equal to half the sum of the '$N/4$ and $N/4+1$' values from each end of the ordered sample.

Sample A

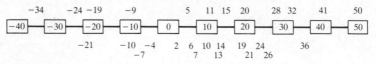

Sample B

Figure 18.2

In our problem, $N/4=25/4=6.25$ is not a whole number and so rule (a) applies: Q_L is the seventh value from the left and Q_U the seventh value from the right side of the ordered sample. Thus $Q_L=-7$ and $Q_U=24$, both of which are actual data values (in fact, both are from sample B) and so, following the remark on page 343, we discard these values from the counting procedure. We see that we have four A values and nine B values in the interquartile range; the resulting contingency table is given below.

	Sample		
	A	B	
Between Q_L and Q_U	4	9	13
Outside Q_L and Q_U	8	4	12
	12	13	25

We now follow the steps for a two-sided test given on pages 340 and 341.

Step 1   Examining the four marginal totals, we find that the smallest is 12; there are two totals with this value, and we arbitrarily choose the first column total; thus $m=12$.

Step 2   Since we are dealing with a two-sided test, we consider in turn the two values, 4 and 8, which make up the column total $m=12$.

Steps 3, 4 and 5 Consider $f=4$. We have $M=13$, this being the other marginal total to which f contributes. Now with $N=25$, Table Z gives $C=3$ and $\alpha=2.6\%$.

          Consider $f=8$. Now $M=12$ and so, with $N=25$, Table Z gives $C=3$ and $\alpha=6.8\%$.

          Clearly, the only value of f worth considering is $f=4$ (being the only one close to its corresponding critical value).

CRITICAL REGION AND CONCLUSION

Following step 6, we have $f=4 > c=3$, and so the result is not significant at the 10% significance level (remembering to double α as discussed in the 'Two-sided tests' section on page 341). In other words, we have no worthwhile evidence to support the alternative hypothesis of a difference in spread between the two investment methods. It is interesting to note that this conclusion is in agreement with the conclusion from the Siegel–Tukey test of Chapter 6.

19
Confidence intervals

Introduction

If you are familiar with books dealing with what we have variously called the classical, standard or traditional approach to statistics, you will probably have noticed a very important difference in emphasis in this book (in addition to the obvious concentration on distribution-free methods). So far, we have dealt exclusively with statistical *tests*, whereas in the traditional approach there is usually a comparable amount of attention devoted to *estimation*, and in particular to the formulation of *confidence intervals*. Indeed, in recent years, some statisticians have spoken for the abolition of statistical tests in favour of estimation methods, claiming that the job done by a test can also be done by an estimation method and, in some senses, the estimation method executes the task more accurately and comprehensively. While not subscribing to such an extreme view, the authors do appreciate these arguments in the classical context, and indeed regard them as a consequence of the lack of generality of the traditional, as opposed to the distribution-free, approach. Nevertheless, there are some situations covered earlier in this book which are more or less conducive to the construction of confidence intervals, and the book would not be complete without some mention of such techniques.

In order to understand why estimation methods are less relevant in a distribution-free context, it is opportune here to spell out in a little more detail the fundamental difference between the two approaches. The techniques in this book, which we have always referred to as 'distribution-free', are often termed 'non-parametric' elsewhere. We prefer the former term because it highlights quite unambiguously the essential feature of the approach (i.e. the lack of distributional assumptions on the populations being sampled), whereas 'non-parametric' is less immediate in its meaning and, in some senses, is not a strictly accurate adjective. On the other hand, most traditional statistical methods are definitely 'parametric', i.e. they are defined entirely in terms of *parameters* (such as the mean and standard deviation) of the underlying distributions.

As opposed to the distribution-free nature of the techniques in this book, traditional methods generally require the assumption that the data are drawn from a specific type, or 'family', of distributions, such as normal distributions (or perhaps binomial or exponential, etc.). The members of these families are 'referenced' or 'indexed' by one or more such parameters so that the specification of the values of these parameters then implies complete knowledge of the distribution; at least, as long as the initial assumptions are correct!

Traditional statistical inference is purely concerned with using the data to give information about these unknown parameters. For example, the parameters of a normal distribution are its mean μ and standard deviation σ, the parameters of a binomial distribution are n and p, and there are a number of families of distributions (e.g. Poisson and exponential) which are indexed by a single parameter, such as the mean. When a family of distributions needs more than one parameter to index its individual members, it may be that in a particular application all but one of the parameters are known (actually or presumed), so that the statistical problem is just concerned with inferences about a single parameter.

There are usually one or more 'obvious' ways of estimating this parameter, in particular by its sample equivalent. Thus one could estimate the population's mean by the mean of the sample, or more relevantly in the current context of distribution-free methods, we could estimate the population's median by the sample median; such single-value estimates are called *point estimates*. The main problem with a point estimate is that no direct indication is given of how close one might expect this estimate to be to the true value. If there is a way of assessing the precision of the estimator, then for many purposes the most sensible way to present the information is by means of a *confidence interval*. As the name implies, this is an interval within which we can be 'confident' that the true value lies. If the basic estimator has high precision (i.e. gives results that are consistently close to the true value) then the corresponding confidence interval will be narrow; but if the estimator is not particularly good (for example, because the sample is too small or because the underlying distribution has large spread) then the confidence interval will be wide. In this context, confidence is quantified by a *confidence level*, which we shall denote by γ, and which represents the level of certainty of the interval containing the true value. The most common (nominal) confidence levels are $\gamma=95\%$ and 99%. Recall that with tests we use 'best conservative' critical regions, i.e. regions whose corresponding significance levels are the nearest available to the nominal level (of, say, 5% or 1%) without exceeding it. In the same way, the actual confidence level of any interval that we shall produce will be the nearest available to the nominal level (of, say, 95% or 99%) but erring 'on the safe side' – that is, the true probability of the interval containing the correct value will be *no less than* the nominal level.

When the statistical problem is simply concerned with inference about a simple parameter (such as the population median), then there is usually an automatic mathematical equivalence between confidence intervals and

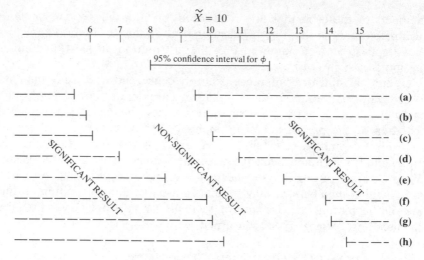

Figure 19.1 Critical regions (broken lines) for testing null hyotheses: (a) ϕ = 7.5; (b) ϕ = 7.9;   (c) ϕ = 8.1;   (d) ϕ = 9.0;   (e) ϕ = 10.5;   (f) ϕ = 11.9;   (g) ϕ = 12.1; (h) ϕ = 12.5.

tests, particularly with two-sided tests. This equivalence is explained by the following rule. Consider testing the null hypothesis H_0 that the parameter is equal to some specific value against the general (two-sided) alternative. *Then H_0 is rejected at the α_2 significance level if and only if this specified value is* not *included in the ordinary confidence interval of level $(100 - \alpha_2)\%$.* So, for instance, any value v_0 contained within the γ=95% confidence interval is such that the two-sided test of the null hypothesis that the parameter is equal to v_0 would not give a significant result.

As an example, suppose that the median $\tilde{X}$ of a sample is equal to 10, and that this happens to produce a 95% confidence interval for the population median ϕ of (8,12). Then the 5% critical regions for testing various null hypotheses for the value of ϕ might be as shown in Figure 19.1. Note that X=10 lies *in* the critical regions in cases (a), (b), (g) and (h), which are the cases where the hypothesized value of ϕ is below 8 or above 12, i.e. outside the confidence interval.

In spite of this apparently simple rule, it turns out that, whereas many distribution-free tests are quick and convenient to use, the same cannot be said of distribution-free confidence intervals. Often the notion of confidence intervals is irrelevant anyway, since the practical situation being analysed may be so general that in no way can a *single* parameter describe it. But, supposing this is possible, distribution-free confidence intervals are often tedious to calculate even for quite small samples, while for larger samples the methods can be extremely cumbersome and impracticable except with the aid of a computer (see the programs at the end of this chapter).

The first of the three methods to be described in this chapter is, however, an exception – this is perhaps not surprising since its theory is linked to that of the sign test. It is a method for finding confidence intervals for a population median ϕ. The second technique concerns the estimation of the difference in location (particularly medians) between two populations; that technique is related to the Mann–Whitney test. Finally we have a method based on Wilcoxon's signed-rank test, which therefore is most usually applied to estimating the average change in a matched-pairs situation (although it is also applicable to estimating the median of a single population if that population's distribution is symmetric – which, if you remember, was the requirement demanded in Chapter 3 if Wilcoxon's test was to be used).

CONFIDENCE INTERVALS FOR THE MEDIAN

Introduction

This unusually easy method for finding confidence intervals for the population median ϕ is based on ideas related to those involved in the sign test. Indeed we shall use the critical values for the sign test (Table C or page 29 of *EST*) as an integral part of the procedure.

PRACTICAL PROBLEM

We shall refer to the problem used to illustrate the sign test in Chapter 3. The data given were the times to process orders in an administrative process; for convenience, we reproduce the data below.

16 h 30 min	14 h 00 min	5 h 40 min	9 h 10 min
11 h 45 min	4 h 20 min	7 h 55 min	10 h 15 min
7 h 45 min	16h 05 min	10 h 05 min	7 h 30 min
9 h 15 min	11 h 55 min	9 h 25 min	10 h 35 min
8 h 20 min	12 h 15 min		

Let us now try to find a confidence interval for the median processing time ϕ; we shall use a confidence coefficient $\gamma=95\%$, which means there is *at least* a 95% chance that the resulting interval will include the true value of ϕ.

METHOD

As may be implied by the rule given in the introduction, we enter the table of critical values for the sign test at the α_2 value given by $\alpha_2=100\%-\gamma$; here we have $\gamma=95\%$, and so the relevant value of α_2 is 5%. For $n=18$, the tabulated entry is 4, but let us denote it by x in general.

The confidence interval is then found as follows. Delete from the sample the x smallest and the x largest values. The required confidence interval is then simply *the interval from the smallest to the largest values that remain*.

Checking with the data given above, and recalling that $x=4$ in this case, the four highest times are 16 h 30 min, 16 h 05 min, 14 h 00 min and 12 h 15 min. After deleting these times, the highest time left is 11 h 55 min. The four shortest times are 4 h 20 min, 4 h 35 min, 6 h 30 min and 8 h 05 min; after deleting these times, the shortest time remaining is 8 h 10 min. Hence the required confidence interval for the median processing time is (8 h 10 min, 11 h 55 min), and we are 95% confident (in the sense defined above) that the median processing time lies in this range.

Discussion

This technique shown for obtaining confidence intervals for ϕ is very easy to carry out. This is certainly not true for most other distribution-free confidence interval methods – including the remaining two to be presented in this chapter, in spite of the fact that they are also based on very well known distribution-free tests.

There is a further point worth mentioning. Classical methods for finding confidence intervals for a population mean μ are restricted to producing intervals having the point estimate (viz. the sample mean $\overline{X}$) at their centre. There is no such restriction here. In the above case, the natural point estimate of ϕ is the sample median $\tilde{X}=\frac{1}{2}(9$ h 25 min $+$ 10 h 05 min$) = 9$ h 45 min, whereas the centre of the confidence interval is at 10 h 02$\frac{1}{2}$ min.

Theory

The easiest way to demonstrate the theory of this technique is first to illustrate it with the above numerical example and then to generalize.

Let us recall the details of the sign test and the interpretation of a critical value. Suppose we were carrying out a *two-sided* test of the null hypothesis H_0 that the median ϕ is equal to some value, m say. (In Chapter 3, m was 8 h.) We represented each observation in the sample by a $+$ or $-$ sign according as to whether it was greater or less than m (to keep this explanation as simple as possible, presume for the moment that there are no observations equal to m). The test statistic was the number of $+$ or $-$ signs, whichever turned out to be the smaller. How exactly, therefore, do we interpret the fact that the critical value corresponding to the $\alpha_2=5\%$ significance level is 4? Referring to the basic formulation of statistical tests in Chapter 2 (if necessary), the meaning is as follows. If H_0 is true, i.e. *$\phi=m$, the total probability of there being 4 or less observations less than m, or 4 or less observations greater than m, is less than or equal to $\alpha_2=5\%$*. In fact, using the binomial tables on page 11 of *EST*, this probability is $2\times0.0154=0.0308$ or 3.08%.

So that we can write this italicized statement in a form more appropriate for the current purpose, it is convenient to introduce a standard notation for the *order statistics* in a sample. This is simply that $X_{(1)}$ represents the minimum value in the sample, $X_{(2)}$ the next smallest, $X_{(3)}$ the third smallest, and so on up to $X_{(n)}$ which is the maximum observation in the sample. With the data in our example, $X_{(1)} = 4$ h 20 min, $X_{(2)} = 4$ h 35 min, $X_{(3)} = 6$ h 30 min, $X_{(4)} = 8$ h 05 min and so on up to $X_{(18)} = 16$ h 30 min.

Referring to the italicized statement above, note that if there are four or less observations less than m, this implies that $X_{(5)}$ must *exceed m*. Similarly, if there are four or less observations that exceed m, this implies that $X_{(14)}$ is *less* than m. We therefore conclude that the probability of either $X_{(5)} > m$ *or* $X_{(14)} < m$ is no greater than $\alpha_2 = 5\%$ (3.08% in this case). By simple logic (or by elementary laws of probability), this statement can be reversed to claim that the probability of both $X_{(5)} \leq m$ *and* $X_{(14)} \geq m$ is no less than $100\% - \alpha_2$, i.e. no less than 95%, and in fact is equal to $(100 - 3.08)\% = 96.92\%$ in our example. But the event now being referred to can be written $X_{(5)} \leq m \leq X_{(14)}$, i.e. m lies in the interval $(X_{(5)}, X_{(14)})$. Therefore, finally, remembering that this argument depends on the truth of H_0: $\phi = m$, it follows that we can claim to have at least 95% confidence that ϕ lies between $X_{(5)}$ and $X_{(14)}$ – and this is precisely what was claimed in the illustration above.

The generalization now follows in a straightforward manner. Given a nominal confidence coefficient $\gamma\%$, we enter the table of critical values of the sign test at $\alpha_2 = (100 - \gamma)\%$, reading off the value c, say. This implies that the probability of there being c or fewer observations less than the true median ϕ, or of there being c or fewer observations greater than ϕ, totals at most α_2. This statement can be reversed to produce the fact that the probability of $X_{(c+1)} \leq \phi \leq X_{(n-c)}$ is at least $100\% - \alpha_2 = \gamma\%$ – and this is precisely what is required for $(X_{(c+1)}, X_{(n-c)})$ to be the required confidence interval.

One can also generalize the above use of the binomial tables to find the *exact* confidence level of any particular interval. The theory both of the sign test and of this method of producing confidence intervals is based on the fact that, in a random sample of size n from a continuous distribution, the number S of observations exceeding the median (or less than the median) is binomially distributed with parameters n and $p = \frac{1}{2}$. We used this in Chapter 3 to find the exact significance level corresponding to any critical region. The method for finding an exact confidence level is as follows. Let the critical value found from Table C (or page 29 in *EST*) be c; then from the cumulative probability tables of the binomial distribution (pages 5, 7, 9 and 11 in *EST*) find $F(c)$, i.e. Prob($S \leq c$). (This is therefore the exact value of α_1, the significance level of the one-sided test having critical region $S \leq c$.) Now double α_1 to obtain α_2 and calculate $\gamma = 100\% - \alpha_2$; this is the required exact confidence level γ.

Large sample sizes
For sample sizes n greater than those in Table C (or the table on page 29 of *EST*), we can use the normal approximation to the binomial distribution. This gives extremely accurate results, providing that the continuity correction is used. In fact, the normal approximation is accurate for much smaller values of n, and it can therefore also be used to estimate the exact confidence level of an interval for those cases not covered by Table C. We demonstrate this idea below.

We have already seen in Chapter 3 how to use the normal approximation to provide critical values for the sign test. So there is really nothing new to learn here. In order to produce a confidence interval of nominal level γ, we find the critical value that would be appropriate for a two-sided test of significance level $\alpha_2 = 100\% - \gamma$, and use it as shown above.

Suppose, for illustration, we had a sample of size $n=120$ and wanted to produce a 99% confidence interval for ϕ; $\gamma = 99\%$ corresponds to $\alpha_2 = 1\%$ and thus to $\alpha_1 = \frac{1}{2}\%$. We would like to find the value of c for which $\alpha_1 = \text{Prob}(S \leqslant c) \approx \Phi[(c + \frac{1}{2} - \frac{1}{2}n)/\frac{1}{2}\sqrt{n}]$ (see Ch. 3); or rather, seeing that we cannot expect to do this exactly, we need to find the value of c such that this probability is just under $\alpha_1 = \frac{1}{2}\%$. From Table A, we find that $\frac{1}{2}\% = \Phi(-2.5758)$, and so we solve the equation

$$\frac{c + \frac{1}{2} - \frac{1}{2}n}{\frac{1}{2}\sqrt{n}} = -2.5758$$

for c, remembering that $n=120$. This gives

$$c = -(\tfrac{1}{2}\sqrt{n}) \times 2.5758 - \tfrac{1}{2} + \tfrac{1}{2}n = 45.39$$

This implies that if we take $c=45$, $\text{Prob}(S \leqslant c)$ will be *less* than $\frac{1}{2}\%$ while if we take $c=46$, $\text{Prob}(S \leqslant c)$ will *exceed* $\frac{1}{2}\%$. Therefore 45 is the critical value that would have been tabulated if the tables had gone as far as $n=120$. Thus the required confidence interval is $(X_{(45+1)}, X_{(120-45)})$, i.e. $(X_{(46)}, X_{(75)})$.

Finally, we show how to use the normal approximation to estimate the exact confidence level of an interval. For illustration, we will use the same case as earlier, i.e. the interval $(X_{(5)}, X_{(14)})$ when $n=18$, which was the interval appropriate for the nominal confidence level $\gamma = 95\%$. We have already evaluated the exact confidence level, using binomial tables, as 96.92%; let us see how close the normal approximation method comes.

The method approximates $\text{Prob}(S \leqslant c) = \text{Prob}(S \leqslant 4)$ by

$$\Phi\left(\frac{(4 + \frac{1}{2} - \frac{1}{2} \times 18)}{\frac{1}{2}\sqrt{18}}\right) = \Phi(-2.121)$$

From Table A, this is equal to 0.0170 or 1.70%. This plays the role of α_1, so that $\alpha_2 = 2\alpha_1 = 3.40\%$ giving $\gamma = (100 - 3.40)\% = 96.60\%$. This differs from the true value by only 0.32%.

CONFIDENCE INTERVALS FOR LOCATION DIFFERENCES

Introduction

As we have seen, a confidence interval is usually constructed in association with a particular test; we have just seen a method of constructing an interval for the population median ϕ based on the sign test. Recall the basic principle that the confidence interval contains all values of the quantity being estimated which would not be rejected by a

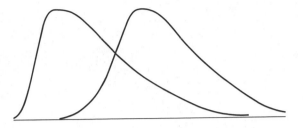

Figure 19.2

two-sided test; the confidence level γ of the interval and the significance level α_2 of the test are complementary, i.e. $\gamma+\alpha_2=100\%$. The 'quantity' being estimated in this section is the difference in location between the two populations that have been sampled. If we assume that the populations' distributions may differ *only* in location, then one distribution is simply a shifted version of the other, as for example in Figure 19.2. It is that shift which is being estimated and, under the above assumption, it is equal to the difference between the two medians, or means (if they exist) or, indeed, the values of any well defined measure of location.

The test associated with the confidence interval method described in this section is the Mann–Whitney test. After first going through the mechanics of the method, we shall then discuss how and why the basic principle just mentioned applies in this case. As we warned you at the beginning of the chapter, the technique is a little unwieldy! It can be carried out graphically or arithmetically; we shall cover both, as it is a matter of personal taste which one prefers.

PRACTICAL PROBLEM

We shall illustrate the technique with the situation and data used in Chapter 5. So now we are attempting to find confidence intervals for the difference between median percentages of the British and Japanese cars breaking down during their first year of use. This is a case where confidence intervals may well be of more interest than the test, because it was virtually certain from the data that H_0 had to be rejected, even without carrying out the tests. The data for this problem, i.e. number of breakdowns, are reproduced below for convenience.

Japanese	3	7	15	10	4	6	4	7				
British	19	11	36	8	25	23	38	14	17	41	25	21

GRAPHICAL METHOD

In Figure 19.3, we have set up scales on ordinary graph paper with the x axis covering the values in sample B and the y axis covering the values in

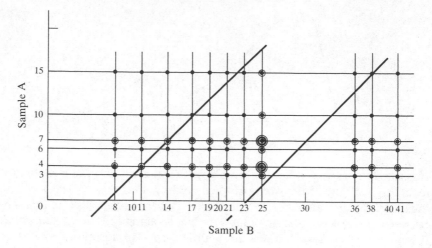

Figure 19.3

sample A. The scales *must* be the same on both axes. We mark sample B's values on the x axis and draw verticals through those points; similarly we mark sample A's values on the y axis and draw horizontal lines through them. If all the observations in each sample are distinct from each other (i.e. there are no tied observations within either sample), there are $n_A n_B$ points of intersection between the vertical and horizontal lines just drawn. If there are ties, the corresponding points should be circled one or more times to indicate such duplication. (Note that in Figure 19.3, points corresponding to pairs of tied values in *both* samples are circled three times, corresponding to quadruple points of intersection.) Thus the total number of points and circles in the diagram is $n_A n_B = 8 \times 12 = 96$. comprising 66 points, 24 single circles and two triple circles (i.e. six circles).

Suppose we want the confidence level γ to be at least 95%. Similarly to finding intervals for ϕ using the sign test, we enter the Mann–Whitney table (Table G or page 30 in *EST*) in the $\alpha_2 = 5\%$ column (remember that $\gamma + \alpha_2 = 100\%$). With sample sizes 8 and 12, the critical value is 22.

Now consider a line, angled at 45° to the horizontal, approaching the graph from the top left-hand corner, and let it travel into the picture until it reaches the place where the number of points above or on it first exceeds 22. This is the upper 45° line shown in Figure 19.3. Similarly, consider a 45° line approaching the graph from the bottom right-hand corner, and move it into the picture until the number of points below or on it first exceeds 22; this is the lower 45° line in Figure 19.3.

A 45° line has an equation of the form $x - y = $ constant, the constant being found by subtracting the y coordinate from the x coordinate of any point on the line. By this means, it is easily seen that the two lines in

Figure 19.3 have equations $x-y=7$ and $x-y=23$. The two constants thus found are the end-points of the 95% confidence interval for the difference between median percentages of cars breaking down. Note that the interval does not include 0, which is of course consistent with the fact that the Mann–Whitney test rejected the null hypothesis of no difference at the $\alpha_2=5\%$ significance level (and also at much more stringent levels).

ARITHMETICAL METHOD

It is quite easy to simulate the graphical method without actually drawing the graph. This is achieved by constructing a table of differences between the A and B values (i.e. B−A) as shown below. The B values are shown in the bottom row of the table, going from smallest to largest; the A values are shown in the left-hand column, with the smallest at the bottom and the largest at the top. Note that tied values are duplicated as appropriate. In the body of the table are displayed the $n_A-n_B=8\times12=96$ differences between the A and B values. (These differences correspond to the $n_A n_B$ comparisons made in the Mann–Whitney test.)

A												
15	−7	−4	−1	+2	+4	+6	+8	+10	+10	+21	+23	+26
10	−2	+1	+4	+7	+9	+11	+13	+15	+15	+26	+28	+31
7	+1	+4	+7	+10	+12	+14	+16	+18	+18	+29	+31	+34
7	+1	+4	+7	+10	+12	+14	+16	+18	+18	+29	+31	+34
6	+2	+5	+8	+11	+13	+15	+17	+19	+19	+30	+32	+35
4	+4	+7	+10	+13	+15	+17	+19	+21	+21	+32	+34	+37
4	+4	+7	+10	+13	+15	+17	+19	+21	+21	+32	+34	+37
3	+5	+8	+11	+14	+16	+18	+20	+22	+22	+33	+35	+38
	8	11	14	17	19	21	23	25	25	36	38	41 B

We now start marking off the differences from the top left-hand corner, beginning with the −7 and then in natural ascending order, i.e. −7 first, then −4, −2 and −1, then the three +1's, the the two +2's, . . . , and so on until we have marked off 23 (one more than the tabulated value of 22) numbers. You will find that there are 18 differences of +6 or less and five of +7. So the 23rd difference marked off is +7; this is then the lower limit of the confidence interval. Next we carry out a similar operation starting from the +38 at the bottom right-hand corner, and then marking off 23 numbers in descending order: +38, +37, +37, +35, +35, +34, +34, +34, +34, +33, etc. You should find the 23rd number marked off in this sequence is +23. The required confidence interval is thus (+7, +23), the same result as obtained by the graphical method.

Discussion
If you compare the graphical and the arithmetical methods, it should be apparent why they are equivalent. In short, the differences in the arithmetical method are marked off in precisely the same order that the 45° lines cross the corresponding

points in the graphical method. The arithmetical method is quickest to carry out if the sample sizes are fairly small, but the graphical method is probably the better choice otherwise. However, you will see that even the graphical method is quite time-consuming when the samples are at all large, since the number $n_A n_B$ of points to consider, and the number (found from the tables) of points to count in from the extremes, both increase sharply with increasing sample sizes.

Theory
The theory of this method may not be quite so easy to understand as that of the one-sample method based on the sign test. This is particularly so because, whereas in the one-sample case it is common to think of testing an H_0 that ϕ equals any specified value, in the two-sample case it is most natural to think of testing just the H_0 that the difference between the population medians is zero. However, we need to broaden our minds here to consider similarly testing the H_0 that the median difference (say, median of B minus median of A) equals any specified value, d. In the Mann–Whitney test, where we were testing that the median difference is zero, the basic argument was that, given a random observation from each process, there is a probability of $\frac{1}{2}$ each that the A is greater or less than the B, i.e. that the B−A difference is positive or negative. Now suppose we are testing H_0 that the median difference is $d=10$, say. If this is true, obviously it is no longer the case that positive and negative differences are equally likely. Instead there are equal probabilities ($\frac{1}{2}$ each) that the difference is greater than or less than 10; equivalently, that *(B value)−(A value)−10 is positive or negative*. If you think for a moment, you will see that a clever way to test this hypothesis is to subtract 10 from all the B values (or, alternatively, add 10 to all the A values), and then carry out the ordinary Mann–Whitney test on the resulting data.

As an exercise, carry out this operation on the car breakdowns data, by adding 10 to the A values. (This will incidentally give you some practice at dealing with ties!) The answer is $U=30$, and there is thus no reason for rejecting this H_0 since the $\alpha_2=10\%$ critical region is $U\leqslant 26$. Hence a median percentage difference of 10% is quite consistent with these data (as opposed to the median difference of 0 which was conclusively rejected).

The same operation can clearly be carried out with any desired hypothesized d. What we need therefore is to find the minimum and maximum values of d which will just permit non-rejection of H_0 (say, at the $\alpha_2=5\%$ level). The table below shows the values of U, calculated as in the above exercise, for several values of d.

d	U	d	U
$d=5$	16	⋮	⋮
$5<d<6$	17	$d=21$	$27\frac{1}{2}$
$d=6$	$17\frac{1}{2}$	$21<d<22$	25
$6<d<7$	18	$d=22$	24
$d=7$	$20\frac{1}{2}$	$22<d<23$	23
$7<d<8$	23	$d=23$	$22\frac{1}{2}$
$d=8$	$24\frac{1}{2}$	$23<d<26$	22
$8<d<9$	26	$d=26$	21
$d=9$	$26\frac{1}{2}$	$26<d<28$	20
⋮	⋮	$d=28$	$19\frac{1}{2}$

Thus, in fact, the range of values of d which would not be rejected at the $\alpha_2=5\%$ level (i.e. which do not result in the value U lying in the critical region $U \leqslant 22$) is $7<d<23$. Notice that there may be end-point discrepancies (e.g. should 7 be included in the confidence interval or not?) between the method as presented above and the theory as presented here but, particularly with continuous distributions, this is of negligible importance. A refinement could be made to the method to produce an exact correspondence.)

The general justification of the method is thus as follows. The 45° lines in the graphical method have equations of the form $x-y=d$, each line corresponding to a different value of d (for example, given by the x coordinate of the point where the line intersects the x axis). As a 45° line moves into the picture from either extreme, the number of points crossed by the stage at which its equation is $x-y=d$ is the value of the U statistic when testing the H_0 that the median difference is d. Before the line starts moving into the picture, no points have been crossed, i.e. $U=0$, so any corresponding d is obviously an unreasonable value of the median difference. As the line moves into the picture, U steadily increases, and the process is stopped as soon as U exceeds the critical value, i.e. as soon as the test would yield a non-significant result.

Large sample sizes
Critical values may be calculated very accurately from the normal approximation given in Chapter 5. Once obtained, they may then be used as above to provide confidence intervals. As already mentioned, both the graphical and arithmetical methods are rather unwieldy with large samples, with the graphical method being the lesser of the two evils. So in general, for large samples you will need to use the computer program given at the end of this chapter (Program 19.1).

CONFIDENCE INTERVALS FOR A MATCHED-PAIRS DIFFERENCE

INTRODUCTION

Finally, we present a confidence interval method based on Wilcoxon's signed-rank test (see Ch. 8). This is particularly relevant therefore for providing an interval for the average change in a matched-pairs situation. However, it may also be used as an alternative to the first method in this chapter for producing confidence intervals for ϕ, *as long as* the population distribution may be regarded as symmetric. The method is considerably more involved than that based on the sign test, but should generally give narrower intervals.

PRACTICAL PROBLEM

Again for illustration purposes, we shall use the relevant practical problem from earlier in the book; in this case, it is the one in Chapter 8 concerning the improvement in BOD levels after the implementation of anti-pollution controls. The data for this problem are given below.

Site	Before controls	Four years later	Change
1	17.4	13.6	3.8
2	15.7	10.1	5.6
3	12.9	10.3	2.6
4	9.8	9.2	0.6
5	13.4	11.1	2.3
6	18.7	20.4	−1.7
7	13.9	10.4	3.5
8	11.0	11.4	−0.4
9	5.4	4.9	0.5
10	10.4	8.9	1.5
11	16.4	11.2	5.2
12	5.6	4.8	0.6

METHOD

Denoting the n differences by $X_1, X_2, \ldots, X_n$, we calculate the $\frac{1}{2}n(n+1)$ pairwise averages $u_{ij}=\frac{1}{2}(X_i+X_j)$ for $i=1,2,\ldots,n$ and $j=i,i+1,\ldots,n$. Note that these include $X_1, X_2, \ldots, X_n$ themselves, corresponding to $u_{11}, u_{22}, \ldots, U_{nn}$. We then look up a value in the Wilcoxon table (Table D or the second table on page 29 in *EST*), exactly as we did when forming a confidence interval based on the sign test using Table C (or the first table on page 29 in *EST*). Thus here, with $n=12$ and $\gamma=99\%$, say, we enter the table at $\alpha_2=1\%$ and obtain the value $T=7$. Now we proceed precisely as with the previous two techniques in this chapter, but operating on the set of u_{ij} averages defined above. That is, we delete the seven smallest u_{ij} values and the seven largest u_{ij} values. The required confidence interval is then the range of the remaining averages, i.e. from the eighth smallest to the eighth largest average.

The work may be conveniently set out in the triangular table given below. Listed down the left-hand side and in the top row are the 12 changes in BOD levels; the body of the table contains the 78 u_{ij} values. For ease in identifying the smallest and largest u_{ij} for deletion, we have arranged the 12 differences in ascending order before forming the table.

	−1.7	−0.4	0.5	0.6	0.8	1.5	2.3	2.6	3.5	3.8	5.2	5.6
5.6	1.95	2.60	3.05	3.10	3.20	3.55	3.95	4.10	4.55	4.70	5.40	5.60
5.2	1.75	2.40	2.85	2.90	3.00	3.35	3.75	3.90	4.35	4.50	5.20	
3.8	1.05	1.70	2.15	2.20	2.30	2.65	3.05	3.20	3.65	3.80		
3.5	0.90	1.55	2.00	2.05	2.15	2.50	2.90	3.05	3.50			
2.6	0.45	1.10	1.55	1.60	1.70	2.05	2.45	2.60				
2.3	0.30	0.95	1.40	1.45	1.55	1.90	2.30					
1.5	−0.10	0.55	1.00	1.05	1.15	1.50						
0.8	−0.45	0.20	0.65	0.70	0.80							
0.6	−0.55	0.10	0.55	0.60								
0.5	−0.60	0.05	0.50									
−0.4	−1.05	−0.40										
−1.7	−1.70											

Then the smallest (or rather, largest negative) u_{ij} values will be found at the bottom of the table and the largest positive towards the right-hand corner. You may check that the eighth smallest u_{ij} is 0.05, and the eighth largest is 4.10; the required confidence interval for the average decrease in BOD is therefore (0.05, 4.10). Note that 0 is just outside this confidence interval, reflecting the fact that the null hypothesis of no change was rejected in Chapter 8 at the $\alpha_1 = \frac{1}{2}\%$.

Discussion
As with the previous method related to the Mann–Whitney test, this technique becomes very laborious with large sample sizes, and so the computer routine (Program 19.2) will be particularly useful here. Note, however, that it is not necessary in practice to complete the whole of the table of u_{ij} values; having seen where the largest and smallest u_{ij} are found, one can, with care, concentrate on calculating just the u_{ij} values in those two parts of the table.

Theory
The theory of this technique is perhaps a little tricky to follow. Recall that the statistic for Wilcoxon's signed-rank test was the sum of the ranks of either the positive or negative differences, the differences being ranked irrespective of sign. Let us first establish the link between these ranks and the u_{ij} used in forming the confidence interval.

Consider the rank of a typical difference (irrespective of sign) in our example, say the 1.5; its rank is 5. Now focus attention on all those u_{ij} which involve 1.5. The averages of 1.5 with the four smaller differences (-0.4, 0.5, 0.6 and 0.8) are 0.55, 1.00, 1.05 and 1.15; note, in particular, that they must all be non-negative and less than 1.5. The other u_{ij} involving the 1.5 must either be negative or be greater than 1.5 (except the u_{ij} involving 1.5 twice, which must of course be equal to 1.5). Therefore we see that there are precisely five u_{ij} values involving 1.5 which lie between 0 and 1.5 inclusive; and five happens to be the rank of 1.5. This rule is immediately generalizable. The rank of any observation, x say, in the current context (i.e. ignoring signs) is between 0 and x inclusive. (The rule needs some refinement in the case of tied observations, but we will ignore that complication here as it turns out to be irrelevant to the main argument.)

Now refer to the table of u_{ij} values. Notice first that all the u_{ij} in any column must be greater than or equal to the difference at the top of the column. In particular, if we consider a column headed by a *negative* difference (either of the first two columns in this example), it follows that the rank of that difference is simply given by the number of negative u_{ij} in that column (so the rank of -1.7 is 6 and the rank of -0.4 is 1). The remaining columns cannot contain any negative differences. Therefore we obtain the very important result that *the sum of the ranks of the negative differences is equal to the total number of negative u_{ij} in the* table. A similar argument involving rows instead of columns shows that the sum of the ranks of the positive differences is equal to the total number of positive u_{ij} in the table. This is consistent with the fact that these two sums of ranks must add up to $1+2+3+\ldots+n = \frac{1}{2}n(n+1)$, which is of course equal to the total number of u_{ij} that have been defined. The two rank sums in the examples are respectively 7 and 71, which agrees with the value of $T=7$ found in Chapter 8.

Now, as with the previous method based on the Mann–Whitney test, we must broaden our minds to consider what would happen if we wished to test the null hypothesis that the average value of the change (B value minus A value, say) were equal to some non-zero value d. The obvious way to adjust the test procedure is to replace the 'B minus A' differences used previously by 'B minus A minus d', and then proceed as usual. Suppose we take $d=2.5$. Then, retaining the natural ordering of the differences used above, they become:

$$-4.2 \quad -2.9 \quad -2.0 \quad -1.9 \quad -1.7 \quad -1.0 \quad -0.1 \quad +0.1 \quad +1.0 \quad +1.3 \quad +2.7 \quad +3.1$$

If you carry out the signed-rank test on these data, you will find that T is now $29\frac{1}{2}$ (given by the sum of the ranks of the positive differences; the sum of the ranks of the negative differences is $48\frac{1}{2}$), which is not significant. Therefore, an average improvement in BOD of 2.5 is consistent with the data.

However, of more importance in the current context, let us now construct the table of u_{ij} values for these new differences $(B-A-d)$. These are given in the table below.

	−4.2	−2.9	−2.0	−1.9	−1.7	−1.0	−0.2	0.1	1.0	1.3	2.7	3.1
3.1	−0.55	0.10	0.55	0.60	0.70	1.05	1.45	1.60	2.05	2.20	2.90	3.10
2.7	−0.75	−0.10	0.35	0.40	0.50	0.85	1.25	1.40	1.85	2.00	2.70	
1.3	−1.45	−0.80	−0.35	−0.30	−0.20	0.15	0.55	0.70	1.15	1.30		
1.0	−1.60	−0.95	−0.50	−0.45	−0.35	0	0.40	0.55	1.00			
0.1	−2.05	−1.40	−0.95	−0.90	−0.80	−0.45	−0.05	0.10				
−0.2	−2.20	−1.55	−1.10	−1.05	−0.95	−0.60	−0.20					
−1.0	−2.60	−1.95	−1.50	−1.45	−1.35	−1.00						
−1.7	−2.95	−2.30	−1.85	−1.80	−1.70							
−1.9	−3.05	−2.40	−1.95	−1.90								
−2.0	−3.10	−2.45	−2.00									
−2.9	−3.55	−2.90										
−4.2	−4.2											

Note first that there are altogether 48 negative u_{ij}, 29 positive u_{ij} and one 0. We shall count the 0 as half a plus and half a minus, so obtaining $48\frac{1}{2}$ negatives and $29\frac{1}{2}$ positives, consistent with the test result above.

Now the crux of the matter is to observe that we *could* very easily have computed these new sums of ranks directly from the previous table of u_{ij}. It is apparent that the new u_{ij} are simply 2.5 $(=d)$ less than the original u_{ij}. Thus the *criterion of whether a new u_{ij} is positive or negative is identical to the criterion of whether the corresponding old u_{ij} is greater or less than 2.5 (or d, in general).*

So if we wanted to compute the statistic for several different values of d, the hypothesized average change, this gives us a much more efficient method than having to recalculate and rerank the differences (or form a new table of u_{ij}) each time. For any given value of d, all we do is to count the number of original u_{ij} which are less than, or greater than, d.

We can now apply this principle to justify the confidence interval technique. As usual, the confidence interval of level γ should contain those values of d which would not be rejected by a two-sided test of level $\alpha_2=100\%-\gamma$. It is easy to see that any value of d less than 0.5 would result in T being less than or equal to 7 (because there are seven u_{ij} values less than 0.5). But as soon as d gets to 0.5, T reaches 8 and becomes non-significant at the $\alpha_2=1\%$ level. Similarly, any value of d exceeding 4.10 gives $T \leq 7$, because there are just seven u_{ij} values greater than 4.0. Thus we indeed have $0.5 \leq d \leq 4.10$ as the range of values of d which are not rejected by a two-sided test with $\alpha_2 = 1\%$.

The generalization to all other n and γ is immediate.

Large sample sizes
For n beyond the range of the tables, we may find critical values using the normal approximation illustrated in Chapter 8; these critical values are then used in the same way as those read directly from the tables for smaller values of n.

Assignments

Construct appropriate 90% confidence intervals for: (a) assignments 1 and 2 of Chapter 3; (b) assignment 3 of Chapter 5.

1   Pain-relieving drugs
A pharmaceutical company sponsored an experiment to compare the effects of two pain-relieving drugs (identified as A and B) for the treatment of a certain disease. Ten patients took part in the experiment, each of them being given both drugs at different times. The number of hours of relief gained by each patient after the administration of each drug is given in the following table.

Patient	Drug A	Drug B
1	2.8	3.8
2	4.6	3.5
3	3.7	5.7
4	5.1	4.8
5	5.6	5.2
6	1.2	2.1
7	6.3	8.6
8	1.4	2.0
9	3.4	5.3
10	4.8	5.4

Task: Construct a 90% confidence interval for the average difference in performance between the drugs.

Program 19.1   Confidence interval for difference between two samples

```
100 REM *** CONFIDENCE INTERVAL FOR DIFFERENCE BETWEEN TWO SAMPLES ***

120 REM ** INPUT SAMPLES **
130 INPUT "SIZE OF SAMPLE A ? ";NA
140 DIM A(NA)
150 PRINT "INPUT SAMPLE A"
160 FOR I=1 TO NA
170 INPUT A(I)
180 NEXT I
190 PRINT
200 INPUT "SIZE OF SAMPLE B ? ";NB
210 LET N=NA*NB
220 DIM B(NB),D(N)
230 PRINT "INPUT SAMPLE B"
240 FOR I=1 TO NB
250 INPUT B(I)
260 NEXT I

270 REM ** CALCULATION OF THE DIFFERENCES **
280 LET L=0
290 FOR I=1 TO NB
300 FOR J=1 TO NA
310 LET L=L+1
320 LET D(L)=B(I)-A(J)
330 NEXT J
340 NEXT I
350 GO SUB 2000

360 REM ** CALCULATION OF THE INTERVAL **
370 PRINT
380 INPUT "CRITICAL VALUE ? ";C
390 PRINT
400 PRINT "CONFIDENCE INTERVAL IS "; D(C+1),D(N-C)
410 STOP

2000 REM ** SORT THE DIFFERENCES - USE LINES 2000-2160 OF PROGRAM 10.1 **
```

Program 19.2   *Confidence interval for matched-pairs differences*

```
100 REM *** CONFIDENCE INTERVAL FOR MATCHED PAIRS ***

120 REM ** INPUT SAMPLES **
130 INPUT "NUMBER OF PAIRS ? ";N
140 LET N2=N*(N+1)/2
150 DIM A(N),B(N),X(N),D(N2)
160 PRINT "INPUT THE PAIRS OF OBSERVATIONS"
170 FOR I=1 TO N
180 INPUT A(I),B(I)
190 NEXT I
200 PRINT

210 REM ** CALCULATION OF THE DIFFERENCES **
220 FOR I=1 TO N
230 LET X(I)=A(I)-B(I)
240 NEXT I
250 LET L=0
260 FOR I=1 TO N
270 FOR J=I TO N
280 LET L=L+1
290 LET D(L)=(X(I)+X(J))/2
300 NEXT J
310 NEXT I
320 GO SUB 2000

330 REM ** CALCULATION OF THE INTERVAL **
340 PRINT
350 INPUT "CRITICAL VALUE ? ";C
360 PRINT
370 PRINT "CONFIDENCE INTERVAL IS "; D(C+1),D(N-C)

2000 REM ** SORT THE DIFFERENCES - USE LINES 2000-2160 OF PROGRAM 10.1 **
```

PART VII
Tables

Table A Probabilities and percentage points of the standard normal distribution.

$$\Phi(z) = \int_{-\infty}^{z} (1/\sqrt{2\pi})\exp\,(-u^2/2)\ du = P(Z \leqslant z)$$

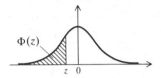

$\Phi(z)$

Probabilities

z	0	1	2	3	4	5	6	7	8	9
−3.0	0.0013	0.0010	0.0007	0.0005	0.0003	0.0002	0.0002	0.0001	0.0001	0.0000
−2.9	0.0019	0.0018	0.0017	0.0017	0.0016	0.0016	0.0015	0.0015	0.0014	0.0014
−2.8	0.0026	0.0025	0.0024	0.0023	0.0023	0.0022	0.0021	0.0020	0.0020	0.0019
−2.7	0.0035	0.0034	0.0033	0.0032	0.0031	0.0030	0.0029	0.0028	0.0027	0.0026
−2.6	0.0047	0.0045	0.0044	0.0043	0.0041	0.0040	0.0039	0.0038	0.0037	0.0036
−2.5	0.0062	0.0060	0.0059	0.0057	0.0055	0.0054	0.0052	0.0051	0.0049	0.0048
−2.4	0.0082	0.0080	0.0078	0.0075	0.0073	0.0071	0.0069	0.0068	0.0066	0.0064
−2.3	0.0107	0.0104	0.0102	0.0099	0.0096	0.0094	0.0091	0.0089	0.0087	0.0084
−2.2	0.0139	0.0136	0.0132	0.0129	0.0126	0.0122	0.0119	0.0116	0.0113	0.0110
−2.1	0.0179	0.0174	0.0170	0.0166	0.0162	0.0158	0.0154	0.0150	0.0146	0.0143
−2.0	0.0228	0.0222	0.0217	0.0212	0.0207	0.0202	0.0197	0.0192	0.0188	0.0183
−1.9	0.0287	0.0281	0.0274	0.0268	0.0262	0.0256	0.0250	0.0244	0.0238	0.0233
−1.8	0.0359	0.0352	0.0344	0.0336	0.0329	0.0322	0.0314	0.0307	0.0300	0.0294
−1.7	0.0446	0.0436	0.0427	0.0418	0.0409	0.0401	0.0392	0.0384	0.0375	0.0367
−1.6	0.0548	0.0537	0.0526	0.0516	0.0505	0.0495	0.0485	0.0475	0.0465	0.0455
−1.5	0.0668	0.0655	0.0643	0.0630	0.0618	0.0606	0.0594	0.0582	0.0570	0.0559
−1.4	0.0808	0.0793	0.0778	0.0764	0.0749	0.0735	0.0722	0.0708	0.0694	0.0681
−1.3	0.0968	0.0951	0.0934	0.0918	0.0901	0.0885	0.0869	0.0853	0.0838	0.0823
−1.2	0.1151	0.1131	0.1112	0.1093	0.1075	0.1056	0.1038	0.1020	0.1003	0.0985
−1.1	0.1357	0.1335	0.1314	0.1292	0.1271	0.1251	0.1230	0.1210	0.1190	0.1170
−1.0	0.1587	0.1562	0.1539	0.1515	0.1492	0.1469	0.1446	0.1423	0.1401	0.1379
−0.9	0.1841	0.1814	0.1788	0.1762	0.1736	0.1711	0.1685	0.1660	0.1635	0.1611
−0.8	0.2119	0.2090	0.2061	0.2033	0.2005	0.1977	0.1949	0.1922	0.1894	0.1867
−0.7	0.2420	0.2389	0.2358	0.2327	0.2297	0.2266	0.2236	0.2206	0.2177	0.2148
−0.6	0.2743	0.2709	0.2676	0.2643	0.2611	0.2578	0.2546	0.2514	0.2483	0.2451
−0.5	0.3085	0.3050	0.3015	0.2981	0.2946	0.2912	0.2877	0.2843	0.2810	0.2776
−0.4	0.3446	0.3409	0.3372	0.3336	0.3300	0.3264	0.3228	0.3192	0.3156	0.3121
−0.3	0.3821	0.3783	0.3745	0.3707	0.3669	0.3632	0.3594	0.3557	0.3520	0.3483
−0.2	0.4207	0.4168	0.4129	0.4090	0.4052	0.4013	0.3974	0.3936	0.3897	0.3859
−0.1	0.4602	0.4562	0.4522	0.4483	0.4443	0.4404	0.4364	0.4325	0.4286	0.4247
−0.0	0.5000	0.4960	0.4920	0.4880	0.4840	0.4801	0.4761	0.4721	0.4681	0.4641

Continued overleaf

Table A *Continued*

Probabilities

z	0	1	2	3	4	5	6	7	8	9
0.0	0.5000	0.5040	0.5080	0.5120	0.5160	0.5199	0.5239	0.5279	0.5319	0.5359
0.1	0.5398	0.5438	0.5478	0.5517	0.5557	0.5596	0.5636	0.5675	0.5714	0.5753
0.2	0.5793	0.5832	0.5871	0.5910	0.5948	0.5987	0.6026	0.6064	0.6103	0.6141
0.3	0.6179	0.6217	0.6255	0.6293	0.6331	0.6368	0.6406	0.6443	0.6480	0.6517
0.4	0.6554	0.6591	0.6628	0.6664	0.6700	0.6736	0.6772	0.6808	0.6844	0.6879
0.5	0.6915	0.6950	0.6985	0.7019	0.7054	0.7088	0.7123	0.7157	0.7190	0.7224
0.6	0.7257	0.7291	0.7324	0.7357	0.7389	0.7422	0.7454	0.7486	0.7517	0.7549
0.7	0.7580	0.7611	0.7642	0.7673	0.7703	0.7734	0.7764	0.7974	0.7823	0.7852
0.8	0.7881	0.7910	0.7939	0.7967	0.7995	0.8023	0.8051	0.8078	0.8106	0.8133
0.9	0.8159	0.8186	0.8212	0.8238	0.8264	0.8289	0.8315	0.8340	0.8365	0.8389
1.0	0.8413	0.8438	0.8461	0.8485	0.8508	0.8531	0.8554	0.8577	0.8599	0.8621
1.1	0.8643	0.8665	0.8686	0.8708	0.8729	0.8749	0.8770	0.8790	0.8810	0.8830
1.2	0.8849	0.8869	0.8888	0.8907	0.8925	0.8944	0.8962	0.8980	0.8997	0.9015
1.3	0.9032	0.9049	0.9066	0.9082	0.9099	0.9115	0.9131	0.9147	0.9162	0.9177
1.4	0.9192	0.9207	0.9222	0.9236	0.9251	0.9265	0.9278	0.9292	0.9306	0.9319
1.5	0.9332	0.9345	0.9357	0.9370	0.9382	0.9394	0.9406	0.9418	0.9430	0.9441
1.6	0.9452	0.9463	0.9474	0.9484	0.9495	0.9505	0.9515	0.9525	0.9535	0.9545
1.7	0.9554	0.9564	0.9573	0.9582	0.9591	0.9599	0.9608	0.9616	0.9625	0.9633
1.8	0.9641	0.9648	0.9656	0.9664	0.9671	0.9678	0.9686	0.9693	0.9700	0.9706
1.9	0.9713	0.9719	0.9726	0.9732	0.9738	0.9744	0.9750	0.9756	0.9762	0.9767
2.0	0.9772	0.9778	0.9783	0.9788	0.9793	0.9798	0.9803	0.9808	0.9812	0.9817
2.1	0.9821	0.9826	0.9830	0.9834	0.9838	0.9842	0.9846	0.9850	0.9854	0.9857
2.2	0.9861	0.9864	0.9868	0.9871	0.9874	0.9878	0.9881	0.9884	0.9887	0.9890
2.3	0.9893	0.9896	0.9898	0.9901	0.9904	0.9906	0.9909	0.9911	0.9913	0.9916
2.4	0.9918	0.9920	0.9922	0.9925	0.9927	0.9929	0.9931	0.9932	0.9934	0.9936
2.5	0.9938	0.9940	0.9941	0.9943	0.9945	0.9946	0.9948	0.9949	0.9951	0.9952
2.6	0.9953	0.9955	0.9956	0.9957	0.9959	0.9960	0.9961	0.9962	0.9963	0.9964
2.7	0.9965	0.9966	0.9967	0.9968	0.9969	0.9970	0.9971	0.9972	0.9973	0.9974
2.8	0.9974	0.9975	0.9976	0.9977	0.9977	0.9978	0.9979	0.9979	0.9980	0.9981
2.9	0.9981	0.9982	0.9982	0.9983	0.9984	0.9984	0.9985	0.9985	0.9986	0.9986
3.0	0.9987	0.9990	0.9993	0.9995	0.9997	0.9998	0.9998	0.9999	0.9999	1.0000

Percentage points

	10%	5%	1%	0.1%	0.01%	0.001%
One-sided	1.2816	1.6449	2.3263	3.0902	3.7190	4.2649
Two-sided	1.6449	1.9600	2.5758	3.2905	3.8906	4.4172

Table B Upper-tail probabilities of the chi-squared (χ^2) distribution.

	α			α	
ν	5%	1%	ν	5%	1%
1	3.841	6.635	26	38.885	45.642
2	5.991	9.210	27	40.113	46.963
3	7.815	11.345	28	41.337	48.278
4	9.488	13.277	29	42.557	49.588
5	11.070	15.086	30	43.773	50.892
6	12.592	16.812	31	44.985	52.191
7	14.067	18.475	32	46.194	53.486
8	15.507	20.090	33	47.400	54.776
9	16.919	21.666	34	48.602	56.061
10	18.307	23.209	35	49.802	57.342
11	19.675	24.725	36	50.998	58.619
12	21.026	26.217	37	52.192	59.893
13	22.362	27.688	38	53.384	61.162
14	23.685	29.141	39	54.572	62.428
15	24.996	30.578	40	55.758	63.691
16	26.296	32.000	45	61.656	69.957
17	27.587	33.409	50	67.505	76.154
18	28.869	34.805	60	79.082	88.379
19	30.144	36.191	70	90.531	100.43
20	31.410	37.566	80	101.88	112.33
21	32.671	38.932	90	113.15	124.12
22	33.924	40.289	100	124.34	135.81
23	35.172	41.638			
24	36.415	42.980			
25	37.652	44.314			

Table C Critical values for the sign test.

n	$\alpha_1 =$ $\alpha_2 =$	5% 10%	2½% 5%	1% 2%	½% 1%	n	$\alpha_1 =$ $\alpha_2 =$	5% 10%	2½% 5%	1% 2%	½% 1%
1		–	–	–	–	26		8	7	6	6
2		–	–	–	–	27		8	7	7	6
3		–	–	–	–	28		9	8	7	6
4		–	–	–	–	29		9	8	7	7
5		0	–	–	–	30		10	9	8	7
6		0	0	–	–	31		10	9	8	7
7		0	0	0	–	32		10	9	8	8
8		1	0	0	0	33		11	10	9	8
9		1	1	0	0	34		11	10	9	9
10		1	1	0	0	35		12	11	10	9
11		2	1	1	0	36		12	11	10	9
12		2	2	1	1	37		13	12	10	10
13		3	2	1	1	38		13	12	11	10
14		3	2	2	1	39		13	12	11	11
15		3	3	2	2	40		14	13	12	11
16		4	3	2	2	41		14	13	12	11
17		4	4	3	2	42		15	14	13	12
18		5	4	3	3	43		15	14	13	12
19		5	4	4	3	44		16	15	13	13
20		5	5	4	3	45		16	15	14	13
21		6	5	4	4	46		16	15	14	13
22		6	5	5	4	47		17	16	15	14
23		7	6	5	4	48		17	16	15	14
24		7	6	5	5	49		18	17	15	15
25		7	7	6	5	50		18	17	16	15

Table D Critical values for the Wilcoxon signed-rank test.

n	$\alpha_1 =$ $\alpha_2 =$	5% 10%	2½% 5%	1% 2%	½% 1%	n	$\alpha_1 =$ $\alpha_2 =$	5% 10%	2½% 5%	1% 2%	½% 1%
1		–	–	–	–	26		110	98	84	75
2		–	–	–	–	27		119	107	92	83
3		–	–	–	–	28		130	116	101	91
4		–	–	–	–	29		140	126	110	100
5		0	–	–	–	30		151	137	120	109
6		2	0	–	–	31		163	147	130	118
7		3	2	0	–	32		175	159	140	128
8		5	3	1	0	33		187	170	151	138
9		8	5	3	1	34		200	182	162	148
10		10	8	5	3	35		213	195	173	159
11		13	10	7	5	36		227	208	185	171
12		17	13	9	7	37		241	221	198	182
13		21	17	12	9	38		256	235	211	194
14		25	21	15	12	39		271	249	224	207
15		30	25	19	15	40		286	264	238	220
16		35	29	23	19	41		302	279	252	233
17		41	34	27	23	42		319	294	266	247
18		47	40	32	27	43		336	310	281	261
19		53	46	37	32	44		353	327	296	276
20		60	52	43	37	45		371	343	312	291
21		67	58	49	42	46		389	361	328	307
22		75	65	55	48	47		407	378	345	322
23		83	73	62	54	48		426	396	362	339
24		91	81	69	61	49		446	415	379	355
25		100	89	76	68	50		466	434	397	373

Table E Critical values for the Kolmogorov–Smirnov goodness-of-fit test (for completely specified distributions).

n	$\alpha_1 =$	5%	$2\frac{1}{2}\%$	1%	$\frac{1}{2}\%$	n	$\alpha_1 =$	5%	$2\frac{1}{2}\%$	1%	$\frac{1}{2}\%$
	$\alpha_2 =$	10%	5%	2%	1%		$\alpha_2 =$	10%	5%	2%	1%
1		0.9500	0.9750	0.9900	0.9950	16		0.2947	0.3273	0.3657	0.3920
2		0.7764	0.8419	0.9000	0.9293	17		0.2863	0.3180	0.3553	0.3809
3		0.6360	0.7076	0.7846	0.8290	18		0.2785	0.3094	0.3457	0.3706
4		0.5652	0.6239	0.6889	0.7342	19		0.2714	0.3014	0.3369	0.3612
5		0.5094	0.5633	0.6272	0.6685	20		0.2647	0.2941	0.3287	0.3524
6		0.4680	0.5193	0.5774	0.6166	21		0.2586	0.2872	0.3210	0.3443
7		0.4361	0.4834	0.5384	0.5758	22		0.2528	0.2809	0.3139	0.3367
8		0.4096	0.4543	0.5065	0.5418	23		0.2475	0.2749	0.3073	0.3295
9		0.3875	0.4300	0.4796	0.5133	24		0.2424	0.2693	0.3010	0.3229
10		0.3687	0.4092	0.4566	0.4889	25		0.2377	0.2640	0.2952	0.3166
11		0.3524	0.3912	0.4367	0.4677	26		0.2332	0.2591	0.2896	0.3106
12		0.3382	0.3754	0.4192	0.4490	27		0.2290	0.2544	0.2844	0.3050
13		0.3255	0.3614	0.4036	0.4325	28		0.2250	0.2499	0.2794	0.2997
14		0.3142	0.3489	0.3897	0.4176	29		0.2212	0.2457	0.2747	0.2947
15		0.3040	0.3376	0.3771	0.4042	30		0.2176	0.2417	0.2702	0.2899

Table F Critical values for Lilliefors' normality test.

n	$\alpha_1 =$	5%	$2\frac{1}{2}\%$	1%	$\frac{1}{2}\%$	n	$\alpha_1 =$	5%	$2\frac{1}{2}\%$	1%	$\frac{1}{2}\%$
	$\alpha_2 =$	10%	5%	2%	1%		$\alpha_2 =$	10%	5%	2%	1%
1		–	–	–	–	16		0.1954	0.2129	0.2332	0.2476
2		–	–	–	–	17		0.1901	0.2071	0.2270	0.2410
3		0.3666	0.3758	0.3812	0.3830	18		0.1852	0.2017	0.2212	0.2349
4		0.3453	0.3753	0.4007	0.4131	19		0.1807	0.1968	0.2158	0.2292
5		0.3189	0.3431	0.3755	0.3970	20		0.1765	0.1921	0.2107	0.2238
6		0.2972	0.3234	0.3523	0.3708	21		0.1725	0.1878	0.2060	0.2188
7		0.2802	0.3043	0.3321	0.3509	22		0.1688	0.1838	0.2015	0.2141
8		0.2652	0.2880	0.3150	0.3332	23		0.1653	0.1800	0.1974	0.2097
9		0.2523	0.2741	0.2999	0.3174	24		0.1620	0.1764	0.1936	0.2056
10		0.2411	0.2619	0.2869	0.3037	25		0.1589	0.1730	0.1899	0.2018
11		0.2312	0.2514	0.2754	0.2916	26		0.1560	0.1699	0.1865	0.1981
12		0.2225	0.2420	0.2651	0.2810	27		0.1533	0.1670	0.1833	0.1947
13		0.2148	0.2336	0.2559	0.2714	28		0.1507	0.1642	0.1802	0.1915
14		0.2077	0.2261	0.2476	0.2627	29		0.1483	0.1615	0.1773	0.1884
15		0.2013	0.2192	0.2401	0.2549	30		0.1460	0.1589	0.1746	0.1855

Table G Critical values for the Mann–Whitney test.

n_1	n_2	$\alpha_1 = 5\%$ $\alpha_2 = 10\%$	$2\tfrac{1}{2}\%$ 5%	1% 2%	$\tfrac{1}{2}\%$ 1%
2	2	–	–	–	–
2	3	–	–	–	–
2	4	–	–	–	–
2	5	0	–	–	–
2	6	0	–	–	–
2	7	0	–	–	–
2	8	1	0	–	–
2	9	1	0	–	–
2	10	1	0	–	–
2	11	1	0	–	–
2	12	2	1	–	–
2	13	2	1	0	–
2	14	3	1	0	–
2	15	3	1	0	–
2	16	3	1	0	–
2	17	3	2	0	–
2	18	4	2	0	–
2	19	4	2	1	0
2	20	4	2	1	0
3	3	0	–	–	–
3	4	0	–	–	–
3	5	1	0	–	–
3	6	2	1	–	–
3	7	2	1	0	–
3	8	3	2	0	–
3	9	4	2	1	0
3	10	4	3	1	0
3	11	5	3	1	0
3	12	5	4	2	1
3	13	6	4	2	1
3	14	7	5	2	1
3	15	7	5	3	2
3	16	8	6	3	2
3	17	9	6	4	2
3	18	9	7	4	2
3	19	10	7	4	3
3	20	11	8	5	3
4	4	1	0	–	–
4	5	2	1	0	–
4	6	3	2	1	0
4	7	4	3	1	0
4	8	5	4	2	1
4	9	6	4	3	1
4	10	7	5	3	2
4	11	8	6	4	2
4	12	9	7	5	3
4	13	10	8	5	3
4	14	11	9	6	4
4	15	12	10	7	5
4	16	14	11	7	5
4	17	15	11	8	6
4	18	16	12	9	6
4	19	17	13	9	7
4	20	18	14	10	8
5	5	4	2	1	0
5	6	5	3	2	1
5	7	6	5	3	1
5	8	8	6	4	2
5	9	9	7	5	3
5	10	11	8	6	4
5	11	12	9	7	5
5	12	13	11	8	6
5	13	15	12	9	7
5	14	16	13	10	7
5	15	18	14	11	8
5	16	19	15	12	9
5	17	20	17	13	10
5	18	22	18	14	11
5	19	23	19	15	12
5	20	25	20	16	13
6	6	7	5	3	2
6	7	8	6	4	3
6	8	10	8	6	4
6	9	12	10	7	5
6	10	14	11	8	6
6	11	16	13	9	7
6	12	17	14	11	9
6	13	19	16	12	10
6	14	21	17	13	11
6	15	23	19	15	12
6	16	25	21	16	13
6	17	26	22	18	15
6	18	28	24	19	16
6	19	30	25	20	17
6	20	32	27	22	18
7	7	11	8	6	4
7	8	13	10	7	6
7	9	15	12	9	7
7	10	17	14	11	9
7	11	19	16	12	10
7	12	21	18	14	12
7	13	24	20	16	13
7	14	26	22	17	15
7	15	28	24	19	16
7	16	30	26	21	18
7	17	33	28	23	19
7	18	35	30	24	21
7	19	37	32	26	22
7	20	39	34	28	24

Continued overleaf

Table G *Continued*

n_1	n_2	$\alpha_1 =$ 5% $\alpha_2 =$ 10%	2½% 5%	1% 2%	½% 1%
8	8	15	13	9	7
8	9	18	15	11	9
8	10	20	17	13	11
8	11	23	19	15	13
8	12	26	22	17	15
8	13	28	24	20	17
8	14	31	26	22	18
8	15	33	29	24	20
8	16	36	31	26	22
8	17	39	34	28	24
8	18	41	36	30	26
8	19	44	38	32	28
8	20	47	41	34	30
9	9	21	17	14	11
9	10	24	20	16	13
9	11	27	23	18	16
9	12	30	26	21	18
9	13	33	28	23	20
9	14	36	31	26	22
9	15	39	34	28	24
9	16	42	37	31	27
9	17	45	39	33	29
9	18	48	42	36	31
9	19	51	45	38	33
9	20	54	48	40	36
10	10	27	23	19	16
10	11	31	26	22	18
10	12	34	29	24	21
10	13	37	33	27	24
10	14	41	36	30	26
10	15	44	39	33	29
10	16	48	42	36	31
10	17	51	45	38	34
10	18	55	48	41	37
10	19	58	52	44	39
10	20	62	55	47	42
11	11	34	30	25	21
11	12	38	33	28	24
11	13	42	37	31	27
11	14	46	40	34	30
11	15	50	44	37	33
11	16	54	47	41	36
11	17	57	51	44	39
11	18	61	55	47	42
11	19	65	58	50	45
11	20	69	62	53	48

n_1	n_2	$\alpha_1 =$ 5% $\alpha_2 =$ 10%	2½% 5%	1% 2%	½% 1%
12	12	42	37	31	27
12	13	47	41	35	31
12	14	51	45	38	34
12	15	55	49	42	37
12	16	60	53	46	41
12	17	64	57	49	44
12	18	68	61	53	47
12	19	72	65	56	51
12	20	77	69	60	54
13	13	51	45	39	34
13	14	56	50	43	38
13	15	61	54	47	42
13	16	65	59	51	45
13	17	70	63	55	49
13	18	75	67	59	53
13	19	80	72	63	57
13	20	84	76	67	60
14	14	61	55	47	42
14	15	66	59	51	46
14	16	71	64	56	50
14	17	77	69	60	54
14	18	82	74	65	58
14	19	87	78	60	63
14	20	92	83	73	67
15	15	72	64	56	51
15	16	77	70	61	55
15	17	83	75	66	60
15	18	88	80	70	64
15	19	94	85	75	69
15	20	100	90	80	73
16	16	83	75	66	60
16	17	89	81	71	65
16	18	95	86	76	70
16	19	101	92	82	74
16	20	107	98	87	79
17	17	96	87	77	70
17	18	102	92	82	75
17	19	109	99	88	81
17	20	115	105	93	86
18	18	109	99	88	81
18	19	116	106	94	87
18	20	123	112	100	92
19	19	123	113	101	93
19	20	130	119	107	99
20	20	138	127	114	105

Table H Critical values for the Tukey test for location-differences.

$\alpha_1 = 5\%,\ \alpha_2 = 10\%$

$n_1\backslash n_2=$	20	19	18	17	16	15	14	13	12	11	10	9	8	7	6	5	4	3	2	
2	11	11	11	11	11	11	10	10	10	10	9	9	8	9	8	7	–	–	–	
3	10	10	9	9	9	9	9	9	8	8	8	7	7	7	6	6	7	6	–	
4	9	9	9	8	8	8	8	8	7	7	7	7	7	6	6	6	6			
5	8	8	8	8	7	7	7	7	7	7	6	6	6	6	6				9	20
6	8	8	8	7	7	7	7	6	6	6	6	6	6				9	9	9	19
7	7	7	7	7	7	7	6	6	6	6	6	6					9	9	9	18
8	7	7	7	7	7	6	6	6	6	6					9		9	9	9	17
9	7	7	7	7	6	6	6	6	6					9	9	9	9	9	9	16
10	7	7	7	6	6	6	6	6				9	9	9	9	9	9	9	9	15
11	7	7	6	6	6	6	6			9	9	9	9	9	9	9	9	9	10	14
12	7	6	6	6	6	6			9	9	9	9	9	9	9	9	9	9	10	13
13	6	6	6	6	6			9	9	9	9	9	9	9	9	9	10	9	10	12
14	6	6	6	6		8		9	9	9	9	9	9	9	10	10	10	10	11	11
15	6	6	6		6	8	8	9	9	9	9	9	9	10	10	10	10	10	11	10
16	6	6			8	8	8	9	9	9	9	9	10	10	11	11	11	11	11	9
17	6	6		8	8	8	9	9	9	9	9	10	10	10	11	11	11	11	12	8
18		–	8	8	8	9	9	9	9	9	10	10	11	11	12	12	12	12	13	7
19	–	–	9	9	9	9	9	10	10	10	11	11	12	13	13	14	13	13	14	6
20	–	–	–	–	8	9	9	10	10	11	12	12	14	15	15	15	16	17	20	5
	–	–	–	–	–	–	–	–	–	–	–	15	16	17	18	19	20	19	20	$2=n_1$
$n_2=$	2	3	4	5	6	7	8	9	10	11	12	13	14	15	16	17	18	19	20	

$\alpha_1 = 1\%,\ \alpha_2 = 2\%$

Continued overleaf

Table H *Continued*

$\alpha_1 = 2\tfrac{1}{2}\%,\ \alpha_2 = 5\%$

$n_2=$	20	19	18	17	16	15	14	13	12	11	10	9	8	7	6	5	4	3	2
$n_1=$ 2	17	16	16	15	15	14	13	13	12	13	12	11	10	–	–	–	–	–	–
3	14	13	13	13	12	12	11	11	10	10	10	9	8	8	7	8	–	–	–
4	12	12	11	11	11	10	10	10	9	9	9	8	8	7	7	7	8	–	10
5	11	11	10	10	10	9	9	9	9	8	8	8	7	7	7	7	–	10	10
6	10	10	9	9	9	9	8	8	8	8	8	7	7	7	7	–	10	10	10
7	9	9	9	8	8	8	8	8	7	7	7	7	7	7	–	10	10	10	10
8	9	9	9	8	8	8	8	7	7	7	7	7	7	–	10	10	10	10	11
9	9	8	8	8	8	8	8	7	7	7	7	7	–	10	10	10	10	10	11
10	8	8	8	8	8	8	7	7	7	7	7	–	10	10	10	10	10	10	11
11	8	8	8	8	8	7	7	7	7	7	–	10	10	10	10	10	10	11	11
12	8	8	8	8	8	7	7	7	7	–	10	10	10	10	10	10	11	11	11
13	8	8	8	8	7	7	7	7	–	10	10	10	10	10	11	11	11	11	12
14	8	8	8	7	7	7	7	–	10	10	10	10	10	11	11	11	11	12	12
15	8	8	7	7	7	7	–	10	10	10	10	10	11	11	11	12	12	12	13
16	8	7	7	7	7	–	9	10	10	10	10	11	11	11	12	12	13	13	13
17	7	7	7	7	–	9	9	10	10	10	11	11	12	12	13	13	13	14	14
18	7	7	7	–	9	9	10	10	11	11	11	12	12	13	13	14	14	15	15
19	7	7	–	10	9	10	10	11	11	12	12	13	13	14	15	15	16	16	17
20	7	–	–	10	10	11	10	12	13	13	12	14	15	15	16	17	18	21	22

$n_2=$	2	3	4	5	6	7	8	9	10	11	12	13	14	15	16	17	18	19	20

$\alpha_1 = \tfrac{1}{2}\%,\ \alpha_2 = 1\%$

$2 = n_1$

Table I Critical values for the Tukey-type test for dispersion differences.

$$\alpha_1 = 5\%, \quad \alpha_2 = 10\%$$

n_1	2	3	4	5	6	7	8	9	10	11	12	13	14	15	16	17	18	19	20
2	–	–	–	2	2	2	2	2	2	2	2	2	2	2	2	2	2	2	2
3	–	–	–	3	3	3	3	2	2	2	2	2	2	2	2	2	2	2	2
4	–	–	4	4	4	3	3	3	3	3	2	2	2	2	2	2	2	2	2
5	–	–	5	5	4	4	4	3	3	3	3	3	3	3	2	2	2	2	2
6	–	–	6	5	5	5	4	4	4	4	3	3	3	3	3	3	3	2	2
7	–	7	7	6	6	5	5	4	4	4	4	3	3	3	3	3	3	3	3
8	–	8	8	7	6	6	5	5	5	4	4	4	4	4	3	3	3	3	3
9	–	9	8	7	7	6	6	5	5	5	5	4	4	4	4	4	4	3	3
10	–	10	9	8	7	7	6	6	5	5	5	5	4	4	4	4	4	4	4
11	–	11	10	9	8	7	7	6	6	6	5	5	5	5	4	4	4	4	4
12	–	12	11	9	9	8	7	7	6	6	6	5	5	5	5	4	4	4	4
13	–	13	11	10	9	8	8	7	7	6	6	6	5	5	5	5	5	4	4
14	–	14	12	11	10	9	8	8	7	7	6	6	6	5	5	5	5	5	5
15	–	14	13	11	10	9	9	8	8	7	7	6	6	6	6	5	5	5	5
16	–	15	14	12	11	10	9	8	8	7	7	7	6	6	6	6	5	5	5
17	–	16	14	13	12	10	10	9	8	8	7	7	7	6	6	6	6	5	5
18	–	17	15	13	12	11	10	9	9	8	8	7	7	7	6	6	6	6	5
19	–	18	16	14	13	12	11	10	9	9	8	8	7	7	7	6	6	6	6
20	–	19	17	15	13	12	11	10	10	9	8	8	8	7	7	7	6	6	6

Continued overleaf

Table I *Continued*

$$\alpha_1 = 2\tfrac{1}{2}\%, \quad \alpha_2 = 5\%$$

n_1	n_2																		
	2	3	4	5	6	7	8	9	10	11	12	13	14	15	16	17	18	19	20
2	–	–	–	–	–	–	2	2	2	2	2	2	2	2	2	2	2	2	2
3	–	–	–	–	3	3	3	3	3	3	3	2	2	2	2	2	2	2	2
4	–	–	–	4	4	4	4	4	3	3	3	3	3	3	3	3	3	2	2
5	–	–	–	5	5	5	4	4	4	4	4	3	3	3	3	3	3	3	3
6	–	–	–	6	6	5	5	5	4	4	4	4	4	3	3	3	3	3	3
7	–	–	7	7	6	6	5	5	5	5	4	4	4	4	4	4	4	3	3
8	–	–	8	7	7	6	6	6	5	5	5	5	4	4	4	4	4	4	4
9	–	–	9	8	8	7	7	6	6	6	5	5	5	5	5	4	4	4	4
10	–	–	10	9	8	8	7	7	6	6	6	5	5	5	5	5	5	4	4
11	–	–	11	10	9	8	8	7	7	6	6	6	6	5	5	5	5	5	5
12	–	12	11	10	10	9	8	8	7	7	7	6	6	6	5	5	5	5	5
13	–	13	12	11	10	9	9	8	8	7	7	7	6	6	6	6	5	5	5
14	–	14	13	12	11	10	9	9	8	8	7	7	7	6	6	6	6	6	5
15	–	15	14	13	11	11	10	9	9	8	8	7	7	7	6	6	6	6	6
16	–	16	15	13	12	11	10	10	9	9	8	8	7	7	7	7	6	6	6
17	–	17	15	14	13	12	11	10	10	9	9	8	8	7	7	7	7	6	6
18	–	18	15	15	13	12	11	11	10	9	9	8	8	8	7	7	7	7	6
19	–	19	17	15	14	13	12	11	10	10	9	9	8	8	8	7	7	7	7
20	–	20	18	15	15	14	12	12	11	10	10	9	9	8	8	8	7	7	7

$\alpha_1 = 1\%$, $\alpha_2 = 2\%$

n_1	n_2																		
	2	3	4	5	6	7	8	9	10	11	12	13	14	15	16	17	18	19	20
2	–	–	–	–	–	–	–	–	–	–	–	2	2	2	2	2	2	2	2
3	–	–	–	–	–	–	–	3	3	3	3	3	3	3	3	3	3	3	3
4	–	–	–	–	–	4	4	4	4	4	4	4	3	3	3	3	3	3	3
5	–	–	–	–	5	5	5	5	5	4	4	4	4	4	4	4	4	3	3
6	–	–	–	–	6	6	6	5	5	5	5	5	4	4	4	4	4	4	4
7	–	–	–	7	7	7	6	6	6	5	5	5	5	5	5	4	4	4	4
8	–	–	–	8	8	7	7	6	6	6	6	5	5	5	5	5	5	5	4
9	–	–	–	9	8	8	7	7	7	6	6	6	6	5	5	5	5	5	5
10	–	–	10	10	9	9	8	8	7	7	7	6	6	6	6	6	5	5	5
11	–	–	11	11	10	9	9	8	8	7	7	7	7	6	6	6	6	6	5
12	–	–	12	11	11	10	9	9	8	8	8	7	7	7	6	6	6	6	6
13	–	–	13	12	11	11	10	9	9	8	8	8	7	7	7	7	6	6	6
14	–	–	14	13	12	11	10	10	9	8	8	8	7	7	7	7	7	7	6
15	–	–	15	14	13	12	11	10	10	9	9	9	8	8	8	7	7	7	7
16	–	–	16	14	13	12	12	11	10	10	9	9	9	8	8	8	7	7	7
17	–	–	17	15	14	13	12	12	11	10	10	9	9	9	8	8	8	7	7
18	–	–	17	16	15	14	13	12	11	11	10	10	9	9	9	8	8	8	8
19	–	–	18	17	16	14	13	13	12	11	11	10	10	9	9	9	8	8	8
20	–	–	19	18	16	15	14	13	12	12	11	11	10	10	9	9	9	8	8

Continued overleaf

Table I *Continued*

$$\alpha_1=\tfrac{1}{2}\%,\ \alpha_2=1\%$$

n_1												n_2								
	2	3	4	5	6	7	8	9	10	11	12	13	14	15	16	17	18	19	20
2	–	–	–	–	–	–	–	–	–	–	–	–	–	–	–	–	–	2	2
3	–	–	–	–	–	–	–	–	–	–	3	3	3	3	3	3	3	3	3
4	–	–	–	–	–	–	–	4	4	4	4	4	4	4	4	4	4	3	3
5	–	–	–	–	–	–	5	5	5	5	5	4	4	4	4	4	4	4	4
6	–	–	–	–	–	6	6	6	6	5	5	5	5	5	5	4	4	4	4
7	–	–	–	–	7	7	7	6	6	6	6	5	5	5	5	5	5	5	5
8	–	–	–	–	8	8	7	7	7	6	6	6	6	6	5	5	5	5	5
9	–	–	–	9	9	8	8	8	7	7	7	6	6	6	6	6	6	5	5
10	–	–	–	10	10	9	9	8	8	8	7	7	7	6	6	6	6	6	6
11	–	–	–	11	10	10	9	9	8	8	8	7	7	7	7	7	6	6	6
12	–	–	–	12	11	11	10	9	9	9	8	8	8	7	7	7	7	7	6
13	–	–	–	13	12	11	11	10	10	9	9	8	8	8	8	7	7	7	7
14	–	–	14	14	13	12	11	11	10	10	9	9	9	8	8	8	7	7	7
15	–	–	15	14	13	13	12	11	11	10	9	9	9	8	8	8	8	8	7
16	–	–	16	15	14	13	13	12	11	11	10	10	9	9	9	8	8	8	8
17	–	–	17	16	15	14	13	12	12	11	11	10	10	9	9	9	9	8	8
18	–	–	18	17	16	15	14	13	12	12	11	11	10	10	10	9	9	9	8
19	–	–	19	18	16	15	14	14	13	12	12	11	11	10	10	10	9	9	9
20	–	–	20	18	17	16	15	14	13	13	12	12	11	11	10	10	10	9	9

Table J Critical values for the Rosenbaum two-sample test.

$$\alpha_1 = 5\%, \; \alpha_2 = 10\%$$

n_2	1	2	3	4	5	6	7	8	9	10	11	12	13	14	15	16	17	18	19	20
1	–	–	–	–	–	–	–	–	–	–	–	–	–	–	–	–	–	–	1	1
2	–	–	–	–	2	2	2	2	2	2	2	2	2	2	2	2	2	2	2	2
3	–	–	3	3	3	3	3	3	2	2	2	2	2	2	2	2	2	2	2	2
4	–	–	4	4	3	3	3	3	3	3	3	2	2	2	2	2	2	2	2	2
5	–	5	5	4	4	4	3	3	3	3	3	3	3	3	3	2	2	2	2	2
6	–	6	5	5	4	4	4	4	3	3	3	3	3	3	3	3	3	3	2	2
7	–	7	6	5	5	4	4	4	4	4	3	3	3	3	3	3	3	3	3	3
8	–	8	7	6	5	5	5	4	4	4	4	3	3	3	3	3	3	3	3	3
9	–	9	7	6	6	5	5	5	4	4	4	4	4	3	3	3	3	3	3	3
10	–	9	8	7	6	6	5	5	5	4	4	4	4	4	4	3	3	3	3	3
11	–	10	9	8	7	6	6	5	5	5	4	4	4	4	4	4	4	3	3	3
12	–	11	9	8	7	6	6	6	5	5	5	4	4	4	4	4	4	4	3	3
13	–	12	10	9	8	7	6	6	5	5	5	5	4	4	4	4	4	4	4	4
14	–	12	11	9	8	7	7	6	6	5	5	5	5	4	4	4	4	4	4	4
15	–	13	11	10	9	8	7	6	6	6	5	5	5	5	4	4	4	4	4	4
16	–	14	12	10	9	8	7	7	6	6	6	5	5	5	5	5	4	4	4	4
17	–	15	12	11	9	8	8	7	7	6	6	6	5	5	5	5	5	4	4	4
18	–	16	13	11	10	9	8	7	7	6	6	6	6	5	5	5	5	5	4	4
19	19	16	14	12	10	9	8	8	7	7	6	6	6	5	5	5	5	5	5	4
20	20	17	14	12	11	10	9	8	7	7	7	6	6	6	5	5	5	5	5	5

Continued overleaf

Table J *Continued*

$$\alpha_1 = 2\tfrac{1}{2}\%, \ \alpha_2 = 5\%$$

n_2	1	2	3	4	5	6	7	8	9	10	11	12	13	14	15	16	17	18	19	20
1	–	–	–	–	–	–	–	–	–	–	–	–	–	–	–	–	–	–	–	–
2	–	–	–	–	–	–	–	2	2	2	2	2	2	2	2	2	2	2	2	2
3	–	–	–	–	3	3	3	3	3	3	3	2	2	2	2	2	2	2	2	2
4	–	–	–	4	4	4	3	3	3	3	3	3	3	3	3	3	3	3	2	2
5	–	–	5	5	4	4	4	4	4	3	3	3	3	3	3	3	3	3	3	3
6	–	–	6	5	5	5	4	4	4	4	4	3	3	3	3	3	3	3	3	3
7	–	–	7	6	6	5	5	5	4	4	4	4	4	4	3	3	3	3	3	3
8	–	8	7	7	6	6	5	5	5	4	4	4	4	4	4	4	3	3	3	3
9	–	9	8	7	7	6	6	5	5	5	5	4	4	4	4	4	4	4	4	3
10	–	10	9	8	7	7	6	6	5	5	5	5	4	4	4	4	4	4	4	4
11	–	11	10	9	8	7	6	6	6	5	5	5	5	5	4	4	4	4	4	4
12	–	12	10	9	8	7	7	6	6	6	5	5	5	5	5	4	4	4	4	4
13	–	13	11	10	9	8	7	7	6	6	6	5	5	5	5	5	5	4	4	4
14	–	13	12	10	9	8	8	7	7	6	6	6	5	5	5	5	5	5	4	4
15	–	14	12	11	10	9	8	8	7	7	6	6	6	6	5	5	5	5	5	5
16	–	15	13	12	10	9	9	8	7	7	7	6	6	6	5	5	5	5	5	5
17	–	16	14	12	11	10	9	8	8	7	7	7	6	6	6	6	5	5	5	5
18	–	17	15	13	11	10	9	9	8	8	7	7	7	6	6	6	6	5	5	5
19	–	18	15	13	12	11	10	9	8	8	7	7	7	6	6	6	6	6	5	5
20	–	19	16	14	12	11	10	9	9	8	8	7	7	7	6	6	6	6	6	5

$$\alpha_1 = 1\%, \quad \alpha_2 = 2\%$$

n_2										n_1										
	1	2	3	4	5	6	7	8	9	10	11	12	13	14	15	16	17	18	19	20
1	–	–	–	–	–	–	–	–	–	–	–	–	–	–	–	–	–	–	–	–
2	–	–	–	–	–	–	–	–	–	–	–	–	2	2	2	2	2	2	2	2
3	–	–	–	–	–	–	3	3	3	3	3	3	3	3	3	3	3	3	3	3
4	–	–	–	–	4	4	4	4	4	4	3	3	3	3	3	3	3	3	3	3
5	–	–	–	5	5	5	5	4	4	4	4	4	4	3	3	3	3	3	3	3
6	–	–	–	6	6	5	5	5	5	4	4	4	4	4	4	4	4	3	3	3
7	–	–	7	7	6	6	6	5	5	5	5	4	4	4	4	4	4	4	4	4
8	–	–	8	8	7	6	6	6	5	5	5	5	5	4	4	4	4	4	4	4
9	–	–	9	8	8	7	7	6	6	6	5	5	5	5	5	4	4	4	4	4
10	–	–	10	9	8	8	7	7	6	6	6	5	5	5	5	5	5	5	4	4
11	–	–	11	10	9	8	8	7	7	6	6	6	6	5	5	5	5	5	5	5
12	–	–	11	10	9	9	8	8	7	7	6	6	6	6	5	5	5	5	5	5
13	–	13	12	11	10	9	9	8	8	7	7	6	6	6	6	6	5	5	5	5
14	–	14	13	12	11	10	9	8	8	7	7	7	7	6	6	6	6	5	5	5
15	–	15	14	12	11	10	10	9	8	7	7	7	7	6	6	6	6	6	6	5
16	–	16	15	13	12	11	10	9	9	8	8	7	7	7	7	6	6	6	6	6
17	–	17	15	14	12	11	10	10	9	9	8	8	7	7	7	7	6	6	6	6
18	–	18	16	14	13	12	11	10	10	9	9	8	8	7	7	7	7	6	6	6
19	–	19	17	15	14	12	11	11	10	9	9	8	8	8	7	7	7	7	6	6
20	–	20	18	16	14	13	12	11	10	10	9	9	8	8	8	7	7	7	7	7

Continued overleaf

Table J   *Continued*

$$\alpha_1=\tfrac{1}{2}\%,\ \alpha_2=1\%$$

									n_1										
n_2	1	2	3	4	5	6	7	8	9	10	11	12	13	14	15	16	17	18	19	20
1	–	–	–	–	–	–	–	–	–	–	–	–	–	–	–	–	–	–	–	–
2	–	–	–	–	–	–	–	–	–	–	–	–	–	–	–	–	–	–	2	2
3	–	–	–	–	–	–	–	–	3	3	3	3	3	3	3	3	3	3	3	3
4	–	–	–	–	–	4	4	4	4	4	4	4	4	3	3	3	3	3	3	3
5	–	–	–	–	5	5	5	5	4	4	4	4	4	4	4	4	4	4	3	3
6	–	–	–	6	6	6	5	5	5	5	5	4	4	4	4	4	4	4	4	4
7	–	–	–	7	7	6	6	6	5	5	5	5	5	5	4	4	4	4	4	4
8	–	–	–	8	7	7	7	6	6	6	5	5	5	5	5	5	5	4	4	4
9	–	–	9	9	8	8	7	7	6	6	6	6	5	5	5	5	5	5	5	5
10	–	–	10	9	9	8	8	7	7	7	6	6	6	6	5	5	5	5	5	5
11	–	–	11	10	9	9	8	8	7	7	7	6	6	6	6	6	5	5	5	5
12	–	–	12	11	10	9	9	8	8	7	7	7	7	6	6	6	6	6	5	5
13	–	–	13	12	11	10	9	9	8	8	7	7	7	7	6	6	6	6	6	6
14	–	–	14	12	11	11	10	9	9	8	8	8	7	7	7	7	6	6	6	6
15	–	–	14	13	12	11	10	10	9	9	8	8	8	7	7	7	7	6	6	6
16	–	–	15	14	13	12	11	10	10	9	9	8	8	8	7	7	7	7	6	6
17	–	–	16	15	13	12	11	11	10	10	9	9	8	8	8	7	7	7	7	7
18	–	–	17	15	14	13	12	11	11	10	9	9	9	8	8	8	7	7	7	7
19	–	19	18	16	15	14	13	12	11	10	10	9	9	9	8	8	8	7	7	7
20	–	20	19	17	15	14	13	12	11	11	10	10	9	9	9	8	8	8	8	7

Table K Critical values for the Kolmogorov–Smirnov two-sample test.

n_1	n_2	$\alpha_1 =$ 5% $\alpha_2 =$ 10%	2½% 5%	1% 2%	½% 1%	n_1	n_2	$\alpha_1 =$ 5% $\alpha_2 =$ 10%	2½% 5%	1% 2%	½% 1%
2	2	–	–	–	–	4	12	36	36	40	44
2	3	–	–	–	–	4	13	35	39	44	48
2	4	–	–	–	–	4	14	38	42	48	48
2	5	10	–	–	–	4	15	40	44	48	52
2	6	12	–	–	–	4	16	44	48	52	56
2	7	14	–	–	–	4	17	44	48	56	60
2	8	16	16	–	–	4	18	46	50	56	60
2	9	18	18	–	–	4	19	49	53	57	64
2	10	18	20	–	–	4	20	52	60	64	68
2	11	20	22	–	–	4	21	52	59	64	72
2	12	22	24	–	–	4	22	56	62	66	72
2	13	24	26	26	–	4	23	57	64	69	76
2	14	24	26	28	–	4	24	60	68	76	80
2	15	26	28	30	–	4	25	63	68	75	84
2	16	28	30	32	–						
2	17	30	32	34	–	5	5	20	25	25	25
2	18	32	34	36	–	5	6	24	24	30	30
2	19	32	36	38	38	5	7	25	28	30	35
2	20	34	38	40	40	5	8	27	30	35	35
2	21	36	38	42	42	5	9	30	35	36	40
2	22	38	40	44	44	5	10	35	40	40	45
2	23	38	42	44	46	5	11	35	39	44	45
2	24	40	44	46	48	5	12	36	43	48	50
2	25	42	46	48	50	5	13	40	45	50	52
						5	14	42	46	51	56
3	3	9	–	–		5	15	50	55	60	60
3	4	12	–	–	–	5	16	48	54	59	64
3	5	15	15	–	–	5	17	50	55	63	68
3	6	15	18	–	–	5	18	52	60	65	70
3	7	18	21	21	–	5	19	56	61	70	71
3	8	21	21	24	–	5	20	60	65	75	80
3	9	21	24	27	27	5	21	60	69	75	80
3	10	24	27	30	30	5	22	63	70	78	83
3	11	27	30	33	33	5	23	65	72	82	87
3	12	27	30	33	36	5	24	67	76	85	90
3	13	30	33	36	39	5	25	75	80	90	95
3	14	33	36	39	42						
3	15	33	36	42	42	6	6	30	30	36	36
3	16	36	39	45	45	6	7	28	30	35	36
3	17	36	42	45	48	6	8	30	34	40	40
3	18	39	45	48	51	6	9	33	39	42	45
3	19	42	45	51	54	6	10	36	40	44	48
3	20	42	48	54	57	6	11	38	43	49	54
3	21	45	51	54	57	6	12	48	48	54	60
3	22	48	51	57	60	6	13	46	52	54	60
3	23	48	54	60	63	6	14	48	54	60	64
3	24	51	57	63	66	6	15	51	57	63	69
3	25	54	60	66	69	6	16	54	60	66	72
						6	17	56	62	68	73
4	4	16	16	–	–	6	18	66	72	78	84
4	5	16	20	20	–	6	19	64	70	77	83
4	6	18	20	24	24	6	20	66	72	80	88
4	7	21	24	28	28	6	21	69	75	84	90
4	8	24	28	32	32	6	22	70	78	88	92
4	9	27	28	32	36	6	23	73	80	91	97
4	10	28	30	36	36	6	24	78	90	96	102
4	11	29	33	40	40	6	25	78	88	89	107

Continued overleaf

TABLES

Table K *Continued*

n_1	n_2	$\alpha_1 =$ 5% $\alpha_2 =$ 10%	2½% 5%	1% 2%	½% 1%	n_1	n_1	$\alpha_1 =$ 5% $\alpha_2 =$ 10%	2½% 5%	1% 2%	½% 1%
7	7	35	42	42	42	9	22	91	101	113	122
7	8	34	40	42	48	9	23	94	106	117	126
7	9	36	42	47	49	9	24	99	111	123	132
7	10	40	46	50	53	9	25	101	114	125	135
7	11	44	48	55	59						
7	12	46	53	58	60	10	10	60	70	70	80
7	13	50	56	63	65	10	11	57	60	69	77
7	14	56	63	70	77	10	12	60	66	74	80
7	15	56	62	70	75	10	13	64	70	78	84
7	16	59	64	73	77	10	14	68	74	84	90
7	17	61	68	77	84	10	15	75	80	90	100
7	18	65	72	83	87	10	16	76	84	94	100
7	19	69	76	86	91	10	17	79	89	99	106
7	20	72	79	91	93	10	18	82	92	104	108
7	21	77	91	98	105	10	19	85	94	104	113
7	22	77	84	97	103	10	20	100	110	120	130
7	23	80	89	101	108	10	21	95	105	118	126
7	24	84	92	105	112	10	22	98	108	120	130
7	25	86	97	108	115	10	23	101	114	127	137
						10	24	106	118	130	140
8	8	40	48	48	56	10	25	110	125	140	150
8	9	40	46	54	55						
8	10	44	48	56	60	11	11	66	77	88	88
8	11	48	53	61	64	11	12	64	72	77	86
8	12	52	60	64	68	11	13	67	75	86	91
8	13	54	62	67	72	11	14	73	82	90	96
8	14	58	64	72	76	11	15	76	84	95	102
8	15	60	67	75	81	11	16	80	89	100	106
8	16	72	80	88	88	11	17	85	93	104	110
8	17	68	77	85	88	11	18	88	97	108	118
8	18	72	80	88	94	11	19	92	102	114	122
8	19	74	82	93	98	11	20	96	107	118	127
8	20	80	88	100	104	11	21	101	112	124	134
8	21	81	89	102	107	11	22	110	121	143	143
8	22	84	94	106	112	11	23	108	119	132	142
8	23	89	98	107	115	11	24	111	124	139	150
8	24	96	104	120	128	11	25	117	129	143	154
8	25	95	104	118	125						
						12	12	72	83	96	96
9	9	54	54	63	63	12	13	71	81	92	95
9	10	50	53	61	63	12	14	78	86	94	104
9	11	52	59	63	70	12	15	84	93	102	108
9	12	57	63	69	75	12	16	88	96	108	116
9	13	59	65	73	78	12	17	90	100	112	119
9	14	63	70	80	84	12	18	96	108	120	126
9	15	69	75	84	90	12	19	99	108	121	130
9	16	69	78	87	94	12	20	104	116	128	140
9	17	74	82	92	99	12	21	108	120	132	141
9	18	81	90	99	108	12	22	110	124	138	148
9	19	80	89	99	107	12	23	113	125	138	149
9	20	84	93	104	111	12	24	132	144	156	168
9	21	90	99	111	117	12	25	120	138	153	165

Table K *Continued*

n_1	n_2	$\alpha_1 =$ 5% / $\alpha_2 =$ 10%	2½% / 5%	1% / 2%	½% / 1%	n_1	n_1	$\alpha_1 =$ 5% / $\alpha_2 =$ 10%	2½% / 5%	1% / 2%	½% / 1%
13	13	91	91	104	117	17	19	126	141	158	166
13	14	78	89	102	104	17	20	130	146	163	175
13	15	87	96	107	115	17	21	136	151	168	180
13	16	91	101	112	121	17	22	142	157	176	187
13	17	96	105	118	127	17	23	146	163	181	196
13	18	99	110	123	131	17	24	151	168	187	203
13	19	104	114	130	138	17	25	156	173	196	207
13	20	108	120	135	143						
13	21	113	126	140	150	18	18	144	162	180	180
13	22	117	130	143	156	18	19	133	142	160	176
13	23	120	135	152	161	18	20	136	152	170	182
13	24	125	140	155	166	18	21	144	159	177	189
13	25	131	145	160	172	18	22	148	164	184	196
						18	23	152	170	189	204
14	14	98	112	112	126	18	24	162	180	198	216
14	15	92	98	111	123	18	25	162	180	202	216
14	16	96	106	120	126						
14	17	100	111	125	134	19	19	152	171	190	190
14	18	104	116	130	140	19	20	144	160	171	187
14	19	110	121	135	148	19	21	147	163	184	199
14	20	114	126	142	152	19	22	152	169	190	204
14	21	126	140	154	161	19	23	159	177	197	209
14	22	124	138	152	164	19	24	164	183	204	218
14	23	127	142	159	170	19	25	168	187	211	224
14	24	132	146	164	176						
14	25	136	150	169	182	20	20	160	180	200	220
						20	21	165	173	193	199
15	15	105	120	135	135	20	22	160	176	196	212
15	16	101	114	120	133	20	23	164	184	205	219
15	17	105	116	131	142	20	24	172	192	212	228
15	18	111	123	138	147	20	25	180	200	220	235
15	19	114	127	142	152						
15	20	125	135	150	160	21	21	168	189	210	231
15	21	126	138	156	168	21	22	163	183	205	223
15	22	130	144	160	173	21	23	171	189	213	227
15	23	134	149	165	179	21	24	177	198	222	237
15	24	141	156	174	186	21	25	182	202	225	244
15	25	145	160	180	195						
						22	22	198	198	242	242
16	16	112	128	144	160	22	23	173	194	217	237
16	17	109	124	139	143	22	24	182	204	228	242
16	18	116	128	142	154	22	25	189	209	234	250
16	19	120	133	151	160						
16	20	128	140	156	168	23	23	207	230	253	253
16	21	130	145	162	173	23	24	183	205	228	249
16	22	136	150	168	180	23	25	195	216	243	262
16	23	141	157	175	187						
16	24	152	168	184	200	24	24	216	240	264	288
16	25	149	167	186	199	24	25	204	225	254	262
17	17	136	136	153	170	25	25	225	250	275	300
17	18	118	133	150	164						

Table L Critical values for Spearman's rank correlation coefficient.

$$r_S = 1 - \frac{6D^2}{n^3 - n}$$

n	$\alpha_1^R =$ $\alpha_2 =$ 5% 10%	2½% 5%	1% 2%	½% 1%	n	$\alpha_1^R =$ $\alpha_2 =$ 5% 10%	2½% 5%	1% 2%	½% 1%
1	–	–	–	–	26	0.3306	0.3901	0.4571	0.5009
2	–	–	–	–	27	0.3242	0.3828	0.4487	0.4915
3	–	–	–	–	28	0.3180	0.3755	0.4401	0.4828
4	1.0000	–	–	–	29	0.3118	0.3685	0.4325	0.4749
5	0.9000	1.0000	1.0000	–	30	0.3063	0.3624	0.4251	0.4670
6	0.8286	0.8857	0.9429	1.0000	31	0.3012	0.3560	0.4185	0.4593
7	0.7143	0.7857	0.8929	0.9286	32	0.2962	0.3504	0.4117	0.4523
8	0.6429	0.7381	0.8333	0.8810	33	0.2914	0.3449	0.4054	0.4455
9	0.6000	0.7000	0.7833	0.8333	34	0.2871	0.3396	0.3995	0.4390
10	0.5636	0.6485	0.7455	0.7939	35	0.2829	0.3347	0.3936	0.4328
11	0.5364	0.6182	0.7091	0.7545	36	0.2788	0.3300	0.3882	0.4268
12	0.5035	0.5874	0.6783	0.7273	37	0.2748	0.3253	0.3829	0.4211
13	0.4835	0.5604	0.6484	0.7033	38	0.2710	0.3209	0.3778	0.4155
14	0.4637	0.5385	0.6264	0.6791	39	0.2674	0.3168	0.3729	0.4103
15	0.4464	0.5214	0.6036	0.6536	40	0.2640	0.3128	0.3681	0.4051
16	0.4294	0.5029	0.5824	0.6353	41	0.2606	0.3087	0.3636	0.4002
17	0.4142	0.4877	0.5662	0.6176	42	0.2574	0.3051	0.3594	0.3955
18	0.4014	0.4716	0.5501	0.5996	43	0.2543	0.3014	0.3550	0.3908
19	0.3912	0.4596	0.5351	0.5842	44	0.2513	0.2978	0.3511	0.3865
20	0.3805	0.4466	0.5218	0.5699	45	0.2484	0.2945	0.3470	0.3822
21	0.3701	0.4364	0.5091	0.5558	46	0.2456	0.2913	0.3433	0.3781
22	0.3608	0.4252	0.4975	0.5438	47	0.2429	0.2880	0.3396	0.3741
23	0.3528	0.4160	0.4862	0.5316	48	0.2403	0.2850	0.3361	0.3702
24	0.3443	0.4070	0.4757	0.5209	49	0.2378	0.2820	0.3326	0.3664
25	0.3369	0.3977	0.4662	0.5108	50	0.2353	0.2791	0.3293	0.3628

Table M Critical values for Kendall's rank correlation coefficient.

$$\tau = \frac{N_c - N_D}{\frac{1}{2}n(n-1)}$$

n	$\alpha_1^R =$ 5% $\alpha_2 =$ 10%	2½% 5%	1% 2%	½% 1%	n	$\alpha_1^R =$ 5% $\alpha_2 =$ 10%	2½% 5%	1% 2%	½% 1%
1	–	–	–	–	26	0.2369	0.2800	0.3292	0.3600
2	–	–	–	–	27	0.2308	0.2707	0.3219	0.3561
3	–	–	–	–	28	0.2275	0.2646	0.3122	0.3439
4	1.0000	–	–	–	29	0.2217	0.2611	0.3103	0.3399
5	0.8000	1.0000	1.0000	–	30	0.2184	0.2552	0.3011	0.3333
6	0.7333	0.8667	0.8667	1.0000	31	0.2129	0.2516	0.2946	0.3247
7	0.6190	0.7143	0.8095	0.9048	32	0.2097	0.2460	0.2903	0.3226
8	0.5714	0.6429	0.7143	0.7857	33	0.2045	0.2424	0.2879	0.3144
9	0.5000	0.5556	0.6667	0.7222	34	0.2014	0.2371	0.2799	0.3119
10	0.4667	0.5111	0.6000	0.6444	35	0.1966	0.2336	0.2773	0.3042
11	0.4182	0.4909	0.5636	0.6000	36	0.1937	0.2317	0.2730	0.3016
12	0.3939	0.4545	0.5455	0.5758	37	0.1922	0.2282	0.2673	0.2973
13	0.3590	0.4359	0.5128	0.5641	38	0.1892	0.2233	0.2632	0.2916
14	0.3626	0.4066	0.4725	0.5165	39	0.1876	0.2200	0.2605	0.2874
15	0.3333	0.3905	0.4667	0.5048	40	0.1846	0.2179	0.2564	0.2846
16	0.3167	0.3833	0.4333	0.4833	41	0.1805	0.2146	0.2537	0.2805
17	0.3088	0.3676	0.4265	0.4706	42	0.1777	0.2125	0.2497	0.2753
18	0.2941	0.3464	0.4118	0.4510	43	0.1761	0.2093	0.2470	0.2735
19	0.2865	0.3333	0.3918	0.4386	44	0.1734	0.2072	0.2431	0.2685
20	0.2737	0.3263	0.3789	0.4211	45	0.1717	0.2040	0.2404	0.2667
21	0.2667	0.3143	0.3714	0.4095	46	0.1691	0.2019	0.2386	0.2638
22	0.2641	0.3074	0.3593	0.3939	47	0.1674	0.1989	0.2359	0.2599
23	0.2569	0.2964	0.3518	0.3913	48	0.1667	0.1968	0.2323	0.2571
24	0.2464	0.2899	0.3406	0.3768	49	0.1633	0.1956	0.2296	0.2534
25	0.2400	0.2867	0.3333	0.3667	50	0.1624	0.1918	0.2278	0.2506

Table N Critical values for the Kruskal–Wallis test (small sample sizes). Unequal sample sizes

$$H = \frac{12}{N(N+1)} \sum_{i=1}^{k} \frac{R_i^2}{n_i} - 3(N+1)$$

k = 3			k = 4		
Sample sizes	α = 5%	1%	Sample sizes	α = 5%	1%
2 2 2	–	–	2 1 1 1	–	–
			2 2 1 1	–	–
3 2 1	–	–	2 2 2 1	5.679	–
3 2 2	4.714	–	2 2 2 2	6.167	6.667
3 3 1	5.143	–			
3 3 2	5.361	–	3 1 1 1	–	–
3 3 3	5.600	7.200	3 2 1 1	–	–
			3 2 2 1	5.833	–
4 1 1	–	–	3 2 2 2	6.333	7.133
4 2 1	–	–	3 3 2 1	6.244	7.200
4 2 2	5.333	–	3 3 2 2	6.527	7.636
4 3 1	5.208	–	3 3 3 1	6.600	7.400
4 3 2	5.444	6.444	3 3 3 2	6.727	8.015
4 3 3	5.791	6.745	3 3 3 3	7.000	8.538
4 4 1	5.455	7.036			
4 4 3	5.598	7.144	4 1 1 1	–	–
4 4 4	5.692	7.564	4 2 1 1	5.833	–
			4 2 2 1	6.133	7.000
5 1 1	–	–	4 2 2 2	6.545	7.391
5 2 1	5.000	–	4 3 1 1	6.178	7.067
5 2 2	5.160	6.533	4 3 2 1	6.309	7.455
5 3 1	4.960	–	4 3 2 2	6.621	7.871
5 3 2	5.251	6.909	4 3 3 1	6.545	7.758
5 3 3	5.648	7.079	4 3 3 2	6.795	8.333
5 4 1	4.985	6.955	4 3 3 3	6.984	8.659
5 4 2	5.273	7.205	4 4 1 1	5.945	7.909
5 4 3	5.656	7.445	4 4 2 1	6.386	7.909
5 4 4	5.657	7.760	4 4 2 2	6.731	8.346
5 5 1	5.127	7.309	4 4 3 1	6.635	8.231
5 5 2	5.338	7.338	4 4 3 2	6.874	8.621
5 5 3	5.705	7.578	4 4 3 3	7.038	8.876
5 5 4	5.666	7.823	4 4 4 1	6.725	8.588
5 5 5	5.780	8.000	4 4 4 2	6.957	8.871
6 1 1	–	–			
6 2 1	4.822	–			
6 2 2	5.345	6.655			
6 3 1	4.855	6.873			
6 3 2	5.348	6.970			
6 3 3	5.615	7.410			
6 4 1	4.947	7.106			
6 4 2	5.340	7.340			
6 4 3	5.610	7.500			
6 4 4	5.681	7.795			
6 5 1	4.990	7.182			
6 5 2	5.338	7.376			
6 5 3	5.602	7.590			
6 5 4	5.661	7.936			
6 5 5	5.729	8.028			
6 6 1	4.945	7.121			
6 6 2	5.410	7.467			
6 6 3	5.625	7.725			
6 6 4	5.724	8.000			
6 6 5	5.765	8.124			
6 6 6	5.801	8.222			

	$k = 5$				$k = 6$		
Sample sizes	$\alpha =$	5%	1%	Sample sizes	$\alpha =$	5%	1%
1 1 1 1 1		–	–	1 1 1 1 1 1		–	–
2 1 1 1 1		–	–	2 1 1 1 1 1		–	–
2 2 1 1 1		–	–	2 2 1 1 1 1		–	–
2 2 2 1 1		6.750	–	2 2 2 1 1 1		7.600	–
2 2 2 2 1		7.133	7.533	2 2 2 2 1 1		8.018	8.618
2 2 2 2 2		7.418	8.291	2 2 2 2 2 1		8.455	9.227
				2 2 2 2 2 2		8.846	9.846
3 1 1 1 1		–	–				
3 2 1 1 1		6.583	–	3 1 1 1 1 1		–	–
3 2 2 1 1		6.800	7.600	3 2 1 1 1 1		7.467	–
3 2 2 2 1		7.309	8.127	3 2 2 1 1 1		7.945	8.509
3 2 2 2 2		7.682	8.682	3 2 2 2 1 1		8.348	9.136
3 3 1 1 1		7.111	–	3 2 2 2 2 1		8.731	9.692
3 3 2 1 1		7.200	8.073	3 2 2 2 2 2		9.033	10.22
3 3 2 2 1		7.591	8.576	3 3 1 1 1 1		7.909	8.564
3 3 2 2 2		7.910	9.115	3 3 2 1 1 1		8.303	9.045
3 3 3 1 1		7.576	8.424	3 3 2 2 1 1		8.615	9.628
3 3 3 2 1		7.769	9.051	3 3 2 2 2 1		8.923	10.15
3 3 3 2 2		8.044	9.505	3 3 3 1 1 1		8.461	9.564
3 3 3 3 1		8.000	9.451	3 3 3 2 1 1		8.835	10.08
4 1 1 1 1		–	–	4 1 1 1 1 1		7.333	–
4 2 1 1 1		6.733	–	4 2 1 1 1 1		7.827	8.400
				4 2 2 1 1 1		8.205	9.000
				4 2 2 2 1 1		8.558	9.538
				4 2 2 2 2 1		8.868	10.07
				4 3 1 1 1 1		8.053	9.023
				4 3 2 1 1 1		8.429	9.506
				4 3 2 2 1 1		8.742	10.01
				4 3 3 1 1 1		8.654	9.934
				4 4 1 1 1 1		8.231	9.538
				4 4 2 1 1 1		8.571	9.940
				5 1 1 1 1 1		7.909	–
				5 2 1 1 1 1		7.891	8.682

Continued overleaf

Table N *Continued*

Equal sample sizes

$$H = \frac{12}{n^2 k(nk+1)} \sum_{i=1}^{k} R_i^2 - 3(nk+1)$$

	$k = 3$		$k = 4$		$k = 5$		$k = 6$	
n	$\alpha = 5\%$	1%	$\alpha = 5\%$	1%	$\alpha = 5\%$	1%	$\alpha = 5\%$	1%
2	–	–	6.167	6.667	7.418	8.291	8.846	9.846
3	5.600	7.200	7.000	8.538	8.333	10.20	9.789	11.82
4	5.692	7.654	7.235	9.287	8.685	11.07	10.14	12.72
5	5.780	8.000	7.377	9.789	8.876	11.57	10.36	13.26
6	5.801	8.222	7.453	10.09	9.002	11.91	10.50	13.60
7	5.819	8.378	7.501	10.25	9.080	12.14	10.59	13.84
8	5.805	8.465	7.534	10.42	9.126	12.29	10.66	13.99
9	5.831	8.529	7.557	10.53	9.166	12.41	10.71	14.13
10	5.853	8.607	7.586	10.62	9.200	12.50	10.75	14.24
11	5.885	8.648	7.623	10.69	9.242	12.58	10.76	14.32
12	5.872	8.712	7.629	10.75	9.274	12.63	10.79	14.38
13	5.901	8.735	7.645	10.80	9.303	12.69	10.83	14.44
14	5.896	8.754	7.658	10.84	9.307	12.74	10.84	14.49
15	5.902	8.821	7.676	10.87	9.302	12.77	10.86	14.53
16	5.909	8.822	7.678	10.90	9.313	12.79	10.88	14.56
17	5.915	8.856	7.682	10.92	9.325	12.83	10.88	14.60
18	5.932	8.865	7.698	10.95	9.334	12.85	10.89	14.63
19	5.923	8.887	7.701	10.98	9.342	12.87	10.90	14.64
20	5.926	8.905	7.703	10.98	9.353	12.91	10.92	14.67
∞	5.991	9.210	7.815	11.34	9.488	13.28	11.07	15.09

Table O Critical values for Friedman's test.

$$M = \frac{12}{nk(k+1)} \sum_{i=1}^{k} R_i^2 - 3n(k+1)$$

n	k = 3 α = 5%	1%	k = 4 α = 5	1%	k = 5 α = 5	1%	k = 6 α = 5%	1%
2	–	–	6.000	–	7.600	8.000	9.143	9.714
3	6.000	–	7.400	9.000	8.533	10.13	9.857	11.76
4	6.500	8.000	7.800	9.600	8.800	11.20	10.29	12.71
5	6.400	8.400	7.800	9.960	8.960	11.68	10.49	13.23
6	7.000	9.000	7.600	10.20	9.067	11.87	10.57	13.62
7	7.143	8.857	˙7.800	10.54	9.143	12.11	10.67	13.86
8	6.250	9.000	7.650	10.50	9.200	13.20	10.71	14.00
9	6.222	9.556	7.667	10.73	9.244	12.44	10.78	14.14
10	6.200	9.600	7.680	10.68	9.280	12.48	10.80	14.23
11	6.545	9.455	7.691	10.75	9.309	12.58	10.84	14.32
12	6.500	9.500	7.700	10.80	9.333	12.60	10.86	14.38
13	6.615	9.385	7.800	10.85	9.354	12.68	10.89	14.45
14	6.143	9.143	7.714	10.89	9.371	12.74	10.90	14.49
15	6.400	8.933	7.720	10.92	9.387	12.80	10.92	14.54
16	6.500	9.375	7.800	10.95	9.400	12.80	10.96	14.57
17	6.118	9.294	7.800	10.05	9.412	12.85	10.95	14.61
18	6.333	9.000	7.733	10.93	9.422	12.89	10.95	14.63
19	6.421	9.579	7.863	11.02	9.432	12.88	11.00	14.67
20	6.300	9.300	7.800	11.10	9.400	12.92	11.00	14.66
∞	5.991	9.210	7.815	11.34	9.488	13.28	11.07	15.09

Table P Critical values for the M_1 match test.

n	$k = 3$ $\alpha = 5\%$	1%	$k = 4$ $\alpha = 5\%$	1%	$k = 5$ $\alpha = 5\%$	1%	$k = 6$ $\alpha = 5\%$	1%
2	–	–	4	–	5	5	4	6
3	9	–	8	12	7	9	7	9
4	12	18	12	15	11	14	11	14
5	18	20	17	20	17	20	17	20
6	23	29	23	28	23	27	23	27
7	31	39	30	36	30	35	30	35
8	39	48	39	45	39	44	38	44
9	48	57	48	55	48	54	48	54
10	59	67	58	66	58	65	58	65

Critical values for $k \geqslant 3$ and $n \geqslant 11$

n	α 5%	1%
11	70	79
12	83	93
13	97	107
14	112	122
15	127	139
16	144	156
17	162	175
18	180	194
19	200	214
20	220	236

Table Q Critical values for the M_2 match test.

n	$k = 3$		$k = 4$		$k = 5$		$k = 6$	
	$\alpha = 5\%$	1%	$\alpha = 5\%$	1%	$\alpha = 5\%$	1%	$\alpha = 5\%$	1%
2	–	–	8.0	–	8.0	10.0	8.0	10.0
3	9.0	–	10.0	12.0	9.0	11.0	9.0	10.0
4	15.0	18.0	15.0	18.0	15.5	17.5	15.5	17.5
5	24.0	26.0	23.0	26.5	24.0	26.0	24.0	26.5
6	32.0	36.0	33.0	35.5	34.0	36.5	34.5	37.5
7	43.0	51.0	45.0	48.0	48.0	49.0	47.0	50.0
8	56.0	61.0	58.0	61.5	59.5	63.5	61.0	64.5
9	70.0	76.0	73.5	77.5	75.0	79.5	76.5	81.0
10	81.0	92.0	90.0	94.5	92.5	97.0	94.5	99.0
11	105.0	110.0	109.0	114.0	112.0	117.0	114.0	119.0
12	125.0	130.0	129.0	134.5	132.5	138.5	135.5	141.0
13	146.0	152.0	151.5	157.5	155.5	161.5	158.5	164.5
14	169.0	176.0	175.5	181.5	180.5	186.5	183.5	190.5
15	193.0	201.0	201.0	208.0	206.5	213.5	210.5	217.5
16	219.0	227.0	228.5	235.5	234.5	242.0	239.0	247.0
17	247.0	256.0	257.5	265.5	264.5	272.5	269.5	278.5
18	277.0	286.0	288.5	297.0	296.5	305.0	302.0	310.5
19	308.0	318.0	321.0	330.0	330.0	339.0	336.0	345.5
20	341.0	351.0	355.5	365.0	365.5	375.0	372.0	382.0

Table R Critical values for the Terpstra–Johnckheere test.

Unequal sample sizes ($k = 3$)

Sample sizes	5%	1%	Sample sizes	5%	1%	Sample sizes	5%	1%
2 2 2	1	2	3 6 8	26	19	5 6 9	41	31
2 2 3	2	0	3 6 9	29	21	5 6 10	44	34
2 2 4	3	1	3 6 10	32	24	5 7 7	37	28
2 2 5	4	1	3 7 7	26	19	5 7 8	41	32
2 2 6	5	2	3 7 8	30	22	5 7 9	46	35
2 2 7	6	3	3 7 9	34	25	5 7 10	50	39
2 2 8	7	3	3 7 10	37	28	5 8 8	46	36
2 3 3	3	1	3 8 8	33	25	5 8 9	51	40
2 3 4	5	2	3 8 9	38	28	5 8 10	56	44
2 3 5	6	3	3 8 10	42	32	5 9 9	56	44
2 3 6	8	4	3 9 9	42	32	5 9 10	61	49
2 3 7	9	5	3 9 10	47	36	5 10 10	67	53
2 3 8	10	6	3 10 10	51	40			
2 4 4	6	3				6 6 6	33	25
2 4 5	8	5	4 4 4	12	8	6 6 7	37	28
2 4 6	10	6	4 4 5	14	10	6 6 8	41	32
2 4 7	12	7	4 4 6	17	12	6 6 9	46	36
2 4 8	14	9	4 4 7	20	14	6 6 10	51	39
2 5 5	10	6	4 4 8	22	16	6 7 7	42	32
2 5 6	13	8	4 4 9	25	18	6 7 8	46	36
2 5 7	15	10	4 4 10	28	20	6 7 9	52	41
2 5 8	17	12	4 5 5	17	12	6 7 10	57	45
2 6 6	15	10	4 5 6	20	15	6 8 8	52	41
2 6 7	18	12	4 5 7	24	17	6 8 9	57	45
2 6 8	21	14	4 5 8	27	20	6 8 10	63	50
2 7 7	21	15	4 5 9	30	22	6 9 9	63	50
2 7 8	24	17	4 5 10	33	24	6 9 10	69	55
2 8 8	27	20	4 6 6	24	17	6 10 10	75	60
			4 6 7	27	20			
3 3 3	5	2	4 6 8	31	23	7 7 7	47	37
3 3 4	7	4	4 6 9	35	26	7 7 8	52	41
3 3 5	9	5	4 6 10	38	29	7 7 9	58	46
3 3 6	11	6	4 7 7	31	23	7 7 10	63	50
3 3 7	12	8	4 7 8	35	27	7 8 8	58	46
3 3 8	14	9	4 7 9	40	30	7 8 9	64	51
3 3 9	17	11	4 7 10	44	33	7 8 10	70	56
3 3 10	18	12	4 8 8	40	30	7 9 9	70	56
3 4 4	9	5	4 8 9	44	34	7 9 10	76	62
3 4 5	11	7	4 8 10	49	38	7 10 10	83	67
3 4 6	14	9	4 9 9	49	38			
3 4 7	16	11	4 9 10	54	42	8 8 8	64	52
3 4 8	18	12	4 10 10	59	47	8 8 9	70	57
3 4 9	21	14				8 8 10	77	62
3 4 10	23	16	5 5 5	21	15	8 9 9	77	63
3 5 5	14	9	5 5 6	24	18	8 9 10	84	68
3 5 6	17	11	5 5 7	28	21	8 10 10	91	74
3 5 7	19	13	5 5 8	31	24			
3 5 8	22	15	5 5 9	35	26	9 9 9	84	69
3 5 9	25	18	5 5 10	39	29	9 9 10	91	75
3 5 10	28	20	5 6 6	28	21	9 10 10	98	81
3 6 6	20	14	5 6 7	32	24			
3 6 7	23	16	5 6 8	36	28	10 10 10	106	88

Equal sample sizes, n

Number of		α	
samples, k	n	5%	1%
4	2	5	2
	3	14	10
	4	29	23
	5	50	40
	6	75	62
	7	106	90
	8	143	122
	9	184	160
	10	231	203
5	2	10	7
	3	28	21
	4	54	44
	5	90	76
	6	134	116
	7	188	164
	8	250	222
	9	322	288
	10	403	364
6	2	17	13
	3	45	37
	4	86	73
	5	141	123
	6	210	186
	7	292	261
	8	388	351
	9	498	454
	10	623	570

Table S   Critical values for Page's test.

n	k = 3		k = 4		k = 5		k = 6	
	α = 5%	1%	α = 5%	1%	α = 5%	1%	α = 5%	1%
2	28	–	58	60	103	106	166	173
3	41	42	84	87	150	155	244	252
4	54	55	111	114	197	204	321	331
5	66	68	137	141	244	251	397	409
6	79	81	163	167	291	299	474	486
7	91	93	189	193	338	346	550	563
8	104	106	214	220	384	393	640	625
9	116	119	240	246	431	441	718	701
10	128	131	266	272	477	487	793	777
11	141	144	292	298	523	534	869	852
12	153	156	317	324	570	581	946	928
13	165	169	343	350	616	628	1022	1003
14	178	181	369	376	662	674	1098	1078
15	190	194	394	402	708	721	1174	1153
16	202	206	420	428	754	767	1249	1229
17	215	218	446	453	800	814	1325	1304
18	227	231	471	479	846	860	1401	1379
19	239	243	497	505	892	906	1477	1454
20	251	256	522	531	938	953	1529	1552

Table T   Critical values for the L_1 match test for ordered alternatives.

n	$k = 3$		$k = 4$		$k = 5$		$k = 6$	
	$\alpha = 5\%$	1%	$\alpha = 5\%$	1%	$\alpha = 5\%$	1%	$\alpha = 5\%$	1%
2	–	–	6	8	6	8	6	7
3	–	–	7	9	7	9	7	9
4	9	12	9	10	9	10	9	10

$n \geqslant 5$, k any value

	α	
n	5%	1%
5	10	12
6	11	13
7	13	15
8	14	16
9	15	18
10	16	19
11	18	20
12	19	22
13	20	23
14	21	24
15	23	26
16	24	27
17	25	28
18	26	30
19	27	31
20	29	32

Table U Critical values for the L_2 match test for ordered alternatives.

n	$k = 3$ $\alpha = 5\%$	1%	$k = 4$ $\alpha = 5\%$	1%	$k = 5$ $\alpha = 5\%$	1%	$k = 6$ $\alpha = 5\%$	1%
2	6	–	7.0	8.0	6.5	7.5	6.5	8.0
3	8	9	8.5	9.5	8.5	10.0	9.0	10.5
4	10	11	10.5	12.0	11.0	12.5	11.5	13.0
5	12	13	12.5	14.0	13.0	15.0	13.5	15.0
6	14	15	14.5	16.5	15.0	17.0	15.5	17.5
7	16	17	16.5	18.5	17.5	19.5	18.0	20.0
8	18	19	18.5	20.5	19.5	21.5	20.0	22.0
9	20	21	20.5	22.5	21.5	23.5	22.0	24.5
10	22	23	22.5	24.5	23.5	26.0	24.0	26.5
11	24	25	24.5	27.0	25.5	28.0	26.5	28.5
12	25	27	26.5	29.0	27.5	30.0	28.5	31.0
13	27	29	28.5	31.0	29.5	32.0	30.5	33.0
14	29	31	30.5	33.0	31.5	34.5	32.5	35.0
15	31	33	32.5	35.0	33.5	36.5	34.5	37.5
16	33	35	34.5	37.0	35.5	38.5	36.5	39.5
17	35	37	36.5	39.0	37.5	40.5	38.5	41.5
18	36	39	38.0	41.0	39.5	42.5	40.5	43.5
19	38	40	40.0	43.0	41.5	44.5	42.5	45.5
20	40	42	42.0	45.0	43.5	46.5	44.5	47.5

Table V Critical values for the S_1 match test for interaction.

n_1	n_2	α 5%	1%
3	3	0	0
3	4	4	3
3	5	7	6
3	6	11	10
3	7	16	12
3	8	22	18
3	9	29	24
3	10	37	32
4	4	6	5
4	5	9	7
4	6	13	11
4	7	18	15
4	8	24	20
4	9	31	27
4	10	39	34
5	5	12	10
5	6	17	14
5	7	22	18
5	8	28	24
5	9	35	30
5	10	43	38
6	6	21	18
6	7	26	22
6	8	32	28
6	9	39	34
6	10	47	42
7	7	31	27
7	8	37	33
7	9	45	39
7	10	53	47
8	8	44	39
8	9	51	45
8	10	59	53
9	9	58	52
9	10	66	60
10	10	74	68

Table W   Critical values for the S_2 match test for interaction.

n_1	n_2	5%	1%
		α	
3	3	7.0	6.0
3	4	11.5	11.0
3	5	17.5	16.5
3	6	25.5	24.5
3	7	32.5	29.0
3	8	43.0	39.0
3	9	55.5	51.0
3	10	69.0	64.5
4	4	16.0	15.0
4	5	22.5	21.0
4	6	30.5	29.0
4	7	40.0	36.5
4	8	51.0	47.0
4	9	64.0	60.0
4	10	79.0	74.0
5	5	29.0	27.5
5	6	37.5	35.5
5	7	47.5	44.0
5	8	59.5	55.0
5	9	73.0	68.0
5	10	88.0	83.0
6	6	46.0	42.5
6	7	56.5	52.0
6	8	68.5	64.5
6	9	82.5	64.5
6	10	98.0	92.5
7	7	67.5	62.5
7	8	79.5	74.5
7	9	94.0	88.5
7	10	109.5	104.5
8	8	92.5	87.0
8	9	106.5	101.0
8	10	123.0	116.5
9	9	121.5	115.0
9	10	137.5	131.0
10	10	154.5	147.5

Table X Critical values for the runs test.

Lower critical values

$\alpha_1 = 5\%,\ \alpha_2 = 10\%$

$n_1 =$	2	3	4	5	6	7	8	9	10	11	12	13	14	15	16	17	18	19	20	$2 = n_2$
$n_1 = 2$	—	—	—	—	—	—	—	—	—	2	2	2	2	2	2	2	2	2	2	2
3	—	—	—	2	2	2	2	2	2	2	2	3	3	3	3	3	3	3	3	3
4	—	—	2	2	3	3	3	3	3	3	4	4	4	4	4	4	4	4	4	4
5	—	2	2	3	3	3	3	4	4	4	4	5	5	5	5	5	5	5	5	5
6	—	2	3	3	3	4	4	5	5	5	6	6	6	6	6	6	6	6	6	6
7	—	2	3	3	4	4	5	5	5	6	6	6	7	7	7	7	7	7	7	7
8	—	2	3	3	4	5	5	6	6	6	7	7	7	8	8	8	8	8	8	8
9	—	2	3	4	5	5	6	6	6	7	7	8	8	8	8	9	9	9	9	9
10	—	2	3	4	5	5	6	6	7	7	8	8	9	9	9	10	10	10	10	10
11	—	2	3	4	5	6	6	7	7	8	8	9	9	10	10	10	11	11	11	11
12	2	2	3	4	6	6	7	7	8	8	9	9	10	10	11	11	11	12	12	12
13	2	2	4	5	6	6	7	8	8	9	9	10	10	11	11	12	12	12	13	13
14	2	2	4	5	6	7	7	8	9	9	10	10	11	11	12	12	13	13	13	14
15	2	3	4	5	6	7	7	8	9	10	10	11	11	12	12	13	13	14	14	15
16	2	3	4	5	6	7	8	8	9	10	11	11	12	12	13	13	14	14	15	16
17	2	3	4	5	6	7	8	9	9	10	11	11	12	13	13	14	14	15	15	17
18	2	3	4	5	6	7	8	9	9	10	11	12	12	13	14	14	15	15	15	18
19	2	4	5	6	6	7	8	9	10	11	11	12	13	13	13	14	14			19
20	2	4	5	6	7	8	8	9	10	11	12	12	13	13						20

$\alpha_1 = 2\tfrac{1}{2}\%,\ \alpha_2 = 5\%$

$n_2 =$	2	3	4	5	6	7	8	9	10	11	12	13	14	15	16	17	18	19	20
									9										
								9	10	10									
							8	9	10	10	11	11							
						8	9	10	10	11	11	12	12						
						9	9	10	11	11	12	12	13	13					
						9	10	10	11	12	12	13	13	13	14				

Continued overleaf

Table X *Continued*

Critical values (top table, columns headed $n_1 =$, row labels at right $= n_2$):

$n_1 =$	2	3	4	5	6	7	8	9	10	11	12	13	14	15	16	17	18	19	20		$2 = n_2$
	—	—	—	—	—	—	—	—	—	—	—	—	—	—	—	—	—	—	—		2
		—	—	—	—	—	—	—	—	—	—	—	—	—	—	—	—	2	2		3
			—	—	—	—	—	—	—	—	—	—	—	—	2	2	2	3	3		4
				2	2	2	3	3	3	3	3	3	4	4	4	4	4	4	4		5
					2	2	3	3	4	4	4	4	5	5	5	5	5	5	5		6
						3	3	3	4	4	5	5	5	6	6	6	6	6	6		7
							4	4	5	5	5	6	6	6	7	7	7	7	7		8
								4	5	5	6	6	7	7	7	8	8	8	8		9
									5	6	6	7	7	8	8	8	9	9	9		10
										6	6	7	7	8	8	9	9	9	10		11
											7	7	8	8	9	9	9	10	10		12
												7	8	9	9	9	10	10	11		13
													8	9	9	10	10	11	11		14
														9	10	10	11	11	12		15
															10	11	11	11	12		16
																10	11	12	12		17
																	11	12	12		18
																		12	13		19
																			13		20

$n_2 =$	2	3	4	5	6	7	8	9	10	11	12	13	14	15	16	17	18	19	20

$\alpha_1 = \tfrac{1}{2}\%,\ \alpha_2 = 1\%$

Upper critical values

$\alpha_1 = 5\%$, $\alpha_2 = 10\%$

$n_1 =$	2	3	4	5	6	7	8	9	10	11	12	13	14	15	16	17	18	19	20	
2	—	—	—	—	—	—	—	—	—	—	—	—	—	—	—	—	—	—	—	$2 = n_2$
3	—	—	—	—	—	—	—	—	—	—	—	—	—	—	15	15	15	15	17	3
4	—	—	—	—	—	—	—	—	—	—	—	—	13	15	16	16	16	16	18	4
5	—	—	—	—	—	—	—	—	—	—	13	13	14	16	17	17	18	18	19	5
6	—	—	—	—	—	—	—	—	13	14	14	14	16	17	18	18	19	19	20	6
7	—	—	—	—	—	—	—	13	13	15	15	15	17	18	19	19	20	20	21	7
8	—	—	—	—	—	—	13	14	14	15	16	16	17	19	20	20	21	21	22	8
9	—	—	—	—	—	12	13	14	15	16	17	17	18	19	21	21	21	22	23	9
10	—	—	—	—	13	13	14	15	16	17	18	17	19	20	21	22	22	23	24	10
11	—	—	—	13	14	14	15	16	17	18	19	18	20	21	22	23	23	24	25	11
12	—	—	13	14	15	15	16	17	18	19	20	19	21	22	23	23	24	25	25	12
13	—	11	13	14	15	16	17	18	19	20	21	20	22	23	24	24	24	25	26	13
14	—	12	14	15	16	16	17	19	20	21	22	21	23	24	25	25	25	26	27	14
15	—	12	14	15	16	17	18	19	20	22	23	23	24	25	26	26	26	26	27	15
16	—	13	14	16	16	17	19	20	21	22	23	24	25	26	26	26	26	27	27	16
17	—	13	14	16	17	18	19	21	21	23	24	24	25	26	27	27	27	27	27	17
18	—	13	15	17	18	18	20	21	22	23	24	25	26	26	27	27	27	27	27	18
19	—	13	15	17	18	19	20	21	22	23	24	25	26	27	27	27	27	27	27	19
20	—	13	15	17	18	20	21	22	23	24	25	25	26	27	27	28	27	27	27	20

$\alpha_1 = 2\tfrac{1}{2}\%$, $\alpha_2 = 5\%$

$n_2 =$	2	3	4	5	6	7	8

Continued overleaf

Table X *Continued*

$n_1 =$	2	3	4	5	6	7	8	9	10	11	12	13	14	15	16	17	18	19	20	
2	—	—	—	—	—	—	—	—	—	—	—	—	—	—	—	—	—	—	—	2 = n_2
3	—	—	—	—	—	—	—	—	—	—	—	—	—	—	—	—	—	—	—	3
4	—	—	—	—	—	—	—	—	—	—	—	—	—	—	—	—	—	—	—	4
5	—	—	—	—	—	—	—	—	—	—	—	—	—	—	—	—	—	—	—	5
6	—	—	—	—	—	—	—	—	—	—	—	—	—	—	—	—	—	—	—	6
7	—	—	—	—	—	—	—	13	15	—	—	—	—	—	—	—	—	—	—	7
8	—	—	—	—	—	11	13	14	15	15	—	—	—	—	—	—	—	—	19	8
9	—	—	—	—	—	12	14	15	16	15	15	17	—	—	—	—	—	19	20	9
10	—	—	—	—	—	13	14	16	16	16	16	18	17	17	17	19	19	20	22	10
11	—	—	—	—	11	17	19	20	17	17	17	19	18	18	18	20	20	22	23	11
12	—	—	—	10	12	18	19	21	21	18	18	19	19	19	20	21	21	23	25	12
13	—	—	—	15	16	19	20	21	22	18	19	20	20	20	21	22	22	24	26	13
14	—	—	—	15	17	19	20	22	22	23	19	21	21	21	22	22	23	24	26	14
15	—	—	9	16	17	20	21	22	23	23	24	21	21	22	22	23	24	25	27	15
16	—	—	13	16	18	20	21	22	23	24	24	25	22	23	23	24	24	26	27	16
17	—	—	14	16	18	20	22	23	23	24	25	26	26	23	24	24	25	26	28	17
18	—	12	15	17	19	21	22	23	24	25	25	26	27	28	24	25	26	27	28	18
19	—	13	15	17	19	21	22	23	24	25	26	27	27	28	29	26	26	27	29	19
20	11	13	15	17	19	21	22	24	24	25	26	27	28	29	29	30	27	28	29	20
$n_2 =$ 2	3	4	5	6	7	8	9	10	11	12	13	14	15	16	17	18	19	20		

$\alpha_1 = \tfrac{1}{2}\%,\ \alpha_2 = 1\%$

Table Y Critical values for the runs up and down test.

n	$\alpha_1 = 5\%$ $\alpha_2 = 10\%$ Lower	Upper	$\alpha_1 = 2\frac{1}{2}\%$ $\alpha_2 = 5\%$ Lower	Upper	$\alpha_1 = 1\%$ $\alpha_2 = 2\%$ Lower	Upper	$\alpha_1 = \frac{1}{2}\%$ $\alpha_2 = 1\%$ Lower	Upper
3	–	–	–	–	–	–	–	–
4	–	–	–	–	–	–	–	–
5	1	–	1	–	–	–	–	–
6	1	–	1	–	1	–	1	–
7	2	–	2	–	1	–	1	–
8	2	–	2	–	2	–	1	–
9	3	8	3	–	2	–	2	–
10	3	9	3	–	3	–	2	–
11	4	10	4	10	3	–	3	–
12	4	11	4	11	4	–	3	–
13	5	12	5	12	4	12	4	–
14	6	12	5	13	5	13	4	13
15	6	13	6	14	5	14	4	14
16	7	14	6	14	6	15	5	15
17	7	15	7	15	6	16	6	16
18	8	15	7	16	7	16	6	17
19	8	16	8	17	7	17	7	18
20	9	17	8	17	8	18	7	18
21	10	18	9	18	8	19	8	19
22	10	18	10	19	9	20	8	20
23	11	19	10	20	10	20	9	21
24	11	20	11	20	10	21	10	22
25	12	21	11	21	11	22	10	22

Table Z Critical values for Fisher's exact test.

N	m	M	C	α(%)
6	3	3	0	10.00
7	2	5	0	9.5+
7	3	4	0	5.7
8	2	6	0	7.1
8	3	5	0	3.6
8	4	4	0	2.9
9	2	7	0	5.6
9	3	5	0	9.5+
9	3	6	0	2.4
9	4	4	0	7.9
9	4	5	0	1.6
10	2	8	0	4.4
10	3	6	0	6.7
10	3	7	0	1.7
10	4	5	0	4.8
10	4	6	1	23.8
10	5	5	1	20.6
11	2	9	0	3.6
11	3	7	0	4.8
11	3	8	0	1.2
11	4	5	0	9.1
11	4	6	0	3.0
11	4	7	1	17.6
11	5	5	0	2.6
11	5	6	1	13.4
12	2	9	0	9.1
12	2	10	0	3.0
12	3	7	0	9.1
12	3	8	0	3.6
12	3	9	1	25.5-
12	4	6	0	6.1
12	4	7	0	2.0+
12	4	8	1	13.3
12	5	5	0	5.3
12	5	6	0	1.5+
12	5	7	1	9.1
12	6	6	1	8.0
13	2	10	0	7.7
13	2	11	0	2.6
13	3	8	0	7.0
13	3	9	0	2.8
13	3	10	1	21.7
13	4	6	0	9.8
13	4	7	0	4.2
13	4	8	0	1.4
13	4	9	1	10.3
13	5	5	0	8.7
13	5	6	0	3.3
13	5	7	1	17.2
13	5	8	1	6.4
13	6	6	1	15.5+
13	6	7	1	5.0+
14	2	11	0	6.6
14	2	12	0	2.2
14	3	9	0	5.5-
14	3	10	0	2.2
14	3	11	1	18.7
14	4	7	0	7.0
14	4	8	0	3.0
14	4	9	1	19.0
14	4	10	1	8.2
14	5	6	0	5.6
14	5	7	0	2.1
14	5	8	1	12.6
14	5	9	1	4.6
14	6	6	0	1.9
14	6	7	1	10.3
14	6	8	1	3.3
14	7	7	1	2.9
15	2	12	0	5.7
15	2	13	0	1.9
15	3	9	0	8.8
15	3	10	0	4.4
15	3	11	0	1.8
15	3	12	1	16.3
15	4	8	0	5.1
15	4	9	0	2.2
15	4	10	1	15.4
15	4	11	1	6.6
15	5	6	0	8.4
15	5	7	0	3.7
15	5	8	0	1.4
15	5	9	1	9.4
15	5	10	1	3.4
15	6	6	0	3.4
15	6	7	0	1.1
15	6	8	1	7.0
15	6	9	1	2.2
15	7	7	1	6.3
15	7	8	1	1.8
16	2	12	0	10.00
16	2	13	0	5.00
16	2	14	0	1.7
16	3	10	0	7.1
16	3	11	0	3.6
16	3	12	0	1.4
16	3	13	1	14.3
16	4	8	0	7.7
16	4	9	0	3.8
16	4	10	0	1.6
16	4	11	1	12.6
16	4	12	1	5.4
16	5	7	0	5.8
16	5	8	0	2.6
16	5	9	1	15.4
16	5	10	1	7.1
16	5	11	1	2.6
16	6	6	0	5.2
16	6	7	0	2.1
16	6	8	1	11.9
16	6	9	1	4.9
16	6	10	1	1.5+
16	7	7	1	10.9
16	7	8	1	4.1
16	7	9	1	1.1
16	8	8	1	1.0+
17	2	13	0	8.8
17	2	14	0	4.4
17	2	15	0	1.5-
17	3	11	0	5.9
17	3	12	0	2.9
17	3	13	0	1.2
17	3	14	1	12.6
17	4	9	0	5.9
17	4	10	0	2.9
17	4	11	0	1.3
17	4	12	1	10.5+
17	4	13	1	4.5-
17	5	7	0	8.1
17	5	8	0	4.1
17	5	9	0	1.8
17	5	10	1	12.0
17	5	11	1	5.5+
17	5	12	1	2.0-
17	6	6	0	7.5-
17	6	7	0	3.4
17	6	8	0	1.4
17	6	9	1	8.6
17	6	10	1	3.5+
17	6	11	1	1.1
17	7	7	0	1.2
17	7	8	1	7.3
17	7	9	1	2.7
17	7	10	2	10.4
17	8	8	1	2.4
17	8	9	2	8.9
18	2	14	0	7.8
18	2	15	0	3.9
18	2	16	0	1.3
18	3	11	0	8.6
18	3	12	0	4.9
18	3	13	0	2.5-
18	3	14	1	21.6
18	3	15	1	11.3
18	4	9	0	8.2
18	4	10	0	4.6
18	4	11	0	2.3
18	4	12	1	16.7
18	4	13	1	8.8
18	4	14	1	3.7
18	5	8	0	5.9
18	5	9	0	2.9
18	5	10	0	1.3
18	5	11	1	9.5-
18	5	12	1	4.3
18	5	13	1	1.5+
18	6	6	0	10.0-
18	6	7	0	5.0-
18	6	8	0	2.3
18	6	9	1	13.1
18	6	10	1	6.3
18	6	11	1	2.6
18	6	12	2	11.5-
18	7	7	0	2.1
18	7	8	1	11.3
18	7	9	1	5.0-
18	7	10	1	1.8
18	7	11	2	7.7
18	8	8	1	4.6
18	8	9	1	1.5+
18	8	10	2	6.1
18	9	9	2	5.7
19	2	15	0	7.0
19	2	16	0	3.5+
19	2	17	0	1.2
19	3	12	0	7.2
19	3	13	0	4.1
19	3	14	0	2.1
19	3	15	1	19.4
19	3	16	1	10.1
19	4	10	0	6.5+
19	4	11	0	3.6
19	4	12	0	1.8
19	4	13	1	14.2
19	4	14	1	7.5-
19	4	15	1	3.1
19	5	8	0	7.9
19	5	9	0	4.3
19	5	10	0	2.2
19	5	11	1	14.2
19	5	12	1	7.6
19	5	13	1	3.5-
19	5	14	1	1.2

Table Z *Continued*

N	m	M	C	α(%)	N	m	M	C	α(%)	N	m	M	C	α(%)	N	n	N	C	α(%)
19	6	7	0	6.8	20	8	9	1	5.0−	21	9	12	2	1.7	22	9	11	2	8.0
	6	8	0	3.4		8	10	1	2.0−		10	10	2	4.5+		9	12	2	3.4
	6	9	0	1.5+		8	11	2	8.0		10	11	2	1.5−		9	13	2	1.2
	6	10	1	9.9		8	12	2	3.1	22	1	21	0	9.1		10	10	2	7.6
	6	11	1	4.7		9	9	1	1.8		2	17	0	8.7		10	11	2	3.0
	6	12	1	1.9		9	10	2	7.0		2	18	0	5.2		10	12	3	9.1
	6	13	2	9.2		9	11	2	2.5−		2	19	0	2.6		11	11	3	8.6
	7	7	0	3.1		10	10	2	2.3		2	20	1	35.5−	23	1	22	0	8.7
	7	8	0	1.3	21	1	20	0	9.5+		3	14	0	7.3		2	18	0	7.9
	7	9	1	8.0		2	16	0	9.5+		3	15	0	4.5+		2	19	0	4.7
	7	10	1	3.5−		2	17	0	5.7		3	16	0	2.6		2	20	0	2.4
	7	11	1	1.3		2	18	0	2.9		3	17	0	1.3		2	21	1	34.0
	7	12	2	5.8		2	19	1	37.1		3	18	1	14.5+		3	14	0	9.5−
	8	8	1	7.4		3	13	0	8.4		3	19	1	7.5+		3	15	0	6.3
	8	9	1	3.0		3	14	0	5.3		4	11	0	9.0		3	16	0	4.0
	8	10	2	11.0		3	15	0	3.0		4	12	0	5.7		3	17	0	2.3
	8	11	2	4.3		3	16	0	1.5+		4	13	0	3.4		3	18	0	1.1
	9	9	2	10.3		3	17	1	15.9		4	14	0	1.9		3	19	1	13.3
	9	10	2	3.7		3	18	1	8.3		4	15	1	15.3		3	20	1	6.9
20	1	19	0	10.00		4	11	0	7.0		4	16	1	9.2		4	12	0	7.5−
	2	16	0	6.3		4	12	0	4.2		4	17	1	4.8		4	13	0	4.7
	2	17	0	3.2		4	13	0	2.3		4	18	1	2.0−		4	14	0	2.8
	2	18	0	1.1		4	14	0	1.2		5	9	0	9.8		4	15	0	1.6
	3	12	0	9.8		4	15	1	10.5+		5	10	0	6.0		4	16	1	13.4
	3	13	0	6.1		4	16	1	5.5+		5	11	0	3.5+		4	17	1	8.0
	3	14	0	3.5+		4	17	1	2.3		5	12	0	1.9		4	18	1	4.2
	3	15	0	1.8		5	9	0	7.8		5	13	1	13.4		4	19	1	1.7
	3	16	1	17.5+		5	10	0	4.5+		5	14	1	7.9		5	10	0	7.6
	3	17	1	9.1		5	11	0	2.5−		5	15	1	4.1		5	11	0	4.7
	4	10	0	8.7		5	12	0	1.2		5	16	1	1.9		5	12	0	2.7
	4	11	0	5.2		5	13	1	9.5−		5	17	2	11.0		5	13	0	1.5−
	4	12	0	2.9		5	14	1	5.0+		6	8	0	8.0		5	14	1	11.2
	4	13	0	1.4		5	15	1	2.3		6	9	0	4.6		5	15	1	6.6
	4	14	1	12.2		5	16	2	12.6		6	10	0	2.5−		5	16	1	3.5−
	4	15	1	6.4		6	8	0	6.3		6	11	0	1.2		5	17	1	1.6
	4	16	1	2.7		6	9	0	3.4		6	12	1	8.7		5	18	2	9.6
	5	9	0	6.0		6	10	0	1.7		6	13	1	4.6		6	8	0	9.9
	5	10	0	3.3		6	11	1	11.0		6	14	1	2.2		6	9	0	5.9
	5	11	0	1.6		6	12	1	5.9		6	15	2	10.7		6	10	0	3.4
	5	12	1	11.6		6	13	1	2.8		6	16	2	5.1		6	11	0	1.8
	5	13	1	6.1		6	14	1	1.1		7	7	0	7.5+		6	12	1	11.9
	5	14	1	2.8		6	15	2	6.1		7	8	0	4.0		6	13	1	6.9
	5	15	2	14.5+		7	7	0	5.9		7	9	0	2.0+		6	14	1	3.7
	6	7	0	8.9		7	8	0	3.0		7	10	1	11.8		6	15	1	1.7
	6	8	0	4.8		7	9	0	1.4		7	11	1	6.3		6	16	2	9.0
	6	9	0	2.4		7	10	1	8.5+		7	12	1	3.1		6	17	2	4.2
	6	10	0	1.1		7	11	1	4.2		7	13	1	1.3		7	7	0	9.3
	6	11	1	7.6		7	12	1	1.8		7	14	2	6.4		7	8	0	5.2
	6	12	1	3.6		7	13	2	8.2		7	15	2	2.7		7	9	0	2.8
	6	13	1	1.4		7	14	2	3.5−		8	8	0	1.9		7	10	0	1.4
	6	14	2	7.5−		8	8	0	1.3		8	9	1	10.5−		7	11	1	8.9
	7	7	0	4.4		8	9	1	7.5−		8	10	1	5.3		7	12	1	4.8
	7	8	0	2.0+		8	10	1	3.4		8	11	1	2.4		7	13	1	2.3
	7	9	1	11.6		8	11	1	1.3		8	12	2	9.6		7	14	2	10.3
	7	10	1	5.7		8	12	2	5.9		8	13	2	4.4		7	15	2	5.1
	7	11	1	2.5−		8	13	2	2.2		8	14	2	1.7		7	16	2	2.1
	7	12	2	10.4		9	9	1	3.2		9	9	1	4.9		8	8	0	2.6
	7	13	2	4.5−		9	10	1	1.2		9	10	1	2.1					
	8	8	1	10.8		9	11	2	4.8										

Continued overleaf

Table Z *Continued*

N	m	M	C	α(%)	N	m	M	C	α(%)	N	m	M	C	α(%)	N	m	M	C	α(%)
23	8	9	0	1.2	24	5	15	1	9.5−	24	11	11	2	3.4	25	6	16	1	2.4
	8	10	1	7.5+		5	16	1	5.5+		11	12	2	1.2		6	17	1	1.1
	8	11	1	3.8		5	17	1	2.9		11	12	3	10.0−		6	18	2	6.5−
	8	12	1	1.7		5	18	1	1.3		11	13	3	4.1		6	19	2	3.0
	8	13	2	7.3		5	19	2	8.5−		12	12	3	3.9		7	8	0	8.1
	8	14	2	3.3		6	9	0	7.4	25	1	24	0	8.0		7	9	0	4.8
	8	15	2	1.2		6	10	0	4.5−		2	19	0	10.00		7	10	0	2.7
	9	9	1	7.1		6	11	0	2.5+		2	20	0	6.7		7	11	0	1.4
	9	10	1	3.3		6	12	0	1.4		2	21	0	4.0		7	12	1	9.3
	9	11	1	1.4		6	13	1	9.6		2	22	0	2.00		7	13	1	5.3
	9	12	2	5.8		6	14	1	5.6		2	23	1	31.3		7	14	1	2.8
	9	13	2	2.4		6	15	1	2.9		3	16	0	7.3		7	15	1	1.4
	9	14	3	8.3		6	16	1	1.4		3	17	0	4.9		7	16	2	6.9
	10	10	1	1.3		6	17	2	7.6		3	18	0	3.0		7	17	2	3.4
	10	11	2	5.2		6	18	2	3.6		3	19	0	1.7		7	18	2	1.4
	10	12	2	2.0+		7	8	0	6.6		3	20	1	18.3		8	8	0	4.5−
	10	13	3	6.6		7	9	0	3.7		3	21	1	11.3		8	9	0	2.4
	11	11	2	1.9		7	10	0	2.0−		3	22	1	5.8		8	10	0	1.2
	11	12	3	5.9		7	11	1	11.9		4	13	0	7.8		8	11	1	7.5+
24	1	23	0	8.3		7	12	1	6.9		4	14	0	5.2		8	12	1	4.0
	2	19	0	7.2		7	13	1	3.7		4	15	0	3.3		8	13	1	2.0−
	2	20	0	4.3		7	14	1	1.8		4	16	0	2.0−		8	14	2	8.7
	2	21	0	2.2		7	15	2	8.4		4	17	0	1.1		8	15	2	4.4
	2	22	1	32.6		7	16	2	4.1		4	18	1	10.5+		8	16	2	2.0−
	3	15	0	8.3		7	17	2	1.7		4	19	1	6.2		8	17	3	7.8
	3	16	0	5.5+		8	8	0	3.5−		4	20	1	3.2		9	9	0	1.1
	3	17	0	3.5−		8	9	0	1.7		4	21	1	1.3		9	10	1	6.8
	3	18	0	2.0−		8	10	1	10.1		5	11	0	7.5+		9	11	1	3.4
	3	19	1	19.8		8	11	1	5.5−		5	12	0	4.8		9	12	1	1.6
	3	20	1	12.3		8	12	1	2.7		5	13	0	3.0		9	13	2	6.7
	3	21	1	6.3		8	13	1	1.2		5	14	0	1.7		9	14	2	3.2
	4	12	0	9.3		8	14	2	5.7		5	15	1	12.8		9	15	2	1.3
	4	13	0	6.2		8	15	2	2.5+		5	16	1	8.1		9	16	3	5.0+
	4	14	0	4.0		8	16	3	9.5−		5	17	1	4.7		10	10	1	3.2
	4	15	0	2.4		9	9	1	9.6		5	18	1	2.5−		10	11	1	1.4
	4	16	0	1.3		9	10	1	4.9		5	19	1	1.1		10	12	2	5.7
	4	17	1	11.9		9	11	1	2.3		5	20	2	7.5+		10	13	2	2.5+
	4	18	1	7.1		9	12	2	8.9		6	9	0	9.0		10	14	3	8.3
	4	19	1	3.7		9	13	2	4.3		6	10	0	5.7		10	15	3	3.6
	4	20	1	1.5+		9	14	2	1.8		6	11	0	3.4		11	11	2	5.5−
	5	10	0	9.4		9	15	3	6.4		6	12	0	1.9		11	12	2	2.3
	5	11	0	6.1		10	10	1	2.1		6	13	0	1.0+		11	13	3	7.2
	5	12	0	3.7		10	11	2	8.0		6	14	1	7.8		11	14	3	2.9
	5	13	0	2.2		10	12	2	3.6		6	15	1	4.5+		12	12	3	6.8
	5	14	0	1.2		10	13	2	1.4							12	13	3	2.6
						10	14	3	4.9										

Outline Solutions to the Assignments

Chapter 3

1.

Dot diagram:

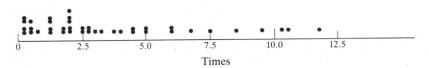

Times

H_0: Median time for the new store is 1.2 min.
H_1: Median time for the new store is greater than 1.2 min.

Test: sign text.
Decision rule: at $\alpha_1 = 5\%$, reject H_0 in favour of H_1 if $S \leq 13$ ($n=37$).
$S = 8$ and this is significant at $\alpha_1 = \frac{1}{2}\%$.

2.

H_0: Population median level of sodium is 140 ppm.
H_1: Population median level of solution is not 140 ppm.

Test: Wilcoxon's signed-rank test.
Decision rule: at $\alpha_2 = 5\%$, reject H_0 in favour of H_1 if $T \leq 46$ ($n=19$).
$T = 79$ and so H_0 cannot be rejected.

Chapter 4

1.

H_0: The mutations are in the ratio $27 : 9 : 9 : 9 : 3 : 3 : 3 : 1$.
H_1: The mutations are not in the ratio $27 : 9 : 9 : 9 : 3 : 3 : 3 : 1$.

Test: chi-squared goodness-of-fit test.
Decision rule: at $\alpha = 5\%$, reject H_0 in favour of H_1 if $\chi^2 \geq 14.067$ ($v=7$).
$\chi^2 = 33.225$, which is significant at $\alpha = 1\%$, examining the differences shows that the theory breaks down with the 'long, red and ebony' mutation.

2.

H_0: The arrival times are normally distributed.
H_1: The arrival times are not normally distributed.

Test: Lilliefors' test.
Decision rule: at $\alpha_2 = 5\%$, reject H_0 in favour of H_1 if $D_{40} \geqslant 0.1305$.
$D_{40} = 0.0994$ and so H_0 cannot be rejected.

Chapter 5

1.

H_0: The median VC is the same for the two populations.
H_1: The median VC is different for the two populations.

Test: Mann–Whitney test.
Decision rule: at $\alpha_2 = 5\%$, reject H_0 in favour of H_1 if $U \leqslant 8$ ($n_1 = n_2 = 7$).
$U = 15.5$ and so H_0 cannot be rejected.

H_0: The median FEV is the same for the two populations.
H_1: The median FEV is different for the two populations.

Test: Mann–Whitney test.
Decision rule: at $\alpha_2 = 5\%$, reject H_0 in favour of H_1 if $U \leqslant 8$ ($n_1 = n_2 = 7$).
$U = 19$ and so H_0 cannot be rejected.

H_0: The median TLC is the same for the two populations.
H_1: The median TLC is different for the two populations.

Test: Mann–Whitney test.
Decision rule: at $\alpha_2 = 5\%$, reject H_0 in favour of H_1 if $U \leqslant 8$ ($n_1 = n_2 = 7$).
$U = 24$ and so H_0 cannot be rejected.

H_0: The median IGV is the same for the two populations.
H_1: The median IGV is different for the two populations.

Test: Mann–Whitney test.
Decision rule: at $\alpha_2 = 5\%$, reject H_0 in favour of H_1 if $U \leqslant 8$ ($n_2 = n2 = 7$).
$U = 24$ and so H_0 cannot be rejected.

2.

H_0: On average, there is no difference in results from the machines.
H_1: On average, the results from the two machines are different.

Test: Tukey's location test.
Decision rule: at $\alpha_2 = 5\%$, reject H_0 in favour of H_1 if $Ty \geqslant 7$.

$Ty=8$ and so H_0 is rejected in favour of H_1.
Test: Mann–Whitney test.
Decision rule: at $\alpha_2=5\%$, reject H_0 in favour of H_1 if $U\leqslant119$.
$U=90$ and so H_0 is rejected in favour of H_1; in fact the result is significant at $\alpha_2=1\%$ and so with this test (not surprisingly) we have strong evidence to support H_1.

3.

H_0: There is no difference between the average heights of the populations of A and B sects.

H_1: There is some difference between the average heights of the populations of A and B sects.

Test: Mann–Whitney test.
Decision rule: at $\alpha_2=5\%$, reject H_0 in favour of H_1 if $U\leqslant26$ ($n_1=9$, $n_2=12$).
$U=32$ and so H_0 cannot be rejected, i.e. there is no evidence to support H_1.

Chapter 6

1.

H_0: There is no difference in spread between the clay and silt contents.

H_1: There is some difference in spread between the clay and silt contents.

Test: Siegel–Tukey test.
Decision rule: at $\alpha_2=5\%$, reject H_0 in favour of H_1 if $U\leqslant30$ ($n_1=n_2=11$).
Site 1: $U=45$ and so H_0 cannot be rejected.
Site 2: $U=28$, which is significant at $\alpha_2=5\%$ but not at $2\frac{1}{2}\%$ and so there is some evidence to support H_1 at this site.
Site 3: $U=37$ and so H_0 cannot be rejected.
Site 4: $U=48.5$ and so H_0 cannot be rejected.
Site 5: $U=52$ and so H_0 cannot be rejected.
Site 6: $U=45$ and so H_0 cannot be rejected.
Site 7: $U=60$ and so H_0 cannot be rejected.
Site 8: $U=55$ and so H_0 cannot be rejected.

2.

H_0: Each method produces the same dispersion.

H_1: The methods produce different amounts of spread (i.e. one is more erratic than the other).

Test: Tukey–type test.
Decision rule: at $\alpha_2=5\%$, reject H_0 in favour of H_1 if $Ts\leqslant6$ ($n_1=n_2=10$). $Ts\dot=8$ and so H_0 cannot be rejected.

Chapter 7

1.

H_0: There is no difference between the clay and silt contents.
H_1: There is some general difference between the clay and silt contents.

Test: Kolmogorov–Smirnov test.
Decision rule: at $\alpha_2=5\%$, reject H_0 in favour of H_1 if $D^*\geqslant77$ ($n_1=n_2=11$).
Site 1: $D^*=77$ and so H_0 is rejected in favour of H_1.
Site 2: $D^*=88$, which is significant at $\alpha_2=1\%$ and so there is strong evidence to support H_1 at this site.
Site 3: $D^*=88$, which is significant at $\alpha_2=1\%$ and so there is strong evidence to support H_1 at this site.
Site 4: $D^*=55$ and so H_0 cannot be rejected.
Site 5: $D^*=77$ and so H_0 is rejected in favour of H_1.
Site 6: $D^*=99$, which is significant at $\alpha_2=1\%$ and so there is strong evidence to support H_1 at this site.
Site 7: $D^*=55$ and so H_0 cannot be rejected.
Site 8: $D^*=88$, which is significant at $\alpha_2=1\%$ and so there is strong evidence to support H_1 at this site.

2.

H_0: The distributions of goals for England and Scotland are the same.
H_1: The distributions are not the same.

Test: Kolmogorov–Smirnov test.
Decision rule: at $\alpha_2=5\%$, reject H_0 in favour of H_1 if $D^*\geqslant2000$ ($n_1=n_2=100$).
$D^*=800$ and so H_0 cannot be rejected.

3.
Dot diagram:

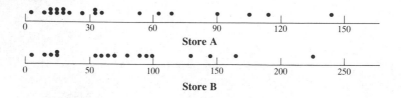

H_0: Both stores are as busy as each other.
H_1: One store is busier than the other.

Test: Rosenbaum's test.
Decision rule: at $\alpha_2=5\%$, reject H_0 in favour of H_1 if $R\geqslant 6$ ($n_1=17$, $n_2=20$).
$R=2\frac{1}{2}$ and so H_0 cannot be rejected.

Chapter 8

1.

H_0: The average gain in weight is the same for both schemes.
H_1: Scheme B produces, on average, greater gain in weight than scheme A.

Test: Wilcoxon signed–rank test.
Decision rule: at $\alpha_1=5\%$, reject H_0 in favour of H_1 if $T\leqslant 21$ ($n=13$).
$T=9\frac{1}{2}$ and so H_0 can be rejected; in fact the result is significant at $\alpha_1=1\%$, giving strong evidence in support of H_1.

2.

H_0: The average percentages of sand and silt are the same.
H_1: There is a difference between the average percentages of sand and silt.

Test: Wilcoxon signed-rank test.
Decision-rule: at $\alpha_2=5\%$, reject H_0 in favour of H_1 if $T\leqslant 13$ ($n=12$).
$T=26$ and so H_0 cannot be rejected.

Chapter 9

1.

H_0: There is no correlation between relative weight and insulin resistance.
H_1: There is positive correlation between relative weight and insulin resistance.

Test: Spearman's test.
Decision rule: at $\alpha_1=5\%$, reject H_0 in favour of H_1 if $r_S\geqslant 0.3805$ ($n=20$).
$r_S=0.3756$ and so H_0 cannot be rejected.

2.

H_0: There is no correlation between the number of awards and the tuberculosis death rate.

H_1: There is negative correlation between the number of awards and the tuberculosis death rate.

Test: Kendall's test.
Decision rule: at $\alpha_1 = 5\%$, reject H_0 in favour of H_1 if $\tau \leqslant -0.4182$ ($n = 11$).
$\tau = -0.9636$, which very significant (more than $\frac{1}{2}\%$) and so there is strong evidence of negative correlation between the variables; but see note (d) on page 184.

Chapter 10

1.

Wind speed (mph)	Gradient	Intercept
5	1.056	−4.611
10	1.211	−21.278
15	1.333	−31.667
20	1.422	−38.889
25	1.489	−44.556
30	1.511	−48.444
35	1.556	−51.111
40	1.600	−53.000
45	1.567	−54.500
50	1.600	−55.000

2.
Rank regression equation is $r(Y) = 13.753 + 0.3603r(X)$.

3.
Rank regression equation is $r(Y) = 0.1154 + 0.984r(X)$.
(a) 67°C, (b) 78°C, (c) 134°C.

Chapter 11

1.

H_0: There is no correlation between blood pressure (X) and heart weight (Y).
H_1: There is positive correlation between X and Y.

Test: Olmstead–Tukey test.
Decision rule: at $\alpha_1 = 5\%$, reject H_0 in favour of H_1 if $C \geqslant 9$.
$C = 29$, which is significant even at $\alpha_1 = \frac{1}{2}\%$ and so there is strong evidence of positive correlation between X and Y.

$\tilde{X}_1=94.5$, $\tilde{Y}_1=385$, $\tilde{X}_2=131.5$, $\tilde{Y}_2=477.5$, giving a first approximate regression line of $Y=2.5X+148.75$.

Chapter 12

1.

H_0: Opinion on physical recreation is independent of region.
H_1: Opinion on physical recreation depends on the region.

Test: chi-squared test.
Decision rule: at $\alpha=5\%$, reject H_0 in favour of H_1 if $\chi^2 \geqslant 16.919$ (9 df).
$\chi^2=15.56$ and so H_0 cannot be rejected.

H_0: Opinion on leisure facilities is independent of region.
H_1: Opinion on leisure facilities depends on the region.

Test: chi-squared test.
Decision rule: at $\alpha=5\%$, reject H_0 in favour of H_1 if $\chi^2 \geqslant 16.919$ (9 df).
$\chi^2=14.05$ and so H_0 cannot be rejected.

H_0: Opinion on sport and health is independent of region.
H_1: Opinion on sport and health depends on the region.

Test: chi-squared test.
Decision rule: (because of low expected frequencies, rows 2 and 3 combined) at $\alpha=5\%$, reject H_0 in favour of H_1 if $\chi^2 \geqslant 7.815$ (3 df).
$\chi^2=7.5$ and so H_0 cannot be rejected.

Chapter 13

1.

H_0: The average copper concentrations is the same at the seven locations.
H_1: At least one location has an average concentration different from the rest.

Test: Kruskal–Wallis test.
Decision rule: at $\alpha=5\%$, reject H_0 in favour of H_1 if $H \geqslant 12.592$ (from chi-squared distribution with 6 df).
$H=9.657$ and so H_0 cannot be rejected.

2.

H_0: The average increase in weight is the same for the three brands.
H_1: At least one brand has an average different from the rest.

Test: Kruskal–Wallis test.

Decision rule: at $\alpha=5\%$, reject H_0 in favour of H_1 if $H\geqslant5.991$ (from chi-squared with 2 df).

$H=4.7965$ and so H_0 cannot be rejected.

or

Test: median test.

Decision rule: at $\alpha=5\%$, reject H_0 in favour of H_1 if $\alpha_2\geqslant5.991$ (2 df).

$\chi^2=3.8$ and so H_0 cannot be rejected.

Chapter 14

1.

H_0: There is no difference in average pulse readings between the patients.

H_1: At least one patient has an average pulse different from the rest.

Test: Friedman's test.

Decision rule: at $\alpha=5\%$, reject H_0 in favour of H_1 if $M\geqslant6.500$ ($k=3$, $n=4$).

$M=3.375$ and so H_0 cannot be rejected.

H_0: There is no difference in average pulse readings between the times.

H_1: At least one time has an average pulse different from the rest.

Test: Friedman's test.

Decision rule: at $\alpha=5\%$, reject H_0 in favour of H_1 if $M\geqslant7.400$ ($k=4$, $n=3$).

$M=8.5$, which is significant at $\alpha=5\%$ but not at 1%, and so there is some, but not strong, evidence to support H_1. Examining the ranked data shows that the average pulse is lowest at 0.600 h and greatest at 1800 h; there is probably no significant difference between times 1000 and 2200 h.

2.

H_0: The average amount of iron absorbed is the same for the four treatments.

H_1: At least one treatment gives an average amount of iron absorbed different from the rest.

Test: the match tests.

Decision rules: (1) at $\alpha=5\%$, reject H_0 in favour of H_1 if $M_1\geqslant39$ ($k=4$, $n=8$),

(2) at $\alpha=5\%$, reject H_0 in favour of H_1 if $M_2\geqslant58$ ($k=4$, $n=8$).

$M_1=51$ and $M_2=72$, both of which are significant at $\alpha=1\%$ and so there is strong evidence to support H_1. Dunn's test shows there to be a significant difference between EO and CN and between CO and CN.

3.

H_0: There are no differences in averages between the students.
H_1: At least one average is different from the rest.

Test: the match tests.
Decision rules: (a) at $\alpha=5\%$, reject H_0 in favour of H_1 if $M_1\geqslant 12$
                      $(k=4, n=4)$,
                 (2) at $\alpha=5\%$, reject H_0 in favour of H_1 if $M_2\geqslant 15$
                      $(k=4, n=4)$.
$M_1=8$ and $M_2=13$ and so using either test means that H_0 cannot be rejected.

H_0: There are no differences in averages between the specimens.
H_1: At least one average is different from the rest.

Test: the match tests.
Decision rules: (1) at $\alpha=5\%$, reject H_0 in favour of H_1 if $M_1\geqslant 12$
                      $(k=4, n=4)$,
                 (2) at $\alpha=5\%$, reject H_0 in favour of H_1 if $M_2\geqslant 15$
                      $(k=4, n=4)$.
$M_1=12$ and $M_2=15\frac{1}{2}$ and so both tests provide some evidence in support of H_1.

Chapter 15

1.

H_0: The average times to complete the jobs are the same for all light conditions.
H_1: The average time to complete the job increases with worsening light conditions.

Test: Tersptra–Jonckheere test.
Decision rule: at $\alpha=5\%$, reject H_0 in favour of H_1 if $W\leqslant 39$ (from the approximation).
$W=60$ and so H_0 cannot be rejected.

2.
(i)
H_0: The average amount of food eaten is the same for all deprivation levels.
H_1: At least one average amount is different from the rest.

Test: the match tests.

Decision rules: (1) at $\alpha=5\%$, reject H_0 in favour of H_1 if $L_1 \geqslant 14$,
(2) at $\alpha=5\%$, reject H_0 in favour of H_1 if $L_2 \geqslant 18$.

$L_1=16$, which is significant at $\alpha=1\%$, while $L_2=18$, which is only significant at $\alpha=5\%$.

(ii)

H_0: The average amount of food eaten is the same for all deprivation levels.

H_1: At least one average amount is different from the rest.

Test: the match tests.

Decision rules: (1) at $\alpha=5\%$, reject H_0 in favour of H_1 if $L_1 \geqslant 14$,
(2) at $\alpha=5\%$, reject H_0 in favour of H_1 if $L_2 \geqslant 18$.

$L_1=16$ and $L_2=20$, both of which are significant at $\alpha=1\%$.

Chapter 17

Assignment 5.3

H_0: There is no difference in height between the boys from the two sects.

H_1: There is some difference between the two sects.

Test: Wald–Wolfowitz runs test.

Decision rule: at $\alpha=5\%$, reject H_0 in favour of H_1 if $T \leqslant 5$ ($n_1=9$, $n_2=12$).

$T=12.83$ (by averaging the different values of T resulting from 'reordering' the tied values) and so H_0 cannot be rejected.

Assignment 6.2

H_0: There is no difference in swimming ability between the two groups.

H_1: There is some difference between the groups.

Test: Wald–Wolfowitz test.

Decision rule: at $\alpha=5\%$, reject H_0 in favour of H_1 if $T \leqslant 6$ ($n_1=n_2=10$).

$T=7$ and so H_0 cannot be rejected.

1.

H_0: The sample values come from a random sequence.

H_1: The sample values do not come from a random sequence.

Test: runs test.

Decision rule: at $\alpha_2 = 5\%$, reject H_0 in favour of H_1 if $T \leq 8$ or $T \geq 19$ ($n_1 = 12$, $n_2 = 13$).
$T = 15$ and so H_0 cannot be rejected.

H_0: The sample values come from a random sequence.
H_1: The sample values do not come from a random sequence.

Test: runs up and down test.
Decision rule: at $\alpha_2 = 5\%$, reject H_0 in favour of H_1 if $U \leq 11$ or $U \geq 20$ ($n = 24$).
$U = 16$ and so H_0 cannot be rejected.

Chapter 19

Assignment 3.1
Based on the sign test, a 90% confidence interval for ϕ is (1.9, 3.7).

Assignment 3.2
Based on the sign test, a 90% confidence interval for ϕ is (138, 144).

Assignment 5.3
A 90% confidence interval for $\phi_A - \phi_B$ is (0, 11).

1.
A 90% confidence interval for $\phi_A - \phi_B$ is (−1.45, −0.1).

References

Ansari, A. R. and R. A. Bradley 1960. Rank-sum tests for dispersion. *Ann. Math. Statist.* **31**, 1174–89.

Arbuthnott, J. 1710. An argument for divine providence taken from the constant regularity observed in the births of both sexes. *Phil. Trans.* **27**, 186–90.

Brown, G. W. and A. M. Mood 1951. On median tests for linear hypotheses. In *Proceedings of the Second Berkeley Symposium on Mathematical Statistics and Probability*, 159–66. University of California Press. (The method was also given in Mood A. M. 1950. *Introduction to the theory of statistics*. New York: McGraw-Hill.

Dunn, O. J. 1964 Multiple comparisons using rank sums. *Technometrics* **6**, 241–52.

Friedman, M. 1937. The use of ranks to avoid the assumption of normality implicit in the analysis of variance. *J. Am. Statist. Assoc.* **32**, 675–701.

Goodman, L. A. 1954. Kolmogorov–Smirnov tests for psychological research. *Psychol. Bull.* **51**, 160–8.

Iman, R. L. and W. J. Conover 1979. The use of the rank transform in regression. *Technometrics* **21**, 499–509.

Jonckheere, A. R. 1954. A distribution-free k-sample test against ordered alternatives. *Biometrika* **41**, 133–45.

Kendall, M. G. 1938. A new measure of rank correlation. *Biometrika* **30**, 81–3.

Kolmogorov, A. N. 1933. Sulla determinazione empirica di una legge di distribuizione. *Giorn. Ist. Ital. Attuari* **4**, 83–91.

Kruskal, W. H. 1952. A nonparametric test for the several sample problem. *Ann. Math. Statist.* **23**, 525–40.

Kruskal, W. H. and W. A. Wallis 1952. Use of ranks in one criterion variance analysis. *J. Am. Statist. Assoc.* **47**, 583–621. 1953. Addendum. *Ibid.* **48**, 907–11.

Lilliefors, W. H. 1967. On the Kolmogorov–Smirnov test for normality with mean and variance unknown. *J. Am. Statist. Assoc.* **62**, 399–402.

Mann, H. B. and D. R. Whitney 1947. On a test of whether one of two random variables is stochastically larger than the other. *Ann. Math. Statist.* **18**, 50–60.

Mood, A. M. 1950. *Introduction to the theory of statistics*. New York: McGraw-Hill.

Mood, A. M. 1954. On the asymptotic efficiency of certain non-parametric two-sample tests. *Ann. Math. Statist.* **25**, 514–22.

Olmstead, P. S. and J. W. Tukey 1947. A corner test for association. *Ann. Math. Statist.* **18**, 495–513.

Page, E. B. 1963. Ordered hypotheses for multiple treatments: a significance test for linear ranks. *J. Am. Statist. Assoc.* **58**, 216–30.

Pearson, K. 1900. On the criterion that a given system of deviations from the probable in the case of a correlated system of variables is such that it can reasonably be supposed to have arisen from random sampling. *Phil. Mag. (5)* **50**, 157–75.

Rosenbaum, S. 1965. On some two-sample non-parametric tests. *J. Am. Statist. Assoc.* **60**, 1118–26.

Siegel, S. and J. W. Tukey 1960. A non-parametric sum of ranks procedure for relative spread in unpaired samples. *J. Am. Statist. Assoc.* **55**, 429–45. 1961. Errata. *Ibid.* **56**, 1005.

Smirnov, N. V. 1939. Estimate of deviation between empirical distribution functions in two independent samples. *Bull. Moscow Univ.* **2**, 3–16.

Spearman, C. 1904. The proof and measurement of association between two things. *Am. J. Psychol.* **15**, 72–101.

Terpstra, T. J. 1952. The asymptotic normality and consistency of Kendall's test against trend when ties are present in one ranking. *Indag. Math.* **14**, 327–33.

Theil, H. 1950. A rank-invariant method of linear and polynomial regression analysis. 1. *Nederl. Akad. Wetensch. Proc. Ser. A* **53**, 386–92.

Tukey, J. W. 1959. A quick, compact, two-sample test to Duckworth's specifications. *Technometrics* **1**, 31–48.

Wald, A. and J. Wolfowitz 1940. On a test whether two samples are from the same population. *Ann. Math. Statist.* **11**, 147–62.

Westernberg, J. 1948. Significance test for median and interquartile range in samples from continuous populations of any form. *Akad. Wetensch. Afdeeling Voor Wis.* **51**, 252–61.

Wilcoxon, F. 1945. Individual comparisons by ranking methods. *Biometrics* **1**, 80–3.

Wilcoxon, F. 1949. *Some rapid approximate statistical procedures.* American Cyanamid Co., Stamford Research Laboratories.

Worthington, P. L. 1982. Match tests for non-parametric analysis of variance problems. PhD Thesis, Nottingham University.

Index